EXPOSING

NUCLEAR PHALLACIES

Pergamon Titles of Related Interest

Brock-Utne EDUCATING FOR PEACE

Related Journals
(Free sample copies available upon request)

REPRODUCTIVE AND GENETIC ENGINEERING: Journal of International Feminist Analysis
WOMEN'S STUDIES INTERNATIONAL FORUM

The ATHENE Series

General Editors
Gloria Bowles
Renate Klein
Janice Raymond

Consulting Editor
Dale Spender

The Athene Series assumes that all those who are concerned with formulating explanations of the way the world works need to know and appreciate the significance of basic feminist principles.

The growth of feminist research has challenged almost all aspects of social organization in our culture. The Athene Series focuses on the construction of knowledge and the exclusion of women from the process—both as theorists and subjects of study—and offers innovative studies that challenge established theories and research.

On Athene—When Metis, goddess of wisdom who presided over all knowledge was pregnant with Athene, she was swallowed up by Zeus who then gave birth to Athene from his head. The original Athene is thus the parthenogenetic daughter of a strong mother and as the feminist myth goes, at the "third birth" of Athene she stops being Zeus' obedient mouthpiece and returns to her real source: the science and wisdom of womankind.

EXPOSING

NUCLEAR PHALLACIES

EDITED BY

DIANA E. H. RUSSELL

PERGAMON PRESS

New York   Oxford   Beijing   Frankfurt   São Paulo   Sydney

Pergamon Press Offices:

U.S.A.	Pergamon Press, Inc., Maxwell House, Fairview Park, Elmsford, New York 10523, U.S.A.
U.K.	Pergamon Press plc, Headington Hill Hall, Oxford OX3 0BW, England
PEOPLE'S REPUBLIC OF CHINA	Pergamon Press, Qianmen Hotel, Beijing, People's Republic of China
FEDERAL REPUBLIC OF GERMANY	Pergamon Press GmbH, Hammerweg 6, D-6242 Kronberg, Federal Republic of Germany
BRAZIL	Pergamon Editora Ltda, Rua Eça de Queiros, 346, CEP 04011, São Paulo, Brazil
AUSTRALIA	Pergamon Press Australia Pty Ltd., P.O. Box 544, Potts Point, NSW 2011, Australia
JAPAN	Pergamon Press, 8th Floor, Matsuoka Central Building, 1-7-1 Nishishinjuku, Shinjuku-ku, Tokyo 160, Japan
CANADA	Pergamon Press Canada Ltd., Suite 271, 253 College Street, Toronto, Ontario M5T 1R5, Canada

First edition 1989

Library of Congress Cataloging in Publication Data

Exposing nuclear phallacies / edited by Diana E.H. Russell. -- 1st ed.
    p.   cm. -- (Athene series)
  Bibliography: p.
  Includes index.
  ISBN 0-08-036476-4 :   ISBN 0-08-036475-6 (soft) :

  1. Nuclear disarmament. 2. Antinuclear movement. 3. Women and peace I. Russell, Diana E.H. II. Series.
JX1974.7.E97 1989
327.1' 7--dc19   88-39941
                                        CIP

Printed in the United States of America

∞™ The paper used in this publication meets the minimum requirements of American National Standard for Information Sciences -- Permanence of Paper for Printed Library Materials, ANSI Z39.48-1984

*To all the women who are working
to save us from a nuclear holocaust.*

"We can best help you to prevent war not by repeating your words and following your methods but by finding new words and creating new methods. We can best help you to prevent war not by joining your society but by remaining outside your society but in cooperation with its aims."
Virginia Woolf, *Three Guineas* (1938).

Contents

PART 4: FEMINIST ANTI-NUCLEAR ACTIONS

PART 5: WHAT NEXT?

Acknowledgments

This book was inspired by the women I met in the spring of 1984 at the Puget Sound Women's Peace Camp near Seattle, Washington, particularly Susan James, Louise Chernin, Joan Tierney, Kate Thayer, and most of all Sandra Jo Palm, who gave to me so generously of her time. My brief but affecting experience with them will be described in the following pages.

Donna Warnock was extremely helpful in the early stage of this project, opening up her files to me, lending me articles, putting me in touch with people, and sharing the expertise that she had accumulated after many years of working against militarism as a feminist. I invited her to co-edit this anthology, but alas, her many other projects kept her too busy to participate.

The enthusiasm of Renate Klein and Gloria Bowles, editors of the Athene Series in which this volume appears, came at a time when I was feeling very discouraged by this project. I am grateful to these two women for their key role in the publication of this book, as well as for lifting my spirits. I have had the pleasure of working closely with Gloria during the final stages of this work. She has been extremely helpful in assisting me with such hard decisions as what to include and when to ask for revisions, and she has also been responsible for finding two of the pieces in this anthology. She has been very accessible and responsive to my many calls, and her genuine interest in the material helped keep me from losing myself in all the mundane paperwork involved in editing an anthology.

I want to thank the many people who gave me substantive or editorial feedback on one or more of the pieces that I wrote for this anthology: Gloria Bowles, Sandra Butler, Jill Hall, Meredith Maran, Jeffrey Masson,

Elissa Melamed, Laura Tow, Donna Warnock, and Jane Futcher. I am also grateful to Marny Hall for her suggestion that I use the pun, nuclear "phallacies" in the title of this book.

Several people have helped me by providing sympathetic ears when I needed them, especially Sandra Butler, Marny Hall, Jill Hall, Maryel Norris, and Barbara Roberts. Darlene Pagano advised me about material to consider for inclusion. And Jan Dennie has done her usual excellent word processing job on the parts of the manuscript that required it.

Finally, I am very grateful to those authors and publishers who waived their usual permission fees, and to my publisher, whose last minute contribution will enable me at least to give small honoraria to the contributors. Any royalties that may accrue from the sale of this book after expenses have been paid will be donated to help continue the work of the women at Greenham Common.

Introduction

Diana E. H. Russell

The urgency of halting the growing threat of nuclear war or nuclear accidents has been articulated extremely well by Helen Caldicott in *Nuclear Madness* (1978), Jonathan Schell in *The Fate of the Earth* (1982), Robert Lifton and Richard Falk in *Indefensible Weapons* (1982), and many others. However, these authors fail to recognize the significance of culturally determined gender differences in the origin and perpetuation of, as well as the solution to, the threat of a nuclear holocaust. Excellent as their books are, this defect in their analysis is serious; it means that their conclusions about what must be done to save us from this nightmare are also flawed.

In her second book, *Missile Envy*, Helen Caldicott does at last observe that gender differences are crucial to an understanding of the nuclear crisis. But she does so from a biologically determinist standpoint that holds women to be *by nature* more peace-loving and nurturant, and men more aggressive and fascinated by death. I, like many feminists, subscribe to the more optimistic view that these differences are primarily the result of social conditioning and the unequal power relationship between men and women imbedded in our social structure.

Gender differences in attitudes to nuclear war and in responses to our having to live with this danger have also been ignored by most social scientists. In one exceptional study of students at the University of Oregon, sociologists Denise Lach and Patricia Gwartney-Gibbs (1988) found that gender was the only demographic factor of several they examined that was associated with attitudes toward nuclear war. (The variables that were unrelated to attitudes to nuclear war were race/ ethnicity, age, marital status, religion and religiosity, academic major and grade point average.) More specifically, these researchers found that women students were significantly more pessimistic than males about the probability of nuclear war and less frequently wanted to survive such a war (see also Gwartney-Gibbs, 1985). In addition, the pessimistic women were much more likely than the optimistic women to report a desire to remain childless. In contrast, the degree of pessimism or optimism had no impact on the paternal aspirations of the male students. Lach and Gwartney-Gibbs' study suggests that feminists are correct in our assumption that research on gender and nuclear war would likely yield many significant and valuable findings.

The women's liberation movement in this country has also largely failed to understand that the nuclear threat is in part a consequence of sexism, and is therefore a feminist issue. The polarization of the sexes into two different roles, two different psyches, and two different sets of standards—one for men and one for women—has had a profound effect on what men and women have done with their lives. This includes the respective parts each sex has played in bringing about our current predicament.

In the discussion that followed ABC-TV's nationally syndicated program "The Day After"—one of the most watched television movies in history—Ted Koppel used his role as the moderator of the other six white men on the panel to emphasize above all else the imperative need to remain unemotional about the possibility of nuclear war. Such a split between thinking, feeling, and morality—as well as the denigration of feelings—is particularly characteristic of the masculine mentality. In contrast, many women find it both foreign and unhealthy to advocate remaining unemotional about the possibility that our leaders could blow us up at any moment and destroy the entire planet. Emotion *is* needed. We must become de-anesthetized, then actively engage in efforts to eradicate the danger of a nuclear holocaust.

In March 1984, I decided to spend my spring vacation from teaching college at Puget Sound Women's Peace Camp near Seattle, Washington. Despite its name, this meant sleeping on a mattress in a small rented house with only three or four other women "peace-campers." Although more than two thousand women had passed through this peace camp since the summer of 1983, when it really *was* a camp, winter had seen the end of visitors, and many of the peace campers themselves had returned to the more normal existence of jobs and family life in Seattle. Nevertheless, that week at the camp was very moving and inspirational; it was there that I decided to do this book.

The spirit and commitment of the women there inspired me. Spending twenty-four hours a day with people who devote all their time and energy to trying to save the planet from nuclear war or nuclear accidents was a new and challenging experience. Being around such people broke through my own resistance to facing our nuclear reality. Another powerful factor was being removed from my regular life with all its structure, obligations and routines. I felt more open to the truth of Helen Caldicott and Jonathan Schell's warning that we are living on borrowed time. I began to change my life accordingly.

With this knowledge, many peace workers have changed their lives dramatically. Take Sandra Jo Palm, for example. She dropped into the Puget Sound Peace Camp one afternoon to participate in an action and never went home, leaving her family, her career as an artist, and virtually all her worldly goods in Portland, Oregon. Such behavior doesn't make sense to the vast majority of people who continue to do "business as usual." But if we had the courage to face the terrible possibility that we and our planet may not survive another decade, many more of us would follow Sandra Jo's example, and there'd be a much greater likelihood that we *wouldn't* die in a nuclear holocaust. (Interviews with Sandra Jo Palm and Susan James appear in chapter 17.)

I responded to my stay at the peace camp by working to develop this feminist anthology on nuclear war. Because I believed that I would have become involved in this issue much sooner had such a book been available to me, I hoped that my book, explaining why nuclear war is a relevant concern of feminists, would help to mobilize the women's movement on this issue. Perhaps it will move people in the same way that feminist analyses of pornography mobilized the women's movement in the 1970s.

Although I had been involved in the anti-nuclear movement prior to 1984 (see my account of FANG, a feminist anti-nuclear action group, in chapter 20), 1984 was a difficult time for a relative newcomer. My relatively new state of unnumbing coincided with a growing sense of futility and despondency on the part of many people. Yet I felt that the nuclear threat was so serious and so urgent that I chose to put all my other work aside. Ironically, I found myself involved in a more prolonged search for a publisher than I had ever experienced. Rejection letters, which often tell little, made one point very clear: sexism, according to several publishers, is not relevant to an understanding of the nuclear crisis. They could understand the need for a feminist analysis of rape or abortion, but not of nuclear war.

Alas, my awakening to our nuclear reality had come at a time when many other women and men were returning to a state of denial. In August 1984, the same year I went to Puget Sound, I spent a few days at the Women's Peace Encampment at Seneca in New York state. I had seen a marvelous slide show about women's actions at the camp the previous summer when thousands of women engaged in civil disobedience to show the strength of their feelings about the danger of nuclear war (see Grace Paley's article, chapter 16). By the time I arrived at Seneca, however, the spirit had definitely changed. There was only one spontaneous demonstration outside the entrance of the nearby military facility while I was there, and I found women's energy quite depleted in terms of nuclear issues. The women who were there at the time were primarily involved in efforts to retain legal rights to remain a camp. Workshops were offered, but none that I can recollect were on the threat of nuclear war.

Why the peace movement waned in 1984, including the all-women's segment of it, is a matter of speculation. Many people consider the failure to stop the deployment of Cruise and Pershing II missiles in Europe on December 12, 1984, to have been the event responsible. A number of peace activists had said it would be the last straw if this happened; and then it happened.

It took me over three years to find a publisher for this book. Ironically, my first title was *Living on Borrowed Time* — perhaps too threatening, even then. The peace movement in this country, and internationally, is still experiencing a severe lull, and with the exception of the Women's Peace Encampment at Seneca, which still survives, I am aware of no specifically feminist peace activities currently going on in this country. Most feminists who were involved in the women's peace camps, for example, have moved on to other concerns. The group I started in 1983 (FANG) died in 1984, having existed for less than a year.

I don't know what chord in women's hearts will be touched by this book. As I write, the summit meeting between Reagan and Gorbachev at which they agreed to destroy all intermediate-range nuclear weapons has just concluded. As Gorbachev said, this is "the first step down the road leading to a nuclear-free world" (Perlman, 1987). It is a first step that likely would not have happened but for the efforts of the peace movements in different countries. Indeed, Gorbachev frequently referred to the "climate of opinion" against these missiles as a motivating factor for the INF treaty. But it has come such a long time after the most intense efforts by the peace movement, particularly those occurring before the deployment of Cruise and Pershing II missiles in Europe in 1984, that even activists may fail to recognize it as our victory.

A greater and far more serious danger is the possibility that people may use this success as a pretext for stopping or slowing down their efforts to achieve a nuclear-free world. We must not allow this to happen. We still have long-range missiles and Star Wars to contend with, as well as short-range missiles and the threat posed by the nuclear arsenals of other countries. Even if the INF treaty were implemented tomorrow, journalist David Perlman points out:

> Europe remains a nuclear battlefield, stocked with tactical nuclear weapons whose ranges can be as short as a few miles. . . . Britain and France maintain their own independent nuclear forces, and China too, is a true nuclear power. Israel is known to have both warheads and the missiles to deliver them. South Africa, India and Pakistan are believed to possess small nuclear weapons. . . . Libya, Brazil and Iraq seek the ability to build nuclear arms. Fuel for a bomb can be made in a civilian reactor, and anyone can learn to build a bomb by reading an encyclopedia (1987).

Feminist anti-nuclear work is as needed now as it ever was. Perhaps this book will help to inspire some women to engage in future efforts similar to the actions described here. Hopefully, the social climate will change soon, and more women and men will once again be willing to mobilize their energies to try to make nuclear war impossible. Perhaps this book will even help to foster the return of a greater receptivity to its message.

I believe that the kinds of feminist perspectives on the nuclear threat included in *Exposing Nuclear Phallacies* have gone unheard in this country for two major reasons: first, most feminists still believe that working against nuclear weapons is a diversion from women's issues; and, second, the peace movement is largely integrated (men and women) and male-dominated. Feminist voices are rarely given the attention they deserve in such settings. This view is amply documented by many of the essays in editor Pam McAllister's *Reweaving the Web of Life* (1982). Integrated organizations have never been particularly hospitable to the development of feminist perspectives and analysis.

In contrast to the United States, many women in England who became active in the nuclear disarmament movement in the last decade organized separately from men. Particularly well-known is the women's peace camp at Greenham Common, the location of a US military base where Cruise missiles are now deployed. Organizing separately has facilitated the recognition by many British women of the connections between sexism and the nuclear threat. In addition, this separatism has greatly empowered many of the women involved. Ignored at first, people now generally recognize that the courage and commitment of the women of Greenham Common has had an enormous impact on the anti-nuclear struggle throughout Europe.

The special role that women have played in the nuclear disarmament movement in England is reflected in the number of books published there by and about women in the peace movement in the past few years (see the Bibliography). Despite this relative profusion of British books on women and peace, I know of none that specifically articulates a sustained analysis of the relationship between feminism and the nuclear crisis. Nor do any of them thoroughly address the argument presented here: that all people who want to end the nuclear threat must recognize the role of sexism in its development, perpetuation, and acceleration. These books also fail to spell out the implications of this theory for the anti-nuclear movement as a whole.

Furthermore, these books were written for a British or European audience. I felt there was an urgent need for a book that would also provide American feminist analyses which would speak to the particular role of the United States in the development of the nuclear terror, and to the special obligation of those of us who live in the US to try to end it.

Although the US women's liberation movement has not mobilized as a whole to try to prevent a nuclear holocaust, many individual feminists have been very active. But their perspective on why feminists should fight the nuclear threat has rarely been articulated and is even more rarely heard. *Exposing Nuclear Phallacies* brings together feminist articles and voices, most of which have been muffled or buried. Together they present a challenge to the women's liberation movement to actively respond to this historic crisis; an incentive and a guide for the transformation of the anti-nuclear movement; and more generally, a catalyst for change that may literally help to save all of us and the planet on which we live.

The nuclear fallacies exposed in this book include the belief that nuclear weapons make us more secure; that the more weapons we have the safer we are; that the etiology of the nuclear crisis has nothing to do with gender; that the threat of nuclear war isn't a woman's issue, and particularly not a feminist issue; that if feminists want to be active in trying to bring about a nuclear-free world, we will have to put aside our feminist beliefs; and that ignoring the danger of a nuclear holocaust is an acceptable response because we can't do anything about it anyway.

It seems fitting to open the first of the five parts of *Exposing Nuclear Phallacies* with a piece by Helen Caldicott, who has probably done more than any other human being alive today to alert the world to the dangers of a nuclear holocaust. "Nuclear Madness" is an excerpt from her farewell speech to the National Women's Studies Association Meetings in 1986. She delivered it shortly before she returned to Australia to recover from what she describes as "a male coup" at Physicians for Social Responsibility, one of the organizations that she had founded.

I first came across the term *omnicide* in Rosalie Bertell's excellent book, *No Immediate Danger* (1985). "The concept of species annihilation," Bertell writes, "means a relatively swift (on the scale of civilization), deliberately induced end to history, culture, science, biological reproduction and memory. It is the ultimate human rejection of the gift of life, an act which requires a new word to describe it, namely omnicide"

(p. 2). She goes on to point out that nuclear war is not the only threat to our survival. The production of nuclear energy and nuclear weapons also threatens our species. In the interview with Bertell included in this volume, she describes how she became involved in conducting research on this subject, its special significance for Third World Countries and peoples, and what she hopes to achieve through her work for change.

The articles by Caldicott and Bertell set the stage by reminding us of the danger of omnicide that we currently face. In Part 2, Fran Peavey and I describe our personal denial of this reality and how we broke through this numbing process. We have to be willing to *feel* the importance of working to create a safer world. Intellectual recognition alone is not enough. In Part 3 several feminists explain why we believe that nuclear war is a feminist issue. Especially striking is the variety of very different approaches, despite their feminist perspectives. Because so many people have ignored the roles of patriarchy and sexism as causative factors in the nuclear crisis, I and the other contributors to this section of the book have given our primary attention to these factors. This does not mean that I consider imperialism and nationalism, for example, unimportant in the etiology of the nuclear arms race. However, the purpose of this book is to rectify a dangerous oversight, not to undertake a comprehensive analysis of all the causes.

Part 4 provides some inspiring examples of feminist anti-nuclear actions, particularly the twenty-four-hours-a-day peace camps. Included here is a chapter about the women's camp at Greenham Common, surely one of the century's most impressive examples of women's tenacity and creative strategizing. The anthology concludes with some ideas about where we go from here, a bibliography, and information about the contributors to this volume.

REFERENCES

Bertell, Rosalie, *No Immediate Danger* (London: The Women's Press, 1985).

Caldicott, Helen, *Nuclear Madness* (New York: Bantam Books, 1978).

Caldicott, Helen, *Missile Envy: The Arms Race and Nuclear War* (New York: William Morrow, 1984).

Gwartney-Gibbs, Patricia, "Student Attitudes Studied." *Lane County Nuclear News Bureau*, Vol. 3, No. 5 (1985).

Lach, Denise and Gwartney-Gibbs, Patricia, "Attitudes Toward Surviving Nuclear War." Unpublished paper presented at the National Women's Studies Association Conference, Minneapolis, Minnesota (June 23, 1988).

Lifton, Robert and Falk, Richard, *Indefensible Weapons* (New York: Basic Books, 1982).

McAllister, Pam (ed.), *Reweaving the Web of Life: Feminism and Nonviolence* (Philadelphia: New Society Publishers, 1982).

Perlman, David, "The INF Treaty's Promise and Problems," *San Francisco Chronicle* (9 December 1987).

Schell, Jonathan, *The Fate of the Earth* (New York: Avon Books, 1982).

Part 1

THE DANGER OF OMNICIDE

[T]his threat of self-destruction and planetary destruction is not something that we will pose one day in the future, if we fail to take precautions; it is here now, hanging over the heads of all of us at every moment. The machinery of destruction is complete, poised on a hair trigger, waiting for the 'button' to be 'pushed' by some misguided or deranged human being or for some faulty computer chip to send out the instruction to fire. That so much should be balanced on so fine a point—that the fruit of four and a half billion years can be undone in a careless moment—is a fact against which belief rebels. Jonathan Schell, *The Fate of the Earth* (1982), pp. 181–182.

Nuclear Madness: Helen Caldicott's Farewell Speech*

Edited by Barbara Gerber

Dr. Caldicott spoke at the Plenary Session "Women Working for Change: Feminist Education and Global Responsibility." She was introduced by Bernice Carroll, whose remarks follow.

Our last speaker tonight is Dr. Helen Caldicott. We welcome her with a mixture of great pride and regret. Regret that she has decided to retire from her public role in this country and to return to Australia; and pride that she has chosen this conference, the NWSA Eighth Annual Convention, as the forum for her farewell address.

Helen Caldicott has been a truly catalytic figure in the nuclear freeze movement and peace movement in this country. Author of Nuclear Madness and Missile Envy, *she was recipient of the Ghandi Peace Prize in 1980. She was Founder and President Emeritus of Physicians for Social Responsibility and Founder of WAND, Women's Action for Nuclear Disarmament. Dr. Caldicott:*

Thank you. It's appropriate, since this is my last major public address here, to talk to women, because I do believe that the future lies with us, in a very deep way. One of the reasons I'm stopping is that I have to go away and work out how we do it. Because we've done nothing yet. We

---

*Previously published in *National Women's Studies Association Perspectives, *Vol. 4, No., 4 (Fall 1986).
(Editor's Note: Women's Action for Nuclear Disarmament [WAND], PO Box 153, New Town Branch, Boston, Mass. 02258, 617–643–6740.)

talk all this equal rights, and we've achieved nothing. Fifty-two percent of us are women. Where is the proportional representation in the Congress? Nowhere, and that's not right. We're very smart. In fact most of us are smarter than men. I want you to stop and think. Think of one strong man that you know. Now think of how many strong women you know. So why are we where we are? Because we haven't got any guts. Do you know why I'm retiring? Because partly men did me in. At Physicians for Social Responsibility there was a male coup, a palace overthrow, done with hidden agendas behind my back. They stabbed me in the back. They didn't have the guts to tell me to my face. They lied to me. I picked it up intuitively, but I didn't have the guts to go and take them on. By the time it happened, I was so done in, emotionally, that I resigned. Then do you know what they did? They got the Nobel Prize: for the work I had done! Yeah!

There've been five previous occasions where women have done the work, and men have gotten the Nobel Prize. One of them is Lisa Mitner, who learned about uranium and radioactivity. As goes PSR and me, so goes the world; because if the feminine principle is destroyed, not just women, but the feminine principle, what bloody hope is there for the world?

The question is, how do we save the earth when we get done in? I'm grieving; I have to go away and get over it. You have to go through your grief as if you lost a baby. It's ridiculous not to grieve because otherwise you will have a nervous breakdown five years hence. I think I'll write a book about it called, *A Lesson for Women*. We've got to stop begging men for equal rights. We have to take over the Congress and determine the law of the land ourselves.

Okay, now let's get on with the issue of the day. The issue of the day is that we're all about to die, be murdered. We did a study at WAND to find out why the freeze failed. It failed because the media killed it. Although 80 percent of Americans for four years have wanted a freeze, the media and Congress killed it. This is not a democracy. Now what I'm going to describe is all male thinking, and male logic, so go with me. All right?

I want to mention Chernobyl: Chernobyl is the first. There's a 50 percent chance of a major meltdown in this country in the next ten years. There's a one in three chance of a meltdown in the world every year. As Chernobyl goes, so others will go, and this Northern hemisphere is going to become very radioactive. I was in Sweden last week and the meat there is radioactive. I think I ate some radioactive reindeer meat, which has given me many sleepless nights. I understand how many people in Europe are feeling. If you get some radioactive material in your body, like strontium 90, it stays there for a long time. Strontium

90 has a half life of twenty-eight years; which means that if you have a pound of it, in twenty-eight years it decays so you have half a pound, In twenty-eight more years a quarter pound. So it is active for 600 years.

The nuclear industry says nobody's died as a result of nuclear power in this country. They say that because they are either medically, biologically and genetically ignorant, in which case they have no right to speak, or they're lying. Mostly they're lying because they are businessmen and they're after profit.

I often think that Chernobyl should have occurred here, because one Russian life does not equal one American life. What a sad commentary. I think that we're going to have to have thousands of Americans dying of acute radiation sickness as the Russians are dying, day after day, and will for six weeks following the Chernobyl accident. That's what happens because the radiation is so intense, the dose they get kills the actively dividing cells of the body, which are in the hair, the skin, the gut, and the blood cells that form in the bone marrow. Five years later, there's going to be an epidemic of leukemia, just as there was in Hiroshima, and fifteen years later there's going to be a high incidence of solid cancer, like thyroid, breast, lung, and other organs, as in Hiroshima. The incidence of cancer is still rising in Hiroshima. It hasn't peaked yet, forty years after the bomb was dropped!

Nuclear power is the pimple on the pumpkin, folks. The pimple on the pumpkin; and the pumpkin is nuclear weapons!

Now. America's got 30,000 hydrogen bombs. In the sixties Robert McNamara said if America had 200 bombs that would be enough to kill one third of the Russians and destroy two thirds of their industry. At that time the Air Force had all the bombs, and the Army and Navy were jealous. So they decided everyone could have their own little bombs. That's why I call my book *Missile Envy*, after Freud. That's the dynamic: mine's bigger than yours, or I want one that's as big as yours. So they diversified and now we've got 30,000 hydrogen bombs, when 200 was enough to kill hundreds of millions of sons and daughters of God. Russia got 20,000. They've always seemed behind, but they've got enough to do it within an instant.

The issue of the arms race really has nothing to do with Communism. We've got to clarify our thinking. If Russia destroys us, when we're all dead, we've got enough bombs at the end to bomb them back and kill all of them. I mean, it's a juvenile four year old, little boy, mentality; but that's what's called deterrent.

But anyway we've changed; now the US policy is to fight and win a protracted nuclear war, fought over a six months period. That's Reagan's policy, and although it will induce nuclear war and the death of all life on earth, it's very exciting and we're proceeding to do it. Star

Wars is part of that. Nuclear war will take about one hour to complete bilaterally.

I want you to imagine; I want you to shut your eyes for a minute and imagine that the bomb is going to land here in ten minutes. I want you to shut your eyes and think. What are you going to do now? Where will you go? Where are your children? Where is your family? Those that you love? What do you value the most about your life? Think of the Spring and the flowers and the planet. Don't forget. The weapons ARE being built, I won't go into them all now, because you can read about them in *Missile Envy*.

Now let me give you a bit of background on your country. It's the only democratic country in the world without a party that represents the people. The only country without a Labor party or a Socialist party. In Australia we have a Socialist government, right now; in New Zealand they have a Socialist government. Maggie Thatcher is going to be replaced by a Socialist. In Germany, there's a Socialist party. Socialism means looking after the people, it means health care clinics, it means clinics to look after children, it means adequate education paid for by the government. In Australia, no operation costs more than five dollars, including heart operations and brain operations. In Australia, education is free. We don't have to pay for it. Well, we do pay for it with our tax dollars.

Your money goes into building these weapons to blast the world. That's where it goes. Only six percent of the Pentagon contracts are competitively bid, all the rest is straight government handout. So, it's Socialism for the corporations, and capitalism for the people. That's the truth. I'm being tough tonight, but I'm telling you the truth. I know it might be hard for some of you to hear, but it's the truth. And you've got to hear it if you want to live. I'm your doctor. I'm telling you, you have a fatal disease, and unless you listen to me, you're going to die. This country is a total military economy, period. Just like Germany used to be. Only this time it's not just localized gas ovens, it's a global gas oven.

This is such a rich country, and most people don't realize what's going on because it is a filtered, trickle-down system where most people can get enough; however, twenty-two percent of the children in this country live in poverty. Twenty-two percent. Thirty four million live in poverty and they're almost all women and children and Black. Fifteen million old women live on an amount of $5,000 a year or less. Fifteen million old women! In the richest country in the world. NOW.

So, what are we going to do now, folks? I came tonight because it's up to us. And I mean no more complaining, no more grizzling and whining. Let's get stuck into it. Now WAND, Women's Action for Nuclear Disarmament teaches you how to run for the Congress and the Senate. Okay. You come from all over this country. It's time we took over the Congress. So, you should all join WAND because you've got big work to do. It's time to stop being polite. It's time to put ourselves on the line. Non-violent disobedience. Why don't we sit at the feet of the civil rights leaders, and find out what they did, and not reinvent the wheel? Maybe it's up to the five million of us to take over Washington and take over the Congress; give up our jobs, and stay there until we stop the arms race. Do you know what? It would only take a couple of months.

How many of you are prepared to try to save the world? If you don't you will not die at peace with yourself or with your maker. You will never live comfortably from this time on, because you will know that you are denying reality, and doing the wrong thing with your life. You and I were only conceived and born to save the earth. We will know, in our lifetime, if we succeeded or failed. If we live, and die of natural causes, we'll know we succeeded. It's our responsibility; an aroused woman is unstoppable. We know how to do it. We are the curators of all life on earth. We hold it in the palms of our hands, and it's our decision whether it lives or dies. I want you to sit down tonight and write a letter. If you've got your own children: to them. If you haven't: to the children of the earth. Tell them what you're going to do to save their lives. And don't let a day pass from now on until you die without doing something. I'm asking for total commitment to save the world. The age of women has arrived, it's now on our shoulders, it is our responsibility to save the earth!

3

Interview
with Rosalie Bertell*

Third World First

Your book No Immediate Danger *alerted Third World First to the importance of producing a publication on the costs* **now** *to the planet and to human health of nuclear technology. Can you tell us how you first became aware of these dangers?*

My original research had to do with the dangers of ordinary medical X-rays. I had specially collected data on about 16 million people, followed over a three year period, and I was not really concerned about the nuclear issue. I thought nuclear power plants were totally contained, whether or not they had an accident.

I think I had a very strong pacifist tendency—I know my home was one of the few after World War II where there was very little rejoicing and I remember my mother saying they shouldn't have dropped the bombs on Hiroshima and Nagasaki. I was about fourteen and didn't know too much about what was going on, but I knew there was a contrast between my situation and everyone ringing church bells and rejoicing out in the streets. It was a good thing that the war was over, but I also knew that there was something wrong about the way it happened.

After I had spent about nine years studying the hazards of medical diagnostic X-rays in a large research center, there was a proposal to build a nuclear power plant near my home town. The citizens' group

---

*Previously published by Third World First, *Links*, Issue 26 (1986).

wanted someone to come to a public hearing and talk about radiation. I went to that hearing saying I'd talk about radiation but I didn't know anything about nuclear power plants.

When I arrived I got a very quick education in manipulated public meetings. They handed me a printed program in which the five men from the nuclear power plant were down with their names, degrees, publications, and then there was an empty place marked "Citizens Committee" with no names or anything. I was also handed a list of questions which the members of the Niagara County legislature had decided to ask the experts from the nuclear station who had had them for two weeks. We sat in the audience and the five men from the power plant sat on the stage. When I asked for an overhead projector, I was told there weren't any; meanwhile, the men from the power plant were putting their movies up in a projection room. First, the five men spoke. They each took exactly fifteen minutes and showed movies of this ultra-clean, white environment—all the radiation handled by remote control equipment and all the workers looking very happy. They said the routine low-level radiation given to the public and workers would be just like a few medical X-rays, which I had just been studying for nine years. They assumed that since your doctor gave you medical X-rays they were harmless. I was really overwhelmed at the public relations approach to this serious subject.

I learned that this plant was being built next to the Cornucopeia Farms where they grow Gerber's baby food. The men from the power plant were surprised to learn this. They hadn't looked at the farms nearby, as they were really looking at Lake Ontario and all the nice cold water for their power plant. Because of the whole selling angle, I spoke rather eloquently that night and the audience responded to the three women that spoke for the citizens' group and not to the five men from the power plant. The next day the Niagara County legislature voted the first moratorium on nuclear power in the US. This was back in about 1973.

After that, I experienced a smear campaign in the newspapers. I experienced reprisals at the cancer research hospital—being carpeted, told that I had to go through certain officials before I talked to the press, etc. They didn't want people in the audience to think I was representing the official position of the institute. Given my fairly low-key, innocent speech, I was taken aback that I got such a strong reaction. It was new to me that nuclear industries were permitted by law to expose people to ionizing radiation routinely. The whole thing made me suspicious. I started to look back to see where these 'permissible levels' started and who said it was okay. Where did these regulations come from and how much were they really releasing?

I discovered they were started in 1950 by the British, American and Canadian physicists who had worked on the Manhattan project, which produced the first nuclear bombs. They had, right after World War II, and as early as 1946, started exploding nuclear bombs in the Pacific. They had four left when the war was over and they immediately went out to Bikini and set two off. They had this theory that the radioactive fallout would only go halfway around the world, but they discovered that it not only went around the world, it went around two and a half times. So they were dropping radioactive material on all the countries of the northern hemisphere. Every country had its own radiation protection regulations and they were violating some of these. In fact, Britain, Canada and the US had three different sets of numbers. So between 1946 and 1950 the physicists hammered out a compromise which they believed would allow them to do the weapons testing. They could then establish themselves as an international recommending body accepted by other countries. They even state quite clearly that this might not be protective of public health, but they could find that out later. Meanwhile, they could undertake all the activities they needed to build nuclear bombs and test them. So these regulations, which are anything but protective of health, were passed and accepted around 1951. There has never been a convenient time for changing them and the further we get away from the original compromise, the more these things take on a kind of magical significance.

Most other nations just accept these regulations and think everything is safe as long as they follow these numbers. They have no idea, for example, that the permissible level of radiation for members of the general public would be a bone marrow dose of five millirem, which is equivalent to the bone marrow dose of 100 chest X-rays a year. I don't think anyone would claim that is safe. Nuclear industry workers are allowed ten times as much.

When the medical and biological community started complaining about the regulations in the late 1960s, they introduced a philosophy. They said we don't really pay attention to these numbers; we really operate ALARA—As Low As Reasonably Achievable, given the economic and social benefits of the activity. This gave a licence to pollute and a philosophy that says if it doesn't cost too much we'll reduce.

So we now have such things as the Chernobyl accident—although radioactive pollution from the local industries is sometimes greater than from Chernobyl—but each thing is individually judged against these unreal standards. When it comes to an accident, there isn't any way to achieve a lower level, so they just make it acceptable—because you don't have an alternative food supply. If you dump your milk in the Irish Sea, the pollution comes back in the fish; if you bury it in ground, it will come up in the next set of crops.

We have now built up carelessness into a no-win situation with radioactive materials, where it becomes acceptable to have cancer deaths; where it becomes acceptable to have deformed children and miscarriages. There is nothing else we can do because we need this 'benefit'. The 'benefit', oddly enough, is not really the medical benefit, nor is it electricity—it is nuclear bombs. They use the same set of regulations for all three industries and, when it comes to the bottom line, the cost benefit ratio is calculated on the basis of preventing a ten megaton blast on London or Paris or New York. If you put that on one side and say we have to have people to handle radioactive material in uranium mining, making bombs, testing bombs, handling them, etc., and if you only have one set of regulations, the final judgement becomes what is needed for national security.

Now we find ourselves in a very strange situation, where the military strategy to save the industrialized countries is not only destroying the environment and the gene pool of those countries, but also destroying the biosphere as radioactive material is circulated in the air, water, and food. It becomes an insane, self-destructive system of poisoning, whether or not we have a nuclear war, whether or not we have a nuclear accident. It is just a matter of substituting a slow poison for a rapid disintegration of the biosphere and the gene pool.

So I have moved rapidly from research looking at low level radiation damage, to realizing that we are doing two things at the same time—we are slightly damaging the next generation, which makes them physically less able to cope, at the same time as we are approving of the pollution that they would have to cope with. That is not a situation that stabilizes, even at a higher level of ill health; that is something which gets progressively worse. That is what brought me out of the research laboratory into trying to make people aware of what was happening before it was too late to reverse it.

We hear in the media of 'acceptable', 'permissible', and 'safe' levels of radiation, often reassuringly related to background levels of radiation. Can you comment on these reassurances from the nuclear industry and the political establishment?

I think that we need to recognize that what is natural is not necessarily harmless. There are things in our natural environment, like arsenic, which just because it is there, doesn't give us a right to increase it in someone's tea! There certainly is a health cost to be paid because of natural background radiation. The most obvious one is ageing. People recognize that most of the cancers are old age diseases and your chronological age is a very good measure of how much natural background radiation you have been exposed to. As you begin to accumulate it, you also accumulate the kinds of ill health that are connected with natural background exposure, including, primarily, damage to the DNA of cells.

When we look at natural background radiation, we are talking about the natural radionuclides in their natural state, which is deep under the earth where they are less hazardous to people. However when we mine uranium, radium or thorium, we bring them up to the surface. We pulverize them into very small particles and they blow in the wind or wash down into drinking water or irrigation ditches. Also, the gaseous form, radon, is released into the air which increases lung cancers and makes cigarettes and other things more hazardous. All of this is called natural background radiation even when it is not in its natural state.

One of the characteristics of natural radionuclides, even when they are taken into the body, is that they spread the dose rather homogeneously throughout all the tissue. On the other hand we have now, since 1945, all these man-made radionuclides which are really chemicals that never used to exist in a radioactive form in our ordinary environment. They are not only giving off radiation, but they are on chemical carriers. These act differently in the body. So, where naturally-occurring potassium would spread through the whole body, if you take in radioactive iodine, which is a man-made fission product, it tends to concentrate in the thyroid gland, giving a big dose to the thyroid. These substances cause different biological effects and they can't just be directly compared to natural background radiation.

Calculated Thyroid Dose to Infants in Millirads Resulting
from Iodine—131 Concentration in Milk

	1966	1967	1968	1969	1970	1971	1972	1973	1974
Chiba, Japan	5	32	17				4	10	
United Kingdom		7							
Sebastian City, USA	107								
Houston, USA		43							
Buenos Aires, Argentina	310	50	28		52	48	81	20	97
Malanda, Australia	127	120	52		67	62	2	1	28
La Paz, Bolivia					120	30	44	60	35
Suva, Fiji	210	33	51		43	33	5	5	28
Diego-Suarez, Madagascar	160	22	80			75			
Noumea, New Caledonia		5			40	30			184
Arequipa, Peru			70		90	35			
Lima, Peru	70	23	50		10	13			
Apia, Samoa	170	97	38		71	84	5	13	51
Tahiti, French Polynesia		55	60		130	210	12	130	680
Pretoria, South Africa					92	127			

(Source: United Nations Scientific Committee on the Effects of Atomic Radiation, 1977, Annex C, page 139)

NB: French nuclear weapons testing began in French Polynesia in 1966.

There are other implications of the use of language, that 'natural' background radiation is anything that is not 'man-made' regardless of its state or bio-availability. 'Background radiation' now means both natural materials and also fission products from the nuclear industry and that includes between 400 and 500 chemicals that give off radioactive or ionizing particles. One year after they have been released into the environment by the nuclear bomb tests, they are included in background radiation. When the Chernobyl accident happened, they compared radioactive iodine with background levels of radioactive iodine. Well, there shouldn't be any radioactive iodine in our environment. Anything new that is being added is being reported as only a small percentage of background, which is really meaningless, because background just keeps going up. Also the health effects are quite different from the health effects of the naturally occurring radionuclides so this kind of reporting is just self-deception.

What are the chief sources of radiation danger affecting the Third World?

When I think of the Third World I think of indigenous people of the First World as well as countries that are labelled 'Third World' or 'developing'. The two major sources of pollution are uranium mining and milling which are often carried out on the land of indigenous peoples, such as Roxby Downs on the land of the aboriginal people in Australia. South Africa is exploiting the Namibian people at the Rossing mine. In North America, it is usually the land of American Indians that is mined for uranium. All the radioactive material left at the mine entrance is on their land, so they live with it too.

Nuclear weapons testing was carried out in the Third World at Bikini, Enewetak and other atolls in the Pacific islands. The US and Britain set off some 200 nuclear blasts in the Pacific and the French have set off about 150 now. There have been two nuclear bombs, one atomic and one hydrogen, exploded off the coast of South Africa. In the most recent reports from the United Nations, the increase in background radiation in the southern hemisphere is greater than the increase in the northern hemisphere.

Many other Third World countries that don't have uranium mining or are used for nuclear testing have been affected too. One might think of Brazil, which has thorium mining, or the southern hemisphere as a whole, which has been blanketed with the French nuclear weapons testing in French Polynesia. In terms of direct radionuclides, Peru has already reported finding radionuclides in their fish to the United Nations and the fish industry is one of their major industries; the Baja Peninsula in Mexico has reported fish contaminated with radionuclides; there has been very high fallout of radioactive iodine in Bolivia—again, most likely from the French testing. These are all direct effects.

The indirect effects would include thermal pollution. When you set off nuclear bombs, you change the temperature of the air. If you set them off underwater, you change the ocean temperature. The ocean current, coming up from the South Pole along the South American Pacific coast in 1983, came up warm instead of cold, causing what was called the El Niño effect in Peru with landslides and rains. It also changed the direction of the trade winds at the equator and caused the monsoons to miss Australia and Fiji, which led to drought on the western side of the Pacific and rains and landslides on the eastern side. These are major disasters for Third World peoples. The seed was lost of entire crops for which there is no replacement in any seed bank, besides the direct loss of life that occurred in these rainfalls. There are many direct and indirect kinds of problems that are happening in the Third World that are part of the First World's military survival strategy—that are altering the radiological environment, altering food and quality of food, altering climate and temperature. These are very severe difficulties for countries that already have food problems.

If reactors are as dangerous as you suggest, why are they being sought by Third World governments?

I think you have to look at which Third World governments are looking for nuclear power and then you also have to look at the strategies of First World governments whose domestic nuclear industry has collapsed. The First World wants to sell its unwanted technology and the Third World is a good dumping place. Most of the First World is now moving to the Star Wars scenario or to laser beam or fission-materated fusion reactors, so they want to sell their fission technology—which they've always admitted was not a good answer to the energy crisis—to the Third World.

If you look at Third World countries you'll find that many of them have already discovered that they don't want nuclear power. Some are being forced into decisions in favor of nuclear power, despite their own studies. I'm thinking of countries such as the Philippines, where, in a major internal study of their energy needs, they prioritized energy sources and at the bottom of the pile was the nuclear option. However, when it came to trying to get loans from the export-import bank or the World Bank, they could only get a loan for a nuclear power plant. They couldn't get loans for any of their other preferred energy strategies. So that is an example of a country that was somewhat forced into nuclear power which they are now cancelling.

Other interested countries are traditional enemies of countries that have developed nuclear power. Korea, for example, is very uncomfortable with mainland China testing and stockpiling nuclear bombs, so Korea has one of the most aggressive nuclear power programs that can easily be moved into nuclear weapons. You also find an active program in Pakistan, a traditional enemy of India which is developing nuclear bombs. You find South Africa developing the whole nuclear fuel cycle including nuclear weapons. You find the two traditional enemies in South America, Argentina and Brazil, developing nuclear technology and Peru trying to compete. Again the countries that have moved in to the nuclear field have had a rather thinly veiled desire for nuclear weapons and they are for the most part totalitarian and militaristic regimes.

As a member of the study commission for the World Council of Churches (WCC), we looked into the argument, the original policy of the WCC, that demanded that the benefits of nuclear power be given to Third World countries. They formed this policy in 1972. However, in about 1979, there were 61 Third World countries that directly petitioned the WCC to change their policy and not to promote the transfer of nuclear technology to the Third World. Subsequently, the WCC did officially change their position on this issue. Unfortunately, the Catholic Church has not yet changed and I think the Catholic Church is now the only one demanding nuclear technology transfer to the Third World, and I am sure it is coming out of ignorance.

In No Immediate Danger *and earlier in this interview, you distinguished two hazards in radionuclides, their radioactivity and their chemically toxic character. Should the efforts to alert the public to radiation effects be separated from the dangers of toxic chemicals such as dioxin or MIC, or is it just a question of scale?*

I think there are probably three things to be said in answer to that. One is that, back in the 1920s, Herman Muller, a famous geneticist who received a Nobel Prize for demonstrating the genetic effects of radiation, announced that he could produce in his laboratory in two months all the kinds of genetic damage that large numbers of scientists had taken twenty years to produce. Irradiation is the most efficient of the mutagens and of course that is what is most important in the long run for species survival.

There is another property of radiation. When chromosomes are damaged and then damaged a second time before they have had a chance to repair, then you have some of the most bizarre of chromosome problems. These are considered peculiar to radiation—chemicals don't produce these double breaks within a four to six hour period—and they produce some of the most damaged children. The UN has made an attempt to bridge between the toxicity of radiation and the toxicity of other chemicals. Incidentally, most of the toxic chemicals were created to kill the earth. In the Vietnam war there were herbicides, pesticides and defoliants, all military productions and they can be pretty awful. The United Nations has proposed using radionuclides as a scale of toxicity, fitting the chemicals in where they belong on that scale, since the basic range is covered by the large number of radioactive chemicals we now have.

I would encourage chemists who have never worked with radiation to begin thinking about radioactive chemicals, because they often give the impression that a given chemical is the worst possible hazard to life on the planet. If you talk to them you'll find that they've only studied nonradiological chemicals because that is their field. On the other hand, if you talk to radio biologists, they often don't know anything at all about the dioxins or other toxic chemicals, so there needs to be dialogue between these different fields because human life is threatened. They are all serious but I think I would put radiation and carelessness with radiation at the top of the list.

You direct research into low level radiation at the Institute in Toronto, you have written extensively on the subject, you are involved in practical health programs in the Pacific islands, and you are at this moment engaged in an extended program of talks and meetings in Britain and Europe. What do you ultimately hope to achieve?

Reflecting on the situation, I perceive that our present path is one headed towards death—and I mean species death—whether this is fast, with nuclear war or technological disaster, or whether it is a slow poison. I see people reacting as they react to death generally, either by denial or by anger and frustration or by a certain barter where they will try to come terms with it, but not fully. A few people have accepted that this is what we are doing and are considering changing their ways. I don't think that, as a species, we're depraved or locked into committing mass suicide or omnicide. I think we're stupid enough to do it, I think we're capable of doing it, but I don't think there is anything necessitating our doing it.

When I look at past history, I realize that there were times when you might have been tempted to say human beings have always had slavery and so they always will have slavery, or human beings always practiced cannibalism so they always will practice cannibalism, or they always had colonialism so they always will practice colonialism, and I see that these things have changed. I don't accept that just because we have always had war, we need always have war. There are societies that have never had war, have no history of war, have no word in their language for enemy and who thrive on cooperation rather than competition. We have this ability. So what I try to do is two things. Firstly, to motivate change by making visible the damage that we are doing to ourselves and the life support environment, and, secondly, to begin to build the infrastructure for a global village which is where we have to go if we are not going to have war. There are things about nationalism that we can keep, like customs, language, life-style, food. There are many beautiful things, but there is no reason why we need to raise standing armies and there is no reason why we need to kill people that don't agree with the system.

What we are talking about giving up is the right of a nation to force its own people to kill others, whether this be internally or externally. That is a very simple thing. Yet if we could do that we could begin to organize on the basis of a global village which would not only respect diversity but be glad of it because diversity gives us survival potential and our monoculture is another form of suicide. Survival comes from diversity and an ability to cope with many changing situations, an ability to share when one part of the world has abundance and another part has need. We have much of the infrastructure in place, we have global communication, we have transportation, we know the way to cure most diseases, we have one and a half times as much food as we need for the global population. There is no reason for our present stalemate except that we seem to be unable to get rid of this militaristic head and attitude, so what I am trying to do is raise consciousness and provide alternative survival structures globally.

Part 2

TIME TO READ
THE WRITING
ON THE WALL

[I]f we are honest with ourselves we have to admit that unless we rid ourselves of our nuclear arsenals a holocaust not only *might* occur but *will* occur—if not today, then tomorrow; if not this year, then the next. We have come to live on borrowed time: every year of continued human life on earth is a borrowed year, every day a borrowed day. Jonathan Schell, *The Fate of the Earth* (1982), p. 183.

4

Unnumbing Ourselves

Diana E. H. Russell

> When one tries to face the nuclear predicament, one feels sick, whereas when one pushes it out of mind, as apparently one must do most of the time in order to carry on with life, one feels well again. But this feeling of well-being is based on a denial of the most important reality of our time, and therefore is itself a kind of sickness. A society that systematically shuts its eyes to an urgent peril to its physical survival and fails to take any steps to save itself cannot be called psychologically well. (Jonathan Schell, *The Fate of the Earth*, [1982], p. 8).

I have spent a great deal of time and energy avoiding the reality and implications of the nuclear threat. The problem was first brought to my reluctant attention by Britain's Committee on Nuclear Disarmament when I was living in England in the late 1950s. Once aware, I deliberately refused to think about it for any length of time. I found that dwelling on it, either emotionally or intellectually, was too incapacitating, too threatening to my ability to proceed with the rest of my life.

This kind of denial and suppression was encouraged by most of the people and institutions that were part of my daily life in England at that time. As a student at the London School of Economics, I had to turn in my assignments on time. Lectures in economics were conducted as if the world economy were not in jeopardy. Careers were determined by one's grades. One was still expected to arrive at work with a psyche that was sufficiently intact to enable one to do a competent job and to appear undisturbed. Everyone else I knew acted as if there were no threat. Not once did the subject of nuclear war come up as a relevant topic in psychology or sociology classes.

When I came to the United States in 1963 I could not ignore the yellow and black bombshelter signs that were scattered around the town of Cambridge, Massachusetts. But nobody I met appeared to take them very seriously. Again, the danger of nuclear war was never mentioned or discussed in my graduate school classes in psychology, sociology, or government at Harvard University.

This indifference to the nuclear crisis did not apply to other issues, for me or for many Americans. The Civil Rights movement was at an apex, and it was followed by rising protests against the Vietnam War. I was far from apathetic politically. My primary political activity had long been focused on opposing the system of apartheid in South Africa—the country where I was born and raised. Upon coming to the United States, my commitment entailed working with various groups to try to encourage US divestment in South Africa.

My political activity in South Africa had led to my arrest for participating in an anti-apartheid demonstration in that country. Being unwilling to stay in South Africa until my trial, I left the country illegally, for which I was found guilty of contempt of court. Far more serious than that was my participation in the African Resistance Movement (ARM), a revolutionary group that, along with the African National Congress and other groups, decided the time had come to go beyond non-violent methods of resistance. Passive resistance had proven futile in a society where the ruling caste was determined to keep virtually all power and privilege in white hands. We confined ourselves to the sabotaging of government property as a first step in this new phase of the struggle for justice in that country. Fortunately for me, I left South Africa just prior to the capture of many ARM members and the complete destruction of this movement.

In 1971 I became active in the women's liberation movement. Since then my research, writing and speaking has focused on rape, child sexual abuse, pornography, wife abuse, and other forms of violence against women. My organizational work has focused on international feminism and pornography (I was one of the organizers of the International Tribunal on Crimes Against Women in 1976 and in 1977 I helped to found a San Francisco-based group called Women Against Violence in Pornography and Media [WAVPM]—the first feminist organization to make an attack on pornography its major goal). Throughout all those years and all that activity, I continued largely to ignore the threat of nuclear extermination or to see the connections between it and the work I was doing.

As a sociology professor at Mills College, a small private women's college in Oakland, California, I have sometimes taught a course on the sociology of oppression. The only interruption in my almost total denial of the nuclear danger was my inclusion of material on that issue. In conjunction with readings on the dropping of atomic bombs on Japan, I would show the film "Hiroshima and Nagasaki." This documentary includes footage long suppressed by the US government of scenes in a hospital where victims of the atomic bomb went for treatment or to die. The images of these charred and mutilated human beings, shockingly silent and uncomplaining, are some of the most painful and haunting that I have ever seen. However, until 1983, I did not allow myself to move from my concern about the bombing of Hiroshima and Nagasaki to consciousness of the growing possibility that we could all be victims of such a fate at any moment.

What finally shook me out of my dream world? The growing anti-nuclear movement, though generally underplayed and discounted by the mass media, began to penetrate my defenses by the early 1980s. Nevertheless, I still considered the nuclear threat to be a "people's" issue rather than a feminist one. Reading Helen Caldicott's book *Nuclear Madness* had a considerable impact. Her portrayal of the devastating effects of a nuclear war, of the increasing likelihood that one will occur, of the link between the development of nuclear energy and the risk of a nuclear holocaust, and of the urgent need to take action, were frightening and convincing.

I was particularly intrigued by an observation Caldicott made on television that more women than men are opposed to nuclear weapons. To explain this Caldicott argued that it is much more common for men to suffer from a split between their thinking and their emotions. She nicely captured this analysis in the slogan, "Take the Toys Away from the Boys!" Much to my disappointment, Caldicott did not develop this preliminary feminist analysis in *Nuclear Madness*. Indeed, Caldicott didn't even include those points in her book. Reading Jonathan Schell's *The Fate of the Earth* also moved me greatly, pushing me to more active and serious involvement in disarmament work. I realized that the sexual abuse research I was pursuing at that time assumed a future that I had no right to assume.

In January 1983 I started looking for an anti-nuclear group to work with. I wanted to be part of an all-women's feminist anti-nuclear organization because I didn't want to have to struggle with male sexism at the same time that I tried to deal with what was for me the most difficult of all issues. When I found none existed in the San Francisco bay area, I began one myself, creating FANG (Feminist Anti-Nuclear Group) in October 1983. (FANG's activities are described in chapter 20 of this volume.) It was also during this period that I visited the Puget Sound Women's Peace Camp in Washington and decided to undertake this anthology.

My disappointment over the demise of FANG in 1984 combined with my failure to find a publisher for this anthology deflected me from these concerns once again. Jonathan Schell eloquently describes how extraordinarily difficult it is to continually face contemporary nuclear reality.

> It is as though life itself were one huge distraction, diverting our attention from the peril to life. In its apparent durability, a world menaced with imminent doom is in a way deceptive. It is almost an illusion. Now we are sitting at the breakfast table drinking our coffee and reading the newspaper, but in a moment we may be inside a fireball whose temperature is tens of thousands of degrees. Now we are on our way to work, walking through the city streets, but in a moment we may be standing on an empty plain under a darkening sky looking for the charred remnants of our children. Now we are alive, but in a moment we may be dead. Now there is human life on earth, but in a moment it may be gone (1982, p. 182).

In a random sample survey of 468 University of Oregon students conducted in the winter of 1984, sixty-one percent admitted that they sometimes or often blocked out their feelings or emotions about the possibility of nuclear war (Gwartney-Gibbs, 1985, p. 9). Only fourteen percent claimed never to do this.

Sayre Sheldon conceives of the unnumbing process as a "conversion experience" (1983, p. 30). She believes that most people who are working for nuclear disarmament have had such an experience. She describes it as "a specific realization that nuclear weapons are real, and that they will be used if we continue to act like people picnicking on a railroad track with the train approaching" (1983, p. 30). Sheldon describes her conversion experience as follows:

> . . . I was driving to work one perfect May morning two years ago. I was enjoying the river and the trees when the scene abruptly vanished— blotted out, gone forever, no more springs with milky blue skies and pale new leaves—gone only for an instant but I could not forget it. . . . [F]or a moment I *knew* that the natural world could disappear (1983, p. 30).

Sheldon describes another woman's unnumbing in the following way:

> [S]he happened to have her car radio on while driving her children home from school and heard a doctor describe the drugs that were being stock-piled in Washington to dispense after a nuclear attack, so that people could kill their suffering families. She saw herself lining up her children on the bed and giving them the pills. For a moment she *knew* how it would feel to kill her children. . . . (1983, p. 30).

Seeing a film changed the life of Vivienne Verdon-Roe, director of the award-winning anti-nuclear documentary, "Women—For America, For the World."

Personally, up until four years ago, I was a political blob . . . an ostrich with my head buried firmly in the sand. I felt there was nothing I could do about the world's problems, so I looked away. Then I saw a documentary film – *The Final Epidemic* – which showed what would happen to a city and its inhabitants if just one nuclear bomb was dropped. The film changed my life: it forced me to face *reality*, to look at the nuclear problem straight on (Paulson, 1986, p. 114).

The problem with applying the notion of a conversion experience to the nuclear threat is that it doesn't capture the day-to-day or week-to-week fluctuations in denial that many people experience. In addition, it implies that the converted cannot progress to a greater degree of enlightenment or commitment to work for disarmament. Helen Caldicott, for example, was already highly aware of the danger of a nuclear holocaust when she obtained information that led her to make an even deeper commitment to try to change the nuclear mentality. She writes: "At the moment when I learned that our world would be controlled by computers by late 1983 or 1984 and that cruise missiles signal the practical end of arms-control treaties, I knew that I would have to leave medicine" (1984, p. 17). At the time, Caldicott specialized in the treatment of children suffering from cystic fibrosis. She found herself asking the question: "What was the use of keeping these children alive for another five to twenty years by the application of meticulous and loving medical care, when during this time they could be vaporized in a nuclear war?" (1984, p. 19).

After emphasizing that "there is no issue more important than the avoidance of nuclear war," Carl Sagan points out that denial is "one of the most serious problems we face. If everyone had a profound and immediate sense of the actual consequences of nuclear war, we would be much more willing to confront and challenge national leaders, of all nations, when they present narrow and self-serving arguments for the continuation of mutual, nuclear terror" (Paulson, 1987, p. 13).

Despite the pain and distress of facing the ever present danger of nuclear war, I agree with Jonathan Schell's argument that avoidance and inertia produce much more serious despair and indifference.

At present, most of us do nothing. We look away. We remain calm. We are silent. We take refuge in the hope that the holocaust won't happen, and turn back to our individual concerns. We deny the truth that is all around us. Indifferent to the future of our kind, we grow indifferent to one another. We drift apart. We grow cold. We drowse our way toward the end of the world. But if once we shook off our lethargy and fatigue and began to act, the climate would change. Just as inertia produces despair – a despair often so deep that it does not even know itself as despair – arousal and action would give us access to hope, and life would start to mend: not just life in its entirety but daily life, every individual life. At that point, we would begin to withdraw from our role as both the victims and the perpetrators of mass murder. We would no longer be the destroyers of mankind but, rather, the gateway through which the future generations would enter the world (1982, p. 230).

The term "numbing" was coined by Robert Lifton (1982) to describe the defense mechanism that enables so many of us to refuse to confront the ever present danger of nuclear war. But nuclear war is not the only issue to which we have become numb. Most of us live as if millions of people in the world aren't starving, including people in the United States. If we think at all about the many children who are being beaten and sexually molested, or all the women who are being battered and raped, it is usually as some shocking statistic about which we don't allow ourselves to feel.

By definition, when we are in the grip of numbness or denial, we don't recognize it, just as we don't know when we are engaging in psychological repression. Yet, it is exactly this process which makes possible the continuation of some of the worst cases of oppression. For this reason it is helpful to look at examples of mass numbing that hindsight has made conspicuous. History's most striking case of such widespread numbing occurred in prewar Nazi Germany.

Adolf Hitler's virulent anti-Semitism was a matter of public record. His book *Mein Kampf* revealed the extremity of his hatred of Jews as did his speeches. The fact that many other Germans were also extremely anti-Semitic became increasingly clear in the late 1930s when discrimination and overt physical attacks on Jews escalated dramatically. Although some Jews read the writing on the wall and saved their lives by leaving Germany, many more did not. Many of those who stayed, as well as many of the non-Jewish Germans opposed to Hitler, were classic victims of denial: they simply could not believe that Hitler and his Nazi supporters would carry out their murderous threats against Jews.

The motivations behind denial were different for Jews and non-Jews. For non-Jews, denial eliminated the need to risk opposing the Nazi regime. These risks included death and torture or economic catastrophe for oneself and one's family. On a less extreme level, denial meant not having to feel responsibility or guilt. A powerful motivation for denial among Jews was the enormous sacrifices they would have had to make in order to leave their country, particularly as anti-Semitism escalated. Departing from Germany meant abandoning most of one's money and worldly goods, starting from scratch in a new country where a different language was spoken, searching for work in a society ravaged by the Depression and where many prospective employers and potential neighbors were likely to be both anti-Semitic and xenophobic. It meant deserting relatives and friends, and, as time went on, leaving became increasingly difficult.

To read the writing on the wall also required recognition of the monstrous depths to which anti-Semitism can descend, and the sadistic cruelty and barbarity of which ordinary people are capable. The behavior displayed during the Nazi era is often described as "inhuman"— that is, as impossible for human beings to perform. But the very notion that certain kinds of acts are inhuman demonstrates denial of the human capacity for evil.

The consequence of blocking out reality in pre-World War II Germany was that millions of Jews were subjected to the "final solution." Understandable as this numbing is, it proved to be a fatally dysfunctional defense mechanism. Those Jews who miraculously survived the Nazi inferno were permanently scarred, having witnessed atrocities against their people, usually including members of their own families or friends and other loved ones.

The dangerous effects of pornography in the West provide a less extreme example of numbing that is more difficult to recognize because it has not yet been illuminated by hindsight. This particular form of woman-hating has not been articulated in such a manifesto as *Mein Kampf.* But it is spewed forth by a multibillion dollar industry which publishes millions of books and magazines and sells thousands of movies and videotapes every year, among them many examples of unadulterated misogyny of the most extreme nature.

Considerable research on the effects of pornography has been conducted in recent years by reputable scholars. Again and again studies demonstrate the connection between exposure to pornography and violent behavior toward women.[1] Even before such research had been conducted, the simple application of the laws of learning suggested that pornography, like any other media, conditions attitudes and behavior. Logic also suggests that if we believe racist propaganda promotes racism—which most liberals and radicals believe—then sexist propaganda must promote sexism. Similarly, society has not tried to solve the problem of physical abuse of children by having movie houses and "parent" book stores in every town filled with materials showing parents beating up their children and children loving it. But when a sexual element is introduced into the scenario and women are the victims, logic flies out of the window and the material is described as harmlessly cathartic and defended as free speech.

---

[1] I have undertaken a detailed analysis of the causal connection between pornography and rape elsewhere (Russell, 1988).

The irrational and dangerous arguments used to defend pornography have lulled many women into a numbing tolerance of men's avid consumption of it. *Hustler, Playboy,* and *Penthouse* accumulate in millions of homes across the nation each month. Snuff movies, which provide realistic portrayals of women being disemboweled and murdered for the sexual pleasure of men, caused a protest among feminists, but our voices have failed to stop their continuing production. Larry Flynt responded to feminist attacks on pornography by presenting on the cover of *Hustler* a picture of a woman being ground up in a meat grinder. Next to the picture was the quip: "We will no longer hang women up like pieces of meat." The implication is that men will kill women instead. I believe that such misogyny has resulted in the murder of many women in this country.[2]

Although pornography using children as models is against the law in the United States, an endless supply of incest-promoting books is easily available. Following are some of the titles available in one "adult" bookstore in downtown Berkeley, California: "Daddy's Slave Girl," "Docile Daughters," "Seduced by Mom," "Joanie's Lust for Dad," "Incest Discipline: Trained Daughters," "Raped Mom: Degraded Daughter," "Incest: Abused Innocence," "Mom's Incest Urges," "Family Sex Trip," "The Nympho Stepmom," "Raped Daughter." And extrafamilial child sexual abuse is celebrated as enthusiastically in pornography as is incestuous abuse. For example: "Teasing Teens: Forced to Please," "Pedophilia: Soft Young Flesh Case Studies," "Too Young for Marriage," "The Child Bride," "School Girl in Bondage."

Numbing to pornography is so prevalent that even people who vociferously oppose racism when they encounter it fail to denounce the extreme racism that characterizes some pornography. As Alice Walker has pointed out, "Where white women are depicted in pornography as "objects," Black women are depicted as animals. Where white women are at least depicted as human bodies if not beings, Black women are depicted as shit" (1980, p. 103). Here is a sample of book or magazine titles about Afro-American women—found in the same Berkeley store and a store in Livermore, California: "Jungle Babies," "Black Cunts," "Dark Meat," "Big Black Knockers," "Chocolate Whoppers," "Black Pussy," "Big Black Juggs," "Fat, Black and Sassy," "Chocolate Milk," "Sweet Tasting Chocolate Twats," "Oreo: A Magazine for Adults who Love Dynamic Afro-sex."[3]

Racist stereotypes in pornography become even clearer when the

---

[2]Jill Radford and I are currently completing an anthology on this subject titled *Femicide: The Politics of Woman-Killing* to be published by Twayne Publishers, 1989.
[3]Alice Mayall gave me the titles from the Livermore store.

titles about different racial and ethnic groups are compared. For example, common titles about Asian women portray them as sweet and demure, unlike those about Afro-American women: "Asian Dolls," "Oriental Kittens," "Spring Blossom," "Oriental Delight." Bondage of Asian women is another popular theme in pornography, for example: "Oriental Captives," "Teen Slaves of Saigon." Examples of anti-Semitic pornography include "Nazi Bondage Tortures," "Sluts of the SS," "Gestapo Mistresses," "Auschwitz Terror," "Gestapo Sex Crimes," "Swastika She-Devil," "Gestapo Training School," "Nazi Sex Captives," "Gestapo Stud Farm."

The following paragraph appears on the back cover of one of these books, *Soul Slave* (1981): "When the white man tied the ropes around me, I moaned with a deep sense of satisfaction in my heart. I felt the ropes cutting into my wrists and I shivered with desire. I was just a nigger bitch, and this white man knew just how a nigger bitch should be treated." Here is a small sampling of the kind of racist material inside the covers of this book.

Rance [a white man] looked down at me and said, "Get naked, Nigger!" And those words were like the greatest poetry in the world to me. Those words were the most fascinating and sexy words that any man had ever spoken to me (p. 20). . . . He smiled at me again, and I could tell that he appreciated something about my nigger soul, something that I had never known was deep in there before. It was like that man had dug down there in the deepest part of me and found something that was ultimate nigger, ultimate bitch, ultimate pain-loving whore (p. 23).
"I am going to give you the fucking of your worthless, nigger life," he said (p. 27). . . . Then he cleared his throat and he spit at me. A glob of spittle landed on one of my big, nigger tits (p. 28). . . . I had never felt more alive in my life, my worthless, nigger life (p. 30). . . . One of them [white boys] told me that I was a special nigger, that I could take more cock into my pussy than any dozen Southern belles. I thought about that and it gave me pride. There was little else that I could be proud of (p. 57).
"Yeah, you nigger bitch," the white boy who was fucking me growled. "You nigger whore." And I fell in love with those words of abuse. . . . I was a nigger, and I knew that no white boy in Birmingham would ever have the courage to take me out in public. But they were going to keep coming around, driving around the nigger section of the city, looking for me on Saturday night, and I knew that that made me special to them. . . . I thought that there was nothing better in the world than a good white cock coming in a nigger cunt (pp. 67–68).

And so it goes on for 180 pages.

The sick mentality that such books appeal to, is, unfortunately, too widespread to dismiss as the pathology of a few individuals. Racism, anti-Semitism and misogyny are social diseases. Only a tiny fraction of women are aware that the kind of titles quoted above are commonplace in pornographic bookstores. Most women would prefer not to know. The rage it arouses is uncomfortable, and it is deeply alienating and disturbing to try to comprehend that such material is purchased by many men for sexual entertainment and gratification. But refusing to acknowledge the existence and proliferation of such anti-woman and racist literature is a form of numbing that has permitted this industry to grow and flourish under our very noses with little resistance from women. While numbing is an understandable defense mechanism, it serves us poorly. At the same time that some women are helping rape victims, battered women, and victims of child sexual abuse to cope with their traumatic experiences, pornography undermines their work and promotes the very crimes they are endeavoring to combat. And a great deal more money is invested every year in pornography than is used to try to prevent or ameliorate the violence and sexual abuse that it causes.

There are many feminists who have been willing to unnumb themselves to pornography. Far fewer have woken up to the fact that all our lives are at risk because of nuclear weapons and the danger of a nuclear war or accident. I hope that by examining two monumental cases of numbing—the diabolical depths of anti-Semitism in Nazi Germany and the vicious and violence-promoting nature of pornography—more people will recognize the widespread defenses that we use to deny the fact that we are all living on borrowed time.

As well as showing my sociology of oppression class at Mills College a movie on the consequences of the bombing of Hiroshima and Nagasaki, I show films about Nazi Germany and its concentration camps and what white people are doing to black people in apartheid South Africa. Students are invariably shocked by the extremity of violence and brutality in these situations and very critical of all the non-Jewish Germans and white South Africans who did or do nothing to try to stop it. But when I raise the question of why so few of them are doing anything to try to stop their own government—or any other government—from committing genocide or omnicide by threatening to use nuclear weapons, they are taken aback. They have learned to live with this horror by denying its existence. It does not seem nearly as serious and odious to them as atrocities in Nazi Germany and South Africa.

When my students' denial starts to crumble in the face of the facts and figures about nuclear war, they then talk about how powerless they feel to change the situation. I point out that working with others, or even on one's own, to try to change the government's policies in this country is infinitely easier and involves infinitely less personal risk than what it took to do the same in Nazi Germany, where being sent to a concentration camp was the common fate of a political activist, or in South

Africa, where detention without trial is an everyday reality. Why are so many of us appalled by the apathy of the Germans and white South Africans, but do nothing to try to stop the obliteration of the entire planet here and now? After all, we live in the country that is most responsible for getting us in this predicament in the first place; it is certainly one of the most able to get us out of it. Indeed, there is no hope of getting out of it without the cooperation of the United States.

The reality is that there may be no future generation to judge us for doing nothing if we allow ourselves to numb out and give in to feelings of powerlessness. At some point, our numbing becomes our collusion. When we are both aware of and able to do something about the nuclear threat but do nothing, we become like the "good" Germans who were bystanders during the Nazi holocaust.

REFERENCES

Caldicott, Helen, *Nuclear Madness* (New York: Bantam Books, 1978).

Caldicott, Helen, *Missile Envy* (New York: William Morrow, 1984).

Cochran, Rita, *Soul Slave* (New York: Star Distributors, 1981).

Gwartney-Gibbs, Patricia, "Student Attitudes Studied," *Lane County Nuclear News Bureau*, Vol. 3, No. 5 (1985).

Jones, Lynne (ed.), *Keeping the Peace* (London: The Women's Press, 1983).

Lifton, Robert and Falk, Richard, *Indefensible Weapons* (New York: Basic Books, 1982).

Paulson, Dennis, *Voices of Survival in the Nuclear Age* (Santa Barbara: Capra Press, 1986).

Russell, Diana, "Pornography and Rape: A Causal Model," *Political Psychology*, Vol. 9, No. 1 (March 1988).

Schell, Jonathan, *The Fate of the Earth* (New York: Avon Books, 1982).

Sheldon, Sayre, "Organizing a National Campaign: Women's Party for Survival, USA," in *Keeping the Peace*, edited by Lynne Jones (London: The Women's Press, 1983).

Walker, Alice, "Coming Apart," in *Take Back the Night*, edited by Laura Lederer (New York: William Morrow, 1980).

5

The Hidden Member
of Our Family*

Fran Peavey

What would I do with my last few minutes if the sirens went off? Would I look out my window and watch it all go, waiting that fraction of an eternity for the wave to evaporate me? Would I grab whoever is nearby and give them all the love I have? Or would I lie down on the hill near my house, hug the earth like a dying lover, and apologize?

When you build a house yourself, it always feels a little more fragile than other buildings you visit. You look at a wall and see the individual two-by-fours and sheetrock. You know what's keeping the windows from falling out, how the siding is nailed in place. This is how I felt about the house I remodeled and lived in on Potrero Hill in San Francisco.

One day in 1980, I was sitting in my living room reading the newspaper. President Carter was threatening the Soviet Union with nuclear weapons because the Soviets had invaded Afghanistan. I felt cold and afraid. It started to sink into my consciousness that the nuclear threat was serious and close, that our president was really thinking about using those bombs. During the Cuban Missile Crisis I'd felt certain that neither side would be stupid enough to use nuclear weapons. During the Vietnam War some people worried that the United States would use nuclear bombs. Not me. Even while protesting against

*Previously published in Fran Peavey, *Heart Politics* (Philadelphia: New Society Publishers, 1986).

nuclear power in the late seventies, I didn't give much thought to the other nuclear menace. But the way Carter was talking scared me.

Then it happened: the house rattled with a boom. It was a sharp jolt, and I knew that a nuclear bomb had exploded—over in Oakland, I guessed. In panic I dived to the floor below the window. As I cowered there, everything I had ever learned about nuclear bombs came into my mind. Don't look at the explosion or your eyes will melt and run down your checks. The concussion will be coming soon, then the wind and firestorm. My poor house, and poor me! I waited and waited. How would I know how long to keep from looking out? After what seemed an eternity, I poked my head up to the window and peeked out between my fingers. Where was the mushroom cloud? I looked again, went outside, and climbed up on the roof, but the sky was clear. Back inside, I turned on the radio and found out that we'd just had an earthquake.

In those moments I had literally been shaken out of my nuclear denial.

I had a vested interest in denying the nuclear threat. In the late sixties I was working on my doctoral dissertation at the University of Southern California, in Los Angeles. My field was innovation theory and techno-logical forecasting—I was almost obsessively interested in the future. At the time, some forecasters were beginning to project a period of declining growth. This worried me. I feared that the need to cut back would create a nasty reaction: instead of gracefully tightening our belts, we in the United States would want more and would pursue reckless growth. Would stock market investors or trade unions be willing to accept limits? Could politicians make decisions that acknowledged limits and still hope to be re-elected? The notion of "more" seemed imbedded in our national psyche. We might even be willing to go to war for more. I envisioned hysteria, social dysfunction, people losing their civility—reactions that would fan the flames of war fever. At some level I knew that if there were a war, it might be a nuclear war.

I led a workshop at San Francisco State that scared me further. The theme was how to teach about the future, and the participants were junior high and high school social studies teachers. They seemed able to look at only the most optimistic, unlimited-growth projections of the future. When I tried to suggest other possibilities, they were visibly uncomfortable. It was inconceivable to them that our standard of living wouldn't keep improving indefinitely. That had been their experience in the past, and they weren't prepared to consider any other scenario. I felt frustrated and discouraged: I couldn't see how to help people explore alternative options for the future. So I put my futures work on hold and focused instead on learning about how people and societies change.

Not long after the earthquake shook me out of my denial, I was invited to join a small study group being formed to figure out how to prevent nuclear war. The other four people in the group were, like me, innovators and achievers. The fact that the nuclear situation hadn't been defused by the efforts of lots of other brilliant people over the past thirty-five years didn't discourage us. We had a can-do attitude; we were going to solve it.

And we had a new approach: we would try to accept the likelihood that at least a few nuclear bombs would be detonated, by accident if not by design. For a long time we had been living in a make-believe world where the possibility of nuclear war did not exist. We were not alone in that fantasy world. Even some of the serious political efforts to prevent nuclear war seemed rooted in denial, relying on frenzied activity to keep the prospect of nuclear destruction out of mind. We reasoned that surrendering our consciousness to the worst scenario might liberate some of the energy tied up in denial. It occurred to us that we were applying the principles of the Japanese martial art *aikido*—taking the energy of the nuclear threat, going with it, and using the energy against the threat itself.

This approach led us to dream up what now seems like a very strange strategy. We planned to go around the world training firefighters, police, doctors, and other professionals to deal with the aftermath of a nuclear attack. Once these service people moved out of *their* denial and experienced how awful nuclear war would be, we reasoned, the international will to stop the arms race would be aroused. Convinced that this was the approach that would prevent nuclear war, we began meeting every day to prepare ourselves to lead the training programs. Hour after hour, day after day, we pored over technical material on the human and environmental effects of nuclear weapons, watched government films on bomb tests and civil defense procedures, and read analytical essays on deterrence and defense strategies. We immersed ourselves in nuclear war.

The process we went through now appears similar to the invention of homeopathy. When homeopathy was being developed, researchers experimented with consuming small amounts of toxic substances, then watching their bodies' responses. We began to take the nuclear poison into ourselves. As we did, we noticed that our responses fell into several categories:

1. Persistent denial and numbness. We were all reading *The Effects of Thermonuclear War*, a grisly and detailed book put out by the US Government's Office of Technological Assessment. Although I was accustomed to whipping through technical information, I couldn't get through this book. After a paragraph or two my eyes would stop, and

blank staring and daydreaming would take over. For a while we all pretended we were reading the book, but finally we sheepishly admitted to each other we hadn't been able to. It was as if our minds had overload switches.

2. A semi-hysterical mental flailing ("We've gotta do something!"), always followed by a voidy question ("But what will really work?").

3. Absolute bewilderment about how we got into this mess as a human family. ("If I am going to be blown up in an instant, I want to know what happened here.") Where did our human ancestors go wrong? What in our culture allowed us to create a crisis with such high stakes?

4. Fear of losing our dear ones in a nuclear war, and feelings of deep love and connection to all creatures who must live under this terrible threat.

5. A sense some days that small tasks were overwhelmingly meaningless in the face of the nuclear threat. Why vacuum the floor if all life is going to be wiped out? This would be followed by: Why do anything?

6. Plotting, in some dark corner of the mind, how to survive a nuclear war. Investigating civil defense, I was relieved to realize that I lived in the shadow of a hill that might deflect the concussion following a nuclear explosion. If they bombed the weapons storage facilities in Oakland, maybe I'd be safe. But if they bombed the defense industries to the south, I'd be done for. I found myself wondering whether my basement would provide protection from the blast. I felt glad about all the earthquake preparations I had made.

7. Rage about the nuclear predicament, often directed at military people. One weekend, feeling profoundly disturbed by the nuclear threat, I went to Berkeley, sat in coffeehouses, walked in the woods, and wrote angry poetry:

> Whoever of us remain, let us make a pact
> whoever comes out of the shelters whole and able
> we swear to all the dead others
> we shall go and find them—the men in the brass stars and tin smiles
> and tear them limb from limb. They shall not survive the wrath of the
> survivors. I know I can count on you.
> Set your jaw, narrow your eyes, walk straight in there and shout:
> "The rent on the planet is due, and it's *you*."
> Go for their eyes, their throats and when they are gasping for breath shove
> it to them in the stomach for the kids and for all our softer selves . . .
> And know that I am proud of you
> Wherever I am . . .

8. Gratitude to the bomb for what it can teach us. By threatening us all, the bomb shows us our commonality and connection. All beings

around the world have a common interest in making sure that nuclear war doesn't happen.

9.   Curiosity about Soviet people. I wanted to go to the Soviet Union (or at least the Soviet Embassy in San Francisco) and ask people their views of the nuclear predicament; I wanted to meet some Soviet people. But I was afraid of harassment by the US government: would I be suspected of selling secrets? And I noticed my shyness, too, about meeting Soviet people. (I am still working on overcoming this shyness and visiting the Soviet Embassy and the Soviet Union.)

10.   Repeated questioning about strategy. Is there a way to allow nuclear weapons to be used for threatening but not for killing? If a few nuclear weapons are used, can all-out nuclear war be prevented? If global nuclear war is inevitable (after this introductory clause there would be a half-hour digression about whether in fact it was inevitable), then what should we do in the time we have left?

After meeting for several months, the group decided to spend four full days together to explore the nuclear threat even more intensively. We went to Forest Farm, a beautiful seminar center in Marin County. Fortunately it rained the entire time, so we weren't seduced by the swimming pool or hot tub.

We confessed our fears about exploring the nuclear land inside of us. It felt like the back forty acres of our hearts and minds: wild, out of control, a tangle of overgrown weeds, thistles, and discarded rubbish. We saw several films about nuclear war, talked about them, and heard a lecture from Bob, a physicist in the group, about how nuclear bombs are built and how they work. It didn't seem so hard to create a nuclear explosion, especially if plutonium could be stolen from a nuclear power plant. The more we learned, the worse the situation seemed to us. And as we shared that truth with each other, we felt more vulnerable. Sometimes we found ourselves wishing "they" would do it quickly and get it over with. Other times we wondered whether we were just ruining the time we had left with our obsessive research. We felt empathy for the fanatical hobbyist who escapes into a tiny niche to avoid looking at the big, frightening picture.

John suggested we take turns telling our "nuclear stories"—our life histories as seen through the nuclear prism. I didn't like the idea. What would we say? What would I say? What did nuclear weapons have to do with me?

The nuclear stories turned out to be the most revealing and powerful part of our retreat. People reported having been fascinated with explosives and power, having had nuclear nightmares that had left them helpless for days, having surreptitiously made decisions about where to live based on anticipated fallout patterns. In revealing our secrets we discovered that several of us had friends or relatives who had helped develop the bomb, assembled nuclear weapons, or transported or maintained them. And we had all been paying for them through federal taxes. Nuclear weapons were a hidden member of our family.

Deep in our barely conscious minds we had been facing nuclear destruction alone for years, and it was eating us up. Now, facing the beast together, we felt immeasurable sadness and anger, terror and hopelessness. It was as though the bomb were going off inside of us, as though we were already nuclear victims. The bomb had exploded on the quality of our lives, threatened our relationships and our confidence in the future. This was a very expensive weapons system!

One night it was Alia's turn. In her nuclear story, she talked about why it was so hard for her to come across the bay to meetings in San Francisco. She was afraid that if there was a nuclear war, and her children were horribly injured, the babysitter would not love the children enough to put them out of their misery. That fear encapsulated the nuclear situation for us. It was the most gruesome thing we could think of. Should we keep poisons or painkillers with us at all times? In the aftermath of a nuclear war, how would we decide whether to use them? We sat together for a long time, crying, talking about our deepest fears for the future.

Then something happened. We started laughing. From deep inside of us a roar erupted as we began wildly to burlesque the situation. We invented nuclear laxatives (to really get things moving). We played with the idea of packing little pieces of nuclear weapons into cereal boxes for children to collect, so that by the time they grew up they could have their own bombs. We considered uses of personal nuclear weapons, like nuking your neighbor for parking in your driveway or for starting a lawnmower at seven o'clock on Saturday morning. As we stood in front of the biggest beast and roared with laughter at its absurdity, our hearts and minds came alive. We had gone through our numbness, we had hit rock bottom, and now we were bouncing up. We stayed awake until 2:00 am. Our muscles were weak from laughing.

We awoke the next morning with a new perspective and a sense of renewal; we felt transformed. After months of tiptoeing around the edges of our nuclear darkness, we had faced the terrible truth. And at the core of that truth we had found a part of our humanity that had been choked by our fear. By saying how deeply we feared nuclear war, we had told each other and ourselves how much we loved life. We had said, in effect: "We are passionate human beings!"

There is something about the nuclear threat that says, "You will be destroyed if you face this." Somehow we had walked through that land of terror—and we had survived! The experience filled me with an inner calm and determination. I knew that I had the resources to keep going, to do what was needed to help prevent nuclear war, no matter what my fears.

After the retreat, I began working very hard for human survival. I started developing nuclear comedy sketches with my friend Charlie, traveled around the world to see how people in other cultures viewed the survival crisis, and led workshops similar to the one we had designed for ourselves at Forest Farm.

I have now listened to hundreds of people tell their nuclear stories, speaking of their fear, anger, and hopelessness, and of their intense passion for life. I see all of us struggling to tell the truth about living in the nuclear age and, by doing so, to reclaim our lives and the consequences of our collective actions. For if we acquiesce in the death of our planet, then who are we?

A fifteen-year-old student in western Massachusetts eyes me squarely as she says, "I don't have a very long nuclear story, but I want to know one thing. When I dream about nuclear war, why is it always in black and white, and silent?" Overwhelmed by her question, I say nothing.

Another student tells about a dream of the moments just before a nuclear attack. She remembers that a Russian woman lives alone at the bottom of the hill. Not wanting her to face this alone, she goes to be with her.

A third student reports a dream in which the Soviet premier is awakened from a drunken slumber with some news and, without really thinking it through, orders Soviet missiles to be launched. Then, realizing what he's done, the premier shoots himself.

A woman in Colorado says, "I want to promise my children that I'll protect them, and I can't."

A farmer in California's Central Valley breaks down sobbing. For him it is almost a sacred duty to feed his fellow citizens. "If my land and water are ruined," he says, "what will I do? How will I grow anything?"

A Jewish woman who left Germany just before World War II says: "We know that the worst *is* possible."

One day at Sixth Street Park, as Ben and I are discussing the nuclear threat, a hurt look comes over him. "They wouldn't really do that, would they?" he asks.

We each have a direct, ongoing relationship with the survival of the planet. Just as we have family lives, and work lives, and sex lives, now we have "nuclear lives," or "planet-survival lives." I have noticed that my planet-survival life goes in cycles. There is an "outward" part of the cycle, when inspiration is at hand, the focus of my work is clear, and I feel powerful and passionate, ready to call forth all possible resources to increase the odds of human survival.

During the "inward" part of the cycle, denial, powerlessness, and confusion take over. I feel smaller, more overwhelmed, more in touch with suffering. There are some weeks when despair seems to be on every plate, in every dream, in every wrinkle of the fabric of life. I need to sleep more, rest from the struggle, and notice what I'm avoiding thinking about. I read, examine my work, doubt myself. I talk with my friends about what I'm experiencing. I've come to see this part of the cycle as a time of seed-planting. I try to be patient, to value these explorations, to know that in time they may flower into action.

In both parts of the cycle, I see flashes of possible extinction and flashes of life's power. A loud plane overhead sends a chill through me. Is it about to drop a bomb? Driving, I see the panorama of San Francisco and imagine it gone in an instant. Walking among redwood trees that are hundreds of years old, I'm filled with the terror of extinction. I wonder: Do these trees know that their species is threatened *right now?*

The next moment I am overwhelmed by the trees' beauty. The possibility of nothingness reminds me that at one time there was nothing. It makes me feel entirely alive and allied with life. I watch with wonder and appreciation as my chickens lay eggs, tomato plants grow in the garden, a fellow human being tells the heartfelt truth. Like someone sanding her fingertips to make them more sensitive to braille, I sand away my nuclear denial and become more sensitive to the powerful pulls of life and extinction. My own life becomes richer and more intense. And I am forced to wonder: If there were no nuclear threat, would I be able to appreciate life's miracle as fully? Do we as a species need such an immediate and terrible threat in order to value and honor life? To what extent am I attached to this threat and the thrills it brings me?

My planet-survival life is one of many questions. I burn to know what it is that has got us into this situation, what will help us get out, and what part of that work is mine. I want to be able to hold these questions so easily and gently that my creativity can address them continuously.

Can we actually uninvent something like nuclear weapons? This was one of the early questions I explored. Then I spent a long time wondering why it was Western civilization that had developed these weapons. I read with excitement about Japan's successful ban on gunpowder in the seventeenth century. But had the ban caused a militaristic reaction that, in the long term, may have been worse? Often even great ideas have unexpected consequences.

What are the effects of nuclear proliferation? Might the mere possession of such a powerful weapon make a leader or a nation more cautious or mature? As less wealthy countries get nuclear weapons, might they gain a more equitable share of the world's power? Have we finally invented something so disgusting and inconceivably horrible that we will have to learn new ways to share power and resources?

Why has war been developed? Is it a result of the desire for novelty? The need to trade in order to satisfy insatiable desires for variety has caused a lot of trouble. Do wars stem from some countries' meddling in the affairs of others so as to get reliable supplies of resources at artificially low prices? Is it possible to reverse that trend, to reduce the number of things in our lives that come to us at other people's expense? What if we gave up bananas grown on US-owned plantations in Central America? Might that help keep our government from meddling with people there?

I started wondering what in my own life made war more likely. I really love bananas. Would I be willing to give them up if that would reduce the risk of war and put more food on a Central American table?

Are there kinds of international trade that may mitigate against war? If the United States sells grain to the Soviet Union, does that reduce the likelihood of conflict?

Albert Einstein said: "The splitting of the atom has changed everything save our mode of thinking . . ." What are all the ways our thinking needs to change? How do I change my way of thinking? *Can* people decide to change their ways of thinking? How?

Would the key change be to give up defensiveness as an attitude? To stop coveting the lands and resources of others? To stop feeling powerless? To consider the consequences of our actions at every step? Or to see actions and individuals as interconnected rather than as discrete? Sometimes it seems logical to consider this a new time in human history, to start a new calendar for the years after the bomb, and call this year 40 A.B.

All this pondering has helped me make choices in my life and work. I continue to perform nuclear comedy. I work with Interhelp, an international network that is helping people break through nuclear numbness and denial. I started a support group for a bunch of people who are doing work for the world. I often help peace groups plan strategy. I spent two weeks in jail for participating in a blockade of the Lawrence Livermore Lab, where nuclear weapons are designed. But I'm still asking questions and not satisfied with my current conclusions. The search is a continuing process, leading me (I hope) to more and more responsible and appropriate behavior in the world. I expect to be fighting nuclear war for the rest of my life, and I hope that's a long time.

I now think that it may take four or five generations for our species to learn to make change without war.

Often I think about these things while sitting on the toilet. In the Renaissance, I sometimes imagine, there must have been a woman a little bit like me, trying to make sense out of a very confusing time. What was she thinking about as she sat on the toilet? What were her questions?

Or I picture a woman like me in the Soviet Union, sitting on the toilet, trying to figure out how the Soviets and the Americans can do better, how we can get out of the nuclear predicament.

Or I think of a woman in the future, thinking about the world. What are the questions on her mind as she sits on the toilet? And what does the new design of the toilet look like?

Every day I am barraged with grim news about people violating the life on this planet: wars, murders, suicides, rapes, ecological disasters. And, in my brief snatch of time on this beautiful planet, I have to contemplate the possibility that all this beauty could end in a puff of radioactivity.

Yes, the danger is real, and we may not get through it. But instead of cowering in the face of doom, I choose to face the mushroom cloud and roar with laughter. That laughter slices into the nuclear silence and penetrates even my own numbness.

Part 3

NUCLEAR WAR AS
A FEMINIST ISSUE

War is as anachronistic as cannibalism, slavery and colonialism. . . .
The present national constraints to life and growth in the developing
world—hunger, poverty and repression—and those in the developed
world—unemployment, cancer and nuclear threat—are clearly interrelated. Rosalie Bertell, *No Immediate Danger* (1985), p. ix.

6

Naming the Cultural Forces that Push Us Toward War*

Charlene Spretnak

In the current wave of peace activism, speakers are sometimes heard to say that the movement is attempting something new in the history of humankind: peace. That view is inaccurate. The "killer ape" theory of early human society has been displaced in anthropology by evidence that cooperation was the key to survival. In Neolithic Old Europe, according to archaeologists, no evidence of fortifications and warfare has been found prior to the invasions of the patriarchal, nomadic, Indo-European barbarians from the Eurasian steppes, beginning around 4500 B.C. (Gimbutas, 1974, 1981). The matrifocal Old European societies thrived peacefully for thousands of years, leaving behind sophisticated goddess-oriented art and egalitarian graves. In a survey of 156 more recent tribal societies studied by anthropolgists, Peggy Reeves Sanday (1981) has presented numerous cultural patterns ranging from habitually violent to habitually peaceful. Clearly, making war is not a genetic imperative for the human race.

Women and men can live together and can relate to other societies in any number of cultural configurations, but ignorance of the configurations themselves locks a populace into blind adherence to the status quo. In the nuclear age, such unexamined acceptance may be fatal as

*This article was published originally in the *Journal of Humanistic Psychology*, Vol. 23, No. 3 (Summer 1983).

certain cultural assumptions in our own society are pushing us closer
and closer to war. Since a major war now could easily bring on massive
annihilation of almost unthinkable proportions, why are discussions in
our national forums addressing the madness of the nuclear arms race
limited to matters of hardware and statistics? A more comprehensive
analysis is badly needed—unless, as the doomsayers claim, we collectively harbor a death wish and do not *really* want to look closely at the
dynamics propelling us steadily toward the brink of extinction.

The cause of nuclear arms proliferation is militarism. What is the
cause of militarism? The traditional materialist explanation is that the
"masters of war" in the military-industrial complex profit enormously
from defense contracts and other war preparations. A capitalist economy periodically requires the economic boon that large-scale government spending, capital investment, and worker sacrifice produce during
a crisis of war. In addition, American armed forces, whether nuclear or
conventional, are stationed worldwide to protect the status quo, which
involves vast and interlocking American corporate interests.

Such an economic analysis alone is inadequate, as are the recent
responses to the nuclear arms race that ignore the cultural orientation of
the nations involved: They are patriarchies. Militarism and warfare are
continual features of a patriarchal society because they reflect and instill
patriarchal values and fulfill essential needs of such a system. Acknowledging the context of patriarchal conceptualizations that feed militarism
is a first step toward reducing their impact and preserving life on Earth.

(1) First, patriarchy—at the level of individuals, groups, or nations—
operates on the model of dominance or submission. Respect is thought
to be gained only through superiority and control. Every situation is
perceived as hierarchical; occupying any position other than the pinna-
cle of the imagined hierarchy creates great anxiety. A clearly visible
element in the escalating tensions among militarized nations is the
macho posturing and the patriarchal ideal of *dominance*, not parity,
which motivates defense ministers and government leaders to "strut
their stuff" as we watch with increasing horror. The Reaganite/New
Right/Christian Right forces are determined to "make America a man
again." They are baffled when the European peace movement views
their John Wayneisms as warmongering rather than awesome virility.

A dominance mode requires dehumanizing "the other"—women,
people of color, or foreign nations—and idealizing oneself. A common
refrain in America during the Cold War of the 1950s was "Nobody wants
war—except the Russians." Our government and military leaders convinced themselves that the Japanese are so monstrously base as to

justify our being the first nation to build an atomic bomb and explode it among civilians. The American decision to drop the first atomic bomb into the centers of Hiroshima and Nagasaki, instead of rural areas, was not made hastily; rather, our leaders considered those civilians so "other" that our military designated those cities as "virgin targets," never to be subjected to conventional bombing, on which we would eventually test our new weapon. The obsession with dominance led to our initiating still higher levels of potential destruction with the hydrogen bomb and multiple warheads, and to our refusal to renounce the principle of first use. The cult of dominance and toughness also deeply influenced our policies during the war in Vietnam (Fasteau, 1975). In March 1983, we witnessed the continuation of this patriarchal *leitmotif* in President Reagan's call for American military control of space, using "killer lasers," particle-beam weapons, and microwave devices.

A dominance mode requires the brandishing of symbols of force and power. During the Carter administration, according to William Perry, then undersecretary of defense, military lobbyists flooded the decision makers in the legislative and executive branches with a kit produced by Boeing that provided upright models of Soviet and American missiles. Theirs, alas, were much larger than ours and although this initially stemmed from their lagging technology (the new Soviet SS-20s are much smaller), the message was that we "suffered an inferiority"(Stern, 1982). Senator Gary Hart (D-CO), a member of the Senate Armed Forces Committee, recalls that the central image during that period of successful lobbying was a "size race," which became "sort of a macho issue" (Stern, 1982). More bluntly, political analyst William Greider (1982) has recently noted, "The glossy ads from defense manufacturers nearly always feature a phallus of destruction." Maintaining that men are no less susceptible to hidden sexual appeals than are women, he posits a correlation between such public lobbying and the fact that opinion polls show a much higher proportion of men than women supporting President Reagan's "bloated defense budget."

But symbolism alone does not breed satisfaction: The only circumstance in which the military can *prove* its superiority and dominance is the state of war. Conveniently, the military believes war, even if "limited," to be inevitable, and it is not alone in our patriarchal society. Eugene Rostow, former director of the US Arms Control and Disarmament Agency, has been widely quoted regarding his insistence that we are now living in "a pre-war world and not a post-war world" (Scheer, 1982). Many military personnel have been conditioned to consider the question of war as "when" rather than "if." Recent interviews with National Guardsmen, who are now being equipped with new, sophisticated weaponry in a program to make them "partners" with the Army, reveal an alarming eagerness to prove dominance: "We're ready to go over there and beat those guys!" (National Public Radio, 1982).

(2) Warfare is held by many people to be the ultimate initiation into true adulthood and full citizenship. This deeply rooted belief surfaced as an unexpected element in the struggle to pass the Equal Rights Amendment, for instance. Feminist lobbyists in state legislatures throughout the 1970s were repeatedly informed, "When you ladies are ready to fight in a *war*, we'll be ready to discuss equal rights." These same legislators vociferously oppose the admission of women to military academies and careers. War is *their* game, a private father-son ritual of sadism. The winners can take their place in the patriarchal hierarchy; the losers are buried or made to beg for crumbs from the slashed budget of the Veterans Administration.

Certainly the pressures to go to Vietnam without examining very deeply the rationale for the war were great. The boys (the average American soldier there was a working-class 19-year-old) knew something about war, they thought, from Hollywood renditions of it, and finally they too could proudly swap war stories "like Dad." Most of all, their families and society simply expected them to "do the manly thing." So they went. Among those assigned to European bases, discontent and depression were common if they could not get sent to Vietnam to "prove their manhood" on a battlefield. The young soldiers who did go to Vietnam found the actual experience of guerrilla warfare to be cruelly ironic: It was so hellish that anyone with any sense was very scared every single day of his year-long tour of duty, causing him to wonder whether he had failed the grand initiation. This is one reason so many of those veterans remain conflicted about their combat experience and refuse to discuss it, even with their families. Their brutal Prussian-style training had radically altered their psyches in order to prepare them for situations that they found did not exist (Eisenhart, 1977). There have been as many suicides among Vietnam veterans since the war as there were combat fatalities (Capps, 1982).

Is there any evidence to indicate that the new generations of sons are suddenly being raised without the age-old macho glorifications of doing "a man's duty" in a war? Or are those pressures still nurtured among our citizenry on a vast scale even though a major war in the nuclear age would very likely mean the poisoning of the planet and the extinction of all life? Although the people who protested against the war in Vietnam—and they were primarily middle class—are probably raising their sons to resist cultural glamorization of the soldier's role, many Vietnam veterans have expressed the unshaken opinion that most of the protesters were simply afraid to "be a man" and to go to war (CBS Special Report: "What Vietnam Did to Us," 1981). Presumably, this belief is being passed on to their sons. Several veterans at the dedication of the Vietnam veterans' monument in Washington, DC, in November 1982 shouted, "Give us a war, and we'll win it!" (*New York Times*). Other veterans are bitterly disillusioned. As one man told a reporter at the dedication, "We all have children now, and we don't want them to march off like tin soldiers without thinking again" (AP release). This father's views are probably in the national minority if the recent boom in the sales of war toys is any indication.

(3) The experience of basic training traditionally implants patriarchal values by reviling women as a foul and lowly class (Eisenhart, 1977; Bliss, 1981; Gerzon, 1982). Recruits and soldiers who fail to perform are scornfully called by derogatory terms for female genitalia. They are continually addressed as "faggot" or "girl" by a screaming drill instructor. The ultimate patriarchal insult of being woman-like has often been imposed throughout history by castrating the vanquished, literally or figuratively. Lyndon Johnson buoyantly told a reporter the day after ordering the bombing of North Vietnamese PT-boat bases and oil depots, the first act of war against North Vietnam: "I didn't just screw Ho Chi Minh. I cut his pecker off" (Fasteau, 1975).

In basic training, harshness and insensitivity are praised; raw aggression and dominance are equated with masculinity. After serving his (patriarchal) country in this fashion, a young man returns to society with certain deeply etched beliefs. In addition to identifying security with hierarchy and well-defined chain of command (a concept the 30 million veterans in this country often apply to business and political situations; Bliss, 1981), the men have learned that "feminine" sensitivity and women, in the world beyond Mom, are not respected and that women are certainly not viewed as equals.

In more extreme cases, which were legion after the Vietnam War, many young veterans were horrified if they happened to feel sensitivity or empathy or other responses valued by women. They feared they might be slipping down into the denigrated class, where such weakness would render them vulnerable. A very common behavior pattern reported among both disturbed and relatively well-adjusted Vietnam veterans is simply their refusal to "open up" to women. Many of the wives at the reunion of "Charlie Company" in 1981 spoke of this loss of psychological intimacy. "I wouldn't say the Army made my husband a man; it made him a different man," said one woman sadly. Several other wives nodded in agreement (CBS Special Report: "What Vietnam Did to Us," 1981). A wide range of this response has been documented by psychologists and therapists working with veterans (Lifton, 1972; Meredith, 1982).

(4) The ritual of the archetypal father slaying his son is as old as patriarchy itself. In classical Greece, young warriors were raised with myths of fathers and sons being treacherous, deadly rivals: Uranus, the Sky Father (mate of Gaia, the Earth Mother, whose mythology long predates his) hurled his rebellious sons, the Cyclopes, into the under-world. Cronus, another son of Uranus, castrated his father as he slept. Laius attempted the murder of his son Oedipus, yet was himself murdered later by that son. In the Judeo-Christian tradition, the Holy Bible sanctified stories of the Great Father ordering Abraham to murder his only son Isaac, ordering all men among the faithful similarly: "The firstborn of thy sons thou shalt give unto me" (Exodus 22:28). Such demands culminated in the Great Father's sacrificing his own son, Jesus. The son's last words were a poignant cry to his father, echoed millions of times in the minds of dying young soldiers: Why has thou forsaken me?

Psychoanalysts recognize that many fathers (in patriarchal/ hierarchical cultures, where men must constantly compete with one another) are wrenched by a horrible jealousy toward their sons, so compelling that they *must* murder them, symbolically if not actually. The sons are rivals who will grow up to compete with and perhaps surpass them. These dynamics of the patriarchal family are currently being championed by the Christian Right, who oppose all statutes establishing children's rights—and, of course, women's rights—on the grounds that such legislation disrupts "God's line of authority in the home." The late Brother Roloff, who was director of the Lighthouse home for errant children in Texas, advised national radio audiences on fundamentalist Christian fatherhood: "A child needs enough punishment to break his stubborn will and let him throw up the white flag and say, 'Daddy, you win; I surrender.' " One can observe numerous individual exceptions to the model of father-son antagonism and there is obviously great richness and spiritual sustenance in the Judeo-Christian teachings, but the desire of the fathers to break the sons is a constant in patriarchal culture.

(5) Patriarchal culture alienates men from the life-giving processes, so their concern becomes the other half of the cycle: death. To be present at and assist in a birth, to cuddle and soothe a baby, to be involved intrinsically in a child's slowly flowering maturation over the years—all of this is denigrated as "women's work." Quite apart from such endeavors, (patriarchal) men focus their attention on the eventual but imminent arrival of death, dwelling on it as an obsessive theme in much

of their art and literature. In patriarchal tribal cultures, men display their kills, whether an animal, a human head, or a scalp, with the same pride that women show in holding up a newborn (Sanday, 1981). Birth imagery for the most horrifying death machine ever devised was used frequently in the Manhattan Project; finally, the men were able to cable President Truman: BABY IS BORN (Gerzon, 1982).

Otto Rank observed that the death-fear of the ego is lessened by the killing of another; that is, acting in the dominant role of giver of death distances one from the role of receiving it. Such action would be particularly appealing to people who are culturally forced into an obsession with death, for example, men under patriarchy. The only situation wherein large-scale killing is not merely allowed but enthusiastically encouraged is war.

(6) The bloody "red badge of courage" that warriors wear signifies honorable access to flowing blood in patriarchal cultures. During the June 12 peace marches in New York, San Francisco, and other cities in 1982, many of the demonstrators wore T-shirts or political buttons with the message *War Is Menstruation Envy.* Surely that is going too far! What does it mean? It refers to the extremely ancient association of blood with honor, sanctity, and power—which occurs in patriarchal culture only in a male context wrenched from women's procreative power. The blood mysteries of woman—her bleeding in rhythm with the moon, her growing *people* from her very flesh while she withheld the sacred blood and grew round as the full moon, her transforming her own blood into milk for the newborn—were the sacred foundation of humankind's first and longest lasting religion, dating from about 25,000 B.C. When the invading waves of patriarchal, nomadic horsemen, the Indo-Europeans, migrated from the Eurasian steppes into peaceful, matrifocal Old Europe (c. 4500 B.C.), they introduced a religion centered on the warrior's glorious death in battle, bathed in his flowing blood.

Like other proponents of the new Indo-European religions, the Judaic fathers determined to invert and co-opt the power of sacred blood. They announced that woman was actually a "foul sink," while the truly sacred blood was to be found in men's new imitative ritual of drawing blood from the male genital in circumcision. The invention of Christian mythology also played upon humankind's 25,000-year-old tradition of revering the sacred blood: Christ displayed his bleeding wounds, and the faithful drink it as their transubstantiated wine. The flowing blood of the soldier is celebrated on nearly every flag of our patriarchal nations. "Blood and Honor" was the motto of the Hitler Youth Movement, inscribed on a phallic implement of destruction, a dagger, and presented to each boy when he completed the initiation. Wartime spectacles of "blood'n'guts'n'glory" are the High Mass of patriarchy. *"You say that a good cause will even sanctify war; but I tell you, it is the good war that sanctifies every cause"* (Nietzsche).

The pressures of patriarchal values and assumptions entangle men in a closed system of possibilities. Most men are uncomfortable with the six "necessary" conditions named here, but their very identity is so intermingled with patriarchal ideology that they cannot effectively critique the system that has pushed us so close to annihilation. After I had spent more than a year delineating the cultural forces of modern patriarchy that continue to feed militarism, I came across Professor Sanday's (1981) anthropological work, which identifies many of the same dynamics in those tribal cultures that are patriarchal and violent:

> Male dominance in myth and everyday life is associated with fear, conflict, and strife. . . . In these societies [described in *Female Power and Male Dominance*], males believe that there is an uncontrollable force that may strike at any time and against which men must be prepared to defend their integrity. The nature of the force and its source are not well defined, but often they are associated with female sexuality and reproductive functions. Men believe it is their duty to harness this force, with its power over life and death, to prevent chaos and to maintain equilibrium. They go to extraordinary lengths to acquire some of the power for themselves so that they will not be impotent when [not *if*] it is time to fight. Men attempt to neutralize the power they think is inherent in women by stealing it, nullifying it, or banishing it to invisibility.

Most men in our patriarchal culture are still acting out old patterns that are radically inappropriate for the nuclear age. To prove dominance and control, to distance one's character from that of women, to survive the toughest violent initiation, to shed the sacred blood of the hero, to collaborate with death in order to hold it at bay—all of these patriarchal pressures on men have traditionally reached resolution in ritual fashion on the battlefield. But there is no longer any battlefield. Does anyone seriously believe that if a nuclear power were losing a crucial, large-scale conventional war it would refrain from using its multiple-warhead nuclear missiles because of some diplomatic agreement? The military theater of a nuclear exchange today would extend, instantly or eventually, to all living things, all the air, all the soil, all the water.

If we believe that war is a "necessary evil," that patriarchical assumptions are simply "human nature," then we are locked into a lie, paralyzed. The ultimate result of unchecked terminal patriarchy will be nuclear holocaust.

We have choices. The question is whether we have enough time to achieve a major shift in thinking before any of the 50,000 nuclear warheads around us are exploded. The debates and discussions on the proposed nuclear freeze have revealed and strengthened a vast and complex nationwide network of citizens concerned with the probability of nuclear war. Those grassroots forums on current political and economic influences on war should be broadened to include such topics as: Do the boys and young men in our community, including our National Guardsmen, associate manhood with going to war? Shall we oppose films and advertising that portray war and warheads as sexy and glamorous? Are our children playing with war toys and our teenagers with videogames such as "Missile Command," on which they practice dispatching and destroying multiple-warhead missiles as if they were as benign as model trains? Do we consider qualities of sensitivity and emotional/psychological intimacy so unmanly that boys should serve a certain amount of time in the military in order to have such "feminine" tendencies squelched? If we refuse to play our-missiles-are-bigger-than-yours anymore, are we willing to devote attention to sane alternatives for structuring human relations, from local to international levels? Do we consider the Russian people "other" than fully human, hence deserving of the most destructive devices we can invent? Is the patriarchal ideal of dominance a self-destructive posture that terrorizes opponents into retaliation? Can we honor heroes who do not shed blood? Shall we honor our peacemakers as much as our famous generals?

The causes of recurrent warfare are not biological. Neither are they solely economic. They are also a result of patriarchal ways of thinking, which historically have generated considerable pressure or standing armies to be used. The inclusion of this fundamental dimension in our efforts to contain militarism and build a secure peace is not going to be initiated by the White House or the Congress; it is a "trickle up" raising of consciousness that has already begun. We can only hope it isn't too late—for the prenuclear, patriarchal assumptions that still guide our society are part of the deadly time lag Albert Einstein warned us about nearly thirty years ago: "The unleashed power of the atom has changed everything save our modes of thinking and we thus drift toward unparalleled catastrophes."

REFERENCES

Bliss, Shepherd, "Between men." (Review of a film on basic training.) *Peacework*, Journal of the American Friends Service Committee of New England (September 1981). (Available from United Documentary Film, P.O. Box 315, Franklin Lane, NJ 07417.)

Capps, Walter H., *The unfinished war: Vietnam and the American conscience* (Boston: Beacon, 1982).

Eisenhart, R. W., "Flower of the dragon: An example of applied humanistic psychology." *Journal of Humanistic Psychology* Vol. 17, No. 1 (1977).

Fasteau, Marc Feiger, *The male machine* (New York: Delta, 1975).

Gerzon, Mark, *A choice of heroes: The changing faces of American manhood.* (Boston: Houghton Mifflin 1982).

Gimbutas, Marija, *Goddesses and gods of Old Europe, 6500–3500 B.C.* (London/Berkeley: Thames & Hudson/University of California Press, 1974).

Gimbutas, M., "Old Europe in the fifth millennium B.C.: The European situation on the arrival of Indo-Europeans," in *Proceedings of the Conference on the Indo-Europeans in the Fourth and Third Millennia, University of Texas, February 1980* (Ann Arbor, Mich.: Karoma 1981). Abridged as "Women and culture in goddess-oriented old Europe," in C. Spretnak (Ed)., *The politics of women's spirituality: Essays on the rise of spiritual power within the feminist movement* (Garden City, N.Y.: Doubleday, 1982).

Greider, William, "Women vs. Reagan," *Rolling Stone* (19 August 1982).

Lapp, R., "The Epstein letter that started it all," *New York Times Magazine* (2 August 1964).

Lifton, Robert Jay, *Home from the war* (New York: Simon & Schuster, 1972).

Meredith, N., "Veterans for whom the war still rages," *California Living Magazine, San Francisco Examiner and Chronicle* (30 May 1982).

National Public Radio, *All things considered* (4 July 1982).

Sanday, Peggy Reeves, *Female power and male dominance: On the origins of sexual inequality* (Cambridge: Cambridge University Press, 1981).

Scheer, Robert, *With enough shovels: Reagan, Bush, and nuclear war* (New York: Random House, 1982).

Stern, Andrew, *How much is enough?* (Film on the nuclear arms buildup shown on PBS national television network as part of the *Crisis to crisis* series) 6 August 1982.

"What Vietnam did to us: Survivors of Charlie Company relive the war and the decades since," *Newsweek* (14 December 1981). (The reunion was also filmed and televised nationally as a CBS Special Report, 12 December 1981.)

7

Sexism, Violence, and the Nuclear Mentality*

Diana E. H. Russell

> The bombs are not the cause of the problem, but only the symptom of the deranged thought processes of man's mind (Helen Caldicott [1984], p. 287).

Fifteen years before the explosion of the first atomic bomb on July 16, 1945, gave birth to the nuclear age, Sigmund Freud concluded his book *Civilization and Its Discontents* with a prophetic statement:

> Men have gained control over the forces of nature to such an extent that with their help they would have no difficulty in exterminating one another to the last man. They know this, and hence comes a large part of their current unrest, their unhappiness and their mood of anxiety (Schell, 1982, pp. 155–156).

Although Freud probably didn't intend to place the entire responsibility for control over nature on men, his use of sexist language makes him more accurate on the issue of gender responsibility than he deserves credit for. Certainly women too experience the unrest and unhappiness he describes. But it is primarily men who have sought to gain control over the forces of nature, and it is men who invented nuclear weapons capable of destroying the whole world in a very short time.

Throughout *The Fate of the Earth* (1982), Jonathan Schell, like Freud, uses the terms "man," "mankind," and "men," generically. Like Freud,

---

*This chapter is an edited version of an article previously published in *Atlantis: A Women's Studies Journal*, Vol. 12, No. 2 (1987).

he fails to recognize that women have played a very different role from men, not only in the development of nuclear weapons, but in the arms race and in war in general. The polarization of the sexes into two different roles, two different psyches, and two different sets of standards, has helped to bring us to the brink of annihilation. In this chapter, I will explain and substantiate this statement.

In her chapter "Etiology: Missile Envy and Other Psychopathology," Helen Caldicott (1984) offers one of the best analyses I have ever read of how and why men have brought the world to the nuclear crisis we face today. However, I disagree with her on the issue of biological versus sociological causation. No one has yet proved that "One of the reasons women are so allied to the life processes is their hormonal constitution" as Caldicott maintains (1984, p. 294). Nor do I believe that men and boys are *naturally* more fascinated by killing (1984, p. 296).

It *is* true, however, that some of the real or imagined biological differences between the sexes have been used as a justification for sexism. Common attitudes about these differences have made it more difficult for women to pursue our own interests (for example, mothers have universally been assigned the primary responsibility for child rearing, which in turn often results in women doing what is best for their children rather than for themselves. While this may be commendable behavior from a moral point of view, it has put women at a great power disadvantage vis-à-vis men.) Whether or not women are "naturally" more emotional and nurturant than men, or men are "naturally" more ambitious and violent than women is a subject for future research. What we know for sure now is that the entire social structure and mainstream culture assumes these differences and reinforces them.

According to Schell:

> It means something that we call both pornography and nuclear destruction "obscene." In the first, we find desire stripped of any further human sentiment or attachment—of any "redeeming social value," in the legal phrase. In the second, we find violence detached from any human goals, all of which would be engulfed in a holocaust—detached, that is, from all redeeming social value (1982, p. 158).

It also means something that pornography has so little appeal to women, and that one aspect of the polarization of the sexes is the greater inclination of males than females to be violent. Since nuclear annihilation—and the threat of it that hangs over our heads—is the ultimate act of violence, this relationship between gender and violence is an important one deserving further elaboration.

My study of violence, a subject I have been working on for the past seventeen years, has enabled me to see the relevance of gender to the nuclear threat. This study has also led me to view both violence and the nuclear threat as feminist issues.

The extent of male violence is a striking phenomenon. For several years now, nine out of ten people arrested for violent crimes in the United States have been males (*Uniform Crime Reports*, annual)[1]. If there were an ethnic group or social class that were responsible for 90 percent of all violent crimes, the members of that group would be considered pariahs and subjected to severe prejudice and discrimination. But since males hold virtually all the power in our society, the primarily male face of violence is rarely acknowledged. When I point out these facts to audiences I address, I am frequently treated as if I am being hostile toward men. Sometimes people question the validity of the statistics, implying that police throughout the nation are so chivalrous toward women that they refuse to arrest them for violent crimes.

Although the rape rate in the United States increased over the years prior to 1981 at a more rapid rate than other major crimes of violence on which national statistics are available, *all* these crimes—homicide, aggravated assault, robbery, and rape—increased alarmingly up until that year. (The decline since 1981 is attributed by many to the fact that males born during the baby boom are no longer at the most violence-prone stage of their lives.[2]) For example, the rate of homicides per 100,000 nearly doubled from 1959 to 1981 (Russell, 1984, p. 143).

In addition to the increase in crimes of violence reported to the police, the homicide rate per 100,000 people in the United States—probably the most reliable single indicator of the overall rate of violent crimes—is substantially higher than that of any other western nation (Wolfgang and Ferracuti, 1967). In 1960, for example, when the homicide rate in the United States was 4.5 per 100,000, it was 1.8 in West Germany, 1.7 in France, 1.5 in Australia, 1.5 in Greece, 1.4 in Canada, 1.4 in Italy, 1.1 in New Zealand, .9 in Portugal, .9 in Switzerland, .8 in Spain, .7 in Belgium, .7 in Sweden, .6 in England, .5 in Denmark, .5 in Norway, .3 in the Netherlands, and .2 in Ireland (1967, p. 275). This means that the homicide rate in 1960 was 23 times higher in the United States than in Ireland.

Not only do most people ignore the fact that males are much more

---

[1]One reason that the percentage of females arrested for crimes of violence is as *high* as 10 percent is that when women kill, it is frequently in self-defense. This explains why in one major study, almost as many women killed men as men killed women (16% and 18%, respectively). This virtual equality in the inter-gender murder rate contrasts with the finding that 62 percent of all the known murders were male on male, and only 4 percent were female on female (intra-gender) (Mulvihill and Tumin, 1969, p. 210).

[2]See my book, *Sexual Exploitation* (1984) p. 143ff, for a more thorough discussion of these statistics.

disposed to use violence than females, but they regard the majority of crime's perpetrators—men—as the superior sex, as better equipped to play leadership roles in the home and in society at large. Clearly our culture embodies the old adage that "might makes right." One manifestation of this domination is that what is considered truth and reality is established by the dominating force itself. Thus, the relationship between maleness and violence is ignored.

I observed this denial when I served as an expert consultant to the California Commission on Crime Control and Violence Prevention. In 1980 the State assigned this Commission the awesome task of trying to discover the root causes of crime. From this understanding they hoped to develop strategies for preventing and controlling crime in California. Despite the availability, credibility, and validity of the statistics that show a 9:1 ratio of male to female perpetrators of crimes of violence, the Commission refused to acknowledge or try to explain this fact. Since the gender factor is perhaps the single most important one in analyzing violent crime, their proposed solutions were largely irrelevant and thousands of dollars were wasted.

In addition to the greater willingness of males to use violence, the patterns of violence differ for men and women. Quite frequently stories appear in the press about men who, when their desire to get what they want is thwarted, kill the person they cannot control rather than accept defeat. Sometimes these men then kill themselves. Women, on the other hand, more often kill in self-defense, or because they believe homicide is the only way to prevent continuing abuse and persecution.[3]

Here I shall cite two examples of the male pattern, which—because most of the leaders of nuclear nations are men—could lead to the instigation of a nuclear war.

Despondent over the failure of his third marriage, 42-year-old Gilbert Macias killed his wife Jennifer, their baby daughter, and two other people. He then shot himself. According to Captain Alex Michaelis: "He said he couldn't live without her. For that reason, he killed her and his daughter" (Carroll and Magagnini, 1981).

Shortly before the homicides, Macias took his fourteen-month-old daughter with him to visit his estranged teenage wife in a futile attempt to win a reconciliation with her. An argument ensued whereupon Macias shot his wife with a .22 caliber pistol, hitting her in the head and abdomen. He telephoned his sister and told her that he had killed his wife and planned to kill the baby and himself. His sister notified the police. After forcing their way into Macias' home, the police found the

---

[3]For example, see Jones (1980); McNulty (1980); and Browne (1987).

bodies of four people—the child, Macias himself, Macias' former roomate and the roommate's girlfriend.

Macias' suicide note partially blamed the couple he murdered for his wife's disaffection. Mrs. Macias had moved out of their $150,000 home on the morning of the murder. Captain Bob Dale commented on the case: "My gut feeling is that it's a marital problem, a guy with a pretty heavy marital problem" (Carroll and Magagnini, 1981).

Gilbert may well have had serious marital problems; so did his wife. Macias' response to feeling that he could not live without her went beyond despair; he killed himself, his wife and three other people, including his own daughter.

The next example of this mentality involves a father who tried to kill his son. In February 1983, seven year-old David Rothenberg was taken on vacation in Southern California by his father. According to a newspaper account, David was dragged from a burning motel room on March 3. His father had intentionally set the room on fire because he was disturbed by fears that his estranged wife would not allow him to visit his son again. Mr. Rothenberg pleaded guilty to attempted murder and arson and received the maximum 13-year sentence (*San Francisco Chronicle*, 24 September 1983).

Mr. Rothenberg appears to have found it easier to burn his son alive than to accept the possibility that his ex-wife might prevent him from seeing his child again. He found it preferable to suffer the permanent loss of his child than to allow his ex-wife to control the situation.

This kind of mentality is similar to 'Better Dead than Red' thinking, which holds that it's better for the whole world to be annihilated than for the United States to lose a war. This predominantly male pattern of killing loved ones or other innocent people out of fear of losing them is one which places all our lives in jeopardy. There is no way of knowing which of our leaders might react to the threat of a personal or political loss by attempting to take the whole world along.

Just as most people appear to ignore the fact that violent crimes are predominantly perpetrated by males, so most people refuse to acknowledge that men in power are largely responsible for the nuclear world in which we now live, and for the imminent danger of annihilation that we face. In order to correct this situation, we need to understand its historical roots.

Male domination preceded the invention of nuclear weapons by many centuries. The development of these lethal arms is the culmination of a long history of male-dominated governments for whom military superiority over other nations justified the expenditure of enormous resources—even while people living in these countries starved. The male leaders of the United States—as well as those who govern some other patriarchal countries—have been willing to consider sacrificing the lives of millions of people in the pursuit of what they perceive as our national self-interest. Some of our leaders still purport to believe that we can survive such a catastrophe. Although war technologies are not new, the lethality of nuclear weapons is so much greater than all other weapons that they deserve a unique analysis and response.

Some argue that only ruling-class white males are responsible for the development of nuclear weapons and the concomitant threat to our survival. These people believe that it is therefore inappropriate to point a finger at the male gender as a whole.

But while not all males are violent, most studies indicate that the perpetrators of interpersonal violence, such as murder, rape, robbery with violence, and aggravated assault, are not more prevalent in the upper class (for example, Brownmiller, 1975; Straus et al., 1980; Russell, 1984). But since upper-class men have more power than men in other classes, their violence is often expressed differently, and it frequently has considerably more destructive consequences. For example, some cigarette manufacturers place their desire for economic profit above people's lives to such an extent that they are now distributing free cigarettes with very high nicotine content to ten-year-olds in some Third World countries in order to try to get them addicted to this lethal habit. Similar examples are so common-place in the history of capitalism that they seem inseparable from it.

However, since men in powerless positions in society are even more prone than men in powerful positions to commit personal crimes of violence (such as murder, rape, robbery with violence, and aggravated assault), there is no reason to believe that most lower-class men would behave differently from upper-class men if they had the power that upper-class men have. While this does not make lower-class men responsible for the behavior of their upper-class brothers, it does suggest that social change that results in the replacement of upper-class men by lower-class men would not ameliorate the problem of violence in this society, including nuclear violence.

Given the way males and females are socialized, there *is* reason to believe that fewer women would behave as men do if they had the same social power that men enjoy (for example, see Russell, 1975; Russell, 1984). On the other hand, if women were subjected to the same socialization as men in this culture, they would presumably behave like men.

The explanation commonly given for the overrepresentation of lower-class men among rapists is that physically coercive tactics are the chief tools of conquest available to them (Brownmiller, 1975; Russell, 1975). Furthermore, since conquest and subjugation are recognized ways of asserting masculinity in this society, rape is often a relatively easy way to prove "manhood" for lower-class men. Middle- and upper-class men are, of course, responsible for a great deal of rape. However, they can more readily buy power or obtain sexual favors by virtue of their economic resources. In addition, they have more ways to assert their masculinity, for example, through economic and political conquests.

A study of the behavior of males in all-male institutions is instructive on this point. For example, numerous studies and personal accounts reveal the widespread occurrence of rape in male prisons and jails. These studies also show that the rapists are the ones who are regarded by other inmates as having proven their manhood because of the power, conquest, and subjugation involved in rape. In contrast, inmates regard the victims as having lost their manhood. Indeed, prisoners often refer to them as women. (For example, see Scacco, 1975; Scacco, 1982.)

The findings of the few studies conducted on women in prison bear little resemblance to the findings on men. Although violence and even rape are reported in female prisons, their occurrence is minute compared to what happens in male prisons. Instead, women inmates reportedly organize themselves into pseudo-family arrangements which involve strong affective ties, with or without sexual relationships (Russell, 1984). Women in and out of prison are not nearly as prone to violence as men. Behaving in a dominant and aggressive fashion plays no equivalent role in reestablishing their sexual identity. On the contrary, violent behavior generally undermines the sexual identity of females.

Nuclear war is the ultimate act of violence. Since men in patriarchal cultures have been and continue to be the perpetrators of most violent acts, it would be very surprising if more women than men were willing to risk initiating this most catastrophic form of violence. The thesis of this chapter is that the same factors that account for the greater willingness of men than women to behave violently in personal situations are important in understanding the nuclear mentality. Indeed, I believe that the nuclear mentality is a perverted outgrowth of this culture's notion of masculinity.

My assumption that there is a connection between men's propensity to commit personal acts of violence and the nuclear mentality is supported by a finding of psychologists Neil Malamuth, John Briere, and James Check. In an experiment using 367 male psychology students, they found that subjects who endorsed the use of nuclear weapons were significantly more likely to report being sexually aroused by "forcing a female to do something she didn't want to" (1986, p. 333 and p. 337).

Just what are the factors that account for men's greater propensity for violence? First and foremost is the prevalent definition of masculinity, of what it takes to qualify as a successful male in this society. Aggression, toughness, strength, determination, adventurousness, daring, fearless-ness, courage, competitiveness, are all examples of "masculine" qualities. When ruling-class men lose a war or some economic or foreign policy venture, this often entails a concomitant blow to their sense of mascu-linity. Conversely, they may *engage* in certain ventures in an effort to prove their manhood. The 1983 invasion of Grenada by the US govern-ment is an example of symbolic biceps-flexing, following almost imme-diately, as it did, a surprise attack and heavy losses of American soldiers in Beirut. Women's gender identity, on the other hand — including women in powerful positions — is not threatened in the same way when they fail to get what they want (although token women like Margaret Thatcher may try to prove they are "man" enough for their jobs).

Masculinity is also defined as the absence of "feminine" qualities such as tenderness, vulnerability, empathy, compassion, sensitivity, and nurturance. The traits identified as masculine may be either positive or negative, constructive or destructive, appropriate or inappropriate, depending on the context within which they occur. Being fearless, for example, in the face of real danger can be fatal, while at other times it can save lives. Being adventurous can lead to useful discoveries or provide fun and laughter, but being adventurous about the use of nuclear weapons can lead to mass murder.

As with qualities that our culture regards as masculine, most of those defined as feminine may also be positive or negative, constructive or destructive, appropriate or inappropriate in different contexts. To feel compassion for one's oppressor, for example, can result in doing nothing to stop the oppression, while to feel compassion toward people who are starving can lead to developing assistance programs or trying to change the policies responsible for their plight.

However, since men who demonstrate these so-called feminine qualities are considered unmasculine — and since to be unmasculine is considered a terrible defect deserving of pity or contempt — many men are unwilling to behave in a way that suggests "femininity" even when it would be appropriate. Similarly, women often will not act in ways regarded as masculine, even when appropriate, for fear that they will be regarded as masculine.[4]

---

[4]Women who behave in a "masculine" way are not viewed as negatively as men who

This division of human qualities into male and female categories results in inappropriate behavior by both males and females. When compassion is what is called for in men, they may not have enough of it. When aggression or assertiveness is called for in women, they may be unable to rise to the occasion. Living, as we do, on the threshold of oblivion, the implications of this polarization for our current predicament are enormous. For the rule of masculine qualities, cut off from the feminine ones, has contributed greatly to our current tragic situation that Caldicott so aptly calls "nuclear madness." It has resulted in a kind of culturally-induced insanity that could lead to the demise of the whole planet. An important step toward the prevention of such a catastrophe is to end the polarization of human characteristics. We must change popular notions of masculinity and femininity. Attempts to meet the masculine ideal too often result in violence, on personal, national and international levels. Caldicott expresses a similar view in a somewhat derogatory fashion:

> These hideous weapons of killing and mass genocide may be a symptom of several male emotions: inadequate sexuality and a need to continually prove their virility plus a primitive fascination with killing (1984, p. 297).

However, we must also recognize that our culture's notions of masculinity and femininity do not exist in a vacuum. They are attached to the roles of the powerful and the powerless, the dominant and the subordinate. It won't be possible to rid ourselves of these ideas completely while men continue their rule over women.

Nor is the integration of equal numbers of women into previously male-dominated hierarchical organizations a satisfactory solution. These hierarchical organizations are a product of this polarization. If there were a true integration of so-called masculine and feminine qualities, the structures of our society would be different. For example, if men were to take equal responsibility for the rearing of their children (which will certainly be necessary if we are to end the polarization of traits and roles discussed), the occupational structure would have to be radically altered, the notion of what constitutes full-time work would have to be transformed, etc.

Nuclear war is a feminist issue; the risk of a nuclear holocaust is very much related to the fact that the United States is a patriarchal nation in a community of patriarchal nations. Despite a few token women leaders, the governments that have participated in the development and buildup

---

behave in a feminine way. Joan of Arc, for example, gained some of the status that accrued to the more powerful male role. Men who behave in a "feminine" way have nothing to gain, except in the eyes of feminists.

of nuclear arms are now and have always been male-dominated. Given the correlation between the masculine mentality and the nuclear mentality, it is hardly surprising that the nuclear mentality pervades world leadership.

An example of the intricate interconnectedness of the masculine mentality and the nuclear mentality is presented by Schell in *The Fate of the Earth*:

> It is a symptom of the schism between what Einstein called our "thinking" and the reality around us that when our strategists set out to think their "unthinkable" thoughts they feel obliged to quite deliberately leave the rest of their human equipment—their feelings, their moral sense, their humanity—behind. For the requirements of strategy in its present form force them to plan actions that from any recognizable moral point of view are indefensible. One strategic thinker, in a striking inversion of the usual understanding of ethical obligation, has said that an "iron will" is required if one is to recommend the slaughter of hundreds of millions of people in a nuclear attack—a point of view that is uncomfortably close to that of Heinrich Himmler, who told the commanders of the SS that in order to carry out the extermination of the Jews they had to be "superhumanly inhuman." In both statements, it is not obedience to our moral feelings but resistance to those feelings that is presented as our obligation, as though moral feeling were a siren call that it would be weak to give in to and that it is our duty to resist. Once the "strategic necessity" of planning the death of hundreds of millions of people is accepted, we begin to live in a world in which morality and action inhabit two separate, closed realms. All strategic sense becomes moral nonsense, and vice versa, and we are left with the choice of seeming to be either strategic or moral idiots (1982, pp. 194–195).

Schell appears unaware that he is describing a split between thinking, feeling and morality that is particularly characteristic of the masculine mentality. Our educational institutions foster this split, focusing as they do on the development of the mind, and ignoring feelings and morality—except in so far as they themselves are the subject of study. It is not surprising then that feminists have attacked these values in academia and have worked to invent new pedagogical techniques that integrate thinking, feeling, and morality. Schell's insightful remarks are flawed only by his failure to understand the significance of gender to his analysis.

Ronald Reagan authorized the expenditure of millions of dollars in 1984 to set up a national center to help state and local police track down serial murderers who, by the way, are all, to our knowledge, male (*San Francisco Chronicle*, July 11, 1984). There is an even more urgent need for a national center to study people who contemplate mass murder such as Reagan, other members of his administration, past US presidents and their advisors, as well as many of our military leaders. As Helen Caldicott points out:

In this society anybody who contemplates murdering a single individual is considered either mentally unstable or a potential criminal. But people within this administration are making statements about nuclear war that contemplate the death of hundreds of millions of human beings. The same moral and legal restraints should be applied to these people as to ordinary citizens who contemplate the death of only one human being (1984, p. 35).

Scholar Jane Caputi argues that there is a direct connection between the nuclear crisis and a certain kind of misogynist murder that she refers to as "sex crimes":

It is particularly the Nuclear Age which is bonded to the Age of Sex Crime, for nuclearism's inevitable goal of the mutilation and devastation of the Earth is the precise macrocosmic parallel to the crimes of Jack the Ripper and his complete mutilation and devastation of the individual female body (1987, p. 12).

Referring to the members of Congress in 1984, Caldicott explains why she thinks our leaders are so criminally inclined: "These people, mostly men, practice psychic numbing. . . . They have never morally, ethically, or emotionally contemplated the logical consequences of their daily actions as they vote to prepare the earth for a global holocaust" (1984, p. 302). Caldicott also observes that:

It is never the people who make the decision to kill who get killed. It is the boys who usually don't even know what the dispute is about, let alone understand the intricacies of international politics. The old men act out their fascination with killing, their need to prove their toughness and sexual adequacy by using innocent pawns. This dynamic has been occurring for thousands, if not millions, of years. Now it must stop because any conventional superpower war will almost certainly escalate to nuclear war (1984, p. 306).

Although it isn't quite true that it is *never* the people who make the decision to kill who get killed, Caldicott's overall analysis here is sound. But I don't agree with Caldicott's explanation for why male leaders have always been so cavalier about other people's deaths:

How many leaders of the world have ever watched the miracle of the birth of a baby? How many leaders of the world have helped a child to die and supported the parents in their grief before and forever after? Each life is as precious as any other, and the magnitude of suffering involved in a single death is vast. Yet because these men do not understand these values in their souls, they have produced the lethal equipment and ordered the deaths of hundreds of thousands of people in the past and possibly hundreds of millions in the future (1984, p. 306).

No. It is not enough that men witness the birth of a baby, the death of a child, and the grief of parents. The distorted values and psyches to which Caldicott refers are a product of the sexist society and the sexist world in which we live.

In conclusion, the threat of nuclear war is a threat to the survival of all human beings on this planet. The oppression of women, people of color, poor or lower-class people, lesbians and gay men, young and old, disabled people—all become secondary in the face of the possibility (or probability) of the total annihilation of large portions of the human race in a nuclear holocaust.

But the very real threat to everyone's survival posed by nuclear war is not what makes it a feminist issue. Nuclear war is a feminist issue because the threat of nuclear obliteration is a consequence of the distorted values, psyches, and institutions that sexist arrangements have bred. This insight provides a guide to more effective and radical efforts to prevent a nuclear catastrophe. We must face the fact that at this point in history the nuclear mentality and the masculine mentality are one and the same. To rid ourselves of one, we must rid ourselves of the other.

REFERENCES

Browne, Angela, *When Battered Women Kill* (New York: Free Press, 1987).

Brownmiller, Susan, *Against Our Will* (New York: Simon and Schuster, 1975).

Caldicott, Helen, *Missile Envy* (New York: William Morrow, 1984).

Caputi, Jane, *The Age of Sex Crime* (Bowling Green, Ohio: Bowling Green State University Popular Press, 1987).

Carroll, Rick and Magagnini, Stephen, "5 Slain in Bay Shootings," *San Francisco Chronicle* (24 April 1981).

Federal Bureau of Investigation, *Uniform Crime Reports* (Washington, DC: US Government Printing Office, Annual).

Jones, Ann, *Women Who Kill* (New York: Holt, Rinehart and Winston, 1980).

Malamuth, Neil, Briere, John, and Check, James, "Sexual Arousal in Response to Aggression: Ideological, Aggressive, and Sexual Correlates," *Journal of Personality and Social Psychology*, Vol. 50, No. 2 (1986).

McNulty, Faith, *The Burning Bed* (New York: Harcourt, Brace and Jovanovich, 1980).

Mulvihill, Donald and Tumin, Melvin, *Crimes of Violence: A Staff Report Submitted to the National Commission on the Causes and Prevention of Violence*, Vol. 11 (Washington, DC: US Government Printing Office, 1969).

Russell, Diana, *Sexual Exploitation: Rape, Child Sexual Abuse, and Workplace Harassment* (Beverly Hills: Sage Publications, 1984).

Russell, Diana, *The Politics of Rape* (New York: Stein and Day, 1975).

Scacco, Anthony (Ed.), *Male Rape* (New York: AMS Press, 1982).

Scacco, Anthony, *Rape in Prison* (Springfield, IL: Charles C Thomas, 1975).

Straus, Murray, Gelles, Richard, and Steinmetz, Suzanne, *Behind Closed Doors: Violence in the American Family* (Garden City, NY: Anchor Books, 1980).

Schell, Jonathan, *The Fate of the Earth* (New York: Avon Books, 1982).

Wolfgang, Marvin E. and Ferracuti, Franco, *The Subculture of Violence* (London: Tavistock Publications, 1967).

8

Ideologies of Madness*

Susan Griffin

Nuclear War has been described as a form of madness. Yet rarely does one take this insight seriously when contemplating the dilemma of war and peace. I wish to describe here the state of mind that has produced nuclear weaponry as a species of socially accepted insanity. This is a state of mind born of that philosophical assumption of our civilization which attempts to divide human consciousness from nature. Exploring the terrain of this state of mind one will find in this geography, in the subterranean and unseen region that is part of its foundation and history, the hatred of the other in the quite literal forms of misogyny (the hatred of women), racism and anti-Semitism.

If one approaches the explosion of a nuclear weapon as if this were symptomatic of an underlying mental condition, certain facets begin to take on metaphorical meaning. Even the simplest physical aspects of a nuclear chain reaction carry a psychological significance. In order for a chain reaction to be created, the atom must be split apart. The fabric of matter has to be torn asunder. In a different vein, it is important to realize that the first atomic weapons were dropped over a people regarded in the demonology of our civilization as racially inferior. Tangentially, and carrying a similar significance, the first nuclear device exploded over Bikini Atoll had a pin-up of Rita Hayworth pasted to its surface. And then, taking from a history that has largely been forgotten or ignored, the prototype of the first missiles capable of carrying nuclear

---

*This is a revised version of Susan Griffin's Schumacher Lecture delivered in London in November 1983, and published in *Green Line*, Nos. 20 and 21 (March–April, 1984).

warheads was invented and designed in the Third Reich. And those first rockets, the German V-2 rockets, were produced in underground tunnels by prisoners of concentration camps who were worked to death in this production.

These facets of the existence of nuclear weaponry can lead us to a deeper understanding of the troubled mind that has created our current nuclear crisis. To begin at one particular kind of beginning, with the history of thought, one can see the philosophical roots of our current crisis in the splitting of the atom. In the most basic terms, what occurs when the atom is split is a division between energy and matter. Until this century, modern science assumed matter and energy to be separate. This assumption began not with scientific observation but out of a religious bias. Examining the early history of science, one discovers that the first scientists were associated with and supported by the church (as was most scholarship at that time) and that they asked questions derived from Christian theology. "What is the nature of light?" a question intimately bound up with the theory of relativity and quantum physics began as a religious question. And the guiding paradigm of the religion that posed this question has been a fundamental dualism between matter and spirit. Matter, or body and earth, were the degraded regions, belonging to the devil and corruption. Spirit, or the realm of pure intellect and heavenly influence, belonged to God, and was, in human experience, won only at the expense of flesh.

Of course, science does not recognize the categories of spirit and matter any longer, except through a process of translation. In the new vocabulary, though, the old dualism has been preserved. Now, matter is conceived of as earthbound and thus subject to gravity, and energy, the equivalent of spirit, is described as a free agent, inspiring and enlivening. Newtonian physics continued the old dualism, but Einsteinian physics does not.

When Einstein discovered the formula that eventually led to the development of the atomic bomb, what he saw was a continuum between matter and energy, instead of a separation. What we call solid matter is not solid, nor is it static. Matter is, instead, a process of continual change. There is no way to divide the energy of this motion from the physical property of matter. What is more, energy has mass. And not only is there no division between matter and energy as such, but to divide any single entity from any other single entity becomes an impossibility. No particular point exists where my skin definitely ends and the air in the atmosphere begins and this atmosphere ends and your skin begins. We are all in a kind of field together. And finally, with the new physics, the old line between subject and object has also disappeared. According to Heisenberg's Principle of Uncertainty, whatever we observe we change through our participation. Objectivity with its implied superiority and control has also vanished.

One might imagine that with the disappearance of a scientific basis for dualism and the appearance of a physical view that is unified and whole, a different philosophy might arise, one which might help us make peace with nature. But instead what this civilization chose to do with this new insight was to find a way to separate matter from energy (it is spoken of as "liberating" the energy from the atom). And this separation has in turn produced a technology of violence which has divided the world into two separate camps who regard each other as enemies.

The real enemy, however, in dualistic thinking, is hidden: the real enemy is ourselves. The same dualism which imagines matter and energy to be separate also divides human nature, separating what we call our material existence from consciousness. This dualism is difficult to describe without using dualistic language. Actually, the mind cannot be separated from the body. The brain is part of the body, and is affected by blood flow, temperature, nourishment, muscular movement. The order and rhythm of the body, bodily metaphors, are reflected in the medium of thought, in our patterns of speech. Yet, we conceive of the mind as separate and above the body. And through a subtle process of socialization since birth, we learn to regard the body and our natural existence as something inferior, and without intelligence. Most of the rules of polite behavior are designed to conceal the demands of the body. We excuse ourselves, and refer to our bodily functions through euphemism.

From this dualistic frame of mind two selves are born: one acknowledged and one hidden. The acknowledged self identifies with spirit, with intellect, with what we imagine is free of the influence of natural law. The hidden self is part of nature, earthbound, inextricable from the matrix of physical existence. We have become very seriously alienated from this denied self. So seriously that our alienation has become a kind of self-hatred, and this self-hatred is leading us today toward the suicidal notion of nuclear combat.

Of course, the body and mind are not separate. And ironically, the warfare incipient between our ideas of who we are and who we really are is made more intense through this unity. Consciousness cannot exclude bodily knowledge. We are inseparable from nature, dependent on the biosphere, vulnerable to the processes of natural law. We cannot destroy the air we breath without destroying ourselves. We are reliant on one another for our survival. We are all mortal. And this knowledge comes to us, whether we want to receive it or not, with every breath.

The dominant philosophies of this civilization have attempted to posit a different order of being over and against this bodily knowledge. According to this order of being, we are separate from nature and hence above natural process. In the logic of this order, we are meant to dominate nature, control life, and in some sense felt largely unconsciously, avoid the natural event of death.

Yet, in order to maintain a belief in this hierarchy one must repress bodily knowledge. And this is no easy task. Our own knowledge of our own natural existence comes to us not only with every breath, but with hunger, with intimacy, with dreams, with all the unpredictable eventualities of life. Our imagined superiority over nature is constantly challenged by consciousness itself. Consciousness emerges from and is immersed in material experience. Consciousness is not separable from perception, which is to say sensuality, and as such cannot be separated from matter. Even through the process of the most abstract thought, we cannot entirely forget that we are part of nature. In the biosphere nothing is ever entirely lost. Death itself is not an absolute end, but rather a transformation. What appears to be lost in a fire becomes heat and ash. So, too, no knowledge can ever really be lost to consciousness. It must remain, even if disguised as a mere symbol of itself.

If I choose to bury a part of myself, what I bury will come back to haunt me in another form, as dream, or fear, or projection. This civilization, which has buried part of the human self, has created many projections. Out of the material of self-hatred several categories of otherness have been fashioned. Existing on a mass scale and by social agreement, these categories form a repository for our hidden selves.

The misogynist's idea of women is a fundamental category of otherness for this civilization. In the ideology of misogyny, a woman is a lesser being than a man. And the root cause of her inferiority is that she is closer to the earth, more animal, and hence, material in her nature. She is thus described as more susceptible to temptations of the flesh (or devils, or serpents), more emotional and hence less capable of abstract thought than a man. Similarly in the ideology of racism, a person with dark skin is perceived as, at one and the same time, more sensual and erotic and less intelligent.

During the rise of fascism in Europe, a fictitious document was created called the *Protocols of the Elders of Zion*. In this "document" Jewish elders plan to corrupt and eventually seize Aryan bloodlines through the rape and seduction of Aryan women. If one has projected a part of the self upon another, one must always be afraid that this self will return, perhaps even entering one's own bloodstream. But what is equally significant about this myth, and much of the racist and anti-Semitic imagination, is that a sexual act, and especially rape, lies at the heart of its mythos.

It was in writing a book on pornography that I first began to understand the ideology of misogynist projection. Since so much in pornography is violent, I began to ask myself why sexual experience is associated with violence. This is a question which poses itself again in the context of nuclear weaponry, not only because Rita Hayworth's image happened to adorn an experimental nuclear bomb, nor simply because of the phallic shape of the missile, nor the language employed to describe the weapons—the first atomic bomb called "little boy," the next "big boy"—but also because of the sexualization of warfare itself, the eroticization of violence in war, the supposed virility of the soldier, the test of virility which is supposed to take place on the battlefield, and the general equivalency between masculine virtues and prowess in battle.

Over time in my study of pornography I began to understand pornographic imagery as an expression of the fear of sexual experience itself. Sexual experience takes one back to a direct knowledge of nature and of one's own body before culture has intervened to create the delusion of dominance. It is part of the nature of sexual pleasure and of orgasm to lose control. And finally the feel of a woman's breast, or of human skin against bare skin at all, must recall infancy and the powerlessness of infancy.

As infants we all experience an understanding of dependence and vulnerability. Our first experience of a natural, material power outside ourselves was through the bodies of our mothers. In this way we have all come to associate nature with the body of a woman. It was our mother who could feed us, give us warmth and comfort, or withhold these things. She had the power of life and death over us as natural process does now.

It was also as infants that we confronted what we have come to know as death. What we call death—coldness, isolation, fear, darkness, despair, trembling—is really the experience of an infant. What death really is lies in the dimension of the unknown. But from the infantile experience of what we call death, one can see the psychological derivation of civilization's association between women and death. (One sees this clearly in the creation myth from Genesis, as Eve the seductress brings death into the world.) In this sense, too, sexual experience returns one to a primal fear of death. And through this understanding one can begin to see that at the center of the impulse to rape is the desire to dominate the power of sexual experience itself, and to deny the power of nature as this is felt through sexual experience.

The connection between sexuality and violence exists as a kind of subterranean theme in the fascist and authoritarian mentality. In several places in Jacobo Timmerman's book, *Prisoner Without a Name, Cell Without a Number*, he points out a relationship between the violence of the dictator and a pornographic attitude toward sexuality. Imprisoned and tortured himself, he recalls that those who did not do "a good scrubbing job" when ordered to clean the prison floors, were forced to "undress, lean over with their index finger on the ground and have them rotate round and round dragging their finger on the ground without lifting it. You felt," he writes, "as if your kidneys were bursting." Another punishment was to force prisoners to run naked along the passageway "reciting aloud sayings dictated" to them, such as "my mother is a whore, I masturbate, I respect the guard, the police love me."

That, to the fascist mind, "the other" represents a denied part of the self becomes clear in the following story about Adolf Hitler. In a famous passage in *Mein Kampf* he describes the moment when he decided to devote his life's work to anti-Semitism. He recounts that while walking through the streets of Vienna, he happened to see an old man dressed in the traditional clothes of Jewish men in that city at that time, i.e., in a Kaftan. The first question he asked was, "Is this man Jewish?" and then he corrected himself, and replaced that question with another, "Is this man German?"

If you are to project a denied self onto another, you must first establish that this other is different from yourself. Were you to notice any similarity, you would be endangered by the perception that what you project may belong to you. The question that Hitler asked himself became a standard part of German textbooks in the Third Reich. A stereotypical portrait of a Jewish man's face was shown under the question, "Is this man German?" and the correct answer the students were taught was, of course, "No." In fact, Germany became a nation rather late. For centuries it existed as a collection of separate tribes, and one of the oldest tribes in that nation was Jewish.

Hitler's story of the man in the Kaftan became a standard part of his orations. He would become nearly hysterical at times telling the story, and is said to have even vomited once. In the light of this history, a seemingly trivial story from Hitler's early life becomes significant. As a young art student he bought his clothes secondhand, because like many students, he was poor. In this period most of those selling secondhand clothing were Jewish and Hitler bought from a Jewish clothes seller one item of clothing that he wore so often that he began to be identified with this apparel. And that was a Kaftan.

What is also interesting historically is that the Kaftan was a form of medieval German dress. Exiled from Germany during a period of persecution, many Jews, who then lived in ghettoes, continued to wear this traditional German dress and were still wearing it when they returned to Germany centuries later. Not only did Hitler fail to recognize an image of himself encountered in the streets of Vienna, but so did an entire generation of Germans. So an entire civilization, that to which we all belong, is in conflict with a part of human nature, which we try to bury and eventually even destroy.

The weapons that now threaten the destruction of the earth and life as we know it were developed because the Allied nations feared that the fascist powers were making them. The missiles which are now part and parcel of nuclear weaponry were first developed in the Third Reich. It is crucial now in our understanding of ourselves and what it is in us that has led to the nuclear crisis that we begin to look at the Nazi holocaust as a mirror, finding a self-portrait in "the other" who is persecuted and denied, and seeing a part of ourselves too in the fascist dictator who would destroy that denied self.

The illusion this civilization retains, that we are somehow above nature, is so severe that in a sense we have come to believe that we can end material existence without dying. The absurdity of nuclear weaponry as a strategy for defense, when the use of those weapons would annihilate us, would in itself argue this. But if you look closely at the particulars of certain strategies within the overall nuclear strategy you again encounter the same estranged relationship with reality. A man who used to be in Reagan's administration, T. K. Jones, actually proposed that a viable method of civil defense would be to issue each citizen a shovel.

It took an eight year old boy to point out that this plan cannot work because after you dig a hole and get into it for protection, someone else must stand outside the hole and shovel dirt on top. The Pentagon refers to its strategies for waging nuclear war as SIOP. One year the Pentagon actually went through the paces of a SIOP plan. As a literary scholar I found the scenario which the Pentagon wrote for this dramatization very disturbing. The Pentagon could write this play any way that they wished, and they wrote that the President was killed with a direct hit to Washington DC. Any student of tragic drama will tell you that what happens to the King, or the President, is symbolic of what happens to the self. But this death is not experienced as real. Though the earthly self dies, in the Pentagon's version, the sky self does not die: The Vice President goes up in an airplane fully equipped to wage nuclear war by computer. There is such a plane flying above us now, and at every hour of the day and night.

The division that we experience from the natural self, the self that is material and embedded in nature, impairs our perceptions of reality. As Timmerman writes:

> The devices are recurrent in all totalitarian ideology, to ignore the complexities of reality, or even eliminate reality, and instead establish a simple goal and a simple means of attaining that goal.

Proceeding both from an alienation from nature, and an estrangement from the natural self, our civilization replaces reality with an idea of reality. Through maintaining the supremacy of the idea, one creates a delusion of a supernatural power over nature.

In the development of this alienation as a state of mind, the delusion of well-being and safety eventually becomes more important than the realistic considerations which will actually effect well-being or safety. Hannah Arendt writes of an illusionary world created by totalitarian movements ". . . in which through sheer imagination uprooted masses can feel at home, and are spared the never-ending shocks which real life and real experience deal to human beings. . . ." Later, in the *Origins of Totalitarianism*, she speaks of the mass state of mind under the Third Reich in which people ceased to believe in what they perceived with their own eyes and ears, prefering the conflicting reports issued by the *Fuhrer*.

One encounters the same failure to confront reality in Stalin's psychology as it is described by Isaac Deutchsher in his biography:[1]

> He [Stalin] was now completely possessed by the idea that he could achieve a miraculous transformation of the whole of Russia by a single *tour de force*. He seemed to live in a half-real and half-dreamy world of statistical figures and indices of industrial orders and instructions, a world in which no target and no objective seemed beyond his and the party's grasp.

During the period of forced collectivization of farms, Stalin destroyed actual farms before the collectivized farms were created. As Deutscher writes, it was as if a whole nation destroyed its real houses and moved "lock, stock and barrel into some illusory buildings."

We are, in fact, now living in such an illusory building. The entire manner in which plans for a nuclear war are discussed, rehearsed, and envisioned, partakes of a kind of unreality, an anesthetized and nearly automatic functioning, in which cerebration is strangely unrelated to experience or feeling. The Generals imagine themselves conducting nuclear war from a room without windows, with no natural light, choosing strategies and targets by looking at enormous computerized maps. The language they use to communicate their decisions is all in code. No one uses the word "war," the word "bomb," the word "death," or the words "blood," "pain," "loss," "grief," "shock," or "horror." In Siegfried Sassoon's[2] recollection of World War I, he remembers encountering a man, a soldier like himself, who has just learned that his brother was killed. The man is half-crazy, tearing his clothes off, and cursing at

---

[1]Isaac Deutscher, *Stalin, A Political Biography* (Oxford: Oxford University Press, 1961).
[2]Siegfried Sassoon, "The Complete Memoirs of George Sherston," as collected in *Sassoon's Long Journey*, edited by Paul Fussell (London: 1983).

war. As Sassoon passed beyond this man into the dark of the war, he could still hear "his uncouth howlings." It is those "uncouth howlings" that those who are planning nuclear war have managed to mute in their imagination.

But of course that howling is not entirely lost. In the shared imagination of our civilization, it is the "other" who carries emotion, the women who howl. And far from wishing to protect the vulnerable and the innocent, it is the secret desire of this civilization to destroy those who feel, and to silence feeling. This hidden desire becomes apparent in pornography where women are pictured in a traditional way as weaker than men and needing protection, and yet, where erotic feeling is freely mixed with the desire to brutalize and even murder women.

One can find a grim picture of the insane logic of the alienated mind of our civilization in the pornographic film "Peeping Tom." The hero of this movie is a pornographic film maker. He has a camera armed with a spear. As he photographs a woman's naked body, the camera releases the weapon and he makes a record of her death agonies. The final victory of the alienated mind over reality is to destroy that reality (and one's experience of it) and replace reality with a record of that destruction. One finds the same pattern in the history of actual atrocities. In California, a man lured women into the desert with a promise of work as pornographic models. There, while he tortured and murdered them, he made a photographic record of the event. The Nazis themselves kept the best documentation of atrocities committed in the concentration camps. And the most complete records of the destruction of native Americans have been kept by the United States military.

Now, the state of conflict in which this civilization finds itself has worsened. The enemy is not simply "the other" but life itself. And it is in keeping with the insane logic of alienation that the Pentagon has found a way that it believes we can win nuclear war. We have situated satellites in space that will record the process of annihilation of life, and the Pentagon counts, as a future victor, that nation which has gathered the best documentation of the destruction.

There is however another form of reflection available to us by virtue of our human nature. We are our own witnesses. We can see ourselves. We are part of nature. And nature is not divided. Matter is intelligent. Feeling, sense, the needs of the body, all that has been consigned to the "other," made the province of women, of darkness, contains a deeper and a sustaining wisdom. It remains for us to empower that knowledge and carry it into the world. In insanity and madness, one is lost to oneself. It is only by coming home to ourselves that we can survive.

9

Seeing Through the Emperor's New Clothes: Two Women Look at the Nuclear Issue

Patricia Ellsberg
Elissa Melamed

As women, we approach the Bomb from our personal histories. Our "nuclear stories" tell who we are and how we woke up to the nuclear threat. They bear witness to the deep personal impact of this issue.

PATRICIA'S NUCLEAR STORY

I grew up with a sense of gratitude to the nuclear bomb. When I was an adolescent, my father told me that nuclear weapons would make the world safe from world wars, because they made starting a large-scale war suicidal. His words carried great weight with me, not only due to his authoritative personality, but also because in the thirties he had befriended many of the men who were to become the great generals of World War II. Eisenhower, Bradley, Marshall, LeMay, Gruenther, and "Drop the Bomb" O'Donnell were all dear friends of his and godfathers to my younger brothers.

Around the time of the Korean War, when my older brother faced the draft, I remember feeling relieved when my father assured us that nuclear weapons would protect us from protracted war with the Communists. Perhaps he knew at the time what Americans were to learn later from memoirs: that his friend, President Eisenhower, was threatening to use nuclear weapons against the Chinese to bring about a truce in the Korean War.

I believed over the years that our buildup of nuclear weapons was essential to defend us against nuclear attack—a necessary evil that provided security through a balance of terror. If we did not remain strong, the imbalance would make nuclear attack more likely.

Only in the last few years have I come to re-examine these beliefs. Even though my husband, Daniel Ellsberg, returned his attention to the dangers of nuclear weapons (the focus of his professional life before the war in Vietnam) soon after the end of the Pentagon Papers trial in the mid-seventies, I was too absorbed with the birth and raising of our young son to be able to face the horrible realities of the nuclear threat. I remember sometimes as I was nursing Michael, my husband would talk about the likelihood that some nuclear weapons would explode somewhere within the next two decades. I would feel suffocated and begin to cry. I asked him to stop talking about it, as if silencing him would make the threat go away.

As Michael grew, so did the anti-nuclear movement, and I was asked to speak on the issue. One night after preparing a speech for a Mother's Day rally, I had a nightmare in which I was watching a documentary film. I saw a young boy reaching out in slow motion to his teddy bear, while a calm male voice announced, "In a radioactive blast, even this teddy bear is radioactive." The glass eyes of the teddy bear began to glow as the child reached out to it for comfort. The child screamed in terror and pain.

Even though the film speeded up in the dream and the child was all right, I woke up in a cold sweat and could not sleep the rest of the night. The thought came to me that when I was my son's age, there were no nuclear weapons on the face of the earth. Now there are over 50,000 of them, with a combined force of one million times the explosive power of Hiroshima. That night I felt in my guts for the first time that unless we change our course, Michael will not live to be my age without witnessing and perhaps being consumed by a nuclear explosion. It was then that I awoke to the nuclear issue, and ever since then I have been placing some of my passion and love for our son into actions that may help assure that he has a future.

ELISSA'S NUCLEAR STORY

Daddy was the greatest, he knew everything, he was always right. Until he stopped us, my sister and I stood on the corner across from the schoolyard handing out his business cards and announcing to the passing parade, "Dr. Isaacson is the best dentist in the world." Even now, I sometimes find it difficult to believe fully that Daddy (read Teacher, Husband, Doctor or Political Leader) can be wrong—not just a little off-base, but tragically, desperately wrong. It is a lesson I have had to learn over and over again.

I think it finally sunk in when I woke up one spring day to find myself in the Nuclear Age. I was living in Paris, cut loose from my moorings, forced to see the world in a fresh light. Trying to improve my French, I was watching television. What I saw that morning was much in the ordinary way of things—in fact, it was its very ordinariness that made it frightening. Carter and Khomeini were eyeball to eyeball in the tiresomely familiar shoot-out scenario, only this time Main Street was the world bristling with nuclear weapons and "click!" there was Daddy again—this time incarnated as two suddenly naked Emperors, one American, one Iranian. In case I missed the point, it was then hammered home by a zillion Iranian men shaking their fists at me.

What had "clicked" for me was this: in the name of various abstractions—like God, country, honor, winning—these men were putting all of existence in jeopardy. I got up, went out to continue my ordinary life, and found that it was gone. Walking down the Avenue de la Bourdonnaise, looking for an orthodontist for my daughter, I felt half-crazed, wondering if she would be around long enough to enjoy her straight teeth. That day was the beginning of a passage through fear.

Along with the dread of nuclear holocaust, I was dealing with more subtle fears. The fear of daring to believe I had seen something real, even though I alone was seeing it, or so it seemed at the time. And the even more frightening corollary that if I *was* seeing something real, I would have to do something about it. I would have to take Daddy on.

I am still discovering where this realization is leading me. And with the fear I also now feel the joy of committing to something really worth doing. But the struggle to retain my integrity of vision never ends. Each time, there is a moment of "how dare I?" as I expose Daddy for all the world to see.

THE EMPEROR HAS NO CLOTHES

Nuclear weapons are a product of the male mind, being 100 percent conceived, developed, administered and utilized by men. Like most other weapons, they resemble male sexual anatomy—in this case, to an uncanny and ludicrous degree. But their dreaded orgasms seed not life, but death: an eternal "nuclear winter" if we unleash even a small fraction of our present arsenal.

In general, men feel a fascination with these and all weapons that women just do not have. As women, we know that these are not *our* weapons. We simply recoil in horror. We stay as far away from the bombs as we can; we don't even like to talk or think about them. Even when we demonstrate against them, we do so from the *outside*. For the most part, the nuclear debate goes on between male hawks and doves. We act as if we don't belong there and have nothing special to contribute.

Subjects of the Emperor

We stand silently on the sidelines while the Emperor struts down the street. Others admire his robes or criticize the flimsiness of the material. But why are we not shouting, *"He has no clothes on?"* Why are we not saying that the entire male system of so-called "protection" poses the greatest threat on earth today?

If we did not doubt our eyes, that is what we would be doing. For women have a special perceptiveness about this issue that we hide — even from ourselves.

It's complicated for us to "come out" about the Bomb and speak with our full voice for several reasons. To do so requires us to say, "We are different," an uncomfortable position for women to take. We tend to define ourselves in terms of connection rather than separation, as Carol Gilligan and others have pointed out. Besides, "different" has usually been seen as "not as good" where women are concerned. And since many women are interested in catching up with men and becoming equal partners in the male system, we haven't wanted to set ourselves in opposition to it. And we have felt so embattled in our struggle for full citizenship that we have not wanted to take on yet another issue, fearing that this would lead to more diffusion of our energies and division in our ranks.

We also defer to male expertise and disqualify ourselves on grounds of technical incompetence. We allow men to define the problem in terms of who has more and what weapons, instead of trusting our own understanding that, in a nuclear age, more weapons only make us less secure. We abdicate, saying in effect, "Daddy knows best." And so we place the nasty world of war and weapons in the male domain. In spite of the many individual women who have played pivotal roles in the peace movement, the organized women's movement and the masses of women living private lives have been slow to see the nuclear issue as a women's issue.

Meanwhile, men with our passive support have created a Doomsday Machine and are now busily refining the trigger. We can no longer rely on them to lead us to safety. It is time to claim this issue as our own, as if our lives and the lives of our children depended upon it—for they do. Far from being divisive, there is no greater potential source of women's unity than to confront the Bomb together. To do so reveals our common vision.

We *do* see things differently. And these differences provide a basis for hope and urgently needed change. Perhaps we are finally secure enough in our equality to affirm them with pride. And a growing body of evidence justifies this new perspective.

Another Way of Thinking

Psychologists (such as A.K. Witkin, Carol Gilligan, Dorothy Dinnerstein, and Nancy Chodorow) are telling us that we don't just *feel* more than men, although this is also probably true, we tend to *think* differently as well.

Connections of all kinds interest women and we grasp them readily. Men find this ability mysterious and label it "women's intuition." This makes it sound like something other than thinking, but in fact it is a perfectly respectable intellectual approach called "systems thinking" when men do it.

This difference between us probably stems at least in part from the different developmental paths we travel in order to become adult men and women. For both boys and girls, Mother is an overwhelming presence in an infant's life. But a boy forges his identity by valuing his difference from Mother and by separating from her. This has myriad implications for the way men come to see reality.

The world becomes divided into Self and Other, often in competition. The Other is always potentially dangerous, incomprehensible, and therefore needs to be controlled. The messiness of real life is neatly quantified and reduced to abstractions, like "nuclear exchanges," "kill ratio," and "acceptable collateral damage."

This analytical way of thinking led to the scientific revolution. But the very technological advances it has generated now threaten our survival. We live in a new world—a world made totally interdependent by the existence of expanding populations, shrinking resources, global pollution, and, of course, nuclear weapons.

Women, by virtue of *our* developmental patterns, grasp this fact readily. We have not had to rupture our primary bond with Mother to find our gender identity, and so the world remains a network of connections for us. We see that the old strategies of competing and abstracting have become suicidal. What we haven't understood is why this is not obvious to men, and to our male leaders especially. And so we have assumed that *we* must be missing something, when the reverse is true.

The relational mode of thinking which women have kept alive must be shared with our brothers. *It must become the norm if we are to survive.* And we can begin by applying it to a re-examination of our nuclear policy.

Exposing the Emperor[1]

When we look at the naked truth it is shocking. The foreign policy of our country, as well as that of most other powerful nations, grows out of a collective psychosis, devoid of any connection to our common humanity or the living reality of flesh and blood. The world is divided into Us versus Them and Good versus Evil. Unlimited violence is permitted against the other.

A swollen sense of nationhood leads us to exaggerated territoriality. As Americans we comprise five percent of the world's population, yet we control forty percent of the world's resources. Our perceived national interest extends to all the corners of the globe. We feel attacked wherever we think we have a vital interest. The difference between offense and defense becomes so blurred as to be meaningless. Often we use our power for coercive rather than defensive purposes, to control and protect what is not rightly ours. The ultimate protection is thought to lie in the ultimate power to destroy.

We clothe our foreign policy in a deceptive garment of justifiable defense, maintaining that we developed our nuclear arsenal to deter nuclear attack by the Soviets. The reality is quite different. We have repeatedly risked world destruction by threatening to initiate the use of nuclear weapons in *non-nuclear* crises. In fact, such threats of first use are the cornerstone of our foreign policy. To maintain our preeminence in places far from our shores, we have substituted nuclear power for manpower.

As Daniel Ellsberg has written, "Again and again, mostly in secret, we have used nuclear weapons in the precise way a gun is used when it is pointed at someone's head in order to get one's way." Since Hiroshima, "every President from Truman to Reagan, with the possible exception of Ford, has seriously considered or actually threatened the first use of nuclear weapons in conventional confrontations" (1981, p. iv). Eisenhower threatened using nuclear weapons against China to end the Korean War. The United States also threatened their first use in the

---

[1]We are indebted to Daniel Ellsberg for his analysis of the nuclear arms race, which has informed our discussion throughout this section of the article.

Quemoy and Matsu, Berlin and Cuban crises, as well as in Vietnam. Our country is currently threatening first use both in Europe through our NATO policy, and in the Middle East, where President Reagan has reaffirmed the Carter Doctrine which commits the US to using "any means necessary" to maintain our vital interests in that region (1981, p. xiv).

In order to play our self-designated role of global policeman effectively, we have built a vast arsenal of nuclear weapons designed not to deter nuclear attack, but to make our threats of first use believable. To maintain our credibility on every level of escalation, we must continually replace or modernize our weapons.

It is true that the Soviet Union has joined us as a full partner in this dance of death. Yet although our government maintains we have only responded to Soviet moves, in fact the Soviets have usually followed our lead. We invented the Bomb and are the only country to have used it in combat. We expanded our arsenal while we had a monopoly of nuclear weapons from 1945–1949, and further increased it while we had an overwhelming superiority through the mid-1960s. As Herb York, former director of Livermore Laboratory states:

> Over the last thirty years we have repeatedly taken unilateral actions that have unnecessarily accelerated the [arms] race. . . . In the large majority of cases, the initiative has been in our hands. Our unilateral decisions have set the rate and scale for most of the individual steps in the strategic arms race (1970, p. 230).

We have consistently exaggerated the Soviet threat. At the time of the so-called "missile gap" and the Berlin Crisis, we had two hundred missiles and three thousand bombers in range of the Soviet Union. They had only *four* intercontinental missiles, and under two hundred bombers capable of striking the US.

And it is little recognized that we have repeatedly rejected opportunities to stop the arms race. We have refused to agree to a Comprehensive Test Ban—which the Soviets have frequently offered. If we had accepted the Soviet offer of a Comprehensive Test Ban in the late 1950s, we would not be facing the ten thousand strategic weapons that threaten us today. If we had signed a treaty in 1963, as Khrushchev urged, we would be facing only a few hundred single warhead missiles. If we had agreed in 1969 to a ban on the testing of MIRVed missiles (missiles with more than one warhead), we would not now be facing thousands of MIRVed warheads threatening our Minuteman missiles. If we now were to accept the Soviets' offer of a mutual comprehensive freeze and a moratorium on testing, we would be spared the development of a first strike capacity by both sides and we would avert the costly and reckless militarization of space.

Of course, there is a concern that if we did not work so hard to stay ahead of the Soviets, they would surpass us and become the dominant world power. Yet the only way to restrain them from developing new weapons systems is to forego these developments ourselves. While the modernization of our nuclear weapons gives us a temporary advantage, the inevitable cost is that the Soviets always catch up. This has been true for almost every technological advance in the arms race: for example, the atom and hydrogen bombs, strategic bombers, and missiles with multiple warheads. It also applies to the highly accurate destabilizing weapons we are now developing and deploying: the MX, Cruise missiles, and the Trident D-5s. Soon both sides will have nuclear weapons so accurate that they are capable of destroying the opponent's land-based missiles while they are in their silos. This greatly reduces the opponent's ability to retaliate and increases the incentive for each side to "use them or lose them," thereby making a preemptive first strike by either side far more likely in a crisis.

Thus, every weapon we develop comes back to haunt us. We then become obsessed with protecting ourselves from the very monsters we have helped to create. And we, along with other major powers, commit human sacrifice on the altar of the state, as more bombs are built while forty million people, most of them children, die each year of starvation and preventable disease. What stakes can justify the possibility of two billion people burned and vaporized, or the destruction of the life chain?

These risks are not acceptable to most women. We know the human costs of the war machine, since we bear the greater share of the economic burdens it imposes. We know we can live well without having to be number one, having done it for centuries. And we know how vengeful and imprudent men can be when their prestige — or virility — is threatened. We recognize that our leaders would not have control of a nuclear exchange any more than they had control in Vietnam, Iran, Lebanon, or now in the Persian Gulf.

We refuse to treat nuclear war as a computer problem. We sense in the cells of our bodies that radiation knows no national boundaries, that the world is an interdependent, interrelated system in which the harm we inflict on others will return to us. We understand that cooperation is a necessity for survival, the *Realpolitik* of our time.

In the words of Carol Gilligan, "The question is whether we finally take ourselves seriously enough to realize that if we see something differently, maybe we are not wrong" (Van Gelder, 1984, p. 40). And the next question is: will we act on what we know?

It is time to place the ending of the nuclear arms race among our highest priorities. As the majority of the electorate, we can effectively support candidates and legislation which further this goal. We can begin to liberate the defense budget for creative and compassionate purposes, and insist that our vast human and material resources be placed in the service of life rather than death. We must demand a defense policy based on the obvious truth that real security lies in improved relations between nations, in mutual security rather than military advantage.

Let us be guided by our *collective wisdom* based on the simple recognition that in the nuclear age, our nuclear family is all the children of the world. The emperor stands trembling and naked at the edge of an abyss. Together we can awaken from the spell he has cast, and proclaim a genuine strategy for survival.

REFERENCES

Ellsberg, Daniel, "Protest and Survive," in E. P. Thompson and Dan Smith (eds.), *Protest and Survive* (New York and London: Monthly Review Press, 1981), pp. i–xxviii.
Van Gelder, Lindsy, "Carol Gilligan: Leader for a Different Kind of Future," *Ms.* (January 1984), pp. 37–40 and 101.
York, Herbert F. *Race to Oblivion: A Participant's View of the Arms Race* (New York: Simon and Schuster, 1970).

10

Feminist Writers Confront the Nuclear Abyss*

Barbara Smith

On June 12, 1982 I marched with a group of friends who had been organizing for several months to express our opposition to the threat of nuclear war and to the US government's ever-increasing commitment to military spending versus basic human needs. This anti-nuclear mobilization, with almost a million participants, was the largest single demonstration in US history. We were the Necessary Bread Affinity Group and our banner read, "NECESSARY BREAD: THIRD WORLD AND WHITE LESBIANS UNITE." We were ". . . northern black and southern white; Anglo, Jewish, daughters of engineers and domestic workers . . . first- and tenth-generation Americans, Cuban immigrants, transplanted Chicanas," all Lesbians.[1] We chose the words for our banner carefully because we planned to use it at other demonstrations for years to come.

As we marched we handed out the statement we had drafted which connected the issues of militarism and disarmament to our concerns as

---

*Previously published in *New England Review, Bread Loaf Quarterly*, Vol. 5, No. 4 (Summer 1983).

[1]Necessary Bread Affinity Group, "Necessary Bread Disarmament Statement," June, 1982. The statement appeared in a number of women's periodicals including *Off Our Backs* and *Feminist Studies*, Vol. 8, No. 3 (Fall, 1982). It will appear in a forthcoming issue of *River Valley Voice*, P.O. Box 1193, Northampton, Ma. 01061.

feminists and Lesbians,[2] actively opposed to all varieties of oppression. Since many of us are writers, we had also sponsored a poetry reading the night before at the YWCA in the Brooklyn neighborhood where some of us live.

Not surprisingly, the reactions to our banner and our presence, both from onlookers and from other demonstrators ranged from applause to undisguised hostility. (Some readers may be having similar reactions at this very moment.) The one appalling word of course was "Lesbians." We could have left it out and passed by without a ripple, but we chose instead to identify exactly who we are to an anti-nuclear movement that has been notoriously white, homophobic, male-dominated, and class-bound. Hundreds of women joined us throughout the day and there were many other Lesbian and gay contingents, as well as thousands upon thousands of individual Lesbians and gay men, out or not. There were also more people of color than I expected from my participation in anti-war activity during the 1960s and 70s. All of us were there—female, poor, colored, and queer—because we knew that if a bomb drops no one will be safe, not even the rich white man who gives the orders to push the button.

The organizing of the Necessary Bread Affinity Group provides a context for my thinking about the question of how contemporary feminists who are also writers view the anti-nuclear struggle. I do not intend to arrive at a definitive statement of how all feminists view this or any other political issue. I will, however, focus upon the work and ideas of feminists whose politics I share—activist Third World and/or Lesbian and/or working-class women—in order to draw some conclusions about how writers like myself confront the nuclear abyss.

At the outset, I must address the assumption that some writers write politically and some do not. Of course there are writers who agree with Toni Cade Bambara that: "A writer, like any other cultural worker, like any other member of the community, ought to try to put her/his skills in the service of the community."[3] There are writers who are fully conscious of and responsible to the political implications of their work. What I question is the deceptive notion that there is such a thing as "pure" art which deals with "universal" themes, untainted by any political concerns whatsoever. All literary art, and other art forms as

---

[2] I capitalize Lesbian to call attention to the importance of Lesbians as a political and social force in contemporary society, and also because the word Lesbian is derived from the Isle of Lesbos, a proper noun.

[3] Bambara, Toni Cade, "What It Is I Think I'm Doing Anyhow," in J. Sternburg, (ed.) *The Writer on Her Work* (New York and London: W. W. Norton, 1980), p. 167. Bambara's novel, *The Salt Eaters* (New York: Random House, 1980), addresses nuclear and environmental concerns among many other issues affecting the Black community.

well, invariably convey the creator's political stance, even if that stance is the typical white-male-élitist one that an artist is above such mundane considerations. The reason that some writers are said to write "protest," for example, while others are said to address "major" and "universal" themes is that those of us who are oppressed write out of our myriad experiences—including our color, sex, class, and culture—and therefore write in critical opposition to the prevailing political system and culture. Those writers who are privileged and therefore uncritical of the very same society, reinforce its politics at every turn. Any Third World feminist critic can pinpoint the politics in the work of so-called mainstream writers. The politics of a Henry James, a T.S. Eliot, a Norman Mailer scream off the page, yet remain invisible to those whose lifestyles, values, and *politics* they support.

A crucial concept for understanding the perspectives delineated here is that of the simultaneity of oppression. Third World feminists, in particular, have worked to analyze and define with great specificity *all* the forces which undermine our lives. Because as women of color we are simultaneously subjected to a range of oppressions, hierarchies of oppression and "primary contradictions" do little to explain our situation or to offer the tools we need to bring about change. In 1977, the Combahee River Collective, a Black feminist organization in Boston of which I was a founding member, wrote:

> The most general statement of our politics at the present time would be that we are actively committed to struggling against racial, sexual, heterosexual, and class oppression and see as our particular task the development of integrated analysis and practice based upon the fact that the major systems of oppression are interlocking. The synthesis of these oppressions creates the conditions of our lives.[4]

From this perspective militarism and nuclear proliferation can be seen as an inevitable outgrowth of a political system historically hostile to human life, one facet of a continuum of violence against us. Nuclear annihilation is not the sole threat we face, but one of a hundred possible bloody ends. The major difference between a nuclear attack and other attacks is that it would be so unselective. One's religion, age, race, nationality, sex, sexuality, or previous condition of servitude will hardly make a difference. If the holocaust occurs, a lot of "privileged" people will die right along with those of us who have always understood that under this system our days are numbered. Unlike white folks with racial, class, sexual, and heterosexual privilege for whom a nuclear

---

[4]The Combahee River Collective, "A Black Feminist Statement," in Hull, Scott & Smith (eds.), *All the Women Are White, All the Blacks Are Men, But Some of Us Are Brave: Black Women's Studies* (Old Westbury: Feminist Press, 1982) p. 13.

disaster might well be the only threat they would ever encounter to their general security and sense of well-being, we are painfully aware, as Black Lesbian feminist poet Audre Lorde writes: "we were never meant to survive."[5]

Experiencing and understanding the simultaneity of our oppression affects our writing in a variety of ways: the subject matter, style, language, and most significantly the incorporation of political questions in an *integrated* and *concrete* fashion. For us, the realities of oppression are not intellectual or theoretical pursuits, but are woven into the very fabric of our existence and our art.

June Jordan's long poem, "From Sea to Shining Sea" comments, for example, on numerous life-threatening situations including nuclear arms. Her initial image of a distorted "natural order" is a supermarket pyramid of pomegranates, ". . . encapsulated plastic looking . . ." not to be touched or eaten. Jordan goes on to warn the reader: *"This was not a good time to be gay,"* or *"Black"* or *"old"* or *"young,"* ". . . *to be without a job,"* or ". . . *to have a job." "This was not a good time to be a woman." "This was not a good time to be a pomegranate ripening on a tree."*[6] She follows each assertion with cryptically phrased proofs:

> *This was not a good time to live in Queens*
> Trucks carrying explosive nuclear wastes will
> exit from the Long Island Expressway and then
> travel through residential streets of Queens
> en route to the 59th Street Bridge, and so on.
>   *This was not a good time to live in Arkansas*
> Occasional explosions caused by mystery
> nuclear missiles have been cited
> as cause for local alarm, among
> other things.
>   *This was not a good time to live in Grand Forks North Dakota*
> Given the presence of a United States' nuclear
> missile base in Grand Forks North Dakota
> the non-military residents of the area feel
> that they live only a day to day distance from certain
> annihilation, etcetera.

After a seemingly overwhelming litany of negatives, the poet suddenly declares, "−Wait a minute−", switches directions and concludes with a positive call to resist:

---

[5]Lorde, Audre, "A Litany For Survival," in *The Black Unicorn* (New York: W. W. Norton, 1978) p. 32.
[6]Jordan, June. "From Sea to Shining Sea," in Smith (ed.), *Home Girls: A Black Feminist Anthology* (Latham, N.Y.: Kitchen Table Press, Box 908, Latham, N.Y. 12110) n.p.

This is a good time
This is the best time
This is the only time to come together

Fractious
Kicking
Spilling
Burly
Whirling
Raucous
Messy
Free

Exploding like the seeds of a natural disorder.

"From Sea to Shining Sea," exemplifies the integration and concreteness of Third World feminist writing inspired by complex political commitments. Typical of Afro-American literature and life, adversity does not lead to existential despair, but to fighting back.

In the prose poem, "i can tomatoes," Jan Clausen, a white Lesbian feminist places her fear of nuclear obliteration within the familiar context of household work. She writes:

> . . . if they wanted to buy me, couldn't i be bought for a strip of good dirt in an unthreatened country?
> but there are no unthreatened countries. in Brooklyn, August, last quarter-century i can tomatoes, sweat sliding into the pots. i am like and unlike other women who've done this: my grandmother canning her way through the Depression, my mother hot for any bargain. i'm of the lumpen now, forever jobless; live on unmentionable revenues; have leisure to shop at the Salvation Army on Myrtle, can tomatoes, think the unthinkable.[7]

Clausen creates emotional reference points for comprehending the horror of no more life.

This poet's use of the details of daily living reflects another characteristic of much feminist writing: the creative use of autobiographical material. Perhaps because the substance of women's lives has been so thoroughly denied, particularly as literary subject matter, contemporary women writers have strongly asserted the legitimacy of the "I." This is not the self-aggrandizing "I" of the author-as-hero, but instead the development of personas and situations derived from the writer's specific identity, her position as outsider. The literature of other oppressed groups has likewise sought to reveal the substance of unknown lives. Black writing, for example, encompasses as-told-to slave narratives, authored autobiographies, and the selective use of an autobiographical stance in creative literature.

---

[7]Clausen, Jan, "i can tomatoes," in *Duration* (New York: Hanging Loose Press, 1983) n.p.

Women writers have further expanded the use of such materials. Cheryl Clarke, a Black Lesbian feminist, uses narrative and other poetic forms to convey the stories of vivid Black women characters in her book, *Narratives: Poems in the Tradition of Black Women*.[8] Audre Lorde terms her most recent work of prose, *Zami: A New Spelling of My Name*, a "biomythography" because it combines elements of biography, fiction, and myth.[9] Poet Judy Grahn has edited two volumes of *True to Life Adventure Stories*, many of them by working-class Lesbians who refuse to be bound by the distinctions between fiction, oral history, and personal narrative.[10] Much of the writing in *This Bridge Called My Back: Writings by Radical Women of Color*, a groundbreaking collection of Third World feminist theory, co-edited by Cherríe Moraga and Gloria Anzaldúa, is solidly based in personal recollection and self-revelation.

In her autobiographical essay, "La Güera," Chicana poet Moraga demonstrates how the naming of herself is both the result of her politics and the motivation to further develop her political understandings:

> When I finally lifted the lid to my lesbianism, a profound connection with my mother reawakened in me. It wasn't until I acknowledged and confronted my own lesbianism in the flesh, that my heartfelt identification with and empathy for my mother's oppression—due to being poor, uneducated, and Chicana—was realized. My lesbianism is the avenue through which I have learned the most about silence and oppression, and it continues to be the most tactile reminder to me that we are not free human beings.
>
> You see, one follows the other. I had known for years that I was a lesbian, had felt it in my bones, had ached with the knowledge, gone crazed with the knowledge, wallowed in the silence of it. Silence *is* like starvation. Don't be fooled. It's nothing short of that, and felt most sharply when one has had a full belly most of her life. When we are not physically starving, we have the luxury to realize psychic and emotional starvation. It is from this starvation that other starvations can be recognized—if one is willing to take the risk of making the connection—if one is willing to be responsible to the result of the connection. For me, the connection is an inevitable one.
>
> What I am saying is that the joys of looking like a white girl ain't so great since I realized I could be beaten on the street for being a dyke. If my sister's being beaten because she's Black, it's pretty much the same principle. We're both getting beaten any way you look at it. The connection is blatant; and in the case of my own family, the difference in the privileges attached to looking white instead of brown are merely a generation apart.

---

[8]Clarke, Cheryl, *Narratives: Poems in the Tradition of Black Women* (Latham, N.Y.: Kitchen Table Press, 1983).

[9]Lorde, Audre, *Zami: A New Spelling of My Name* (Freedom, CA: Crossing Press, 1982).

[10]Grahn, Judy, *True to Life Adventure Stories*, Volumes I & II (Trumansburg, N.Y.: Crossing Press, n.d.)

In this country, lesbianism is a poverty—as is being brown, as is being a woman, as is being just plain poor. The danger lies in ranking the oppressions. *The danger lies in failing to acknowledge the specificity of the oppression.* The danger lies in attempting to deal with oppression purely from a theoretical base. Without an emotional, heartfelt grappling with the source of our own oppression, without naming the enemy within ourselves and outside of us, no authentic, nonhierarchical connection among oppressed groups can take place.[11]

Simultaneity, integration, the integrity of writing out of one's total self lead to a wholeness of vision, a visceral exploration of what oppression feels like, what we must be responsible for, and how we can move to bring about fundamental change. That there is a specifically Lesbian feminist perspective about a variety of social-political issues, including nuclear destruction, may be surprising to some. Yet this new writing nurtured by the women's movement of the last two decades poses some of the most vital political and ethical questions of this era.[12] Those of us who have experienced poverty in all its forms are not so quick to accept business as usual, not so unwilling to ask unsettling questions. We are also not in the least surprised by the build up of nuclear weapons, the latest cogs in the white-European death machine.

This element of unsurprise comes through most clearly in the writing of women of color, Lesbian and non-Lesbian. People of color, especially women, comprehend white-male values and culture in a way that white men have never remotely understood themselves. We have had to strategize our survival based upon a deep understanding of the aliens who have invaded our lands or who have stolen us from our own countries in order to serve them. As the ruling race-sex-class, the majority of white men have no desire to really know who they are, to acknowledge the work of their minds and hands, to comprehend the disasters they have collectively wrought. If nothing else, comprehending and *feeling* the magnitude of these horrors might undermine their stranglehold on power, their unearned "right" to rule. Whether we call them "ghosts," or "wasicu sica," "gringos," or "Mr. Charlie," we

---

[11]Moraga, Cherríe, "La Guera," in Moraga & Anzaldúa (eds.), *The Bridge Called My Back: Writings by Radical Women of Color* (Latham, NY: Kitchen Table Press, 1981, 1983) pp. 28–29.
[12]For a discussion of the ethical vision of Lesbian writing, see: Cherríe Moraga and Barbara Smith, "Lesbian Literature: A Third World Feminist Perspective," in M. Cruikshank (ed.), *Lesbian Studies: Past, Present, and Future* (Old Westbury: Feminist Press, 1982) pp. 55–65. Other important sources of criticism of Lesbian feminist writing are Jan Clausen's *A Movement of Poets: Thoughts on Poetry and Feminism* [Brooklyn, N.Y.: Long Haul Press (Box 592, Van Brunt Station, Brooklyn, N.Y. 11215), 1982] and the introduction to *Lesbian Poetry: An Anthology*, (eds.) E. Bulkin & J. Larkin and *Lesbian Fiction: An Anthology*, E. Bulkin (ed.) both available from Persephone Press.

have been on to the white man and his poisonous capacity for ruin, for centuries.[13]

A traditional attitude toward evil among Afro-Americans that I believe significantly influences our reactions to the possibility of nuclear obliteration is embodied in two passages from Toni Morrison's novel, *Sula*. She writes:

> In spite of their fear, they reacted to an oppressive oddity, or what they called evil days, with an acceptance that bordered on welcome. Such evil must be avoided, they felt, and precautions must naturally be taken to protect themselves from it. But they let it run its course, fulfill itself, and never invented ways either to alter it, to annihilate it or to prevent its happening again. So also were they with people.
>
> What was taken by outsiders to be slackness, slovenliness or even generosity was in fact a full recognition of the legitimacy of forces other than good ones. They did not believe doctors could heal—for them, none ever had done so. They did not believe death was accidental—life might be, but death was deliberate. They did not believe Nature was ever askew—only inconvenient. Plague and drought were as "natural" as springtime. If milk could curdle, God knows robins could fall. The purpose of evil was to survive it and they determined (without ever knowing they had made up their minds to do it) to survive floods, white people, tuberculosis, famine, and ignorance. They knew anger well but not despair, and they didn't stone sinners for the same reason they didn't commit suicide—it was beneath them.
>
> So they laid broomsticks across their doors at night and sprinkled salt on porch steps. But aside from one or two unsuccessful efforts to collect the dust from her footsteps, they did nothing to harm her. As always the black people looked at evil stony-eyed and let it run.[14]

Or as Audre Lorde succinctly puts it, citing a traditional West Indian saying in the opening pages of *Zami*: " 'Island women make good wives; whatever happens, they've seen worse.' " Peoples who have been owned, beaten, raped, chased, starved, mass murdered, and otherwise denied know evil intimately and know also how to survive it.

Certainly this comprehension of the role of evil informs Alice Walker's unique statement, "Only Justice Can Stop a Curse," first delivered at an antinuclear rally in San Francisco in 1982. Walker begins by repeating a traditional curse-prayer collected by Zora Neale Hurston in the 1920s. She then says that given all the evil white men have done, nuclear death and destruction seem for them a peculiarly fitting end:

---

[13]"Ghosts" is the term that Maxine Hong Kingston uses for white people in *The Woman Warrior*. "Wasicu sica" means terrible white people in the Lakota language. See Barbara Cameron's, " Gee, You Don't Seem Like An Indian From the Reservation," in *This Bridge Called My Back*, pp. 46–52.

[14]Morrison, Toni, *Sula*, (New York: Bantam, 1973), pp. 77, 78 & 98.

When I have considered the enormity of the white man's crimes against humanity. Against women. Against every living person of color. Against the poor. Against my mother and my father. Against me. . . . When I consider that at this very moment he wishes to take away what little freedom I have died to achieve, through denial of my right to vote. . . . Has already taken away education, medicine, housing and food. . . . That William Shockley is saying at this moment that he will run for the Senate of my country to push his theory that Blacks are genetically inferior and should be sterilized. . . . When I consider that he is, they are, a real and present threat to my life and the life of my daughter, my people, I think— in perfect harmony with my sister of long ago:*Let the earth marinate in poisons. Let the bombs cover the ground like rain. For nothing short of total destruction will ever teach them anything.*[15]

Walker suggests that ". . . this hope for revenge, finally . . . is at the heart of people of color's resistance to any anti-nuclear movement." Yet she also reasons:

However, just as the sun shines on the godly and the ungodly alike, so does nuclear radiation. And with this knowledge it becomes increasingly difficult to embrace the thought of extinction purely for the assumed satisfaction of—from the grave—achieving revenge.

She concludes by affirming that she will fight ". . . to protect my home," and if the planet does in fact survive, ". . . only justice to every living thing (and everything is alive) will save humankind." "Only Justice Can Stop a Curse" is a perfect example of how "non-mainstream" writers think about the nuclear threat. Walker's opinions are shaped by an integrated understanding of the workings of a pervasive system of oppression/evil and her vision does not stop short with the mere hope that the world will be saved. Instead she demands that if life continues people have to start acting right and work to make this planet habitable for everybody.

I am positive that the way that Morrison and Walker conceive of both evil and hope springs from an African American value system and set of spiritual beliefs vastly different from the ones Euro-Americans have imposed here. Lusiah Teish, a Black feminist writer and seer, describes the initial clash in values during slavery between Blacks and whites in her essay, "Women's Spirituality: A Household Act." She writes:

All West Africans (and I dare say all Africans) believed in an animated universe, that is, that all things are alive on varying levels of existence [and] that all of Nature—Earth, Air, Fire and Water—is sacred and worthy of praise, and responsive to human influence through invocation.[16]

---

[15]Walker, Alice, "Only Justice Can Stop a Curse," chapter 22 of this volume.
[16]Teish, Luisah, "Women's Spirituality: A Household Act," in *Home Girls: A Black Feminist Anthology.*

Surely such an evolved philosophy must have been incomprehensible to white people who viewed both land and people as property, as "wilderness" and "savages" to be tamed. Their arrogant narrowness also clashed with Native American peoples who likewise were aware that they were a part of Nature, not her antagonist. The white man thought that by killing us and pushing us off the land he could kill our beliefs. But we and our values continue and the old ways fundamentally affect our approach to every political and ethical question.

In "No Rock Scorns Me As Whore," Chrystos, a Native American Lesbian, discusses nuclear and environmental destruction in both spiritual and material terms:

> It is clear to me that the use of nuclear power is dangerous—as is almost every other aspect of the dominant culture . . . *Nothing short of completely altering the whole culture will stop it* . . .
> We have lost touch with the sacred To survive we must begin to know sacredness . . .
> I am still in love with the mystery of shadows, wind, bird song The reason that I continue despite many clumsy mistakes, is love My love for humans, or rather my continuous attempts to love, have been misdirected I am not wise However there is no shame when one is foolish with a tree No bird ever called me crazy No rock scorns me as a whore The earth means exactly what it says The wind is without flattery or lust Greed is balanced by the hunger of all So I embrace anew, as my childhood spirit did, the whispers of a world without words
> I realized one day after another nuclear protest, another proposed bill to make a nuclear waste disposal here, that I had no power with those My power rests with a greater being, a silence which goes on behind the uproar I decided that in a nuclear holocaust, for certainly they will be stupid enough to cause one if their history is any example, that I wanted to be planting corn & squash After there will be other beings of some kind They'll still need to eat . . . I will be sad to see the trees & birds on fire Surely they are innocent as none of us has been
> With their songs, they know the sacred I am in a circle with that soft, enduring word In it is the wisdom of all peoples Without a deep, deep understanding of the sacredness of life, the fragility of each breath, we are lost The holocaust has already occurred What follows is only the burning brush How my heart aches & cries to write these words I am not as calmly indifferent as I sound I will be screaming no no no more destruction in that last blinding light[17]

Chrystos' evocative language is solidly rooted in the everyday physical and spiritual longings of people. This is poetic-political writing at its best.

I expect that the ancient female and colored connections that Chrystos and other writers make here may be threatening to some, even to those who say they want an end to nuclear terror. They will say we are "too

---

[17]Chrystos, "No Rock Scorns Me As Whore," in *This Bridge Called My Back*, pp. 243–245.

radical," "too emotional," "too polemical," "too queer." Yet if our perspectives are excluded from the work of this most massive of any recent political movement, whatever its triumphs, it will also fail. This like no other moment is the time for genuine coalitions, an imperative that many will also try to ignore.

But we are not waiting. We are our own movement. We march, chant prayers, dream words.

REFERENCES

Bambara, Toni Cade, "What It Is I Think I'm Doing Anyhow," in J. Sternburg (ed.), *The Writer on Her Work* (New York and London: W. W. Norton, 1980) p. 167. Bambara's novel, *The Salt Eaters* (New York: Random House, 1980) addresses nuclear and environmental concerns among many other issues affecting the Black community.

Chrystos, "No Rock Scorns Me As Whore," in *This Bridge Called My Back*, pp. 243–245.

Clarke, Cheryl, *Narratives: Poems in the Tradition of Black Women* (Latham, N.Y.: Kitchen Table: Women of Color Press, P. O. Box 908, Latham, NY 12110, 1983) n. p.

Clausen, Jan, "i can tomatoes," in *Duration* (New York: Hanging Loose Press, 1983) n.p.

The Combahee River Collective, "A Black Feminist Statement," in Hull, Scott & Smith (eds.), *All The Women Are White, All the Blacks Are Men, But Some of Us Are Brave: Black Women's Studies* (New York: Feminist Press, 1982) p. 13.

Grahn, Judy, *True to Life Adventure Stories*, Volumes I & II (Freedom, Cal.: Crossing Press, n. d.).

Jordan, June, "From Sea to Shining Sea," in Smith (ed.), *Home Girls: A Black Feminist Anthology* (Lathan, N.Y.: Kitchen Table: Women of Color Press) pp. 223–229.

Lorde, Audre, "A Litany for Survival," in *The Black Unicorn* (New York: W. W. Norton, 1978) p. 32.

Lorde, Audre, *Zami: A New Spelling of My Name* (Freedom, Cal.: Crossing Press, 1982).

Moraga, Cherríe, "La Guera," in Moraga & Anzaldúa (eds.), *This Bridge Called My Back: Writings by Radical Women of Color* (Latham, N.Y.: Kitchen Table: Women of Color Press, 1981, 1984).

Morrison, Toni, *Sula*. (New York: Bantam, 1973) pp. 77, 78, & 98.

Necessary Bread Affinity Group, "Necessary Bread Disarmament Statement," June, 1982. The Statement appeared in a number of women's periodicals including *Off Our Backs* and *Feminist Studies*, Vol. 8, No. 3 (Fall, 1982).

Teish, Luisah, "Women's Spirituality: A Household Act," in *Home Girls: A Black Feminist Anthology*, p. 338.

Walker, Alice, "Only Justice Can Stop a Curse," in *Home Girls: A Black Feminist Anthology*, p. 354.

11

It'll Make A Man of You: A Feminist View of the Arms Race*

Penny Strange

INTRODUCTION

The women's peace movement is strong and growing all over Western Europe and the USA. In Britain, inspired by the women's peace camp at Greenham Common, many thousands of women have joined in the struggle for nuclear disarmament. Many women's peace groups are springing up, and there is more acceptance of women's initiatives and women-only groups and actions. However, although the practical effectiveness of women working together is very convincing, there is still little awareness of the connections between war and male values, and how women together are expressing values that are essential to a peaceful society.

These ideas are not new—similar things were being said by Virginia Woolf back in 1937. In her book *Three Guineas* she argues cogently that the best way to promote peace is to contribute to the liberation of women. More recently, feminist writers such as Andrea Dworkin and Barbara Deming have taken up the theme. Yet the ideas are still not widely known. Why is it that although Virginia Woolf is much admired as an author, what she had to say about war and a male-dominated society is so neglected? The answer is that these ideas are hard to accept:

*Previously published as a pamphlet by Mushroom Books, Nottingham, England (1983).

they mean that opposition to war and violence starts at home: that the causes of war are "in here" as well as "out there". My hope is that this chapter will set some people thinking; it is meant as a starting point, not a definitive analysis.

This article grew out of discussions with my friends in Nottingham Women Opposed to Nuclear Technology, a specifically feminist anti-nuclear group. For us, making a feminist analysis of the arms race does not mean blaming it on individual men: rather it means looking at the causes of war in the structures of a male-dominated society, and looking behind those structures to an underlying male cosmology. By cosmology I mean a basic worldview that shapes how we look at everything, and what kinds of patterns and meanings we make of our experiences. Our cosmology is so fundamental that it is usually invisible to ourselves: we think we are talking about "plain facts", and don't realise that a shift in our worldview would change the meanings of our perceptions – even change what we notice and what we are blind to. The male cosmology is the chief concern of this chapter. It so shapes and defines our world that many individual women actually support the male supremacy, either by emulating masculine behavior (like Margaret Thatcher or Indira Gandhi) or by playing the complementary feminine role. On the other hand, some individual men are trying to work against male domination.

Still, all men derive certain benefits from their place in the system, although they are also oppressed by the limitations of their role. Women are doubly oppressed, first by being assigned a role at all, and second by the fact that inferiority is central to that role. In the male supremacist system, human qualities and activities, even natural products and artefacts, are divided between the male sphere and the female sphere, and arranged hierarchically, the male always superior, the female inferior. I hope to show how this dualistic, hierarchical thinking has led to the acceptance and approval of violence, and thus lies at the root of the arms race; and that this kind of thinking itself is a projection of sexual dominance.

Because male dominance is, as I shall show later, based on separation and dominance, men have sought to keep peace by building barriers to keep others out. Hadrian's Wall and the Great Wall of China are monuments to this approach. We still speak of "buffer states" and "zones". But now that physical distance is less significant, separation is maintained through fear, one country trying to keep another afraid of its military strength. The consequence of seeking "peace" and "security" through separation and barriers (known as dissociative peace strategies) is an accelerating arms race.

THE ARMS RACE

The causes and workings of the arms race are very complicated: here I can only make a brief sketch to provide a point of reference. The world arms race has achieved a momentum unparalleled in peacetime. Military spending in 1981 reached somewhere between 600 and 650 billion dollars a year. Nuclear stockpiles are equivalent to a million Hiroshima-size bombs. It is a worldwide phenomenon: there are arms races between India and Pakistan, Iran and Iraq, Argentina and Brazil. In these arms races, it is impossible to say which side is "ahead" – different weapons systems are not comparable, the requirements of each country are different, and above all, military secrecy and lies make the numbers game sheer guesswork. But both sides claim that the other is ahead to justify their increasing arms expenditure. The stated aim of both sides is to keep a little ahead of the enemy in order to deter it from attack, and thus to "keep the peace". In fact, no balance of power can be reached, and the escalation continues.

The same is true of the nuclear arms race between the superpowers, the USA and the USSR and the alliances they lead, the NATO and the Warsaw Pact. The buildup in armaments is an increase partly in the sheer number of weapons and warheads, and more significantly, in their sophistication. Weapons, in particular nuclear weapons, are getting more powerful, more accurate, harder to detect. Estimating each other's forces has become even more difficult, and this arms race can never reach a stable balance and stop. It has no end but a nuclear holocaust.

A major force behind the arms race is, of course, the *military*. New equipment helps to keep morale high, and there is often competition between different branches of the armed forces over which should have the most advanced technology. The military are professionals; their job is to aim for military superiority. They do not consider any other kind of defence than military strategy and equipment; they do not consider the human consequences except in balancing losses against gains. The presupposition of the existence of an enemy which poses an armed threat is the justification for their existence, and their existence keeps this presupposition alive. Military confrontations have a momentum of their own, as was evident during the Falklands Crisis.

Withdrawal from the arms race would be regarded as a sign of weakness, a defeat in itself. Britain's independent nuclear force is a matter of national prestige, conferring membership of the elite nuclear club, which brings with it real political power, not just a boost to national pride. As existing arms invite attack from an "enemy", then even higher levels of "deterrence" must constantly be sought.

All over the world, the military possesses great influence over governments. In many countries, the military *are* the government, in others the government rule with the permission and protection of the armed forces. Even where the military is not so prominent, it still wields power over the government, as a powerful lobby and electoral force. Politicians who resist the demands of the military/industrial/academic/ bureaucratic complex soon find themselves out of office, so their personal status is tied up with that of the military. This complex is also a major employer of both civilians and servicepeople, and, significantly, many ex-servicepeople.

And the influence of the military extends even further, in that its values are shared and admired in many parts of civilian life. The soldier's task is not thought of as a disagreeable necessity but as an heroic field of manly virtue, to be emulated. Some of these military values are: the acceptance of the use of force or the threat of it, and of the necessity and virtue of having superior force; the giving of orders, and unthinking obedience; the importance of winning; the need to be tough, to suppress feelings; the despising of bodily pain, your own or others'; the labelling of some other group of people as "the enemy". Most of these are also regarded as "manly". Social pressures encourage in boys the development of a character that has much in common with the military ideal. The institutions of a male-dominated society are based on these competitive and power-seeking kinds of behavior. Indeed, the military is the model of manhood: the arms race is the collective expression of virility.

High Technology

The arms race is *high technology*. Weapons have become so sophisticated that many of them don't make sense economically or even militarily anymore. You cannot fight a war with nuclear weapons. "Modern military technology" writes Mary Kaldor, "is not advanced; it is decadent. . . . They are incapable of achieving a limited military objective, and they have successively eroded the economy of the US and the economies of those countries that have followed in its wake."[1] Yet despite the devastating economic effects of its massive cost, and its doubtful military value, the technology seems to have a momentum of its own. Every possibility of making weapons more deadly must become a reality. If the researchers supply the technology, the military devise a new scenario to fit, and then this is presented politically as a strategic

---

[1]Mary Kaldor, *The Baroque Arsenal* (New York: Hill and Wang, 1981).

necessity. "First strike" was politically unacceptable, and the justification for nuclear weapons was the deterrent effect of "Mutual Assured Destruction"—until a new generation of accurate missiles made "first strike" a possibility. Now a military and political rationale for striking first has emerged, bringing us one step nearer a nuclear war. Every new missile demands a new antimissile, and it all provides a reliable supply of work and money to research departments. Research teams are kept together after their project has finished: they are a force towards the creation of new military research work. The research establishment is a powerful force, involving a lot of money and a lot of people. Worldwide, over 50% of scientists are working on "defence" contracts.

Big Business

The arms race is also *big business*. Selling arms is the biggest business in the world after oil, and grosses about 130,000 million dollars a year. The industrialized nations, both governments and arms manufacturers and traders, try hard to sell their arms abroad. It makes good profits, cuts down the relative cost of research and development, and gives political influence over the purchaser. Many of these sales are made to Third World countries where the military equipment is frequently used by repressive governments against their own people. No amount of development aid can help poor people while military aid and arms sales are assisting their government to stop them gaining real control over the resources they need for healthy living conditions.

Both these fields, arms research and the arms industry, are highly competitive. The desire to win somehow overrides consideration of the real consequences. For the scientist, there is the challenge of increasing accuracy, increasing control; the consequences of the use of the new technology can be thought of as a side issue, the responsibility of someone else. For the industrialist, money is an acceptable means to power, and the mark of success.

Common to all the elements in the military/political/industrial/academic complex which keeps the arms race going is the desire for mastery and power, the struggle for superiority. This struggle goes on at all levels—between military alliances such as NATO and the Warsaw Pact; between countries within those alliances for leadership; between the armed forces of both sides, and within each of those armed forces; between politicians, for high office and international prestige. These kinds of competition are regarded as healthy, even invigorating. Yet behind them lies a chilling desire to control and master, dangerously cut off from human feelings about the consequences.

THE MEANING OF MASCULINITY

Feminists view the striving for mastery and superiority as a striking feature of a male-dominated society; we see it as not only widespread, but also admired, desired and cultivated in half the human race, and an acceptable mode of political discourse and international relations. It is an obvious but not trivial fact that all the organizations that promote the arms race are male enclaves. Most of the people working in these areas are men, and the women who do work there are generally not in positions of power. Until recently, these occupations were exclusively male. Men set up the structures, and this determines their operation today. Those who enter these occupations must accept the underlying male values.

The Male Cult of Toughness

Violence is not an exclusively male practice, but only for men is it bound up with their identity. Subjugating someone or something becomes the necessary proof of manhood, and the oppression of women perpetuates this false virility. A boy must prove himself, separate himself from the women, principally by toughness and violence. Sometimes this violence is physical; sometimes the power over other people comes from economic or social relationships and no overt physical force is necessary. Physical, economic, political, social power—are all forms of the same underlying dominance, and are convertible one to the other. Perhaps the "macho" male has become such a stock figure that we are in danger of forgetting how profoundly the need to be thought tough and manly infects our political, social and economic life, and now threatens us with destruction. This need is a powerful influence over leaders in all fields. One might almost say that the more powerful the leader, the deeper this anxiety. David Halberstam's account of the behavior of US leaders in the Vietnam War period shows how deeply their decisions were affected by this.

> President Lyndon B Johnson had always been haunted by the idea that he would be judged as being insufficiently manly for the job. . . . He had unconsciously divided people around him between men and boys. Men were the activists, doers, who conquered business empires, who acted instead of talked, who made it in the world and had the respect of other men. Boys were the talkers and the writers and the intellectuals who sat around thinking and criticising and doubting instead of doing. . . . As Johnson weighed the advice he was getting on Vietnam, it was the boys who were most sceptical, and the men who were most sure and hawkish,

and who had Johnson's respect. Hearing that one of the administration was becoming a dove on Vietnam, Johnson said "Hell, he has to squat to piss."[2]

The idea that Johnson's attitude to foreign policy was a projection of sexual dominance is borne out by a boast he made to a journalist after the bombing of North Vietnamese boat bases: "I didn't just screw Ho Chi Minh—I cut his pecker off".[3] He regarded doubt as a feminine quality, and therefore despised it. And this was not just a personal hang-up. In his book *The Male Machine*, Marc Feigen Festeau studies Presidents Kennedy, Johnson and Nixon, and concludes: "Their failure of analysis and readiness to believe the Right, which might accuse them of being too soft and weak if they withdrew from Vietnam, was in large part a result of their personal preoccupation with toughness and the projection of that preoccupation onto the voting public". Taught to believe in the need for "strong" leaders, that voting public gets leaders from whom appearing tough and not weak is worth tremendous sacrifice by the nation. Deliberation and decision-making at the top takes place in a kind of male lodge, where the myths of masculinity are supreme. And these are not just the values of the leaders; they are the ambitions on which the whole society is structured.

THE PATRIARCHAL HIERARCHY

The dream of a male-dominated society is a dream of extending control. Past empires gave it clear political shape: now the power is exercised less blatantly and more diversely through military alliances, economic agreements, aid, the multinational corporations, etc. Science, technology and agriculture are geared to conquer nature and wrest from "her" her secrets and resources. The desire for mastery has written a history of conquest, slavery, exploitation; it has given us nuclear weapons and the strategists who can plan to use them.

Yet it is customarily *celebrated* as an heroic quality. Man's striving to prove himself above nature, above animals, above other races, above women, has been equated with the pursuit of excellence. Philosophers have held it to be the tragedy, pathos and paradox of man's existence that his soaring "soul" is encased in a fleshy body, and attempts to rise above physical nature have been regarded as laudable endeavors. In the Judeo-Christian tradition, the body, nature, women, animals, "primitive" people, have all been seen as lower orders over which the "higher" rightfully have domination. "Thou hast made him a little lower than the angels . . . thou hast put all things under his feet: all sheep and oxen,

---

[2]David Halberstam, *The Best and the Brightest* (New York: Random House, 1972).
[3]Mark Feigen Festeau, *The Male Machine* (New York: Dell Publishing, 1975) p. 174.

yea and the beasts of the field and the fowls of the air and the fish of the sea," says the psalmist in Psalm 8.

The classical eighteenth-century idea of a "Chain of Being" set out a hierarchy very clearly from God at the top right down to the lowest living creatures. The idea thrives today in modern dress. Ernest Becker has studied the major themes of modern philosophy and psychology. He writes:

> Man has a symbolic identity that brings him sharply out of nature . . . This immense expansion, this dexterity, this self-consciousness, gives to man literally the status of a small god in nature . . . Man is literally split in two; he has an awareness of his own splendid uniqueness in that he sticks out of nature with a towering majesty, and yet he goes back into the ground in order blindly and dumbly to rot . . . The lower animals are spared this painful contradiction . . . They merely act and move reflexively as they are driven by their instincts . . . This is what has made it so simple to shoot down whole herds of buffalo or elephant.[4]

This is an entirely male view about Man and nature; women are not deliberately left out of humanity; they are simply invisible. For centuries, it was taught that women lacked the full self-consciousness that according to this theory marks out man from the animal kingdom. In this passage too, we find the hierarchy—man's "towering majesty" over the "lower orders"—and with it, the consequences for the "lower orders": it is "so simple to shoot down whole herds of buffalo or elephant". Easy too to shoot down other human beings, once you have relegated them to an inferior place by calling them "niggers", "commies", "cunts" or "faggots". It is clear too that this is not a gradually ascending hierarchy: there is a qualitative leap between the man's "towering majesty" and the rest, identified with the natural world. On the one hand, the masters, the thinkers, the planners; and on the other, those who are there to be used, to fit into the plan. Not only is it possible to treat the inferior group roughly and violently, but it becomes imperative to do so in order to dissociate oneself from them, lest one be pushed around as they are.

Warring Opposites

This way of perceiving the world as divided into two, one superior, the other inferior, is associated with many destructive splits in human life—mind/body, intellect/emotion, culture/nature. Man has perceived a contradiction between intellectual or spiritual aspirations and physical needs and appetites, and it has been thought virtuous to forswear

---

[4]Ernst Becker, *The Denial of Death* (New York: Free Press, 1973).

physical pleasure, even to cause oneself deliberate pain. (Even the idea of sport is frequently to bring the body under control of the will and push it beyond its normal limits.) It is also regarded as admirable to keep emotion out of decision-making; feelings are thought to be irrational. So those who design, make and use weapons are trained to dismiss any qualms of pity or revulsion as mere emotionalism, although these feelings may be entirely consonant with rational thought about the implications of their work.

This essentially dualistic and hierarchical view of the world leads to a model of relationships based on conflict. The world is conceived of in terms of warring opposites. Those who are different are seen as threatening. It is assumed that there will always be an actively hostile enemy ready to exploit any "weakness". The "answer" is to make sure one is the stronger of the two. This sets off a spiral of fear, violence and preparation for war. This model is the foundation of the theory of deterrence. A nation state always has an enemy, though they change regularly; if an old enemy becomes a friend, then a new enemy will be found. In this model, there is no middle ground—if you do not constantly assert your superior power, then you will be oppressed by the enemy's power.

Debasing the Female

Traditionally, women are associated with the lower part of the hierarchy, the natural world, by virtue of their child-bearing, and have been assigned roles within this sphere—nurture roles rather than glory roles. Women's place in reproducing the mortal body has been used as justification for the low value put upon them and their work, while men's work has been to seek immortality through deeds of glory.

Yet it is unreasonable if not suicidal to place low value on reproductive and survival skills. Rather than accept the usual justification for women's low status, we could turn it on its head and say that nature and survival skills are debased because of their association with women. We know from anthropologists that the tasks assigned to men and women in societies vary greatly, yet always those assigned to men have high status, to women, low status. Rather than women being stigmatized for their association with the natural world, the natural world and survival skills are despised because of their association with women.

If this is true, then such bread-and-butter issues as the setting of economic priorities are directly affected by men's need to put low value on womanly things. In Britain there is not enough money for social services, but always enough for prestigious armaments and nuclear power stations. In the Third World, the West's idea of "development" helps men to grow cash crops, while women's vital subsistence farming is ignored and gets more difficult.

The sociologist Nancy Chodorow offers an explanation of how men come to despise all things womanly. Dependency on an adult, usually female, is a child's first and primary experience, and upon it all other relationships to the outside world are based. This is at first an identification with the mother, in which the child feels at one with her and not separate. When children begin to develop a separate identity girls discover they have made their first identification with someone of the same sex, whereas boys find that they have made their primary identification with someone of the other sex. And not only that—they have also made a deep tie with someone in a group that is treated as inferior. The response is often to come to define masculinity largely in negative terms as that which is not feminine or involved with women. The boy tries to deny his attachment to and dependence on his mother. He does this by repressing whatever he takes to be feminine inside himself, and by denigrating and devaluing whatever he considers to be feminine in the outside world—and this includes rejecting many of the qualities and activities associated with the mother.

Among these despised feminine qualities are survival skills—cooperating, admitting dependence; subsistence farming, preparing food, bringing up children. A boy learns not to show emotion, not to admit dependence: to compete, to try to get the better of others; he learns to value work for money over domestic work, the tending of machines more than the tending of children.

A boy learns to establish his masculine identity by a process of separation: orthodox (male) psychology looks at growing up as progressive individuation. The other side of maturity, discovering oneself in relation to others is a girl's experience, and consequently invisible. Clearly, we have need right now of developing an awareness of our interconnectedness with other people and the rest of the natural world: yet while men are learning that they must achieve selfhood by separation, this awareness can only seem to threaten loss of identity.

Rituals of Growing Up

Training in masculinity, initiation into the male club, begins very early. Anne Marie Fearon in an article "Come In Tarzan Your Time Is Up", traces her horror at the pressures on her young son:

> My son came home from nursery school one day with the information: "Girls are soppies" . . . Then it was his lunch basket—a handy little basket that would hang on his peg; someone told him it was a "girl's" basket, so

it had to go. His orange trousers were next to go; now he can't wear yellow socks to school. Think of it: a child of four or five having to scrutinise every toy, every garment, for signs of "soppiness"; but these signs are so subtle that it must keep them in constant fear and self-doubt. After all, could you define the difference between a "girl's" shoe and a "boy's" shoe?[5]

This is not trivial; the fear of being thought female (or soppy or weak) is a formative influence instilling male violence and the thirst for power. Boys are supposed to hide their fear and hurt; the resulting tension can only be let out in aggression or violence, which are "safe" because they are definitely not "soppy".

Little boys must hide their softer emotions and display aggression on pain of ridicule and ultimate expulsion from the male club. This is commercially exploited by super-hero and war-toys. Little girls, on the other hand, must suppress their assertive behavior: they are taught to be kind and caring, but at the expense of learning self-effacement and lack of physical confidence. They become symbols of all that threatens a boy's claim to masculinity.

Drive to Power

In this process of "making a man of him", there are several processes at work; separating boys from women, girls, and babies; teaching them to fear and deny their own softer emotions; teaching them to identify sexuality with violence, i.e., to get a thrill out of power rather than pleasure; making them compete with each other. The drive to compete and to gain power is formed very early in life, and is addictive. It is a central part of the gender structure. Competition is the basis of our educational system and the driving force of the economy. It is held to be "character-building". It is the dominant mode of the male-dominated society, at play as well as at work. Our society's idea of a game is an aggressive competition between two opponents. "Big-time football manifests the ideal of masculine identity through its aggressive ethos. The weekend trip to the arena is not an escape from the world of corporate America; rather it is a weekly pilgrimage to the national shrines where the virtues of toughness and insensitivity can be renewed".[6]

This is the image of the game that goes on in all spheres of a male dominated culture. And the origin of this game is the denigration of the female. Violence to women is not just a symptom of a violent society—

---

[5]Anne-Marie Fearon, "Come in Tarzan your time is up" in *Shrew* (Summer 1978).
[6]Eugene Bianchi and Rosemary Ruether (eds.), *From Machismo to Mutuality: Essays on Sexism and Woman–Man Liberation* (New York: Paulist Press, 1976).

it is the prototype for men's assault on the world. Eugene Bianchi goes on to say: "Although we don't want to acknowledge it, rape is the prototype example of the masculine game that pervades society. The competitor, the enemy, the opponent, needs to be humiliated, made powerless, made into woman."

WOMAN DESPISED

Rape is an act of war, out on the battlefront, and daily in our streets and houses. Mary Daly writes of the "Unholy Trinity" of rape, genocide and war. She says:

> It is clear that there has always been a connection between the mentality of rape and the phenomenon of war . . . The socialisation of male sexual violence in our culture forms the basis for corporate and military interests to train a vicious military force. It would be a mistake to think that rape is reducible to the physical act of few men who are rapists. All men have their power enhanced by rape, since this instills in women a need for protection. Rape is a way of life.[7]

Soldiers take it as their "privilege" to rape enemy or foreign women. Husbands also take it as their right to rape their wives—to force them to have sex against their will. Although rape is spoken of as a heinous crime, the way that the police and courts treat rapists and their victims shows that the rape of adult women (as opposed to children) is regarded as an extension of normal masculine behavior.

The case of a young man in the Coldstream Guards found guilty of raping a woman, leaving her with a broken rib, bites, bruises and internal injuries, brings out the links between "masculinity" and violence, between rape and war. His sentence was squashed in the Appeal Court, where the judge said that the rapist "clearly was a man who, on the night in question, allowed his *enthusiasm for sex* (my emphasis) to overcome his normal good behaviour. It does not seem to this court that the appellant is a criminal . . ."

Rape is an act of violence, and entirely consistent with the attitudes and practices instilled during the rapist's "excellent service" in the Guards. But the judge does not see this; for him rape is *sex*, the fault of man's "lower nature". Nevertheless, the judge sees nothing inconsistent in the use of violence in the act of sex. Sex in our society is about power, and the ultimate expression of power is violence.

Pornography also expresses men's feelings about the body, the flesh and sexual feelings. The body is despised, as part of woman's sphere, a

---

[7]Mary Daly, *Beyond God the Father: Toward a Philosophy of Women's Liberation* (Boston: Beacon Press, 1973).

connection with mortality, a reminder that man is of woman born. Nakedness is therefore a powerful metaphor for weakness. We have to pause to remind ourselves that it is only a metaphor. Bevan's remark that to abandon our nuclear weapons would be to go "naked into the conference chamber" has been taken as a strong argument for retaining nuclear arms: it gains its power from men's contempt for the body.

Violence against women, and the everyday "petty" harrassment and humiliation they suffer are not "women's issues" separable from the violence of war, and the structural violence of racism, poverty and exploitation. Male sexual dominance and female submission at home and on the streets is the child's early experience of power relations. I have tried to indicate the kind of model this provides—one in which, for the male, the exercise of power by the defeat and humiliation of others is essential to identity. This is the foundation of a society where violence is characteristic and war and preparation for war are major preoccupations and consumers of resources.

MALE VALUES IN THE
WAR-MAKING SYSTEM

The male cult of toughness has deep psychic roots, but the problem is not a question of personal power lust. These masculine values are built into the system—economic, political, social and even moral—and those who reach positions of authority are those who have best played the male game. I want now to look at the way the male-heroic model determines the nature of some of the major systems which mesh together to promote the arms race.

The two major causes of the arms race—the *external* force of nation state rivalry and the *internal* force of the military/industrial/technological complex—cover a range of economic, political and ideological areas. Sex-role division and the male projection of male sexual dominance are significant factors in all these areas. They are not the only factors, but I shall focus on them as a much-neglected area of the relation of sexual politics to the arms race.

The International Hierarchy

Rivalry between the two major power blocs involves economic and ideological competition and the maintenance of *national prestige*. I described earlier the sexual content in the US presidents' preoccupation with personal prestige, and how this helped to determine foreign policy.

These are the leaders who set up and defend national honor, a concept whose strength was made clear in the Falklands Crisis. In the House of Commons debate on April 13, 1982, Julian Amery, speaking of the use of force in the dispute, said: "Nothing else will restore the credibility of the government and wipe the stain from Britain's honor". According to this code of honor and its more modern counterpart credibility, nothing is worse than defeat. "The NATO doctrine is that we will fight with conventional weapons until we are losing, then we will fight with tactical nuclear weapons until we are losing, and then we will blow up the world" (Morton Halperin, former US Deputy Secretary of Defence in A. Grosser, *The Western Alliance*, Papermac, 1980). Better dead than defeated; better to die a manly death (usually one that involves killing others) than to retreat, surrender, appear a softie.

In-Groups

Some of this national rivalry is based on real *ideological differences*, about which people feel passionately. The strength of this feeling is fuelled by the need to belong to the in-group, and the need of the in-group to identify and downgrade the out-group for its own cohesion. (This need led Aldous Huxley to say that the only thing that would stop the nations of the world fighting among themselves was an invasion from Mars.) This process is similar to the initiation of boys into the male club by the rejection of all things womanly, and the expression of contempt and violence towards women. Feeling a member of a superior group gives a sense of power; it is what men get from their treatment of women, and what nations get from having an enemy. National leaders gain particularly from this—an enemy on the horizon produces an internal cohesion in which domestic problems fade. This kind of behavior is learned by men as part of their sex role.

The existence of the *nation state* is a fundamental factor in the arms race. Arms races take place between nation states or groups of nation states: in the latter case, power relations between allies can also help accelerate the arms race. The rise of the nation state is historically associated with a new concept of the military as a large permanent body of professionals, equipped with the latest technology. Maintaining an army prestigious in size, training and equipment is one of the marks of nationhood. It was reported in the *Guardian* that Argentina's military performance in the Falklands War sealed its "coming of age as a nation". Even though they were defeated, they had proved themselves in the same league as Britain, a major power.

The parallel between proving manhood and proving nationhood is clear: both are based on winning power, backed up by the threat or use of violence. National prestige is directly related to military strength: it is the major military powers who have most say in the United Nations; even in peacetime diplomatic negotiating, it is military might that speaks loudest. International politics closely resembles gang fights in the playground. The leader is the one acknowledged to have superior force: his power is then augmented by his position—in effect, the power of all his underlings is added to his own. They give this power to him and get certain benefits—protection, enhanced prestige from the relationship to the leader. Alliances such as NATO function in this way.

There are also real economic interests at stake in a competition for markets and resources. Modern nations are vitally dependent on international trade. This state of affairs is the result of a particular kind of economic growth. Some of it is a legacy of colonialism, which rested on the attitude that other people and other parts of the world are inferior, "underdeveloped", and therefore may legitimately be exploited ("developed"). A similar attitude to natural resources is part of the reason we are accustomed to a life-style that cannot be self-reliant, and this lack of self-reliance is an important cause of insecurity and the resulting build up of arms to "defend national interests". It is a sign of the breakdown of wholeness, the loss of the feeling of being part of the world, working within a self-sustaining system, and its replacement by a sense of superiority and living off conquest and exploitation. Many western economies became dependent on oil when oil was cheap: now they arm themselves to protect their access to oil. There would in fact be more security in changing our life-style so that we could produce our own essentials, but such a change demands a complete change in thinking and the abandonment of the struggle for dominance.

Dependency is actually fostered as part of the power game. Men have deliberately made women dependent on them, economically and physically, and various mechanisms from job discrimination to rape have enforced this means of keeping power. Protection and economic support are used as forms of oppression. So in international relations, self-reliance has been deliberately undermined for political and economic penetration.

Aid is given as means of control, and this brings about alignments that give impetus to the arms race. It is plain to see that the Soviet Union's protection of Warsaw Pact countries brings political control; it is just as true, if less obvious, that the price of US protection for NATO is US dominance in economic and social life. Third World countries are drawn into superpower rivalry through their dependence on aid, economic and military. Thus the whole world is a battlefield, and relatively poor countries spend their resources on military technology for internal repression or an arms race with local rivals. It is arguable that the undermining of self-reliance and the integration of all nations into the international hierarchy is an important reason why the arms race is accelerating now as never before.

Britain's place in the hierarchy now makes it both oppressor and oppressed, and self-reliance politically and economically is a central part of refusing either role. The aim of self-reliance is paralleled by the struggle of many women who refuse to be victims any longer, yet also refuse to become oppressors. What is being struggled against is at root the same thing—a hierarchy grounded in and perpetuated by sexual dominance.

Its a Man's Life

> We talked of the League of Nations and of the prospects of peace and disarmament. On this subject he was not so much militarist as martial. The difficulty to which he could find no answer was that if permanent peace were ever achieved, and armies and navies ceased to exist, there could be no outlet for the manly qualities which fighting developed, and that human physique and human character would deteriorate.[8]

As I said earlier, the military is a great upholder of male values. The army, it is said, will "make a man of you"; "it's a man's life" in the army. The violence it represents is admired because it is regarded as a sign of virility and is held to be character-building. The military is fundamentally a male-bonding institution of specialists in violence, founded on such symbols of power as uniforms, drill, weapons, subordination and command. Within this framework, pressure is on a man to "prove himself" by physical superiority over an enemy or over competitors. "Some men haven't the backbone for it" said one British army advertisement. US Army recruiting offers power in the form of weapons: "If you've never felt invincible, you've never ridden a tank . . . our monsters are things of beauty only to the guys who ride them". The choice of the word "ride" with its sexual connotations (when "drive" would be the more normal verb) is no accident.

Power in the army involves the humiliation and hatred of women. During basic training, recruits are commonly called "faggot" or "girl", the insult screamed at close quarters by a drill instructor. Chants such as "Your sister is a whore, your girlfriend is a whore, and your mother is a whore because she had you", exploit the sexual basis of violence. They prime men up to kill. The gun is a penis, the penis is a gun. "This is my

---

[8]From the biography, *Antony (Viscount Knebworth): A Record of Youth by his Father, the Earl of Lytton*, by Edward A. J. Lytton, Viscount (New York: C. Scribner's, 1936).

rifle, this is my gun; this one's for killing, this one's for fun".[9] Which is which?

The arms race is a mark of the permanence of the military. For many hundreds of years, rulers raised an army only in times of war; full-time soldiers formed what was in effect only an extended bodyguard. Nowadays it is accepted and expected that every country should have a considerable standing army supposedly for defence. For these professionals, war is the purpose of their training and very existence: in the minds of the military, war is going on all the time. A permanent army is the badge of nationhood. Its introduction is linked to the rise of the nation state, increased centralization, state education, and industrialization.

In all these, increased control at the top is linked to increasing fragmentation of tasks at the bottom. There is more division of labor, and professionalism grows: the "experts" rule. The rationale is efficiency; but the real result is alienation, loss of the sense of the whole community, and a shrugging off of responsibility. It teaches obedience and discipline, an unthinking performance of a single narrow task. These are military values, yet they pervade the whole of society. Factories, offices and schools were founded upon them: the patriarchal family instilled them. And although social attitudes have changed, the basic structures still embody these values. The face is kinder, but the power has not been given up.

Women have a special understanding of the division of labor used to take power from some and give more to others, for that is precisely how the sexual division of labor works. For centuries, women were taught that obedience and submission were inextricably connected with the ability to bear children. With the rise of the nation state, the introduction of a standing army, and industrialization came also an even narrower role for women. The household ceased to be thought of as a productive unit. Work and public life were separated from home and private life. Women's place was firmly in the domestic sphere (although many poor women have always had to work outside the home as well). Their part in production was denied, and their role in bringing up children devalued, the prestigious part being taken over by the school.

This fragmentation of tasks and roles, to which the oppression of women is basic, provides a fertile ground for the arms race to flourish. The "professionals"—soldiers, arms designers and manufacturers—depend on war, the threat of it and preparation for it, for their self-esteem, identity, and varying degrees of power. The rest of us are told to "leave

---

[9]Examples quoted by Helen Michalowski in her article "The Army will make a man of you" in *Reweaving the Web of Life*, ed. Pam McAllister (Philadelphia: New Society, 1982).

it to the experts". Many people play their small part in keeping the military machine going, working in an office or factory, without feeling responsible for the end product. They simply take orders.

The domestic sphere is supposed to be the source of emotional satisfaction—at work, you simply get on with the job. Getting on with the job means being blinkered to the death and suffering that are the result of military enterprises, blinkered to the ecological destruction that results from many industries. But it depends on women keeping going the haven of the home. What if women refused to maintain this protected area where men can admire themselves as husbands and fathers regardless of their lives outside?

The Scientific Worldview

Over half the scientists in the world are engaged in military research. How can so much knowledge be devoted to destruction? One answer, of course, is money. The defence establishment has the money to give for research and development, and this in itself is a reflection of priorities. Another answer is that scientists can cut off from the consequences of their work as an arms factory worker can. But there is more than this. Weapons research is consistent with the attitudes underlying the whole scientific worldview, although individual scientists have been people of integrity and desirous of peace. Many have been dedicated to the pursuit of knowledge as an end in itself, and have claimed that the uses to which it is put are outside their responsibility. But the purpose of scientific inquiry within this male-dominated society has always been to master and control the natural world: it has always involved accumulating power to increase control. In traditional ways of thinking the concept of mastery and the master-slave metaphor are the dominant ways of describing man's relationship to nature, as well as to the implements of technology.

There are seldom any reservations about man's rightful role in conquering, vanquishing and subjugating everything natural. This is clearly stated in the writings of Francis Bacon right at the start of the scientific revolution. He makes clear that man should "obey Nature" only as long as it takes to learn "her" secrets; then he will command "her" as a tyrant commands his subjects. The basic approach has been to take the world apart and re-assemble it under the control of men. The model for this approach to the natural world is, as discussed earlier, men's oppression of women. That some of this activity has had obviously dangerous, even disastrous consequences has not slowed it down at all—there is a blind faith that science will solve the problems it creates.

Many scientists have seen their task as conquering nature for the benefit of mankind. Yet we know that, by and large, research resources go to the most prestigious projects, and these are frequently the most daring and difficult (like transplant surgery or space technology) and not the most useful to most people. Research is an intellectual competition, and the race to be first with a new military technology is an exciting challenge. We are told there is "no turning the clock back", that the knowledge of nuclear technology cannot be forgotten—is there also no way of stopping the upward spiral of this knowledge? The realization that something is technologically possible sets scientists to work to make it a reality. This work goes on in secret, and the rest of us are not held fit to question the judgement of "the experts". Meanwhile, the scientists may claim that the technology is neither good nor bad, and disclaim their responsibility. There must be a way of stopping this forward thrust of military research: it involves a different kind of science, in which scientists no longer stand back from the social and political implications of their work—an escape from the patriarchal science in which the conquest of nature is a projection of sexual dominance.

WOMEN AND THE PEACE MOVEMENT

The male cosmology based on separation and hierarchy gives rise to strategies for peace and security based on building barriers and creating fear (a dissociative peace strategy). The result—a never-ending arms spiral. The alternative—a positive peace built on mutual support and cooperation (an associative strategy). Women are not only calling for nuclear disarmament as a first step towards trust-building, we are also showing a new way of working in our organization. Women in the peace movement are now confronting Cruise missiles, the police, prison, with the strength of our sisterhood, and it is a very powerful defense for preserving our values and our freedom.

It is our vision and our practice of a new way to peace that makes women such an important force in the peace movement—not any "natural pacifism" attributed to women. The common belief that women are by nature nonaggressive is itself part of the feminine stereotype of passivity, the complement to the idea that violence and war are "natural" to men. Just as boys are initiated into the male club, so girls are taught to accept male dominance. They learn to distrust their own opinions, and their physical abilities: in place of confidence and assertion, they learn endurance and patience.

But women's existing role also includes many valuable human qualities, particularly those associated with nurture and sensitivity to the needs of others. Under a male-dominated society, however, these are channelled to support male pride, male ego. It has been recognized recently that housework is unpaid work, but it has not been grasped that "love" is also exploited labor. The theft of a woman's sense of herself as an autonomous self-sufficient person produces for the man his surplus sense of himself. The female stereotype provides the environment in which masculine dominance and aggression flourish; it is the mirror in which men see these things as heroic, and themselves more than life-size.

Women are not inherently nonviolent: they are traditionally oppressed, and as an oppressed group, have often turned their anger and violence in upon themselves. Nor are men inherently violent: they are traditionally and structurally dominant, and retain that dominance through the cultivation of toughness and violence. Women are not "Earth Mothers" who will save the planet from the deadly games of the boys—this too is part of the support and nurture role that women are given in the world. Upon the support and silence of women has been built the male edifice of dominance, exploitation and war.

Women have played this role too in Left movements including the peace movement—typing, tea-making, making up the numbers. Yet it has been very difficult to get men in the peace movement and Left groups to accept their own behavior and ways of organizing as part of this male edifice. Difficult to get them to take the hierarchy, the centralism out of their meetings and to use a structure where everyone can take part, be listened to and cared for; where everyone's energy is fully available and not dissipated in frustration or competition. Difficult too to get men to accept the centrality of women's oppression. On the Left, sexism has joined all the other isms—racism, imperialism, capitalism, etc.—but it is often thought of as a private and domestic matter for now, its public side to be sorted out after the revolution or whatever. Women have put sexism on the agenda in the peace movement too: but here, as well, it is frequently regarded as a side issue. There is not the recognition that violence against women—rape, assault, exploitation—and the violence of war and the arms race have common roots: that the violence the peace movement is struggling against is a function of male sexual identity.

Women in Action

Women are playing a leading role in the peace movement today. The Women's March from Cardiff in 1981 set up the first peace camp at Greenham Common. Despite attempts at eviction, women there have endured and their commitment has inspired many others. In December

1982, 30,000 women took part in a demonstration at Greenham Common, surrounding the nine-mile perimeter fence, and hanging on it symbols of the things dear to them that were threatened by nuclear weapons—photos, baby clothes, poems, drawings, flowers. Many women have gone to prison for their part in blockades or actions inside the base: they refuse to be bound over to "keep the peace" since they must continue their protest precisely in order to make peace.

The movement is also strong abroad. In the USA, 2000 women demonstrated at the Pentagon in November 1980. Their statement made clear the connections between the nuclear threat and the daily oppression in women's lives. Women from various European countries formed the core of the European Peace March in 1981: Scandinavian women led the 1982 peace march through the USSR. There are many other women-led peace initiatives, such as Mothers for Peace, and also many women's peace groups. Some groups are well-established, such as the Women's International League for Peace and Freedom (WILPF) and Voice of Women; others have been set up more recently, such as the Women's Peace Alliance, Women for Life on Earth, and Women Oppose the Nuclear Threat (WONT). Some of the women involved are specifically feminist, others are not: WONT is the only declaredly feminist group. Not all would share my analysis. Some work in mixed-sex groups, others in women-only groups, many do both.

Working in an all-women group or taking part in women-only actions gives women the space to recover their autonomy, to gain confidence, to find their identity: the opportunity to work out their own ways of organizing, based on the sharing of power and responsibility and the personal caring that have been features of the women's movement. Any woman who has taken part in a Greenham Common action will know the powerful feeling created by women working together. We also need this chance to work out our analysis, a task we have only just begun.

Women's leading role in the peace movement is (as I said earlier) not an expression of any "natural pacifism" but a measure of their refusal to accept the role division that lies behind this idea. By refusing to be oppressed, they are refusing to allow men to be oppressors.

> We will diminish violence by refusing to be violated. We will repudiate the whole patriarchal system with its institutions . . . its social scenarios of dominance and submission all based on the male-over-female model, when we refuse conscientiously, rigorously and absolutely to be the soil on which male aggression, pride and arrogance can grow like wild weeds.[10]

---

[10]Andrea Dworkin, "Up from Under," *Peace News*, Nov. 21, 1975.

Feminism and Positive Peace

Working together, women are recovering valuable human qualities distorted by male supremacy. Women bring their caring and nurture out of domestic isolation where it feeds male dominance. Our caring for life on earth is not soft or sentimental: it is determined, realistic, political. Our care for each other builds strong groups where work, responsibility and power are shared, and energy is generated. Women refuse to "service" men and provide emotional support for them, not because we spurn giving each other support, but because men must learn to give it to each other. Our vision is of each person a whole person; of women reclaiming their autonomy and self-assertion: no longer seeking "femininity" in submission and helplessness: of men learning to care, to nurture, to show emotion, to admit weakness, no longer having to prove their manhood in acts of domination and violence, instead seeking positive peace through cooperation and confidence-building.

A first step is to encourage the equal participation of more women in the peace movement, whether in women-only groups or in mixed groups. This involves asking how many women go to meetings or demonstrations, and what role they play. It may be necessary to make a policy that office-holders, committees, etc. should be composed of equal numbers of women and men. It involves changing the organization of meetings and the style of demonstrations in the light of the experience of the feminist movement—using meeting structures that encourage equal participation by all and give mutual support, which are not dominated by a few; and demonstrations that make the movement seem open and welcoming to those outside, as well as determined in its struggle.

Beyond this, I believe that all who oppose violence must take seriously the daily violence against women: that all who support liberation must look seriously at how women are oppressed: that all who work for peace must uproot from their own lives the sexual dominance and hierarchical thinking that breed wars. Great changes are demanded in our social, political and economic systems, but they begin at home, in our personal relationships, and how we bring up our children.

At one level, we are creating an alternative sexuality which is not based on dominance but relies on respect for other people, equality of power, sensitivity, and an ability to receive and give generously—to be confident in giving and vulnerable in receiving; a sexuality in which body and mind are one, and equally precious. At another level we are finding alternatives to reliance on increasingly menacing weapons and a highly trained professional group for our defense. These would be based around ideas of self-reliance and peace-building through cooperation between equals, with widespread knowledge of the techniques of nonviolent civilian defense. This is as important for protection against internal repression as against external enemies.

The analysis linking these two levels that I have attempted to explain may seem to complicate the issue of peace and confuse the simple demand for nuclear disarmament. It makes the changes required seem huge. But we would be fooling ourselves to imagine that peace is attainable without massive changes. And on the other hand, this analysis means that we do not have to wait for governments and generals: we can all take a step in the right direction tomorrow, in our personal lives, at our next meeting. To destroy sexual dominance is to undermine the foundations of hierarchy, power-seeking and violence on which war and the preparation of unbelievably destructive arms are based.

12

Sex and Death in the Rational World of Defense Intellectuals*

Carol Cohn

"I can't believe *that*," said Alice

"Can't you?" the Queen said in a pitying tone. "Try again: draw a long breath, and shut your eyes."

Alice laughed. "There's no use trying," she said. "One *can't* believe impossible things."

"I daresay you haven't had much practice," said the Queen.

"When I was your age, I always did it for half-an-hour a day. Why sometimes I've believed as many as six impossible things before breakfast." [Lewis Carroll, *Through the Looking Glass*].

My close encounter with nuclear strategic analysis started in the summer of 1984. I was one of forty-eight college teachers (one of ten women) attending a summer workshop on nuclear weapons, nuclear strategic doctrine, and arms control, taught by distinguished "defense intellectuals." Defense intellectuals are men (and indeed, they are virtually all men) "who use the concept of deterrence to explain why it is safe to have weapons of a kind and number it is not safe to use."[1] They are civilians who move in and out of government, working sometimes as administrative officials or consultants, sometimes at universities and

---

*Previously published in *Signs: Journal of Women in Culture and Society*, Vol. 12, No. 4 (1987).
[1] Thomas Powers, "How Nuclear War Could Start," *New York Review of Books* (17 January 1985) p. 33.

think tanks. They formulate what they call "rational" systems for dealing with the problems created by nuclear weapons: how to manage the arms race; how to deter the use of nuclear weapons; how to fight a nuclear war if deterrence fails. It is their calculations that are used to explain the necessity of having nuclear destructive capability at what George Kennan has called "levels of such grotesque dimensions as to defy rational understanding."[2] At the same time, it is their reasoning that is used to explain why it is not safe to live without nuclear weapons.[3] In short, they create the theory that informs and legitimates American nuclear strategic practice.

For two weeks, I listened to men engage in dispassionate discussion of nuclear war. I found myself aghast, but morbidly fascinated—not by nuclear weaponry, or by images of nuclear destruction, but by the extraordinary abstraction and removal from what I knew as reality that characterized the professional discourse. I became obsessed by the question, How can they think this way? At the end of the summer program, when I was offered the opportunity to stay on at the university's center on defense technology and arms control (hereafter known as "the Center"), I jumped at the chance to find out how they could think "this" way.

I spent the next year of my life immersed in the world of defense intellectuals. As a participant observer, I attended lectures, listened to arguments, conversed with defense analysts, and interviewed graduate students at the beginning, middle, and end of their training. I learned their specialized language, and I tried to understand what they thought and how they thought. I sifted through their logic for its internal inconsistencies and its unspoken assumptions. But as I learned their language, as I became more and more engaged with their information and their arguments, I found that my own thinking was changing. Soon, I could no longer cling to the comfort of studying an external and objectified "them." I had to confront a new question. How can *I* think this way? How can any of us?

Throughout my time in the world of strategic analysis, it was hard not to notice the ubiquitous weight of gender, both in social relations and in

---

[2]George Kennan, "A Modest Proposal," *New York Review of Books*, (16 July 1981) p. 14.
[3]It is unusual for defense intellectuals to write for the public, rather than for their colleagues, but a recent, interesting exception has been made by a group of defense analysts from Harvard. Their two books provide a clear expression of the stance that living with nuclear weapons is not so much a problem to be solved but a condition to be managed rationally. Albert Carnesale and the Harvard Nuclear Study Group, *Living with Nuclear Weapons* (Cambridge, Mass.: Harvard Press, 1984), and Graham T. Allison, Albert Carnesale, and Joseph Nye, Jr. (eds.), *Hawks, Doves, and Owls: An Agenda for Avoiding Nuclear War* (New York: W. W. Norton & Co., 1985).

the language itself; it is an almost entirely male world (with the exception of the secretaries), and the language contains many rather arresting metaphors. There is, of course, an important and growing body of feminist theory about gender and language.[4] In addition, there is a rich and increasingly vast body of theoretical work exploring the gendered aspects of war and militarism, which examines such issues as men's and women's different relations to militarism and pacifism, and the ways in which gender ideology is used in the service of militarization. Some of the feminist work on gender and war is also part of an emerging, powerful feminist critique of ideas of rationality as they have developed in Western culture.[5] While I am indebted to all of these

---

[4]For useful introductions to feminist work on gender and language, see Barrie Thorne, Cheris Kramarae, and Nancy Henley (eds.), *Language, Gender and Society* (Rowley, Mass.: Newbury Publishing House, 1983); and Elizabeth Abel (ed.), *Writing and Sexual Difference* (Chicago: University of Chicago Press, 1982).

[5]For feminist critiques of dominant Western conceptions of rationality, see Nancy Hartsock, *Money, Sex, and Power* (New York: Longman, 1983); Sandra Harding and Merrill Hintikka (eds.), *Discovering Reality: Feminist Perspectives on Epistemology, Metaphysics, Methodology and the Philosophy of Science* (Dordrecht: D. Reidel Publishing Co., 1983); Evelyn Fox Keller, *Reflections on Gender and Science* (New Haven, Conn.: Yale University Press, 1985); Jean Bethke Elshtain, *Public Man, Private Woman: Woman in Social and Political Thought* (Princeton, N.J.: Princeton University Press, 1981); Genevieve Lloyd, *The Man of Reason: "Male" and "Female" in Western Philosophy* (Minneapolis: University of Minnesota Press, 1984), which contains a particularly useful bibliographic essay; Sara Ruddick, "Remarks on the Sexual Politics of Reason," in Eva Kittay and Diana Meyers (eds.), *Women and Moral Theory* (Totowa, N.J.: Rowman & Allanheld, in press). Some of the growing feminist work on gender and war is explicitly connected to critiques of rationality, see Virginia Woolf, *Three Guineas* (New York: Harcourt, Brace, Jovanovich, 1966); Nancy C. M. Hartsock, "The Feminist Standpoint: Developing the Grounds for a Specifically Feminist Historical Materialism," in Harding and Hintikka (eds.), pp. 283–310, and "The Barracks Community in Western Political Thought: Prologomena to a Feminist Critique of War and Politics," in Judith Hicks Stiehm (ed.), *Women and Men's Wars* (Oxford: Pergamon Press, 1983); Jean Bethke Elshtain, "Reflections on War and Political Discourse: Realism, Just War and Feminism in a Nuclear Age," *Political Theory*, Vol. 13, No. 1 (February 1985) pp. 39–57; Sara Ruddick, "Preservative Love and Military Destruction: Some Reflections on Mothering and Peace," in Joyce Trebilcot (ed.), *Mothering: Essays in Feminist Theory* (Totowa, N.J.: Rowan & Allanheld, 1984) pp. 231–62; Genevieve Lloyd, "Selfhood, War, and Masculinity," in E. Gross and C. Pateman *(eds.), Feminist Challenges* (Boston: Northeastern University Press, 1986). There is a vast and valuable literature on gender and war that indirectly informs my work, see, e.g., Cynthia Enloe, *Does Khaki Become You? The Militarization of Women's Lives* (Boston: South End Press, 1984); Jean Bethke Elshtain, "On Beautiful Souls, Just Warriors, and Feminist Consciousness," in Stiehm (ed.), pp. 341–48, Sara Ruddick, "Pacifying the Forces: Drafting Women in the Interests of Peace," *Signs: Journal of Women in Culture and Society*, Vol. 8, No. 3 (Spring 1983), pp. 471–89, and "Drafting Women: Pieces of a Puzzle," in Robert K. Fullinwider, *Conscripts and Volunteers: Military Requirements, Social Values, and the All-Volunteer Force* (Totowa, N.J.: Rowman & Allanheld, 1983); Amy Swerdlow, "Women's Strike for Peace versus HUAC," *Feminist Studies*, Vol. 8, No. 3 (Fall 1982) pp.493–520; Mary C. Segers, "The Catholic Bishops'

bodies of work, my own project is most closely linked to the development of feminist critiques of dominant Western concepts of reason. My goal is to discuss the nature of nuclear strategic thinking; in particular, my emphasis is on the role of its specialized language, a language that I call "technostrategic."[6] I have come to believe that this language both reflects and shapes the nature of the American nuclear strategic project, that it plays a central role in allowing defense intellectuals to think and act as they do, and that feminists who are concerned about nuclear weaponry and nuclear war must give careful attention to the language we choose to use—whom it allows us to communicate with and what it allows us to think as well as say.

STAGE 1: LISTENING

Clean Bombs and Clean Language

Entering the world of defense intellectuals was a bizarre experience—bizarre because it is a world where men spend their days calmly and matter-of-factly discussing nuclear weapons, nuclear strategy, and nuclear war. The discussions are carefully and intricately reasoned, occurring seemingly without any sense of horror, urgency, or moral outrage—in fact, there seems to be no graphic reality behind the words, as they speak of "first strikes," "counterforce exchanges," and "limited nuclear war," or as they debate the comparative values of a "minimum deterrent posture" versus a "nuclear war-fighting capability."

Yet what is striking about the men themselves is not, as the content of their conversations might suggest, their cold-bloodedness. Rather, it is that they are a group of men usually endowed with charm, humor, intelligence, concern, and decency. Reader, I liked them. At least, I liked many of them. The attempt to understand how such men could

---

Pastoral Letter on War and Peace: A Feminist Perspective," *Feminist Studies*, Vol. 11, No. 3 (Fall 1985) pp. 619–47.

[6] I have coined the term "technostrategic" to represent the intertwined, inextricable nature of technological and nuclear strategic thinking. The first reason is that strategic thinking seems to change in direct response to technological changes, rather than political thinking, or some independent paradigms that might be isolated as "strategic." [On this point, see Lord Solly Zuckerman, *Nuclear Illusions and Reality* (New York: Viking Press, 1982)]. Even more important, strategic theory not only depends on and changes in response to technological objects, it is also based on a kind of thinking, a way of looking at problems—formal, mathematical modeling, systems analysis, game theory, linear programming—that are part of technology itself. So I use the term "technostrategic" to indicate the degree to which nuclear strategic language and thinking are imbued with, indeed constructed out of, modes of thinking that are associated with technology.

contribute to an endeavor that I see as so fundamentally destructive became a continuing obsession for me, a lens through which I came to examine all of my experiences in their world.

In this early stage, I was gripped by the extraordinary language used to discuss nuclear war. What hit me first was the elaborate use of abstraction and euphemism, of words so bland that they never forced the speaker or enabled the listener to touch the realities of nuclear holocaust that lay behind the words.

Anyone who has seen pictures of Hiroshima burn victims or tried to imagine the pain of hundreds of glass shards blasted into flesh may find it perverse beyond imagination to hear a class of nuclear devices matter-of-factly referred to as "clean bombs." "Clean bombs" are nuclear devices that are largely fusion rather than fission; they release a somewhat higher proportion of their energy as prompt radiation, but produce less radioactive fallout than fission bombs of the same yield.[7]

"Clean bombs" may provide the perfect metaphor for the language of defense analysts and arms controllers. This language has enormous destructive power, but without emotional fallout, without the emotional fallout that would result if it were clear one was talking about plans for mass murder, mangled bodies, and unspeakable human suffering. Defense analysts talk about "countervalue attacks" rather than about incinerating cities. Human death, in nuclear parlance, is most often referred to as "collateral damage"; for, as one defense analyst said wryly, "The Air Force doesn't target people, it targets shoe factories."[8]

---

[7]Fusion weapons' proportionally smaller yield of radioactive fallout led Atomic Energy Commission Chairman Lewis Strauss to announce in 1956 that hydrogen bomb tests were important "not only from a military point of view but from a humanitarian aspect." Although the bombs being tested were 1,000 times more powerful than those that devastated Hiroshima and Nagasaki, the proportional reduction of fallout apparently qualified them as not only clean but also humanitarian. Lewis Strauss is quoted in Ralph Lapp, "The 'Humanitarian' H-Bomb," *Bulletin of Atomic Scientists*, Vol. 12, No. 7 (September 1956) p. 263.

[8]I must point out that we cannot know whether to take this particular example literally: America's list of nuclear targets is, of course, classified. The defense analyst quoted, however, is a man who has had access to that list for at least two decades. He is also a man whose thinking and speaking are careful and precise, so I think it is reasonable to assume that his statement is not a distortion, that "shoe factories," even if not themselves literally targeted, accurately represent a category of target. Shoe factories would be one among many "military targets" other than weapons systems themselves; they would be military targets because an army needs boots. The likelihood of a nuclear war lasting long enough for foot soldiers to wear out their boots might seem to stretch the limits of credibility, but that is an insufficient reason to assume that they are not nuclear targets. Nuclear targeting and nuclear strategic planning in general frequently suffer from "conventionalization" – the tendency of planners to think in the old, familiar terms of "conventional" warfare rather than fully assimilating the ways in which nuclear weaponry has changed warfare.

Some phrases carry this cleaning-up to the point of inverting meaning. The MX missile will carry ten warheads, each with the explosure power of 300–475 kilotons of TNT: *one* missile the bearer of destruction approximately 250–400 times that of the Hiroshima bombing.[9] Ronald Reagan has dubbed the MX missile "the Peacekeeper." While this renaming was the object of considerable scorn in the community of defense analysts, these very same analysts refer to the MX as a "damage limitation weapon."[10]

These phrases, only a few of the hundreds that could be discussed, exemplify the astounding chasm between image and reality that characterizes technostrategic language. They also hint at the terrifying way in which the existence of nuclear devices has distorted our perceptions and redefined the world. "Clean bombs" tells us that radioactivity is the only "dirty" part of killing people.

To take this one step further, such phrases can even seem healthful/ curative/corrective. So that we not only have "clean bombs" but also "surgically clean strikes" ("counterforce" attacks that can purportedly "take out"—i.e., accurately destroy—an opponent's weapons or command centers without causing significant injury to anything else). The image of excision of the offending weapon is unspeakably ludicrous when the surgical tool is not a delicately controlled scalpel but a nuclear warhead. And somehow it seems to be forgotten that even scalpels spill blood."[11]

In avoiding talking about murder, the defense community has long been ahead of the State Department. It was not until 1984 that the State Department announced it will no longer use the word "killing," much less "murder," in official reports on the status of human rights in allied countries. The new term is "unlawful or arbitrary deprivation of life" [*New York Times*, 15 February 1984, as cited in *Quarterly Review of Doublespeak*, Vol. 11, No. 1 (October 1984) p. 3].

[9]"Kiloton" (or kt) is a measure of explosive power, the number of thousands of tons of TNT required to release an equivalent amount of energy. The atomic bomb dropped on Hiroshima is estimated to have been approximately 12 kt. An MX missile is designed to carry up to ten Mk 21 re-entry vehicles, each with a W-87 warhead. The yield of W-87 warheads is 300 kt, but they are "upgradable" to 475 kt.

[10]Since the MX would theoretically be able to "take out" Soviet land-based ICBMs in a "disarming first strike," the Soviets would have few ICBMs left for a retaliatory attack, and thus, damage to the United States theoretically would be limited. However, to consider the damage that could be inflicted on the United States by the remaining ICBMs, not to mention Soviet bombers and submarine-based missiles as "limited" is to act as though words have no meaning.

[11]Conservative government assessments of the number of deaths resulting from a "surgically clean" counterforce attack vary widely. The Office of Technology Assessment projects 2 million to 20 million immediate deaths. [See James Fallows, *National Defense* (New York: Random House, 1981) p. 159.] A 1975 Defense Department study estimated 18.3 million fatalities, while the US Arms Control and Disarmament Agency, using

White Men in Ties Discussing Missile Size

Feminists have often suggested that an important aspect of the arms race is phallic worship, that "missile envy" is a significant motivating force in the nuclear build-up.[12] I have always found this an uncomfortably reductionist explanation and hoped that my research at the Center would yield a more complex analysis. But still, I was curious about the extent to which I might find a sexual subtext in the defense professionals' discourse. I was not prepared for what I found.

I think I had naively imagined myself as a feminist spy in the house of death—that I would need to sneak around and eavesdrop on what men said in unguarded moments, using all my subtlety and cunning to unearth whatever sexual imagery might be underneath how they thought and spoke. I had naively believed that these men, at least in public, would appear to be aware of feminist critiques. If they had not changed their language, I thought that at least at some point in a long talk about "penetration aids," someone would suddenly look up, slightly embarrassed to be caught in such blatant confirmation of feminist analyses of What's Going On Here.[13]

Of course, I was wrong. There was no evidence that any feminist critiques had ever reached the ears, much less the minds, of these men. American military dependence on nuclear weapons was explained as "irresistible, because you get more bang for the buck." Another lecturer solemnly and scientifically announced "to disarm is to get rid of all your stuff." (This may, in turn, explain why they see serious talk of nuclear disarmament as perfectly resistable, not to mention foolish. If disarmament is emasculation, how could any real man ever consider it?) A professor's explanation of why the MX missile is to be placed in the silos of the newest Minuteman missiles, instead of replacing the older, less accurate ones, was "because they're in the nicest hole—you're not going to take the nicest missile you have and put it in a crummy hole." Other lectures were filled with discussion of vertical erector launchers, thrust-to-weight ratios, soft lay downs, deep penetration, and the comparative advantages of protracted versus spasm attacks—or what one military advisor to the National Security Council has called "releasing 70 to 80

---

different assumptions, arrived at a figure of 50 million [cited by Desmond Ball, "Can Nuclear War be Controlled?" Adelphi Paper No. 169 (London: International Institute for Strategic Studies, 1981)].

[12]The phrase is Helen Caldicott's in *Missile Envy: The Arms Race and Nuclear War* (Toronto: Bantam Books, 1986).

[13]For the uninitiated, "penetration aids" refers to devices that help bombers or missiles get past the "enemy's" defensive systems; e.g., stealth technology, chaff, or decoys. Within the defense intellectual community, they are also familiarly known as "penaids."

percent of our megatonnage in one orgasmic whump."[14] There was serious concern about the need to harden our missiles and the need to "face it, the Russians are a little harder than we are." Disbelieving glances would occasionally pass between me and my one ally in the summer program, another woman, but no one else seemed to notice.

If the imagery is transparent, its significance may be less so. The temptation is to draw some conclusions about the defense intellectuals themselves—about what they are *really* talking about, or their motivations; but the temptation is worth resisting. Individual motivations cannot necessarily be read directly from imagery; the imagery itself does not originate in these particular individuals but in a broader cultural context.

Sexual imagery has, of course, been a part of the world of warfare since long before nuclear weapons were even a gleam in a physicist's eye. The history of the atomic bomb project itself is rife with overt images of competitive male sexuality, as is the discourse of the early nuclear physicists, strategists, and SAC commanders.[15] Both the military itself and the arms manufacturers are constantly exploiting the phallic imagery and promise of sexual domination that their weapons so conveniently suggest. A quick glance at the publications that constitute some of the research sources for defense intellectuals makes the depth and pervasiveness of the imagery evident.

Air Force Magazine's advertisements for new weapons, for example, rival *Playboy* as a catalog of men's sexual anxieties and fantasies. Consider the following, from the June 1985 issue: emblazoned in bold letters across the top of a two-page advertisement from the AV-8B Harrier II—"Speak Softly and Carry a Big Stick." The copy below boasts "an exceptional thrust to weight ratio" and "vectored thrust capability that makes the . . . unique rapid response possible." Then just in case we've failed to get the message, the last line reminds us, "Just the sort of 'Big Stick' Teddy Roosevelt had in mind way back in 1901."[16]

An ad for the BKEP (BLU-106/B) reads:

The Only Way to Solve Some Problems is to Dig Deep.
THE BOMB, KINETIC ENERGY
PENETRATOR

---

[14]General William Odom, "C³I and Telecommunications at the Policy Level," Incidental Paper, Seminar on C³I: Command, Control, Communicationas and Intelligence (Cambridge, Mass.: Harvard University, Center for Information Policy Research, Spring 1980) p. 5.

[15]This point has been amply documented by Brian Easlea, *Fathering the Unthinkable: Masculinity, Scientists and the Nuclear Arms Race* (London: Pluto Press, 1983).

[16]*Air Force Magazine*, Vol. 68, No. 6 (June 1985) pp. 77–78.

"Will provide the tactical air commander with efficient power to
deny or significantly delay enemy airfield operations."
"Designed to maximize runaway cratering by optimizing penetration
dynamics and utilizing the most efficient warhead yet designed."[17]

(In case the symbolism of "cratering" seems far-fetched, I must point out
that I am not the first to see it. The French use the Mururoa Atoll in the
South Pacific for their nuclear tests and assign a woman's name to each
of the craters they gouge out of the earth.)

Another, truly extraordinary, source of phallic imagery is to be found
in descriptions of nuclear blasts themselves. Here, for example, is one
by journalist William Laurence, who was brought to Nagasaki by the Air
Force to witness the bombing. "Then, just when it appeared as though
the thing had settled down in to a state of permanence, there came
shooting out of the top a giant mushroom that increased the size of the
pillar to a total of 45,000 feet. The mushroom top was even more alive
than the pillar, seething and boiling in a white fury of creamy foam,
sizzling upward and then descending earthward, a thousand geysers
rolled into one. It kept struggling in an elemental fury, like a creature in
the act of breaking the bonds that held it down."[18]

Given the degree to which it suffuses their world, that defense
intellectuals themselves use a lot of sexual imagery does not seem
especially surprising. Nor does it, by itself, constitute grounds for
imputing motivation. For me, the interesting issue is not so much the
imagery's psychodynamic origins, as how it functions. How does it
serve to make it possible for strategic planners and other defense
intellectuals to do their macabre work? How does it function in their
construction of a work world that feels tenable? Several stories illustrate
the complexity.

During the summer program, a group of us visited the New London
Navy base where nuclear submarines are homeported and the General
Dynamics Electric Boat boatyards where a new Trident submarine was
being constructed. At one point during the trip we took a tour of a
nuclear-powered submarine. When we reached the part of the sub
where the missiles are housed, the officer accompanying us turned with
a grin and asked if we wanted to stick our hands through a hole to "pat
the missile." *Pat the missile?*

The image reappeared next week, when a lecturer scornfully declared
that the only real reason for deploying Cruise and Pershing II missiles in
Western Europe was "so that our allies can pat them." Some months

---

[17]Ibid.
[18]William L. Laurence, *Dawn over Zero: The Study of the Atomic Bomb* (London: Museum
Press, 1974) pp. 198–99.

later, another group of us went to be briefed at NORAD (the North American Aerospace Defense Command). On the way back, our plane went to refuel at Offut Air Force Base, the Strategic Air Command headquarters near Omaha, Nebraska. When word leaked out that our landing would be delayed because the new B-1 bomber was in the area, the plane became charged with a tangible excitement that built as we flew in our holding pattern, people craning their necks to try to catch a glimpse of the B-1 in the skies, and climaxed as we touched down on the runway and hurtled past it. Later, when I returned to the Center, I encountered a man who, unable to go on the trip, said to me enviously, "I hear you got to pat a B-1."

What is all this "patting"? What are men doing when they "pat" these high-tech phalluses? Patting is an assertion of intimacy, sexual possession, affectionate domination. The thrill and pleasure of "patting the missile" is the proximity of all that phallic power, the possibility of vicariously appropriating it as one's own.

But if the predilection for patting phallic objects indicates something of the homoerotic excitement suggested by the language, it also has another side. For patting is not only an act of sexual intimacy. It is also what one does to babies, small children, the pet dog. One pats that which is small, cute, and harmless—not terrifyingly destructive. Pat it, and its lethality disappears.

Much of the sexual imagery I heard was rife with the sort of ambiguity suggested by "patting the missiles." The imagery can be construed as a deadly serious display of the connections between masculine sexuality and the arms race. At the same time, it can also be heard as a way of minimizing the seriousness of militarist endeavors, of denying their deadly consequences. A former Pentagon target analyst, in telling me why he thought plans for "limited nuclear war" were ridiculous, said, "Look, you gotta understand that it's a pissing contest—you gotta expect them to use everything they've got." What does this image say? Most obviously, that this is all about competition for manhood, and thus there is tremendous danger. But at the same time, the image diminishes the contest and its outcomes, by representing it as an act of boyish mischief.

Fathers, Sons, and Virgins

"Virginity" also made frequent, arresting appearances in nuclear discourse. In the summer program, one professor spoke of India's explosion of a nuclear bomb as "losing her virginity"; the question of how the United States should react was posed as whether or not we should "throw her away." It is a complicated use of metaphor. Initiation into the nuclear world involves being deflowered, losing one's innocence, knowing sin, all wrapped up into one. Although the manly United States is no virgin, and proud of it, the double standard raises its head in the question of whether or not a woman is still worth anything to a man once she has lost her virginity.

New Zealand's refusal to allow nuclear-armed or nuclear-powered warships into its ports prompted similar reflections on virginity. A good example is provided by Retired US Air Force General Ross Milton's angry column in *Air Force Magazine*, entitled, "Nuclear Virginity." His tone is that of a man whose advances have been spurned. He is contemptuous of the woman's protestation that she wants to remain pure, innocent of nuclear weapons; her moral reluctance is a quaint and ridiculous throw-back. But beyond contempt, he also feels outraged— after all, this is a woman we have *paid* for, who *still* will not come across. He suggests that we withdraw our goods and services—and then we will see just how long she tries to hold onto her virtue.[19] The patriarchal bargain could not be laid out more clearly.

Another striking metaphor of patriarchal power came early in the summer program, when one of the faculty was giving a lecture on deterrence. To give us a concrete example from outside the world of military strategy, he described having a seventeen year-old son of whose TV-watching habits he disapproves. He deals with the situation by threatening to break his son's arms if he turns on the TV again. "That's deterrence!" he said triumphantly.

What is so striking about this analogy is that at first it seems so inappropriate. After all, we have been taught to believe that nuclear deterrence is a relation between two countries of more or less equal strength, in which one is only able to deter the other from doing it great harm by threatening to do the same in return. But in this case, the partners are unequal, and the stronger one is using his superior force not to protect himself or others from grave injury but to coerce.

But if the analogy seems to be a flawed expression of deterrence as we have been taught to view it, it is nonetheless extremely revealing about US nuclear deterrence as an operational, rather than rhetorical or declaratory policy. What it suggests is the speciousness of the defensive rhetoric that surrounds deterrence—of the idea that we face an implacable enemy and that we stockpile nuclear weapons only in an attempt to defend ourselves. Instead, what we see is the drive to superior power as a means to exercise one's will and a readiness to threaten the disproportionate use of force in order to achieve one's own ends. There is no question here of recognizing competing but legitimate needs, no

---

[19]USAF Retired General T. R. Milton, "Nuclear Virginity," *Air Force Magazine*, Vol. 68, No. 5 (May 1985) p. 44.

desire to negotiate, discuss, or compromise, and most important, no necessity for that recognition or desire, since the father carries the bigger stick.[20]

The United States frequently appeared in discussions about international politics as "father," sometimes coercive, sometimes benevolent, but always knowing best. The single time that any mention was made of countries other than the United States, our NATO allies, or the USSR was in a lecture on nuclear proliferation. The point was made that younger countries simply could not be trusted to know what was good for them, nor were they yet fully responsible, so nuclear weapons in their hands would be much more dangerous than in ours. The metaphor used was that of parents needing to set limits for their children.

Domestic Bliss

Sanitized abstraction and sexual and patriarchal imagery, even if disturbing, seemed to fit easily into the masculinist world of nuclear war planning. What did not fit, what surprised and puzzled me most when I first heard it, was the set of metaphors that evoked images that can only be called domestic.

Nuclear missiles are based in "silos." On a Trident submarine, which carries twenty-four multiple warhead nuclear missiles, crew members call the part of the submarine where the missiles are lined up in their silos ready for launching "the Christmas tree farm." What could be more bucolic—farms, silos, Christmas trees?

In the ever-friendly, even romantic world of nuclear weaponry, enemies "exchange" warheads; one missile "takes out" another; weapons systems can "marry up"; "coupling" is sometimes used to refer to the wiring between mechanisms of warning and response, or to the psychopolitical links between strategic (intercontinental) and theater (European-based) weapons. The patterns in which a MIRVed missile's nuclear warheads land is known as a "footprint."[21] These nuclear explosives are not dropped; a "bus" "delivers" them. In addition, nuclear bombs are not referred to as bombs or even warheads; they are referred to as "re-entry vehicles," a term far more bland and benign, which is then shortened to "RVs," a term not only totally abstract and

---

[20]I am grateful to Margaret Cerullo, a participant in the first summer program, for reporting the use of this analogy to me and sharing her thoughts about this and other events in the program. The interpretation I give here draws strongly on hers.

[21]MIRV stands for "multiple independently targetable re-entry vehicles." A MIRVed missile not only carries more than one warhead, its warheads can be aimed at different targets.

removed from the reality of a bomb but also resonant with the image of the recreational vehicles of the ideal family vacation.

These domestic images must be more than simply one more form of distancing, one more way to remove oneself from the grisly reality behind the words; ordinary abstraction is adequate to that task. Something else, something very peculiar, is going on here. Calling the pattern in which bombs fall a "footprint" almost seems a willful distorting process, a playful, perverse refusal of accountability—because to be accountable to reality is to be unable to do this work.

These words may also serve to domesticate, to *tame* the wild and uncontrollable forces of nuclear destruction. The metaphors minimize; they are a way to make phenomena that are beyond what the mind can encompass smaller and safer, and thus they are a way of gaining mastery over the unmasterable. The fire-breathing dragon under the bed, the one who threatens to incinerate your family, your town, your planet, becomes a pet you can pat.

Using language evocative of everyday experiences also may simply serve to make the nuclear strategic community more comfortable with what they are doing. "PAL" (permissive action links) is the carefully constructed, friendly acronym for the electronic system designed to prevent the unauthorized firing of nuclear warheads. "BAMBI" was the acronym developed for an early version of an antiballistic missile system (for Ballistic Missile Boost Intercept). The president's Annual Nuclear Weapons Stockpile Memorandum, which outlines both short- and long-range plans for production of new nuclear weapons, is benignly referred to as "the shopping list." The National Command Authorities choose from a "menu of options" when deciding among different targeting plans. The "cookie cutter" is a phrase used to describe a particular model of nuclear attack. Apparently it is also used at the Department of Defense to refer to the neutron bomb.[22]

---

[22]Henry T. Nash, "The Bureaucratization of Homicide," *Bulletin of Atomic Scientists* (April 1980), reprinted in E. P. Thompson and Dan Smith (eds.), *Protest and Survive* (New York: Monthly Review Press, 1981) p. 159. The neutron bomb is notable for the active political contention that has occurred over its use and naming. It is a small warhead that produces six times the prompt radiation but slightly less blast and heat than typical fission warheads of the same yield. Pentagon planners see neutron bombs as useful in killing Soviet tank crews while theoretically leaving the buildings near the tanks intact. Of course,the civilians in the nearby buildings, however, would be killed by the same "enhanced radiation" as the tank crews. It is this design for protecting property while killing civilians along with soldiers that has led people in the anti-nuclear movement to call the neutron bomb "the ultimate capitalist weapon." However, in official parlance the neutron bomb is not called a weapon at all; it is an "enhanced radiation device." It is worth noting, however, that the designer of the neutron bomb did not conceive of it as an anti-tank personnel weapon to be used against the Russians. Instead, he thought it would be useful

The imagery that domesticates, that humanizes insentient weapons, may also serve, paradoxically, to make it all right to ignore sentient human bodies, human lives.[23] Perhaps it is possible to spend one's time thinking about scenarios for the use of destructive technology and to have human bodies remain invisible in that technological world precisely because that world itself now *includes* the domestic, the human, the warm, and playful—the Christmas trees, the RVs, the affectionate pats. It is a world that is in some sense complete unto itself; it even includes death and loss. But it is weapons, not humans, that get "killed." "Fratricide" occurs when one of your warheads "kills" another of your own warheads. There is much discussion of "vulnerability" and "survivability," but it is about the vulnerability and survival of weapons systems, not people.

Male Birth and Creation

There is one set of domestic images that demands separate attention—images that suggest men's desire to appropriate from women the power of giving life and that conflate creation and destruction. The bomb project is rife with images of male birth.[24] In December 1942, Ernest Lawrence's telegram to the physicists at Chicago read, "Congratulations to the new parents. Can hardly wait to see the new arrival."[25] At Los Alamos, the atom bomb was referred to as "Oppenheimer's baby." One of the physicists working at Los Alamos, Richard Feynman, writes that when he was temporarily on leave after his wife's death, he received a telegram saying "The baby is expected on such and such a day."[26] At Lawrence Livermore, the hydrogen bomb was referred to as "Teller's baby," al-

---

in an area where the enemy *did not have* nuclear weapons to use. [Samuel T. Cohen, in an interview on National Public Radio, as reported in Fred Kaplan, "The Neutron Bomb: What It Is, the Way It Works," *Bulletin of Atomic Scientists* (October 1981) p. 6.]

[23]For a discussion of the functions of imagery that reverses sentient and insentient matter, that "exchange[s] . . . idioms between weapons and bodies," see Elaine Scarry, *The Body in Pain: The Making and Unmaking of the World* (New York: Oxford University Press, 1985) pp. 60–157, esp. p. 67.

[24]For further discussion of men's desire to appropriate from women the power of giving life and death, and its implications for men's war-making activities, see Dorothy Dinnerstein, *The Mermaid and the Minotaur* (New York: Harper & Row, 1977). For further analysis of male birth imagery in the atomic bomb project, see Evelyn Fox Keller, "From Secrets of Life to Secrets of Death" (paper delivered at the Kansas Seminar, Yale University, New Haven, Conn., November 1986); and Easlea (n. 15 above), pp. 81–116.

[25]Lawrence is quoted by Herbert Childs in *An American Genius: The Life of Ernest Orlando Lawrence* (New York: E. P. Dutton, 1968) p. 340.

[26]Feynman writes about the telegram in Richard P. Feynman, "Los Alamos from Below," in Lawrence Badash, Joseph O. Hirshfelder, and Herbert P. Broida (eds.), *Reminiscences of Los Alamos, 1943–1945* (Dordrecht: D. Reidel Publishing Co., 1980) p. 130.

though those who wanted to disparage Edward Teller's contribution claimed he was not the bomb's father but its mother. They claimed that Stanislaw Ulam was the real father; he had the all-important idea and inseminated Teller with it. Teller only "carried it" after that.[27]

Forty years later, this idea of male birth and its accompanying belittling of maternity—the denial of women's role in the process of creation and the reduction of "motherhood" to the provision of nurturance (apparently Teller did not need to provide an egg, only a womb)—seems thoroughly incorporated into the nuclear mentality, as I learned on a subsequent visit to US Space Command in Colorado Springs. One of the briefings I attended included discussion of a new satellite system, the not yet "on-line" MILSTAR system.[28] The officer doing the briefing gave an excited recitation of its technical capabilities and then an explanation of the new Unified Space Command's role in the system. Self-effacingly he said, "We'll do the motherhood role—telemetry, tracking, and control—the maintenance."

In light of the imagery of male birth, the extraordinary names given to the bombs that reduced Hiroshima and Nagasaki to ash and rubble—"Little Boy" and "Fat Man"—at last become intelligible. These ultimate destroyers were the progeny of the atomic scientists—and emphatically not just any progeny but male progeny. In early tests, before they were certain that the bombs would work, the scientists expressed their concern by saying that they hoped the baby was a boy, not a girl—that is, not a dud.[29] General Grove's triumphant cable to Secretary of War Henry Stimson at the Potsdam conference, informing him that the first atomic bomb test was successful read, after decoding: "Doctor has just returned most enthusiastic and confident that the little boy is as husky as his big brother. The light in his eyes discernible from here to

---

[28]The MILSTAR system is a communications satellite system that is jam resistant, as well as having an "EMP-hardened capability." (This means that the electromagnetic pulse set off by a nuclear explosion would theoretically not destroy the satellites' electronic systems.) There are, of course, many things to say about the sanity and morality of the idea of the MILSTAR system and of spending the millions of dollars necessary to EMP-harden it. The most obvious point is that this is a system designed to enable the United States to fight a "protracted" nuclear war—the EMP-hardening is to allow it to act as a conduit for command and control of successive nuclear shots, long after the initial exchange. The practicality of the idea would also appear to merit some discussion—who is going to be communicating what to whom after the initial exchange? And why bother to harden it against EMP when all an opponent has to do to prevent the system from functioning is to blow it up, a feat certain to become technologically feasible in a short time? But, needless to say, exploration of these questions was not part of the briefing.
[29]The concern about having a boy, not a girl, is written about by Robert Jungk, *Brighter Than a Thousand Suns*, trans. by James Cleugh (New York: Harcourt, Brace & Co., 1956) p. 197.

Highhold and I could have heard his screams from here to my farm."[30] Stimson, in turn, informed Churchill by writing him a note that read, "Babies satisfactorily born."[31] In 1952, Teller's exultant telegram to Los Alamos announcing the successful test of the hydrogen bomb, "Mike," at Eniwetok Atoll in the Marshall Islands, read, "It's a boy."[32] The nuclear scientists gave birth to male progeny with the ultimate power of violent domination over female Nature. The defense intellectuals' project is the creation of abstract formulations to control the forces the scientists created—and to participate thereby in their world-creating/destroying power.

The entire history of the bomb project, in fact, seems permeated with imagery that confounds man's overwhelming technological power to destroy nature with the power to create—imagery that inverts men's destruction and asserts in its place the power to create new life and a new world. It converts men's destruction into their rebirth.

William L. Laurence witnessed the Trinity test of the first atomic bomb and wrote: "The big boom came about a hundred seconds after the great flash—the first cry of a new-born world. . . . They clapped their hands as they leaped from the ground—earthbound man symbolizing the birth of a new force."[33] Watching "Fat Man" being assembled the day before it was dropped on Nagasaki, he described seeing the bomb as "being fashioned into a living thing."[34] Decades later, General Bruce K. Holloway, the commander-in-chief of the Strategic Air Command from 1968 to 1972, described a nuclear war as involving "a big bang, like the start of the universe."[35]

God and the Nuclear Priesthood

The possibility that the language reveals an attempt to appropriate ultimate creative power is evident in another striking aspect of the language of nuclear weaponry and doctrine—the religious imagery. In a

---

[30]Richard E. Hewlett and Oscar E. Anderson, *The New World, 1939/46: A History of the United States Atomic Energy Commission*, 2 Vols. (University Park: Pennsylvania State University Press, 1962) Vol. 1 p. 386.

[31]Winston Churchill, *The Second World War*, vol. 6., *Triumph and Tragedy* (London: Cassell, 1954) p. 551.

[32]Quoted by Easlea, p. 130.

[33]Laurence (n. 18 above), p. 10.

[34]Ibid., p. 188.

[35]From a 1985 interview in which Holloway was explaining the logic of a "decapitating" strike against the Soviet leadership and command and control systems—and thus how nuclear war would be different from World War II, which was a "war of attrition," in which transportation, supply depots, and other targets were hit, rather than being a "big bang" [Daniel Ford, "The Button," *New Yorker Magazine*, Vol. 61, No. 7 (8 April 1985) p. 49].

subculture of hard-nosed realism and hyper-rationality, in a world that claims as a sign of its superiority its vigilant purging of all nonrational elements, and in which people carefully excise from their discourse every possible trace of soft sentimentality, as though purging dangerous nonsterile elements from a lab, the last thing one might expect to find is religious imagery—imagery of the forces that science has been defined in *opposition to*. For surely, given that science's identity was forged by its separation from, by its struggle for freedom from, the constraints of religion, the only thing as unscientific as the female, the subjective, the emotional, would be the religious. And yet, religious imagery permeates the nuclear past and present. The first atomic bomb test was called Trinity—the unity of the Father, the Son, and the Holy Spirit, the male forces of Creation. The imagery is echoed in the language of the physicists who worked on the bomb and witnessed the test: "It was as though we stood at the first day of creation." Robert Oppenheimer thought of Krishna's words to Arjuna in the *Bhagavad Gita*: "I am become Death, the Shattered of Worlds."[36]

Perhaps most astonishing of all is the fact that the creators of strategic doctrine actually refer to members of their community as "the nuclear priesthood." It is hard to decide what is most extraordinary about this: the easy arrogance of their claim to the virtues and supernatural power of the priesthood; the tacit admission (*never* spoken directly) that rather than being unflinching, hard-nosed, objective, empirically minded scientific describers of reality, they are really the creators of dogma; or the extraordinary implicit statement about who, or rather what, has become god. If this new priesthood attains its status through an inspired knowledge of nuclear weapons, it gives a whole new meaning to the phrase "a mighty fortress is our God."

STAGE 2: LEARNING TO SPEAK THE LANGUAGE

Although I was startled by the combination of dry abstraction and counter-intuitive imagery that characterizes the language of defense intellectuals, my attention and energy were quickly focused on decoding and learning to speak it. The first task was training the tongue in the articulation of acronyms.

Several years of reading the literature of nuclear weaponry and strategy had not prepared me for the degree to which acronyms littered all conversations, nor for the way in which they are used. Formerly, I

---

[36]Jungk, p. 201.

had thought of them mainly as utilitarian. They allow you to write or speak faster. They act as a form of abstraction, removing you from the reality behind the words. They restrict communication to the initiated, leaving all others both uncomprehending and voiceless in the debate.

But, being at the Center, hearing the defense analysts use the acronyms, and then watching as I and others in the group started to fling acronyms around in our conversation revealed some additional, unexpected dimensions.

First, in speaking and hearing, a lot of these terms can be very sexy. A small supersonic rocket "designed to penetrate any Soviet air defense" is called a SRAM (for short-range attack missile). Submarine-launched Cruise missiles are not referred to as SLCMs, but "slick'ems." Ground-launched Cruise missiles are "glick'ems." Air-launched Cruise missiles are not sexy but magical—"alchems" (ALCMs) replete with the illusion of turning base metals into gold.

TACAMO, the acronym used to refer to the planes designed to provide communications links to submarines, stands for "take charge and move out." The image seems closely related to the nicknames given to the new guidance systems for "smart weapons"—"shoot and scoot" or "fire and forget."

Other acronyms work in other ways. The plane in which the president supposedly will be flying around above a nuclear holocaust, receiving intelligence and issuing commands for the next bombing, is referred to as "kneecap" (for NEACP—National Emergency Airborne Command Post). The edge of derision suggested in referring to it as "kneecap" mirrors the edge of derision implied when it is talked about at all, since few believe that the president really would have the time to get into it, or that the communications systems would be working if he were in it, and some might go so far as to question the usefulness of his being able to direct an extended nuclear war from his "kneecap" even if it were feasible. (I never heard the morality of this idea addressed.) But it seems to me that speaking about it with that edge of derision is *exactly* what allows it to be spoken about and seriously discussed at all. It is the very ability to make fun of a concept that makes it possible to work with it rather than reject it outright.

In other words, what I learned at the program is that talking about nuclear weapons is fun. I am serious. The words are fun to say; they are racy, sexy, snappy. You can throw them around in rapid-fire succession. They are quick, clean, light; they trip off the tongue. You can reel off dozens of them in seconds, forgetting about how one might just interfere with the next, not to mention with the lives beneath them.

I am not describing a phenomenon experienced only by the perverse, although the phenomenon itself may be perverse indeed. Nearly everyone I observed clearly took pleasure in using the words. It mattered little whether we were lecturers or students, hawks or doves, men or women—we all learned it, and we all spoke it. Some of us may have spoken with a self-consciously ironic edge, but the pleasure was there nonetheless.

Part of the appeal was the thrill of being able to manipulate an arcane language, the power of entering the secret kingdom, being someone in the know. It is a glow that is a significant part of learning about nuclear weaponry. Few know, and those who do are powerful. You can rub elbows with them, perhaps even be one yourself.

That feeling, of course, does not come solely from the language. The whole set-up of the summer program itself, for example, communicated the allures of power and the benefits of white male privileges. We were provided with luxurious accommodations, complete with young black women who came in to clean up after us each day; generous funding paid not only our transportation and food but also a large honorarium for attending: we met in lavishly appointed classrooms and lounges. Access to excellent athletic facilities was guaranteed by a "Temporary Privilege Card," which seemed to me to sum up the essence of the experience. Perhaps most important of all were the endless allusions by our lecturers to "what I told John [Kennedy]" and "and then Henry [Kissinger] said," or the lunches where we could sit next to a prominent political figure and listen to Washington gossip.

A more subtle, but perhaps more important, element of learning the language is that, when you speak it, you feel in control. The experience of mastering the words infuses your relation to the material. You can get so good at manipulating the words that it almost feels as though the whole thing is under control. Learning the language gives a sense of what I would call cognitive mastery; the feeling of mastery of technology that is finally *not* controllable but is instead powerful beyond human comprehension, powerful in a way that stretches and even thrills the imagination.

The more conversations I participated in using this language, the less frightened I was of nuclear war. How can learning to speak a language have such a powerful effect? One answer, I believe, is that the *process* of learning the language is itself a part of what removes you from the reality of nuclear war.

I entered a world where people spoke what amounted to a foreign language, a language I had to learn if we were to communicate with one another. So I became engaged in the challenge of it—of decoding the acronyms and figuring out which were the proper verbs to use. My focus was on the task of solving the puzzles, developing language competency—not on the weapons and wars behind the words. Although my interest was in thinking about nuclear war and its prevention, my energy was elsewhere.

By the time I was through, I had learned far more than a set of abstract words that refer to grisly subjects, for even when the subjects of a standard English and nukespeak description seem to be the same, they are, in fact, about utterly different phenomena. Consider the following descriptions, in each of which the subject is the aftermath of a nuclear attack:

> Everything was black, had vanished into the black dust, was destroyed. Only the flames that were beginning to lick their way up had any color. From the dust that was like a fog, figures began to loom up, black, hairless, faceless. They screamed with voices that were no longer human. Their screams drowned out the groans rising everywhere from the rubble, groans that seemed to rise from the very earth itself.[37]

> [You have to have ways to maintain communications in a] nuclear environment, a situation bound to include EMP blackout, brute force damage to systems, a heavy jamming environment, and so on.[38]

There are no ways to describe the phenomena represented in the first with the language of the second. Learning to speak the language of defense analysts is not a conscious, cold-blooded decision to ignore the effects of nuclear weapons on real live human beings, to ignore the sensory, the emotional experience, the human impact. It is simply learning a new language, but by the time you are through, the content of what you can talk about is monumentally different, as is the perspective from which you speak.

In the example above, the differences in the two descriptions of a "nuclear environment" stem partly from a difference in the vividness of the words themselves—the words of the first intensely immediate and evocative, the words of the second abstract and distancing. The passages also differ in their content; the first describes the effects of a nuclear blast on human beings, the second describes the impact of a nuclear blast on technical systems designed to assure the "command and control" of nuclear weapons. Both of these differences may stem from the difference of perspective: the speaker in the first is a victim of nuclear weapons, the speaker in the second is a user. The speaker in the

---

[37]Hisako Matsubara, *Cranes at Dusk* (Garden City, N.Y.: Dial Press, 1985). The author was a child in Kyoto at the time the atomic bomb was dropped. Her description is based on the memories of survivors.

[38]General Robert Rosenberg (formerly on the National Security Council staff during the Carter Administration), "The Influence of Policymaking on C³I," Incidental Paper, Seminar on C³I (Cambridge, Mass.: Harvard University, Center for Information Policy Research, Spring 1980) p. 59.

first is using words to try to name and contain the horror of human suffering all around her; the speaker in the second is using words to ensure the possibility of launching the next nuclear attack. Technostrategic language can be used only to articulate the perspective of the users of nuclear weapons, not that of the victims.[39]

Thus, speaking the expert language not only offers distance, a feeling of control, and an alternative focus for one's energies; it also offers escape—escape from thinking of oneself as a victim of nuclear war. I do not mean this on the level of individual consciousness; it is not that defense analysts somehow convince themselves that they would not be among the victims of nuclear war, should it occur. But I do mean it in terms of the structural position the speakers of the language occupy and the perspective they get from that position. *Structurally*, speaking technostrategic language removes them from the position of victim and puts them in the position of the planner, the user, the actor. From that position, there is neither need nor way to see oneself as a victim; no matter what one deeply knows or believes about the likelihood of nuclear war, and no matter what sort of terror or despair the knowledge of nuclear war's reality might inspire, the speakers of technostrategic language are positionally allowed, even forced, to escape that aware-ness, to escape viewing nuclear war from the position of the victim, by virtue of their linguistic stance as users, rather than victims, of nuclear weaponry.

Finally, then, I suspect that much of the reduced anxiety about nuclear war commonly experienced by both new speakers of the language and long-time experts comes from characteristics of the language itself: the distance afforded by its abstraction; the sense of

---

[39]Two other writers who have remarked on this division of languages between the "victims" and the professionals (variously named) are Freeman Dyson and Glenn D. Hook. Dyson, in *Weapons and Hope* (New York: Harper & Row, 1984), notes that there are two languages in the current discussion of nuclear weapons, which he calls the language of "the victims" and the language of "the warriors." He sees the resulting problem as being the difficulty the two groups have in communicating with each other and, thus, in appreciating each other's valid concerns. His project, then, is the search for a common language, and a good portion of the rest of the book is directed toward that end. Hook, in "Making Nuclear Weapons Easier to Live With: The Political Role of Language in Nuclearization," *Journal of Peace Research*, Vol. 22, No. 1 (1985) pp. 67–77, follows Camus in naming the two groups "the victims" and "the executioners." He is more explicit than Dyson about naming these as perspectives, as coming from positions of greater or lesser power, and points out that those with the most power are able to dominate and define the terms in which we speak about nuclear issues, so that no matter who we are, we find ourselves speaking as though we were the users, rather than the victims of nuclear weapons. Although my analysis of perspectives and the ways in which language inscribes relations of power is similar to his, I differ from Hook in finding in this fact one of the sources of the experts' relative lack of fear of nuclear war.

control afforded by mastering it; and the fact that its content and concerns are that of the users rather than the victims of nuclear weapons. In learning the language, one goes from being the passive, powerless victim to the competent, wily, powerful purveyor of nuclear threats and nuclear explosive power. The enormous destructive effects of nuclear weapons systems become extensions of the self, rather than threats to it.

STAGE 3: DIALOGUE

It did not take very long to learn the language of nuclear war and much of the specialized information it contained. My focus quickly changed from mastering technical information and doctrinal arcana to attempting to understand more about how the dogma was rationalized. Instead of trying, for example, to find out why submarines are so hard to detect or why, prior to the Trident II, submarine-based ballistic missiles were not considered counterforce weapons, I now wanted to know why we really "need" a strategic triad, given submarines' "invulnerability."[40] I also wanted to know why it is considered reasonable to base US military planning on the Soviet Union's military capabilities rather than seriously attempting to gauge what their intentions might be. This standard practice is one I found particularly troubling. Military analysts say that since we cannot know for certain what Soviet intentions are, we must plan our military forces and strategies as if we knew that the Soviets planned to use all of their weapons. While this might appear to have the benefit of prudence, it leads to a major problem. When we ask only what the Soviets *can* do, we quickly come to assume that that is what they *intend* to do. We base our planning on "worst-case scenarios" and then come to believe that we live in a world where vast resources must be committed to "prevent" them from happening.

Since underlying rationales are rarely discussed in the everyday business of defense planning, I had to start asking more questions. At first, although I was tempted to use my newly acquired proficiency in

---

[40]The "strategic triad" refers to the three different modes of basing nuclear warheads: at land, on intercontinental ballistic missiles; at sea, on missiles in submarines; and "in the air," on the Strategic Air Command's bombers. Given that nuclear weapons based on submarines are "invulnerable" (i.e., not subject to attack), since there is not now nor in the foreseeable future any reliable way to find and target submarines, many commentators (mostly from outside the community of defense intellectuals) have suggested that the Navy's leg of the triad is all we need to ensure a capacity to retaliate against a nuclear attack. This suggestion that submarine-based missiles are an adequate deterrent becomes especially appealing when it is remembered that the other basing modes—ICBMs and bombers—act as targets that would draw thousands of nuclear attacks to the American mainland in time of war.

technostrategic jargon, I vowed to speak English. I had long believed that one of the most important functions of an expert language is exclusion—the denial of a voice to those outside the professional community.[41] I wanted to see whether a well-informed person could speak English and still carry on a knowledgeable conversation.

What I found was that no matter how well-informed or complex my questions were, if I spoke English rather than expert jargon, the men responded to me as though I were ignorant, simpleminded, or both. It did not appear to occur to anyone that I might actually be choosing not to speak their language.

A strong distaste for being patronized and dismissed made my experiment in English short-lived. I adapted my everyday speech to the vocabulary of strategic analysis. I spoke of "escalation dominance," "preemptive strikes," and, one of my favorites, "subholocaust engagements." Using the right phrases opened my way into long, elaborate discussions that taught me a lot about technostrategic reasoning and how to manipulate it.

I found, however, that the better I got at engaging in this discourse, the more impossible it became for me to express my own ideas, my own values. I could adopt the language and gain a wealth of new concepts and reasoning strategies—but at the same time as the language gave me access to things I had been unable to speak about before, it radically excluded others. I could not use the language to express my concerns because it was physically impossible. This language does not allow certain questions to be asked or certain values to be expressed.

To pick a bald example: the word "peace" is not a part of this discourse. As close as one can come is "strategic stability," a term that refers to a balance of numbers and types of weapons systems—not the political, social, economic, and psychological conditions implied by the word "peace." Not only is there no word signifying peace in this discourse, but the word "peace" itself cannot be used. To speak it is immediately to brand oneself as a soft-headed activist instead of an expert, a professional to be taken seriously.

If I was unable to speak my concerns in this language, more disturbing still was that I found it hard even to keep them in my own head. I had begun my research expecting abstract and sanitized discussions of nuclear war and had readied myself to replace my words for theirs, to be ever vigilant against slipping into the never-never land of abstraction. But no matter how prepared I was, no matter how firm my commitment to staying aware of the reality behind the words, over and

---

[41]For an interesting recent discussion of the role of language in the creation of professional power, see JoAnne Brown, "Professional Language: Words That Succeed," *Radical History Review*, No. 34 (1986) pp. 33–51.

over I found that I could not stay connected, could not keep human lives as my reference point. I found I could go for days speaking about nuclear weapons without once thinking about the people who would be incinerated by them.

It is tempting to attribute this problem to qualities of the language, the words themselves—the abstractness, the euphemisms, the sanitized, friendly, sexy acronyms. Then all we would need to do is change the words, make them more vivid, get the military planners to say "mass murder" instead of "collateral damage" and their thinking would change.

The problem, however, is not only that defense intellectuals use abstract terminology that removes them from the realities of which they speak. There *is* no reality of which they speak. Or, rather, the "reality" of which they speak is itself a world of abstractions. Deterrence theory, and much of strategic doctrine altogether, was invented largely by mathematicians, economists, and a few political scientists. It was invented to hold together abstractly, its validity judged by its internal logic. Questions of the correspondence to observable reality were not the issue. These abstract systems were developed as a way to make it possible to "think about the unthinkable"—not as a way to describe or codify relations on the ground.[42]

So the greatest problem with the idea of "limited nuclear war," for example, is not that it is grotesque to refer to the death and suffering caused by *any* use of nuclear weapons as "limited", or that "limited nuclear war" is an abstraction that is disconnected from human reality but, rather, that "limited nuclear war" is itself an abstract conceptual system, designed, embodied, achieved by computer modeling. It is an abstract world in which hypothetical, calm, rational actors have sufficient information to know exactly what size nuclear weapon the opponent has used against which targets, and in which they have adequate command and control to make sure that their response is precisely equilibrated to the attack. In this scenario, no field commander would use the tactical "mini-nukes" at his disposal in the height of a losing battle; no EMP-generated electronic failures, or direct attacks on command and control centers, or human errors would destroy communications networks. Our rational actors would be free of emotional response to being attacked, free of political pressures from the populace, free from madness or despair or any of the myriad other factors that regularly affect human actions and decision-making. They would act solely on the basis of a perfectly informed mathematical calculus of megatonnage.

---

[42]For fascinating, detailed accounts of the development of strategic doctrine, see Fred Kaplan, *The Wizards of Armageddon* (New York: Simon & Schuster, 1983) and Gregg F. Herken, *The Counsels of War* (New York: Alfred A. Knopf, 1985).

So to refer to "limited nuclear war" is already to enter into a system that is de facto abstract and removed from reality. To use more descriptive language would not, by itself, change that. In fact, I am tempted to say that the abstractness of the entire conceptual system makes descriptive language nearly beside the point. In a discussion of "limited nuclear war," for example, it might make some difference if in place of saying, "In a counter-force attack against hard targets collateral damage could be limited," a strategic analyst had to use words that were less abstract—if he had to say, for instance, "If we launch the missiles we have aimed at their missile silos, the explosions would cause the immediate mass murder of 10 million women, men, and children, as well as the extended illness, suffering, and eventual death of many millions more." It is true that the second sentence does not roll off the tongue or slide across one's consciousness quite as easily. But it is also true, I believe, that the ability to speak about "limited nuclear war" stems as much, if not more, from the fact that the term "limited nuclear war" refers to an abstract conceptual system rather than to events that might take place in the real world. As such, there is no need to think about the concrete human realities behind the model; what counts is the internal logic of the system.[43]

This realization that the abstraction was not just in the words but also characterized the entire conceptual system itself helped me make sense of my difficulty in staying connected to human lives. But there was still a piece missing. How is it possible, for example, to make sense of the following paragraph? It is taken from a discussion of a scenario ("regime A") in which the United States and the USSR have revised their offensive weaponry, banned MIRVs, and gone to a regime of single warhead (Midgetman) missiles, with no "defensive shield" (or what is familiarly known as "Star Wars" or SDI):

> The strategic stability of regime A is based on the fact that both sides are deprived of any incentive ever to strike first. Since it takes roughly two warheads to destroy one enemy silo, an attacker must expend two of his missiles to destroy one of the enemy's. A first strike disarms the attacker. The aggressor ends up worse off than the aggressed.[44]

---

[43]Steven Kull's interviews with nuclear strategists can be read to show that on some level, some of the time, some of these men are aware that there is a serious disjunction between their models and the real world. Their justification for continuing to use these models is that "other people" (unnamed, and on asking, unnameable) believe in them and that they therefore have an important reality ["Nuclear Nonsense," *Foreign Policy*, No. 58 (Spring 1985), pp. 28–52].

[44]Charles Krauthammer, "Will Star Wars Kill Arms Control?" *New Republic*, No. 3, 653 (21 January 1985) pp. 12–16.

"The aggressor ends up worse off than the aggressed"? The homeland of "the aggressed" has just been devastated by the explosions of, say, a thousand nuclear bombs, each likely to be ten to one hundred times more powerful than the bomb dropped on Hiroshima, and the aggressor, whose homeland is still untouched, "ends up worse off"? How is it possible to think this? Even abstract language and abstract thinking do not seem to be a sufficient explanation.

I was only able to "make sense of it" when I finally asked myself the question that feminists have been asking about theories in every discipline: What is the reference point? Who (or what) is the *subject* here?

In other disciplines, we have frequently found that the reference point for theories about "universal human phenomena" has actually been white men. In technostrategic discourse, the reference point is not white men, it is not human beings at all; it is the weapons themselves. The aggressor thus ends up worse off than the aggressed because he has fewer weapons left; human factors are irrelevant to the calculus of gain and loss.

In "regime A" and throughout strategic discourse, the concept of "incentive" is similarly distorted by the fact that weapons are the subjects of strategic paradigms. Incentive to strike first is present or absent according to a mathematical calculus of numbers of "surviving" weapons. That is, incentive to start a nuclear war is discussed not in terms of what possible military or political ends it might serve but, instead, in terms of numbers of weapons, with the goal being to make sure that you are the guy who still has the most left at the end. Hence, it is frequently stated that MIRVed missiles create strategic instability because they "give you the incentive to strike first." Calculating that two warheads must be targeted on each enemy missile, one MIRVed missile with ten warheads would, in theory, be able to destroy five enemy missiles in their silos; you destroy more of theirs than you have expended of your own. You win the numbers game. In addition, if you do not strike first, it would theoretically take relatively few of their MIRVed missiles to destroy a larger number of your own—so you must, as they say in the business, "use 'em or lose 'em." Many strategic analysts fear that in a period of escalating political tensions, when it begins to look as though war may be inevitable, this combination makes "the incentive to strike first" well nigh irresistible.

Incentive to launch a nuclear war arises from a particular configuration of weapons and their hypothetical mathematical interaction. Incentive can only be so narrowly defined because the referents of technostrategic paradigms are weapons—not human lives, not even states and state power.

The fact that the subjects of strategic paradigms are weapons has several important implications. First, and perhaps most critically, there simply is no way to talk about human death or human societies when you are using a language designed to talk about weapons. Human death simply *is* "collateral damage" — collateral to the real subject, which is the weapons themselves.

Second, if human lives are not the reference point, then it is not only impossible to talk about humans in this language, it also becomes in some sense illegitimate to ask the paradigm to reflect human concerns. Hence, questions that break through the numbing language of strategic analysis and raise issues in human terms can be dismissed easily. No one will claim that the questions are unimportant, but they are inexpert, unprofessional, irrelevant to the business at hand to ask. The discourse among the experts remains hermetically sealed.

The problem, then, is not only that the language is narrow but also that it is seen by its speakers as complete or whole unto itself — as representing a body of truths that exist independently of any other truth or knowledge. The isolation of this technical knowledge from social or psychological or moral thought, or feelings, is all seen as legitimate and necessary. The outcome is that defense intellectuals can talk about the weapons that are supposed to protect particular political entities, particular peoples and their way of life, without actually asking if weapons *can* do it, or if they are the best *way* to do it, or whether they may even damage the entities you are supposedly protecting. It is not that the men I spoke with would say that these are invalid questions. They would, however, simply say that they are separate questions, questions that are outside what they do, outside their realm of expertise. So their deliberations go on quite independently, as though with a life of their own, disconnected from the functions and values they are supposedly to serve.

Finally, the third problem is that this discourse has become virtually the only legitimate form of response to the question of how to achieve security. If the language of weaponry was one competing voice in the discussion, or one that was integrated with others, the fact that the referents of strategic paradigms are only weapons would be of little note. But when we realize that the only language and expertise offered to those interested in pursuing peace refers to nothing but weapons, its limits become staggering, and its entrapping qualities — the way in which, once you adopt it, it becomes so hard to stay connected to human concerns — become more comprehensible.

STAGE 4: THE TERROR

As a newcomer to the world of defense analysts, I was continually startled by likeable and admirable men, by their gallows humor, by the bloodcurdling casualness with which they regularly blew up the world while standing and chatting over the coffee pot. I also *heard* the language they spoke—heard the acronyms and euphemisms and abstractions, heard the imagery, heard the pleasure with which they used it.

Within a few weeks, what had once been remarkable became unnoticeable. As I learned to speak, my perspective changed. I no longer stood outside the impermeable wall of technostrategic language and, once inside, I could no longer see it. Speaking the language, I could no longer really hear it. And once inside its protective walls, I began to find it difficult to get out. The impermeability worked both ways.

I had not only learned to speak a language: I had started to think in it. Its questions became my questions, its concepts shaped my responses to new ideas. Its definitions of the parameters of reality became mine. Like the White Queen, I began to believe six impossible things before breakfast. Not because I consciously believed, for instance, that a "surgically clean counterforce strike" was really possible, but instead because some elaborate piece of doctrinal reasoning I used was already predicated on the possibility of those strikes, as well as on a host of other impossible things.[45]

My grasp on what *I* knew as reality seemed to slip. I might get very excited, for example, about a new strategic justification for a "no first use" policy and spend time discussing the ways in which its implications for our force structure in Western Europe were superior to the old versions.[46] And after a day or two I would suddenly step back, aghast that I was so involved with the military justifications for not using nuclear weapons—as though the moral ones were not enough. What I was actually talking about—the mass incineration caused by a nuclear attack—was no longer in my head.

Or I might hear some proposals that seemed to me infinitely superior to the usual arms control fare. First I would work out how and why these proposals were better and then work out all the ways to counter the arguments against them. But then, it might dawn on me that even though these two proposals sounded so different, they still shared a host of assumptions that I was not willing to make (e.g., about the inevitable, eternal conflict of interests between the United States and the USSR, or the desirability of having some form of nuclear deterrent, or

---

[45]For an excellent discussion of the myriad uncertainties that make it ludicrous to assume the targeting accuracies posited in the notion of "surgically clean counterforce strikes," see Fallows (n. 11 above), chap 6.

[46]"No first use" refers to the commitment not to be the first side to introduce nuclear weapons into a "conventional" war. The Soviet Union has a "no first use" policy, but the United States does not. In fact, it is NATO doctrine to use nuclear weapons in a conventional war in Western Europe, as a way of overcoming the Warsaw Pact's supposed superiority in conventional weaponry and troop strength.

the goal of "managing," rather than ending, the nuclear arms race). After struggling to this point of seeing what united both positions, I would first feel as though I had really accomplished something. And then all of a sudden, I would realize that these new insights were things I actually knew *before I ever entered* this community. Apparently, I had since forgotten them, at least functionally, if not absolutely.

I began to feel that I had fallen down the rabbit hole—and it was a struggle to climb back out.

CONCLUSIONS

Suffice it to say that the issues about language do not disappear after you have mastered technostrategic discourse. The seductions remain great. You can find all sorts of ways to seemingly beat the boys at their own game; you can show how even within their own definitions of rationality, most of what is happening in the development and deployment of nuclear forces is wildly irrational. You can also impress your friends and colleagues with sickly humorous stories about the way things really happen on the inside. There is tremendous pleasure in it, especially for those of us who have been closed out, who have been told that it is really all beyond us and we should just leave it to the benevolently paternal men in charge.

But as the pleasures deepen, so do the dangers. The activity of trying to out-reason defense intellectuals in their own games gets you thinking inside their rules, tacitly accepting all the unspoken assumptions of their paradigms. You become subject to the tyranny of concepts. The language shapes your categories of thought (e.g., here it becomes "good nukes" or "bad nukes," not, nukes or no nukes) and defines the boundaries of imagination (as you try to imagine a "minimally destabilizing basing mode" rather than a way to prevent the weapon from being deployed at all).

Yet, the issues of language have now become somewhat less vivid and central to me. Some of the questions raised by the experiences described here remain important, but others have faded and been superseded by new questions. These, while still not precisely the questions of an "insider," are questions I could not have had without being inside, without having access to the knowledge and perspective the inside position affords. Many of my questions now are more practical—which individuals and institutions are actually responsible for the endless "modernization" and proliferation of nuclear weaponry? What role does technostrategic rationality actually play in their thinking? What would a reasonable, genuinely defensive "defense" policy look like? Others are more philosophical. What is the nature of the rationality and "realism" claimed by defense intellectuals for their mode of thinking? What are the many different grounds on which their claims to rationality can be shown to be spurious?

My own move away from a focus on the language is quite typical. Other recent entrants into this world have commented to me that, while it is the cold-blooded, abstract discussions that are most striking at first, within a short time "you get past it—you stop hearing it, it stops bothering you, it becomes normal—and you come to see that the language, itself, is not the problem."

However, I think it would be a mistake to dismiss these early impressions. They can help us learn something about the militarization of the mind, and they have, I believe, important implications for feminist scholars and activists who seek to create a more just and peaceful world.

Mechanisms of the mind's militarization are revealed through both listening to the language and learning to speak it. *Listening*, it becomes clear that participation in the world of nuclear strategic analysis does not necessarily require confrontation with the central fact about military activity—that the purpose of all weaponry and all strategy is to injure human bodies.[47] In fact, as Elaine Scarry points out, participation in military thinking does not require confrontation with, and actual demands the elision of, this reality.[48]

Listening to the discourse of nuclear experts reveals a series of culturally grounded and culturally acceptable mechanisms that serve this purpose and that make it possible to "think about the unthinkable," to work in institutions that foster the proliferation of nuclear weapons, to plan mass incinerations of millions of human beings for a living. Language that is abstract, sanitized, full of euphemisms; language that is sexy and fun to use; paradigms whose referent is weapons; imagery that domesticates and deflates the forces of mass destruction; imagery that reverses sentient and nonsentient matter, that conflates birth and death, destruction and creation—all of these are part of what makes it possible to be radically removed from the reality of what one is talking about and from the realities one is creating through the discourse.[49]

---

[47]For an eloquent and graphic exploration of this point, see Scarry (n. 23 above) p. 73.
[48]Scarry catalogs a variety of mechanisms that serve this purpose (ibid., pp. 60–157). The point is further developed by Sara Ruddick, "The Rationality of Care," in Jean Bethke Elshtain and Sheila Tobias (eds.), *Thinking about Women, War, and the Military* (Totowa, N.J.: Rowman & Allanheld, in press).
[49]My discussion of the specific ways in which this discourse creates new realities is in the next part of this project, entitled, "The Emperor's New Armor." I, like many other social scientists, have been influenced by poststructuralist literary theory's discussion of deconstructing texts, point of view, and narrative authority within texts, and I take the

Learning to speak the language reveals something about how thinking can become more abstract, more focused on parts disembedded from their context, more attentive to the survival of weapons than the survival of human beings. That is, it reveals something about the process of militarization—and the way in which that process may be undergone by man or woman, hawk or dove.

Most often, the act of learning technostrategic language is conceived of as an additive process: you add a new set of vocabulary words; you add the reflex ability to decode and use endless numbers of acronyms; you add some new information that the specialized language contains; you add the conceptual tools that will allow you to "think strategically." This additive view appears to be held by defense intellectuals themselves; as one said to me, "Much of the debate is in technical terms— learn it, and decide whether it's relevant later." This view also appears to be held by many who think of themselves as anti-nuclear, be they scholars and professionals attempting to change the field from within, or public interest lobbyists and educational organizations, or some feminist antimilitarists.[50] Some believe that our nuclear policies are so riddled with irrationality that there is a lot of room for well-reasoned, well-informed arguments to make a difference; others, even if they do not believe that the technical information is very important, see it as necessary to master the language simply because it is too difficult to attain public legitimacy without it. In either case, the idea is that you add the expert language and information and proceed from there.

However, I have been arguing throughout this paper that learning the language is a transformative, rather than an additive, process. When you choose to learn it you enter a new mode of thinking—a mode of thinking not only about nuclear weapons but also, de facto, about military and political power and about the relationship between human ends and technological means.

Thus, those of us who find US nuclear policy desperately misguided appear to face a serious quandary. If we refuse to learn the language, we are virtually guaranteed that our voices will remain outside the "politically relevant" spectrum of opinion. Yet, if we do learn and speak it, we

language and social practice of the defense intellectuals as a text to be read in this way. For a classic introduction to this literature, see Josue Harari, (ed.), *Textual Strategies: Perspectives in Post-structuralist Criticism* (Ithaca, N.Y.: Cornell University Press, 1979) and Jacques Derrida, *Of Grammatology* (Baltimore: Johns Hopkins University Press, 1976).

[50]Perhaps the most prominent feminist proponent of this strategy is Sheila Tobias, see, e.g., "Demystifying Defense: Closing the Knowledge Gap," *Social Policy*, Vol. 13, No. 3 (1983) pp. 29–32 and Sheila Tobias, Peter Goudinoff, Stefan Leader, and Shelah Leader, *What Kinds of Guns Are They Buying for Your Butter?* (New York: William Morrow & Co., 1982).

not only severely limit what we can say but we also invite the transformation, the militarization, of our own thinking.

I have no solutions to this dilemma, but I would like to offer a few thoughts in an effort to reformulate its terms. First, it is important to recognize an assumption implicit in adopting the strategy of learning the language. When we assume that learning and speaking the language will give us a voice recognized as legitimate and will give us greater political influence, *we are assuming that the language itself actually articulates the criteria and reasoning strategies upon which nuclear weapons development and deployment decisions are made.* I believe that this is largely an illusion. Instead, I want to suggest that technostrategic discourse functions more as a gloss, as an ideological curtain behind which the actual reasons for these decisions hide. That rather than informing and shaping decisions, it far more often functions as a legitimation for political outcomes that have occurred for utterly different reasons. If this is true, it raises some serious questions about the extent of the political returns we might get from using technostrategic discourse, and whether they can ever balance out the potential problems and inherent costs.

I do not, however, want to suggest that none of us should learn the language. I do not believe that this language is well suited to achieving the goals desired by antimilitarists, yet at the same time, I, for one, have found the experience of learning the language useful and worthwhile (even if at times traumatic). The question for those of us who do choose to learn it, I think, is what use are we going to make of that knowledge?

One of the most intriguing options opened by learning the language is that it suggests a basis upon which to challenge the legitimacy of the defense intellectuals' dominance of the discourse on nuclear issues. When defense intellectuals are criticized for the cold-blooded inhumanity of the scenarios they plan, their response is to claim the high ground of rationality; they are the only ones whose response to the existence of nuclear weapons is objective and realistic. They portray those who are radically opposed to the nuclear status quo as irrational, unrealistic, too emotional. "Idealistic activists" is the pejorative they set against their own hard-nosed professionalism.

Much of their claim to legitimacy, then, is a claim to objectivity born of technical expertise and to the disciplined purging of the emotional valences that might threaten their objectivity. But if the surface of their discourse—its abstraction and technical jargon—appears at first to support these claims, a look just below the surface does not. There we find currents of homoerotic excitement, heterosexual domination, the drive toward competency and mastery, the pleasures of membership in an elite and privileged group, the ultimate importance and meaning of membership in the priesthood, and the thrilling power of becoming

Death, shatterer of worlds. How is it possible to hold this up as a paragon of cool-headed objectivity?

I do not wish here to discuss or judge the holding of "objectivity" as an epistemological goal. I would simply point out that, as defense intellectuals rest their claims to legitimacy on the untainted rationality of their discourse, their project fails according to its own criteria. Deconstructing strategic discourse's claims to rationality is, then, in and of itself, an important way to challenge its hegemony as the sole legitimate language for public debate about nuclear policy.

I believe that feminists, and others who seek a more just and peaceful world, have a dual task before us—a deconstructive project and a reconstructive project that are intimately linked.[51] Our deconstructive task requires close attention to, and the dismantling of, technostrategic discourse. The dominant voice of militarized masculinity and decontextualized rationality speaks so loudly in our culture, it will remain difficult for any other voices to be heard until that voice loses some of its power to define what we hear and how we name the world—until that voice is delegitimated.

Our reconstructive task is a task of creating compelling alternative visions of possible futures, a task of recognizing and developing alternative conceptions of rationality, a task of creating rich and imaginative alternative voices—diverse voices whose conversations with each other will invent those futures.

---

[51]Harding and Hintikka (eds.) (n. 5 above), pp. ix–xix, esp. p. x.

Part 4

FEMINIST ANTI-NUCLEAR ACTIONS

Instead of teaching "you can win and be a hero in the face of over-whelming odds," the one hundredth monkey theory suggests that "your contribution just might be the crucial link". — Fran Peavey, *Heart Politics* (1986).

13

With Mourning, Rage, Empowerment and Defiance: The 1981 Women's Pentagon Action*

Rhoda Linton
Michele Whitham

On 15 and 16 November 1981, 3500 women gathered in Washington, DC to express their fear, their sorrow and their hope to the warlords of the Pentagon. In a two-day ritual, intricately woven into a symbolic whole, these women poured themselves into their message: ". . . we fear for our lives, we fear for the life of this planet, our Earth, and the life of the children who are our human future . . . we fear for our lives, we fear for the life of this planet, our Earth, and the life of the children who are our human future . . . life on the precipice is intolerable . . . we will not allow these violent games to continue . . ."

For Rhoda Linton, one of the thousands of women present at the ceremony, the 1981 Women's Pentagon Action was a logical moment in a twenty-year political involvement that began when she graduated from college in the late fifties, and culminated with her commitment to grassroots organizing in the sixties, particularly in her four years with the National Welfare Rights Organization. Yet despite a committed and politically active career, Rhoda found herself by the early 1970s search-

*Previously published in *Socialist Review*, Vol. 12 (1982).

ing for a way of making her own life the subject of the struggle. She returned to her home town, a rural community in upstate New York, built a house and became actively involved in organizing activities with the people there. Gradually her life and work came together in the women's movement, and today she is working as a PhD candidate at Cornell University to define a feminist research methodology, with a particular focus in the area of women and criminal justice.

It was out of this extensive history as an organizer that Rhoda arrived at the 1981 Women's Pentagon Action. She came experienced as a participant in and planner of mass demonstrations, seeking little more than the usual opportunity "to stand and declare." What she experienced, however, was an event so powerfully different in its approach to mass political action that she found herself seized by its inventiveness, compelled to try to conceptualize and articulate precisely what it was that made this demonstration so "different" in its approach and its impact on her.

On a rainy day in late March 1982, Rhoda sat with Michele Whitham to relate her experience of the Women's Pentagon Action and to undertake an analysis of its unique "demonstration-ology." Rhoda chose Michele as her collaborator in this effort because of their eight-year friendship, their mutual commitment to social justice and the women's movement, and Michele's professional experience as a Freirian educator and writer on the subject of women's empowerment. What follows, then, is a conversation between two women, friends, sisters, comrades. It is an interaction—not a formal interview— organized around one woman's interpretation of the events of the Women's Pentagon Action, another's spontaneous response and analysis.

THE CONVERSATION

I'd like to start out by talking about what my reasons were for going to the Women's Pentagon Action last November. When Reagan was elected, right directly following that election and before he really took office, I remember talking with friends of mine and saying, "This is a shock to have this actually happening, and the next four years aren't going to be a good time for any kind of social programs. It's going to be a time when we have to hold the line, to try to protect what we have won. There are going to be a lot of times when we are going to have to stand and declare—who we are and what we believe in."

Give witness.

Give witness. And so the reason that I ended up going to the Pentagon Action was because I felt that need to stand and declare. It took a whole year for me to find this place to do it. It wasn't that I was waiting for this particular event, but when I first heard about this demonstration, I heard about it as women against the military. Although I didn't feel that the military was my particular thing, I am very heavily committed to the women's movement and to women. So I saw this as something that I could be connected to that made a statement to the Reagan administration, and as something larger than my personal life and my individual being here in Ithaca.

Did you go into it with any affiliation at all with the nuclear aspect of the demonstration?

No. I had no connection whatsoever to the nuclear issue other than being aware of what is happening in the world. I just decided that this was the time and the place for me to do this and I was going to go. So I went alone in that respect, feeling that it was important to go and be part of something larger, not necessarily my own thing. I didn't really know anything about the sponsoring group, the planning process or any of that. I just had a compelling need to stand and declare.

To stand with other women.

What I didn't realize, however, at the time that I made this decision to go, was that I was about to experience something that was to have a more far-reaching effect on my life and thinking than any of the many other public, mass demonstrations that I have participated in over the last seventeen years. In fact, the Women's Pentagon Action was to be tremendously powerful for me, and it has been very important to me in the months since then to understand why. What I have come to believe through this reflection on the experience is that the Action was so compelling, not by accident, but because it revealed a new dimension of "demonstrationology," a different methodololgy. The major significance of this demonstration for me was the power that it had—through its carefully thought-out elements and process—to simultaneously reflect, reinforce and create anew personal and political consciousness. I believe the Women's Pentagon Action represents a methodology significantly different from our "old ways" and from all I have heard about such recent demonstrations as Solidarity Day and El Salvador. So I'd like to describe here the events as they took place and suggest the methodological significance I saw in the demonstration.

When we arrived in Washington, the first thing that struck me as being very different about this demonstration was that it was a two-day action and that one of the days was a Preparation. I think that derives from women's experience in that women are always involved in the preparation of what is to come.

The kneading, before the baking.

Right. And the baking before the eating. Whereas men have tradition-ally come and sat down at the table to eat, and that's their experience of how the world works. Women have the experience of preparing.

It also seems to me that women would not make major decisions easily for other people. The fact that you don't have a clear sense of who the original planners of the demonstration were seems significant to me. And the fact that everyone came together by design a day early to do that with each other seems significant.

This preparation took place in Washington's Colosseum. The Colos-seum, from an organizer's point of view, is a terrible place to have such an event. It is a huge, cold, gigantic place, and so it was only a quarter to a third full of people once you got inside. Still, people were arriving from all over and there was a sense of excitement that could be felt even in this place. Indeed, there was an air of festivity and the planning was in fact billed as a Women's Festival.

So the planning was a celebration!

Yes, that was how I experienced the intent of it. On the way into the Colosseum, in the entryway, there were many, many tables and everything was jam-packed in there with people selling their buttons and their T-shirts and their albums. And everyone who had some cause or some women's issue to support from all different parts of the country was there handing out their literature and so forth.

It sounds like a fair.

There was free water to drink. Somebody was selling cider. Somebody selling a little bit of food. People in charge of making child care arrangements. People saying what they needed. Other people declaring what they were willing to do. People bringing food that they had brought to contribute to the soup kitchen that was going to be in one of the churches so that people who didn't have money wouldn't be prevented from coming, because there would be a place where they could eat. In fact, the forty women that I had ridden down on the bus with had recruited a lot of food, and people who couldn't go participated by donating to the support of the demonstrators. Maybe that's a different type of "affinity group."

As we entered into this celebration, one of the most impressive things that happened, and one of the things that altered me to the fact that there was definitely something different about the approach that was being taken in this mass demonstration, was that people were being given name tags. Receiving a name tag was an extremely amazing experience to go through at an event of this size, and to think about as an organizer. When I was involved in organizing mass demonstrations in the past, name tags were not even considered as far as I can remember. Yet as I think back, people spontaneously made all kinds of efforts to identify themselves with buttons, banners, placards and who knows what else. Still, for organizers, in a mass demonstration, the purpose was to produce bodies, not to produce individuals. It wasn't important who each person was. It was important that there were a lot of someones there.

It was the total collective force that mattered?

Right. In those demonstrations, people participated as part of a mass. When people went back home to their smaller cities and towns, that mass was gone. They could only reconstruct such events in miniature, without the power or effect. The effect of those mass demonstrations for people afterwards was mainly when you met someone else who had been there, too. The continuing power of those particular events was on a personal basis. The experience had not necessarily become a very significant model or learning event for what anyone would then do at home.

Are you suggesting that being part of the mass somehow absolves individuals of their personal responsibility of becoming committed?

It may be that or it may be being committed in a certain way.

To take individual responsibility for carrying through.

The mass demonstrations are such media events. I don't mean to trivialize them, but they become participatory events that come and go as opposed to something that comes and stays with you and makes a change in you that helps you to do something in your regular life.

So your identity around the event has to do with being part of the mass rather than bringing your identity to it.

Right. That was my experience of the past. Other people may have had other experiences of that. But this time it was different; this time we had name tags. Everyone wore a name tag.

In this huge crowd of people.

In this huge crowd of people. Now, the name tag wasn't some little piece of cardboard enclosed in plastic that no one could ever see. It was an $8\frac{1}{2} \times 11$ piece of paper from a yellow pad, cut in two, that you pinned on yourself with a straight pin. But the powerful part of it was that on the name tag everyone was already supplied with a last name, to which you added your own first name. There were only two last names given to people: one was Silkwood and one was Ward. So every single one of us belonged to either the Silkwood family or the Ward family. That single, tiny little piece of methodology was incredible in terms of what it produced—the unity of that crowd. The unity of those masses was incredible, to say nothing about what the name tags meant in terms of consciousness raising for people. If people who came there did not know who Karen Silkwood was, or did not know who Yolanda Ward was, then they certainly knew it very quickly. And there wasn't any mass announcement of that. Identity was what people talked to each other about: "Who am I?" "Who does this mean I am?" And the fact that one was a white woman and one was a black woman had a further impact on who we were as a crowd. So right off the bat, as far as I was concerned, something very different was going on.

It's interesting, because on the one hand you have the individualization of name tags and on the other hand you have the coming together as Everywoman in the creation of those two family groupings.

Yes, and there was also the further implication—which was to become one of the messages of the whole demonstration—that these were women who were victims of violence within the system, a reality which the women coming to the Pentagon could identify with. The further strength of the Silkwood-Ward symbolism came from the fact that one of the deaths was caused by acts of the corporate world and the other by an act of political violence directed at a black urban organizer. Being suddenly made to identify with these two women struck an incredible message. I just want to mention two more things about this preparation phase that happened at the Colosseum. When we went inside, one of the things people had been asked to bring from home (more preparation at an earlier stage) were pieces of fabric to join together in a braid that was going to be used in one of the phases of the demonstration, the encirclement of the Pentagon. I had heard that that was going to be done and that people were bringing scarves and anything like that that they wanted to bring. So I collected some things from my mother to take along with my own so that there would be some kind of weaving of generations in the braid. Other people had interpreted the instruction in different ways, and they had gone out and sought donations of ends of fabrics so that there were huge piles of fabric lying on the floor in the middle of the Colosseum. As women felt the urge, they went and participated in making this braid even as other people were doing different things all around. I went and wove for awhile, working with women from everywhere, none of whom I knew, tearing pieces of fabric, tying them together and then rolling them up on a piece of cardboard so that they could be ready to take with us the next day. All of that was happening as a result of the energy of the people who came there. It wasn't done by a certain chosen number of people. Everybody brought the ingredients and worked on it and put it together. While this was happening, women who could do things like song leading would get up from time to time and lead a little singing, and people learned different songs that they might not have known before. The music of Holly Near and Cris Williamson and Meg Christian were prominent among those, along with some of the older civil rights songs. In the midst of one of these times when song leading was going on, the song leaders introduced a woman from El Salvador to sing for the group of the struggle in her land, providing a link to a different part of the world. There were also telegrams read from women in other parts of the world. And people were recognized from England and I can't remember where else. All this lent a growing realization that we are not in this alone. The anti-militarism movement is larger than ourselves and our own communities and our own country.

An international movement.

Right. But I think that the most powerful part of that preparation stage for me was the preparation of the materials that were going to be used in the first part of the demonstration at the Pentagon itself on the next day, the mourning phase, namely the preparation of tombstones. Many tombstone shapes had been prepared beforehand out of cardboard. Then, during the preparation period, women were asked to come forward and, with a crude sort of old brush and a paper cup full of black tempera paint, to paint their messages on the blank tombstones commemorating women they had personally known who had died as a result of various types of violence and oppression within our system. People were specifically asked not to commemorate historic figures or national figures, but to put something from their own experience. And so in a wide space on the floor, there were all of these women in all different steps of this process. Some people were just painting the tombstones gray. Other people were writing their messages. Some were putting on very fancy things; others were doing very simple things. Being there was like walking through a cemetery. Of course what happened was that people's personal experiences, when they were put out into the public arena side by side, showed fantastic patterns of similarity. So again it was a way of showing the individual as part of the collective without losing her individuality.

And also of discerning the larger meanings of the events in individual lives.

Exactly. Exactly. When I went through and I saw . . . I was stunned by it. One young woman had written: "Mary Louise, my college roommate. Beaten, raped and killed. May 21, 1981. Rochester, New Hampshire." And from Virginia, and again from a small town in Indiana. On and on. And those women who may have, up until that point, experienced that as a personal thing, could go through that cemetery and see that theirs were not isolated incidents. This is violence against women in this society that is accepted. And what a small representation we are, yet look at what has happened to every one of us in our lives. I saw one which said, I don't remember the name, but it said "My Grandmother died of a self-induced abortion in 1932." I saw another one which said a woman's name and then "My Mother. Died of an illegal abortion in 1964." And into my mind came the image of a woman who was raised with no mother. Her mother must have died at a very young age. And on and on. And there were signs which may have been prepared beforehand which were for the women of Chile. I wrote one for the women in Northern Ireland because I had been at the peace march there in 1977. There were others like mine, but by far the majority were of people's personal experience.

Here in America.

Yes. The one that just wiped me out to the point where I couldn't even stay there any more—and it makes me cry to say on this day four months later—was one which was very crudely written. After I read it, I just stood there and looked at it, imagining the woman who had written it.

She said: "Three unknown Vietnamese women," and underneath that she had written, "Killed by my son."

Dear God.

It was unbelievable. To think about the consciousness of that woman and where she's been and what that meant. It's amazing. To think of the impact that that had on not only that woman, but also all the women who were there to read it. Many of the younger women don't have an experience of the Vietnamese war.

But can learn to identify with it through these personal experiences. The ability, the power of that single activity to capture all of history for each woman is really astonishing to think about.

It was personalizing the world. I was very conscious of the interconnections and of moving back and forth from being an individual to being part of a huge piece of the world. It's nothing like the kind of feeling that I got from the demonstrations that I participated in in the past. I'm not trying to put those down; I'm simply trying to show the way that this was different. In the past it seemed as though we limited what we could experience through our political actions by limiting ourselves in time and space, by designing short-term events that focused only on themselves, on their own moment.

And by surrendering ourselves to the mass also. How can you experience if you're not there as an entity?

Right. Not to be someone who contributes my piece and sees what everybody else's piece is, but limiting ourselves to the words of selected individuals who "represent" us or who somehow lend legitimacy to us because of who they are, not because of who we are.

At many of those demonstrations, others spoke for us.

Right

I'm really understanding the power of the planning together now, because in planning for someone you conceptualize the experience for them. You do the thinking and the interpreting.

You take away from their opportunity to create themselves.

To name their own reality.

Exactly. Yes, it's different. I just keep coming back and saying it's definitely different.

Was there conscious discussion of that? Did people say things to each other about this difference as it was happening?

Standing together and looking at each other, a shaking of the head, tears coming down, saying "Did you see this or that?" That type of communication. I didn't feel that there was an abstraction of it. Not for me.

You used the word "alone." And yet it sounds to me as if you were very much not alone.

I was alone in terms of not being with one or two other people or a group of people that I knew.

But not alone in terms of the power of the identification that you were feeling.

No. Not at all.

The next part of the demonstration was on the same day, Sunday: the march to the Air and Space Museum. In preparation for moving out from the Colosseum we had our first view of the puppets which were to be used in the main demonstration. These puppets I also considered to be part of this very different method. The puppets were papier mâché characters about six or seven feet tall which people carried on their shoulders. There were four of them, and each one embodied one of the four parts of the demonstration; mourning, rage, empowerment and defiance.

Right. These four expressions were what was going to happen on the next day. But when we went on the first march to the Air and Space Museum, it was almost like a practice march in a way, and people had their first experience of walking with the puppets, these huge heads with extremely defined characteristics symbolizing their particular stage of the demonstration. One person would carry the puppet itself and then other people would carry sort of flowing pieces of fabric or whatever else was attached to this puppet to be the rest of its being. The puppets were also used as markers as everyone was assigned to stay near a particular one. In addition to the four head puppets, there were two big white bird puppets which had long white banners that went out to the side and to the rear—really flying. The doves led everything; whenever the demonstration was going to do a different thing, those huge birds would herald the action. The total impact of these several puppets was that, although they provided structure and organization to the march, they also allowed participants to be free to move throughout the demonstration because they knew they could always find their own group back at the assigned puppet. So that whole element in a mass demonstration of losing your group, the fear of being separated from the people you came with, totally disappeared. It just was erased. The security that the puppets provided was something I felt right away. At any given time you, as one small part of this demonstration, could tell where all the other people were. The dimensions of what was happening were also clear because you knew that if you saw the birds and they were going a certain way, you were definitely going to go that way! You could keep track of the whole group quite easily. This was a very different experience for me from the demonstrations in which we used to carry eye-level banners. These puppets were sitting way up in the air and you could always see what was going on. No specific people were assigned to carry these. I saw different people trading off because they were a little bit heavy and it was quite windy. So we marched down from the Colosseum through a neighborhood which must have been northeast because we came down past the Capitol building at some distance, but you could see it, and then came on into the Air and Space Museum and the whole Constitution Avenue area. It seemed as though the neighborhood was empty, somehow. It was a very strange experience to walk through a deserted neighborhood with this group of people. It's not the kind of environment that you're accustomed to when you participate in a demonstration, which is usually planned to take place at one of the busiest times so that it commands attention.

And in a commercial or public area, too. It sounds eerie.

When we got to the Air and Space Museum, another unique aspect of this demonstration was made manifest. As the rally got underway, it became clear that there were no apparent leaders. Indeed, there were no "stars" in this entire demonstration. I could never identify from one day to the next, or from one event to the next, the same people doing whatever leading had to be done. The ritual that took place at the Air and Space Museum I don't remember as being very effective. It was a play, or an acting out of some type, but the setup was such that I and a lot of other people couldn't see or hear very well. A free sound system, which turned out not to be functioning very well, had evidently been donated to the group. The following day the group rectified that situation, which I'll tell you about later; but at this particular time people were complaining that they couldn't hear.

Do you know what the intended purpose of the march to the Air and Space Museum was?

It was to demonstrate against putting money into military spending and to testify to putting money towards human needs.

What made the Museum a particularly appropriate target for that kind of expression?

Well, it's the official museum of the space program. We can put people on the moon, but we can't feed people in this country. That's pretty oversimplified. I realize I'm sort of minimizing this part of the demonstration—it wasn't a part that meant a lot to me. To some people it might have been much more important. One thing that was very important to me there, however, was the dissension that was expressed by a black woman who apparently had been on the planning committee, or had worked on the demonstration or had otherwise had prior involvement. I had the impression that she had been involved the year before, too, in the 1980 demonstration. Almost as soon as we arrived at the Museum, an announcement was made by one of the women that a woman wanted to say something. That was when the black woman took the microphone. She talked about the fact that she felt that she had been excluded from the demonstration, excluded from the planning, that women of color had been downplayed in some way or had not been included in ways she considered important. Although all of this was very hard to hear, the sense I got from further discussion by whoever was responsible for that portion of the action, was that in the previous year's demonstration, the puppet symbolizing mourning was black and this was seen to be the weakest part of the demonstration. Therefore the black women had objected to that, and this year the mourning puppet was white. The puppet that was nearest to being black was a sort of bronze, symbolizing what the people in the demonstration considered to be the strongest expression, defiance. The speaker said that they had tried to work on this, had talked about it and had tried to make a response. She also said that if there was anything that anyone else wanted to say about this or if there was any help anyone could give to try to work on this problem so that we would be unified as women, she and the planning group were very open to it. Disappointment is not the right word: they seemed very upset about it.

Did you have a sense that the original speaker was speaking for women of color? Or was she speaking for herself?

I couldn't be certain. But I believe she was representing more than herself. I can't believe that there was only one woman of color who worked on the demonstration, although the percentage of women of color at the demonstration was definitely very, very small.

This seems like a significant moment to me in that it's a sharp contrast to the sense of participation and mutual planning that you were suggesting in the beginning.

It was disturbing. It was very disturbing to me.

What was your reaction?

Let down.

By the demonstration?

No. By the feeling that we still have so far to go. Even with all that we have done.

So you had this feeling of excitement and ebullience over what you encountered and then suddenly saw some of the realities, the harsh realities that still have to be struggled with.

Yes. So that was a very disturbing moment. The only other thing I remember about that part of the demonstration was that the ritual was performed and it had one period where everyone was killed by some kind of military action, and we all had to lay down and then we all had to rise again. The symbolism sort of escapes me now.

You say "had to." It sounds to me as if this part of it wasn't something that you owned.

This wasn't as meaningful for me, that's true. After that part of the demonstration, everyone split up for the day. Some people volunteered to go to the soup kitchen area to take all the flour that women were asked to bring from all parts of the country to make bread that would be used in the following day's ritual, and to cook dinner for people. Everyone else went off to do whatever they were going to do. Some people, I understand it was about a hundred people, had a candlelight vigil at the White House that night, but I wasn't involved in that.

Before you go on talking about the Pentagon itself, I just want to reflect back on this first day, the day of preparation and some of the other activities. I'm still, in my own mind, mulling over what happened at the Air and Space Museum, and trying to understand the difference between that moment and the earlier moments in the preparation. It seems clear to me from what you've said that there was a planning structure. Obviously it was regionwide. It consisted both of planning centers—you've mentioned Washington, you've mentioned New York—and also local groups that worked on preparing themselves in their own ways and then came together and participated in the final planning at the time of the actual demonstration. So there was this participation that was set in a larger context of long-term thought and reflection that had been going on by a central group of people. What would have made the Air and Space Museum even more viable, do you think?

I don't know. I haven't really thought about it like that and I'm realizing that now, after four months, that part of it has receded from memory.

You lost it.

I lost it; I think that's true. Maybe it was partly due to the fact that it was the end of a long, exciting, tiring day or that I couldn't hear or see very well, or that there was little participation by the total group, or that I was let down from the black woman's statement—or a combination of all of that. It just didn't have the staying power for me. To go on: next morning at seven o'clock we met near the Lincoln Memorial in order to prepare to march across the bridge. That felt very much like old times.

How many times have you marched across that bridge!

People were coming from all directions to join the group. Two things stand out for me at this point. One was really the mood, which had shifted from festive to serious, a very quiet mood. The traffic was going by on its way into the city, a bit slowed due to having one lane of the highway blocked off for us. Nothing was very noisy, though. The people were talking in low tones. There were several thousand people, but you couldn't hear them. There were police cars all around. There were mounted police. I began to have the feeling that something was going to happen or something serious could happen or somebody might do something. For those people who had been involved in other demonstrations, I'm sure it meant those kinds of things. For people who had never been involved, it might have been a little more full of awe. In this context, the Ithaca group, which was suddenly faced with some decision about its internal plans, formed into a circle to talk and to try to reach a consensus on their decision. At the moment that their decision was made, the group, in their own circle with their arms linked, started to sing quietly "You Can't Kill the Spirit; She's Like a Mountain; Old and Strong; She Goes On and On," a refrain that was heard a lot at the demonstration. And as that small group was standing there, with their arms closing their circle, representing a specific group from a specific place, expressing their own specific group-life methodology, other people came and joined them, joined that strong women's symbol, the circle.

The circle is like a magnet.

Yes. Yes. Women felt very comfortable with it. They didn't feel like they were breaking in. It was very easy to get into that circle.

Because the circle didn't mean ownership or possession or exclusion.

No. It expanded. It wasn't expected by the Ithaca group. As I looked around at their faces, I could see from their faces that they felt they had done something special, they knew what was happening, realized that they are not only part of something bigger, but that they were part of making something happen in that context. They had come as this small group and had started this little circle and it was getting bigger and bigger.

It rippled.

And incorporated a diverse group of women.

Diverse in what ways?

Diverse in age, in background, in interest. Another thing I found extremely interesting and so positive was the strong representation of lesbians. It seems to me that that has been a very difficult issue for the women's movement for such a long time. But what I saw was so encouraging—the total acceptance of whoever anybody was. There weren't people who were trying to be separate. People were being very kind to each other and accepting of each other . . . sharing food and all kinds of things.

You're describing a transcendence of internecine warfare that is really powerful.

The Unity Statement reflected such a broad and comprehensive perspective that tells me there must have been some very committed and concentrated work done to arrive at such a position, a lot of drawing people together toward an openness that we may not have seen before.
    Yes. It seems as if, in coming, people accepted that notion of unity and agreed to abide by the values of the demonstration.
    I talked to one woman who came back with us on the bus to Ithaca,

who was apparently from Ithaca but who had been traveling and was in St. Louis before she came to the demonstration. She came from St. Louis on a regular school bus with over thirty women who took turns driving the twenty-five hours it took to come straight through. She talked to me about some of the problems that existed on that bus because of the differences among women, cultural and value differences, things that people couldn't seem to get worked out in that setting. But they made it. And they were still together. I thought, what a miracle. But I need to get on. We marched across the bridge and into Arlington Cemetery. Because we were quite strung out and because the puppets really allowed for delineation and definition of where we were, it was an empowering experience to look back and see this long string of women. When we got to Arlington Cemetery, we were asked not to talk. There was some very quiet talking, some low humming, but overall it was again very, very silent and hushed. It was still quite early in the morning. We found ourselves in the midst of rows and rows of tombstones.

Tombstones — the irony of that beautiful cemetery.

There were men working in the area, men looking at us so curiously, wondering what was happening. Suddenly all that silence was disrupted by the roar of cannons. My first reaction was that we were being attacked! Of course it turned out to be some type of commemoration or honor salute or something. How representative: women's sign of respect was silence; men's a cannon's roar.

"Yea though I walk through the valley of the shadow of death."

When we came out of the cemetery, there was a great cheering — and we arrived at the Pentagon energetic and ready. We went immediately to the front entry, to the lawn in the front of the building. Here the demonstration proper began. The first thing that happened was that the white puppet, symbolizing mourning, came down across the grass. As the puppet came opposite to where you were standing, you would go out and stick your tombstone into the ground. And so, little by little, there was a growing cemetery of women on the front lawn of the Pentagon. We had just come through an entire huge cemetery of men who are honored for dying in war — and these victims of another kind of violence aren't recognized at all.

Both groups, the men at Arlington and the women on the lawn, victims of violence. Yet so different. And responded to so differently by their society.

Validated and unvalidated.

Known and unknown.

Respected and disrespected.

Honored and blamed.

Exactly. Women are seen as having provoked their own death. And are then blamed for that violation.

For being women. May I cry now?

It's your turn! This stage, the mourning stage, was very quiet and very respectful. People brought out tombstones that they had made at home, brought out banners, some finely quilted in beautiful colors and designs, to put up and to stand in silent respect. When that stage was over, the next stage was that of rage. The red puppet came out and women expressed their rage. That part of the demonstration did not particularly engage me. But I certainly saw women who very clearly were enraged and had this opportunity to express that in public and in concert, together.

What's happened to your rage?

I don't know.

Thinking in terms of the process of the demonstration that you're trying to describe, and the way in which the different stages of it parallel our own feelings and our own growth as individuals as we try to become empowered, it seems important to me that each of us learns somehow to express, then come to grips with and find a proper place for each of these feelings—mourning, rage, empowerment and defiance—integrating them into a whole person who can act. So I'm curious about what you did with your rage. Where has it gone? How does one constructively integrate rage so one can act?

It was probably different for each person there.

Yes, and it seems to me that the genius of this demonstration had something to do with the way in which each of those thirty-five hundred individual experiences were woven together into this very powerful collective expression.

Certainly those who were reached at any given point carried the ones who weren't and the ones who weren't reached, were there supporting or being.

Yes. The respect that the mass gives to the individuals at each point along the way is remarkable.

For their individual and personal expression. So that it was truly collective in the sense that everyone was there for each other whether or not that was your particular moment to express. That stands in such sharp contrast to what I've seen in other situations where there is one-upmanship, combatting over . . .

. . . who's going to give a better speech.

Yes. Right. The stars mentality that you were describing earlier. Some people's interpretations and feelings being more important and valued than others.

That's right. None of that. At this point, the group split into two parts. One big white bird went in one direction around the Pentagon and the other bird went the other; people followed in single file. At that point the defiance puppet moved the women who were going to do civil disobedience into position, together with their companion affinity groups of supporters. They moved to the places and the areas where the civil disobedience was going to take place at the same time that the rest of us were encircling the Pentagon. As we walked around the Pentagon, I looked up and saw a sign in one of the windows that made me smile. It said, "Hi, Mom!"—you never know where the next support will come from! One of the things that was done at this time was to have women who were designated as "runners." Their job was to keep running around the Pentagon describing whatever was happening in other places, to support and weave together the separated parts. That was really the only place where I saw things break down. That separation of people from each other by that structure and by the isolation. As soon as the human link, the chain of hands, was broken by the arrival of the braid which the runners brought, which everyone was then supposed to take hold of . . . as soon as that human chain was broken, women started to leave the circle and to turn to the scene where the civil disobedience was happening. People wanted to see what was happening, but they also didn't want to be separated. They didn't want to be "out there," and I think that that's extremely symbolic, that it's very hard to be out on your own, to go back home and continue to do something on your own wherever you are.

That's the other side of being a star. The individual who can stand forward and take responsibility for making her statement, for being public about her commitments.

Right.

Interesting. I wondered about the runners because in the abstract, when I read the descriptions of that portion of the demonstration, I mentally wrestled with what it would mean to maintain communication in a group of that size, involving that kind of activity. And I thought that sounded like a very creative attempt.

It was. It was a real attempt. But at the same time, all it took was a few people to break that line and start walking. I could feel a resentment building in myself toward the women who were walking past me going to see what was going on, when I was still out there by myself or with a few people talking . . .

Taking responsibility.

. . . my responsibility. It was very, very interesting because I don't think I ever felt like that in a mass demonstration before. It didn't even really matter.

What individuals did.

Yes.

So by that time there really was a sense of collective responsibility.

The chain of responsibility, right.

And some people walked away.

Yes. When the braid came around, I tied my scarves into the braid as part of it and left them there for whatever happened to that braid. My mother's and my scarves. Most people then did gather in one of the two places where civil disobedience was going on. At the loading dock site in the rear of the Pentagon, there was a big crowd of people gathering so that people at the back couldn't see what was going on. So two women got together and got another woman up on their shoulders; she then gave a running account of what was going on, where something important was happening but nobody knew it—a real cooperative effort!

What happened, what I saw or heard via this reporter, was that the women who were going to do civil disobedience had balls of string and yarn and parts of the braid and they were attempting to weave a net over the door of the Pentagon. Weaving, a woman's symbol and a symbol of connection. The bright colors that it put on this gray, cold building! People were very happy and festive about it. Then everybody settled down to see what the police would do. As near as I understood what happened, one of the police got a knife and slit the weaving, destroyed this whole net . . . this net-work. There was the slightest hesitation in the group. Then all of a sudden I saw all of these balls of yarn in the air being thrown from the crowd in to the women who were weaving! And they just started over amidst loud, loud cheers! The symbolism of it, I don't know if it was planned or not, but the symbolism of that was wonderful. You can't cut us up; cut us down; cut us out. Because we are going to come back and we are going to keep weaving our safety nets. We are definitely going to be there. Our presence is going to be known. As one woman would go limp or get into a no-go zone and be hauled away by the police, shouts would go up and everybody would cheer. Altogether over fifty women were arrested like that in a relatively brief period of time.

Over fifty women at the loading dock site.

Right. Around in front, in addition to the civil disobedience, there were some women doing other constructive activities. The women from Ithaca constructed out of cardboard a women's community, a community in accordance with the Unity Statement. There was a food co-op and a free health clinic and cheerful, small schools and housing for lesbian mothers and this and that and the other. That was set up right across from the front of the Pentagon where the second group was doing civil disobedience on the steps. There were a lot of women sitting there, together with a huge contingent of police. Things seemed to be at a standstill by the time I arrived. This particular entrance had ascending steps that had handrails, metal handrails, leading up to the doors. the women had taken the balls of yarn and string and braid and had woven a very colorful net all the way across the steps. The net looked like a giant trampoline! There seemed to be some continuing negotiation about keeping one small track open for people to go in and out so the doors were not totally blocked. The women were there, the police were there, but people could still get in and out, although the military brass who were coming and going had to sometimes step over the women. A picture that appeared in the *New York Times* and in other papers showed a military man stepping over a woman's head on those steps. There was a lot of singing by the group on the steps. That went on for what seemed like hours—it was probably two hours or so. This demonstration was way ahead of schedule! I don't know what actually happened or was planned, but it looked like the authorities did not want to arrest the women in this location because of the presence of the media. In all I think only seven or eight, maybe fewer, women were arrested in that location, with the exception of the two or three women who, very early in the civil disobedience, threw blood on the entryway and were immediately taken away.

I'm curious about the norms of that portion of the demonstration. How were decisions made about doing civil disobedience and how was the group organized to be supportive of the people who were doing c.d.? Your description of this whole aspect of the action, from the fragmentation that occurred with the passing of the braid through the c.d., sounds very individualistic.

No, I didn't mean to convey that so totally. Definitely those of us who were not doing c.d. were organized to be supportive. People milled around, true; but there was always a solid group of people who were singing and encouraging and talking. And there was communication between those of us who couldn't see in the crowd and those who were close to the action.

So the defiance portion of the action at the Pentagon was in effect taken by the women doing civil disobedience, with other people acting as a huge support group.

Right. It's interesting that you bring up the question of who organized and managed that portion of the action, because that was really the only place I saw some women really trying to exert direction. As time was wearing on, the support group on the front steps had gotten somewhat impatient and boisterous and was shouting. At that point one of the women, whose words made it seem that she was part of a planning group, got up on one of the steps, higher than the crowd, and spoke, saying that "we" don't want this to get out of hand, that the shouting could cause a violent reaction by the authorities. In fact, she said, it could be that there were people planted in the support group to provoke just such an event. She was warning people that their actions could provoke a confrontation that those doing civil disobedience had not agreed to. There was then discussion back and forth between this woman and the group, some people taking one side and some another. "What are we supposed to do, be meek and good and behave?" versus

"This kind of provocation from the inside will turn this into something that those of us who will take the brunt of the reaction don't want it to be."

There is a statement that was written governing the civil disobedience portion of the demonstration called The Common Thread. It very clearly asked that anyone who came adhere to certain norms of nonviolence so that the women who did take that risk of arrest would be safe.

I'm sure there were a lot of people like myself who hadn't read that.

And just reacted as themselves.

Trying to make something happen. Trying to bring this to some kind of conclusion. The feeling that emerged after a while was "We're going to sit here all day saying You Can't Kill the Spirit. Maybe they can!" It was a frustration, almost a fear of defeat.

It sounds as if it wasn't clear at that point what the purpose of this moment was supposed to be.

I think that the police had out-waited us. Many participants might have had expectations as to what would happen and thought that a "confrontation" would happen quickly.

I can imagine, on the other hand, that there were women in the group who believed that the Presence, for however long it lasted, was what was intended to be.

Yes, the disagreement seemed to be over the purpose of the meaning of defiance. In any case, several women doing c.d. finally decided to provoke arrest and went and lay down. One of them, a gray-haired woman who clearly had a lot of self-confidence and a lot of presence, went and it appeared to me that she was negotiating with one of the head police to come and arrest them already. She was smiling at them and talking with them. I imagined in my mind that she was saying, "Look, do we actually have to lay down? Is this really going to be what it takes? Couldn't you just take us away and we'll go on about our business?"

And what happened to those women once they were arrested? Did the group take responsibility for them?

The affinity groups were organized to follow up on the women who were arrested, to ensure their well-being. At least that was my understanding. Immediately after those arrests, everybody reassembled on the front lawn for the closing ritual. If you can imagine a mass demonstration having a closing ritual, quite different from the usual fading away. Throughout this closing ritual, by the way, reports were made about what was happening to the women who had been arrested, every one of whom was released at the local police station, with the exception of those who had thrown blood. For the closing ceremony people were asked to make a circle on the Pentagon lawn, in amongst the tombstones. At that point, many people produced small bags of salt and made a circle of the salt, the center of which was to symbolize that the deaths and endings and finishings of anything anybody wanted to say were finished, that they were finished with. In trying to explain how this was going to happen, the same old inadequate sound system from the demonstration at the Air and Space Museum was used. Immediately somebody way on the outside of the circle of several thousand began saying "We can't hear." So someone from the circle closest to the center said, "Well, that's easy. Whenever whoever hears whatever is said, repeat it." What an incredible effect as the waves of words washed out over that huge crowd! Not only did everybody get to hear everything that was said; some people got to repeat and to thereby take ownership of what everybody else said, and these things that were said were very personal things. Anyone who wanted to come forward was invited to bring any object, a stone or a shell or whatever, to cast into the circle of endings and finishings and to announce into the microphone what the object symbolized. Again, this was a powerful method of bringing the personal into the public arena, of owning everybody's thinking, of identifying with other people, of expanding one's world. People brought stones and shells from all over the world. Some people who couldn't come had sent stones and shells to their friends to cast into the circle for them. Women talked about wanting to be finished with their fear of other women. Their hatred of themselves. War. Nuclear weapons. Their own timidity, passiveness, their insecurity, their subservience to men. The patriarchy. The murders of women in Chile. The oppression of women everywhere. Some things that are very common to all of us and very much part of each of us, other things that you never thought about in your life. Another thing that was done during the closing ceremony was that flowers were passed around and we put them on the tombstones of the women who were not there. Yet another part of the ceremony was to feed each other with all this bread that had been baked at the soup kitchen with the ingredients brought by women from all over the country. Bread that would nourish us to travel back to all parts of the country to do what we had to do in our everyday lives.

"The common woman is like a common loaf of bread . . . and will rise."

Yes, that symbolism. The ceremony, I won't describe it totally, was organized around the symbols of earth, air, fire and water. Finally, at the end, we had the Beginnings, so that the beginnings were what we took home with us.

I was just going to ask you that. The idea of ending with endings bothered me.

No, we ended with a beginning. Seeds were passed out, all kinds of seeds. I got squash, pumpkin, sunflower.

You plant those and they'll grow!

Exactly! We put little holes down into the Pentagon lawn and gently tucked those seeds down in there. Then we went away and the authorities thought they cleaned up after us by picking up this pile of stones and shells and removing the tombstones. But there's a circle where the salt was that is dead and finished and, right about now, if you go to the Pentagon lawn, there will be some perplexed people there saying "What on earth is this happening? These women are totally crazy!" A Women's Presence remains at the Pentagon, and will grow.

There is a faith that I hear in what you're saying. A faith in the tower of this process that you set in motion. I mean, in any sort of concrete terms, there is the Pentagon.

Concrete.

Concrete, yes, this mountain of stone and weaponry. To combat with flowers and plants, in some ways you understand their amusement and amazement—and yet you're saying something . . .

About life versus death.

Yes. And about a process versus that kind of mass, that kind of immobile . . .

Total oppression.

Right. I find that something to think about. As someone trying to hear and to learn from your experience, I came with a product orientation. I wanted to know about the Women's Pentagon Action. And what I found happening to me as you described the entire process, beginning with your decision to go and then moving on to the preparations and all the events, the Pentagon began to shrink in my mind.

Oh, great!

I lost the Pentagon in the event. It became subsumed and I lost any sense of those moments at the Pentagon as being the most important moments in the ceremony. The process that you describe overtook me.

Imagine the impact if you were there, different for each one of us, but unifying and empowering.

One woman's experience, yet Everywoman's experience. We need to listen to this.

14

Mobilizing Emotions: Organizing the Women's Pentagon Action

Interview with Donna Warnock*

Annie Popkin
Gary Delgado

How did you first get involved in the Women's Pentagon Action?

I was living in upstate New York then and was involved in the Women and Life on Earth network, a loosely affiliated group of women in the Northeastern United States that organized a conference on feminism and ecology in Amherst, Massachusetts, during the early spring of 1980. There a number of participants talked about having a women's demonstration at the Pentagon. That May I was speaking in New York City and Grace Paley called me beforehand and suggested that we use the opportunity to get together a small meeting of women to follow up on the idea of an action. So we did. We knew that we wanted it to be a women's action, to reflect feminist values; to represent as many constituencies as possible; and that, while we were going to the military's headquarters, we wanted to address a wide range of concerns, pointing to the Pentagon sometimes literally, sometimes symbolically.

*Previously published in *Socialist Review*, Vol. 12 (1982).

You said this group of women wanted to organize an action that reflected feminist values. How did you go about that?

First we set the tone for something completely different. We began by deciding it would be an all-women's action. That created a safe space to explore new possibilities because we didn't have to interpret sexism, or explain or argue over basic feminist issues. (Though that happened some, of course. But the nature of it was different because we knew everyone was basically supportive.) Different women involved had different reasons why they wanted a women's action, and I think that was good. There were women who were not necessarily part of the feminist movement, for some this was their first all-women activity. And there were other women who were lesbian separatists, who wouldn't be involved in an action unless it was all women. The action gave us the opportunity to demonstrate our pride in being women, not having to be on the defensive or trying to prove ourselves. Whenever you're acting out of pride you're beginning from a powerful position.

Was the decision to have an all-women's action controversial?

Not among us. It was a bit of a surprise to me that it wasn't controversial among some of the mixed-sex groups women belonged to. I think that was because the groundwork for autonomous feminist organizing had already been laid, especially in the antinuclear movement. Another reason was that we weren't a coalition and we weren't seeking any endorsements. We wanted to make decisions on our own and to define ourselves by what we said and did rather than by with whom we were associated. Our concerns were quite broad; to our knowledge, there were no other organizations that had our politics. But we saw the possibility that with our diverse demands, our creativity and all our good energy, a lot of groups might want to endorse us and treat us like free advertising for *them* having the correct politics. Since we didn't really feel so good about a lot of the politics expressed especially by male-dominated groups, we didn't want to open the whole thing up to that. Also, we had to organize so fast—we did everything in just eight weeks—there really wasn't time for controversy to arise in the other organizations that women belonged to.

Tell me about how feminist ideas were incorporated in the conceptualization of the action.

We began by talking about the ways in which we wanted this action to be different from other demonstrations. First, we wanted it to be a totally participatory event. We'd been to demonstrations having a lot of speakers who basically said the same things, over and over again, oftentimes in rhetoric, then everybody would stand there and applaud, and people didn't learn anything new. Folks don't take any major new step in their own political development, really, by just observing, so we wanted to have it be a totally participatory action which reflected each woman's unique commitment and contribution to the event.

When we were first organizing we talked about whether we were aiming the action at those in the Pentagon, whether we were aiming it at the press, whether we were aiming it at "middle-American" women, whether we were aiming it at feminists, and so forth. What we decided was this: We wanted the language that we spoke, especially in the Unity Statement, to be ordinary language; we wanted our mothers to be able to understand it. What we actually did while we were at the Pentagon, though, we wanted to do for ourselves, and from our own hearts and consciousness. We wanted a real respect for each woman's contribution.

An important part of organizing the action was developing our beautiful Unity Statement. We knew if we were really speaking about the truth, we could find the words to say it to *any* woman. At one of the meetings we posed it in the context of the women in our own lives and we asked the women present to think, "What does my mother, who is not yet political, need to know? What is my sister or my neighbor concerned about? How can we address those needs?"

Over the period of two-and-a-half months in which we worked on the action, the Unity Statement that we developed was discussed among some two hundred women, and consensus was reached. The Unity Statement was changed a number of times and continued to be altered even after the first action. I think this openness enabled us to build an incredible amount of trust among those involved in organizing the action, and the trust, in turn, provided the basis for a lot of creativity. We were fortunate to have Grace Paley writing the Unity Statement. Grace is a wonderful poet, so she was able to transform our ideas into prose. Grace and the other women who took leadership in the action did it in a way that respected and encouraged everyone's contribution.

Do you feel that the Pentagon Action represents a new stage in the relationship between the feminist movement and the left?

Yes. Because the left still doesn't understand sexism, doesn't really understand feminism, feminists within the left have always been in the role of caucus. The Pentagon Action marks a departure from that stage in which we were isolated in an adversary role. This action showed how feminists could recognize our own power and, while retaining our autonomy, move into a leadership role in the left and use that leadership role to demonstrate our understanding of process, of structure, of creativity and of expression of emotion. By no means am I saying that we hadn't proven ourselves before. It's that this action gained us recognition *in* the left, rather than *outside* it. Whereas before we might have been accused of being separatists for doing what we did, this time we were recognized as role models.

Instead of giving in to the sexist stereotype that emotion should not be part of rational thinking, and should not be shown in public, we demonstrated that being in touch with our emotions makes us strong and intelligent. As we recognize the very real pain invoked in us and others by oppression and militarism and allow ourselves to feel it, we're able to transform it into a source of power that the militarists don't understand. In going to the Pentagon, we weren't *appealing* to them, we were *contradicting* them; by being on their property and providing a safe place for women to express their deep, hurtful emotions, we were in effect negating the power of the Pentagon, and affirming our own power instead.

What do you think of the argument of some feminists that women, because of their particular capacities to nurture, are going to be the saviors of the earth and are the most appropriate people to fight against militarism?

There are two sides to that line. The notion that women are more nurturing and, therefore, should participate to save the earth is usually sexist. That's our sex role stereotype. The fact is that everyone has the capacity to nurture. That women have been socialized to do so is a reality, and it's an asset we have going for us. But at the same time we recognize it as a strength, we must deplore it as a mandate. If that's done, then I think we're talking feminism.

Was the infrastructure for the Women's Pentagon Action one that had been developed in the anti-nuclear movement?

It was from both anti-nuclear organizing and the women's movement. Because women came from a number of different movements we were able to get the word out quickly. The lesbian community was very important in organizing.

Was there tension or conflict within the circle of people who were organizing, for instance, between lesbian women and straight women?

Problems seemed to arise primarily in the big cities. There, because the populations are so much larger, there are many more organizations and women are able to be in separate groups. They'll come together for events and argue with each other and then go back to their base groups which will support not only the substantive position, but also organizational divisions. It can really impede unity. Whereas those who came from smaller towns and rural communities have to work together because that's all they've got. In New York City there was a conflict between some lesbians and straight women, but I've heard the action did a lot to bring those women together in a way that has never happened before.

Were the networks that connected women in rural areas the same networks that organized the action in urban areas?

No, because the nature of organizing in urban and rural areas is very different. In the urban areas there was a tendency, as there often is, to see organizing as almost synonymous with publicity. You put up posters, you get announcements in newsletters if you can, get the press releases out to publicize that you're doing something. In the rural areas people have to do more person-to-person organizing (a skill which I wish organizers in the larger urban areas would work to develop too). So it was in the smaller communities where women did things like having the Unity Statement read aloud in church, or going round to all the laundromats and hanging them up and then just talking to the women while the wash was being done, or going to PTA meetings and other gatherings with the Unity Statement. Often, in the bigger metropolitan areas, those things aren't even thought about; not that they weren't done at all, of course, just that, to my knowledge, they weren't relied on in the same way.

Among the participants in the action, were there more people who came from rural areas than from urban areas?

We didn't calculate that. But I'll tell you that when I first started organizing in upstate New York experienced activists there told me I'd be lucky to get twenty or thirty women to go. Two hundred women went.

How do you account for the success of the action?

Having such a powerful Unity Statement as a mobilizing tool, doing things really differently and creatively, being feminists, and having local autonomy all were part of it. In addition to mobilizing people in our areas to go, and raising consciousness about the issues in our Unity Statement in our communities (which, by the way, we saw as a vital part of the action regardless of whether the recipients attended the event), each local area was encouraged to do what it could to contribute in any way to the organizing and events in DC. For example, from Syracuse we brought the Women Harvest Choir; thirty women went and sang during the action, and led women in song all around the Pentagon while the civil disobedience was going on. Not only could we diversify the repertoire and keep everyone on key, but we had harmonies all worked out so it sounded wonderful.

Another example of the contributions that were brought: The first year we were afraid we wouldn't have enough women to encircle the Pentagon, so everyone brought brightly colored scarves which we called "women extenders," to stay connected while we surrounded the Pentagon. It was fun to bring such an offering, and we all admired each other's scarves. We used them in the beginning of the empowerment stage, but it turned out we were plenty enough women to surround the monster, so in the end they just added to the gaiety of the event. They became part of our ritual; in the '81 action, women from all over the country brought cloth and made a braid when they encircled the Pentagon. Also in '81, women from all over sent and brought whole wheat flour, which was kneaded and made into loaves of bread right during the demonstration and sent along to jail with the women who were arrested, to nourish them. So you see what I mean when I say it was a caring action.

If you were going to talk about the ways in which you thought this action was different, what else would you say?

When we first met in September 1980, we were talking about what we could do. Different women were saying what they had done in their own communities. "Well, we could do a balloon release," one woman said. No, that had been done a million times. "We could hold a die-in," another suggested. No, same thing, it's been done too often. Then somebody remarked, "It's always good to have something positive; we could have a safe energy fair."

I'd been sitting there listening to all these different ideas, and I looked up and said, "The problem that I have with the safe energy fair, although I like the idea of being positive, is that you go from one extreme to the next: at one table you see pictures of Hiroshima victims; it's devastating. Then at the next table you have all the solar power stuff and smiling suns. It's really an emotional strain. It clashes inside you."

I realized that if we were going to deal with such emotional issues we had to have a way to make transitions smoothly. And so I said, "Look, why don't we just figure out how we *feel* about all these different issues that we want to address, and then try and group those feelings together and move through them and within each one deal with the issues that are appropriate to those feelings." And so I thought about it for a second and added, "I know some of the emotions that come up for me are grief, anger and power." That really got us rolling. As soon as we decided that we were going to develop the thing emotionally we realized how significant that was and that this way each individual could find her niche.

Because we were dealing with emotions, we were getting to people's humanness. And once you start getting to their humanness, what it means is that the skills that need to be relied on are not the kind of political skills generally used nowadays, except maybe in feminist counseling, especially for targets of rape and battering, for example. We were relying on our skills as friends, as sisters, as mothers, as daughters, as lovers, on very personal levels. And on that level, women are experts. So, as organizers, we were able to treat each other in radically different ways than people have come to expect from politicos.

We decided to begin the day in mourning and then move to rage, next empowerment and, finally, defiance, when women would commit nonviolent civil disobedience by weaving a web which blocked the Pentagon doors. We created appropriate and safe spaces for women to release emotions within this framework.

In mourning we marched through Arlington National Cemetery, surrounded by rows of tombstones of those who died in military service. When we arrived at the Pentagon we set up our own cemetery for women who've died at the hands of patriarchal violence. Participants added epitaphs to the tombstones we'd made commemorating sisters, mothers, friends and lovers, women known and unknown. Because each woman was able to contribute names to those tombstones, and because we created a safe, supportive space, many were able to grieve in ways that have never been done before in a political demonstration. Usually when you're in a space like that it's really hard to let go with whatever you're feeling. But, as I said, we were relating in these very human, sisterly ways. Because of the closeness we felt, when the tombstones were being placed, if you'd see someone crying, even if it were a stranger, you'd go embrace her, and comfort her. We made a space to deal with those needs usually filled only by close friends and, too often, outside their political context. When people are the targets of oppression and they only deal with the grief of that hurt on a personal level—which is what people are taught to do—the result is disempowering; despair, depression, addiction, suicide, crime are the potential results. But the dealing with the personal hurt in a political context, we give the person vital individual support and validation that is energizing and empowering. More than the promises of liberal politicians, we're giving the gifts of hope and caring. It's revolutionary.

Why don't you say something about rage?

Rage is often a necessary step to empowerment. At the time of the Action I thought rage had to follow mourning. But now I feel differently; I'm tending to think that we could have done it the other way around, or we could even have crested it in waves and gone rage, mourning, rage, empowerment. That's because most of the people who come to political demonstrations are generally angry already. Often they haven't reached the point of grief, or they thought they'd left it behind. You get angry because you know these political things, right? The contradictions are apparent to you, and so forth. But then what happens is that you realize how deep the hurt really is and that awareness brings new pain. Being in touch with these feelings is an important source of human energy. I think sensitive people who've been in the movement for a long time would know what I mean. You feel like you know everything about a certain issue or subject, and then you hear it the next time and it hits you completely differently, and it's because you are going back and forth into these different emotional areas.

When you've mourned something you can be more empowered about it. An example for me was working on the Karen Silkwood case. When I first learned about her murder, I was furious. Later I became overcome with fear as I realized the threat to my own life, to those of my friends and all activists. Then came grief. It was so overwhelming; I'd get upset whenever I saw a Honda Civic (the kind of car Karen was killed in), I couldn't step inside one. I'd give speeches about the case and get everyone really depressed. I went through that phase and then, finally, out into a much more positive thing. I could celebrate what Silkwood lived for and why she was important in my life, and in the lives of others. Then my talks began being uppers — linking feminism, ecology, peace and class issues. There was hope. Had I known earlier what I know now I could have gotten to that stage much earlier and been a more effective organizer.

It's really hard to deal with emotions though. At first the Women's Pentagon Action rage wasn't expressed as well as it could have been. We moved into it all right, clearly the need for expression was there, women started yelling and screaming, women in the band started in with their horns. But we're taught not to express anger, and I think that had a bearing on our lack of creativity about expressing rage. We have to deal with that, give people opportunities to let that anger out.

The emphasis on emotions definitely built up the collective feeling so that when it was time for the civil disobedience all of us were involved in a collective effort. The women committing civil disobedience were truly extensions of all of us and we sang and did a lot of work to support each other.

What was it that led you to looking at emotions as a framework through which women could be organized?

I'm an emotional woman. I knew the reason I get involved in things is because they move me emotionally, and it's those emotions that give me power when I speak or write or organize. I think I rely on my emotions much more than talent or skill or experience. If I know what I'm feeling I can mobilize the rest. It's this self-awareness that made me look at how emotions could be dealt with on a larger scale. I draw from a rich tradition of feminists who have historically put a lot of attention on emotions. Lately I've been learning a lot of new approaches to all of this from Ricky Sherover-Marcuse, who conducts workshops on unlearning racism and anti-Semitism. She explains that oppression is locked in place by painful emotional experiences and those experiences act as the glue that secures the oppression.

You see, oppression has two sides. There is the institutional form, and there is the attitudinal form. Both must be dealt with, though generally only the former is addressed. I'm looking for ways we can undo the attitudinal damage because that's what divides the people who need to be united. That's what needs to be undone if we're going to make our movement grow. People have been taught to be racist, sexist, homophobic and chauvinist, so they can unlearn it as well. And the way they need to unlearn it is to recognize and release the emotions that lock it in place.

It's not an intellectual process.

No, not until the end part of it. Unless you deal with your emotions you're just not going to think clearly. Witness the militarists: are they rational? Unrecognized emotions act like fog veiling the brain; because vision is distorted, misinformation is believed. At the Pentagon we were attempting to lift that fog. We were dealing with emotions that we, in fact, had and, consequently, needed to deal with, in order to get to our power and to think intelligently.

It's a form of group therapy.

That's exactly what it is.

There we were, in the shadow of the people who block their emotions the most, and we were crying and raging on their front lawn! We encircled them, not just with our bodies, but also with our spirits. We were a living contradiction just being there dealing with our emotions. That creates a *feeling* of power—it's not an illusion or merely a contrast—it's a sensitivity that is crucial if we're going to turn things around because the reality is that change requires emotional growth that is sometimes painful and the time and place of it can't always be chosen as we had the luxury of doing at the Pentagon. Blocking is the patriarchy's way of dealing with emotions; feeling them is the feminist way to liberation. Only if we understand this are we going to hope to address the problems of oppressed people putting each other down, robbing, competing with and killing each other instead of making a revolution so everyone can be liberated. It's the missing key.

Do you see the women who came together for the Pentagon Action as being involved in any of the other issues that you raised?

The women who organized the action had come from these issues. But the Pentagon Action was a turning point for expressing a wide range of political concerns simultaneously along with the emotions they provoke. It was by no means the perfect action. It was an important one, but just a step. The efforts by women to deal with racism, classism, anti-Semitism, homophobia, ageism and the rights of those who are disabled, psychiatric patients or physically different which are going on right now mark another major step. We're breaking new ground, and it's very exciting. As we incorporate understanding of these oppressions we're going to develop even more sophisticated actions that not only respect but manifest, cherish and represent the diversity of people in this world.

15

On Common Ground:
The Women's Peace Camp
at Greenham Common*

Lynne Jones

THE BEGINNING

It was cold, dark and wet, the first time that I visited the camp at
Greenham, in the November of 1981. I'd heard the stories, legends
rather, for that is what they'd become: how a woman called Anne Pettit,
living on a smallholding in Wales with her husband and two children,
had organized a women's march from Cardiff to RAF Greenham
Common to protest against Cruise missiles. She'd wanted to inspire
"women not necessarily in the women's movement, but who were
worried, anxious and isolated like myself." She called the march
WOMEN FOR LIFE ON EARTH to show that it wasn't just a negative
protest, and succeeded in inspiring 40 women and four men to join her.
They were women like Liz Stocker who'd "never thought much about
the peace thing" and "didn't think women worked well together in
groups." Liz had seen an advertizement for the march in *Cosmopolitan*.
She'd been ill all year and went "to learn something and see if I could
walk that far." They had walked through sunny countryside and
friendly villages "and in 48 hours," Liz went on "we had become a very

*Previously published in Lynne Jones (ed.), *Keeping The Peace: Women's Peace Handbook*
(London: The Women's Press, 1983). The Postscript first appeared in the *New Statesman* (5
September 1986).

close group; all totally different backgrounds yet we worked out our disagreements, cut through the nonessentials with none of the egotripping that you get on male committees." The media, however, had ignored them, so they'd decided to chain themselves to the perimeter fence of the base, saying that they would stay until there was a live television debate between John Nott, Minister of Defense, and themselves on the issue of Cruise missiles. Nothing happened. The issue had "already been debated," they were told that they could stay as long as they liked. More and more women had arrived, however, and local people brought tents and food. "We decided," Anne told me, "that while there might not be much point in chains there was a point in having a permanent peace picket. We called it a Women's Peace Camp and decided to stay, and you know, when we came out of the tent there was an enormous Harvest Moon in the sky and a rainbow, good omens."

There was no rainbow now. Only mud, wet bracken and a huddle of caravans by the main gate of the base. A small shelter had been erected by an open fire, two men sat by it. "Is anyone around?" I asked. "Effie's in her caravan, over there." I knocked on the door, opening it to see a small, frail-looking old lady buried under a heap of blankets. "Hello," she mumbled, waking. "Do come in. It's so cold and I get so tired of making tea for visitors, I thought I'd have a rest. Do sit down." She pushed a heap of clothes aside. "I'm sorry it's so untidy, the girls don't seem to mind, would you like tea? They're all away today." While I drank tea, Effie talked about her grandchildren and her market garden. "We grow tomatoes, shrubs and things. No, I haven't done anything like this before. We're rather remote, you see, we don't have any daily papers but I had begun to realize things were altering. I came because I wanted reassuring. I was one of the ones chained up, you know."

"What was that like?"

"When it was first mooted, I thought it was dreadful. Cold shadows went through me at the thought, but we discussed it . . . It was freezing cold and the traffic was noisy but I didn't mind."

"What made you stay?"

"There are so few here, and my husband doesn't mind, we've been married 30 years. He was a CO in the last war. He paid my train fare. Are you staying?"

"Oh Effie, I'm sorry, I can't. I have to be back on duty at the hospital," I said, feeling guilty.

"Oh well." Effie looked tired.

"I'll go now," I said, "and be down again soon." I stepped out of the caravan feeling depressed and impressed both at the same time. "It can't last," I thought. "It's too difficult."

In early December, Anne wrote to me saying "The camp's going strong. Hundreds of people visit every weekend. Why don't you come down?"

The camp looked different and not just because there were two feet of snow on the ground. Bright signs had been painted saying WOMEN'S PEACE CAMP. NO CRUISE HERE. HONK IF YOU'RE FOR US. There were ten caravans and two teepees. Smoke rose from the fire where about twenty people had gathered around a woman talking. I'd heard of Helen before. She'd caught the media's eye because she'd given up five children, husband and home to live here. She was 44, a midwife and "asleep like everyone else" until she'd gone to an anti-nuclear rally in Wales. "Seeing those young people trying desperately to stop their futures being damaged, I realized my generation hadn't worked hard enough to prevent what's happening. It was a fit of guilt that got me going." Initially she'd joined the Labour Party and had stood as a councillor in Powys, her home county, to get the issue raised. Now she felt it was more important to be here. "People are disillusioned with politics and rightly so. They need something they can focus their attention on and begin to believe in. You can actually draw a line here and make a positive physical statement that cannot be misunderstood: we are not allowing these weapons in. If I'd said it in Powys they wouldn't have listened." She hadn't planned to take direct action. "I never disapproved but I thought the way a lot of women with children think, that I'd a greater responsibility to them than what I felt was right for me. The thought that these missiles could kill all the people I cared about anyway changed that. The only logical thing to do was to make a committed stand. I felt I had the right to make that decision on my own without consulting my husband and children. Obviously they were very upset. The youngest is four and my husband has had to give up his job and go on social security, which he hates, though he understands what I'm doing and he supports the peace movement. I just had to decide whether I was going actively to involve myself in this protest or put it aside for someone else to do because of the children. It's one of those decisions that affects the rest of your life—I chose to become involved."

"Shall we march into Newbury?" she asked us all.

Someone handed out mugs of tea. "How do you organize yourselves here?" I asked, "Who makes decisions? How does it run?"

"Chaotically," Helen said, "and I think that's our greatest strength in a daft way, we never seem to know what we're doing from day to day, which makes it hard for the authorities to know either. The chaos comes from people coming and going. No one sits down and makes rigid plans, which is excellent or you'd be stuck if something happened fast."

"Don't you have rotas or anything?"

"Rotas?" Helen spat out the word with a laugh. "Oh my God! There were rotas but nobody paid attention to them. Somebody had this mania to write them, but nobody took any notice."

"It doesn't run smoothly all the time," a small, dark-haired woman called Shushu joined in. "But mostly it's OK. People simply agree on what needs to be done and do it. We meet most evenings over supper. We don't have a steering committee or hierarchy or all that kind of thing. My CND group did and spent most of its time organizing jumble sales and never doing anything."

"Why did you come?" I asked.

"I've just finished school. I've got the time and energy to do something more than organize jumble sales."

"Once you've accepted the fact that you can live with a greater degree of untidiness and filth you can relax. I think if we were the type of women who gave a high priority to having clean, smooth-running homes, that's where we'd be. Our priority is stopping Cruise."

A woman walked up carrying a large puppet; an enormous woman's head with long red hair and brightly colored hand-painted robes. "This is the Goddess,"she said.

"Right," said Helen, "let's walk to Newbury."

We set off, the Goddess in the lead, bright against snow-laden branches and clear sky. Sara and I took it in turns to carry the Goddess while she told me about herself. She'd been working in a psychiatric rehabilitation hostel in Sheffield, but hadn't seen the point of trying to help people back to the normality of a society that spent millions of pounds on destroying everything. "One woman was having nuclear nightmares every night. She couldn't control her normal life at all and kept having tantrums. The social services saw her as not being able to cope with the world so she had to change to fit it. No one said, "You've got good reason to feel like this." Everything that's valued in our society at present is masculine. The heroics, virility, power. It's lunatic and destructive. We've got to work out a more balanced vision where the feminine is valued by everyone. The Women's Peace Camp seemed to combine all the things I'd been working on so I had to come."

"Was that hard?"

"I knew it was wrong to give up my job and wrong not to come here. They were angry because I was "deserting" them. They thought *I* was crazy coming to live in a teepee in December."

A WOMEN'S CAMP

The women continued to camp out through bitter winter weather. Money, letters of support and food poured in and even Newbury people, not naturally sympathetic, as many of them worked in the nuclear industry, began to be impressed. They stopped by the fire on their way to discos on the base; a local policeman left his phone number for anyone wanting baths, and the media came in droves, from Japan, Australia, the States, Europe and the USSR. Meanwhile the women talked. They talked to the workers on the base: Franny ran a one-woman picket outside the construction workers' gate. Sitting with a primus stove she'd hold out a sign saying "Will you stop and talk?" and another for when they returned saying "How about a cup of tea on the way back then?" Then she'd ask them what they thought of the men who built the gas chambers in Hitler's Germany, or of Claude Eatherly, the man who flew the weather plane on the Hiroshima mission. "These men aren't union men, so the only way you can get through is on a personal basis. I just want them to understand what they're doing building a missile site."

They talked at conferences and meetings all over the world, determined to raise the issue of Cruise missiles. I watched Ev receive a standing ovation from 500 women in Amsterdam when she interrupted a formal conference to tell them about Greenham. One thing the camp was teaching them was to be powerful and effective speakers. "I'd never have had the confidence to speak at massive rallies before," Ev said. "Every time I've been down to the camp I've come away with this great surge of energy, able to do things like set up a Woman's Peace group and get an art show together. Being active helps me confront fear."

"The point of this camp," Sara said, "is to draw attention to the fact that every day men are helping to build missile silos for the American military forces in this country. Those missiles could trigger off a holocaust. Every day hundreds of people go past on that road and have to ask themselves 'What makes those women live here and give up their normal lives?' It's a focus too for all the people in the peace movement, who know what we're up against but are uncertain what to do. They can come here, meet others sympathetic, get inspiration, anything could happen."

Clearly too much was happening. Another peace camp was set up at RAF Molesworth, the second intended Cruise missile site. The idea was catching. Towards the end of January, I read a short column in the *Guardian* saying that Newbury District Council had given the women fourteen days to leave or they would be evicted. I had already planned to go down to the camp that weekend to prepare for a festival and nonviolent blockade of the base in March. The threat of eviction brought hundreds of other supporters as well.

A large marquee had been built since my last visit: a circus-like structure of pieces of clear plastic attached to wooden poles around a poplar tree as centre post. A table was covered with leaflets. Banners, appliqués, poems and paintings hung round the walls, smoke rose from the central fireplace where Franny sat dispensing tea to all comers.

"We're going ahead with the festival and blockade whatever happens," she said.

It wasn't an easy weekend. People couldn't decide whether to focus on the proposed blockade or the eviction. Some felt the women were not providing enough leadership. Underneath all this another difficulty was emerging: the question of Men. A week previously all the women present at the camp had met and unanimously decided that, while under threat of eviction, women only should actually live at the camp. Although up to this point men had been allowed to live there, the march and camp had always been women's initiatives, with women talking to the press, representing the camp and doing the decision-making. Many now felt they should make this position clearer. Others returning the following day were unhappy with the decision, as were the men involved. By Sunday afternoon there was a muttering too loud to ignore and it was going to have to be talked out.

"Men are just as capable of being non-violent as women."

"Yes, but they often provoke more violence because the police pick on them deliberately."

"Or they get upset at women being mistreated! It's a tactical decision, we want the authorities to have to deal very clearly with women. Right or wrong it makes them react differently."

"No one can ask me to leave! We weren't even allowed in the meeting when you made the decision. Anyway this is my home—I've squatter's rights!"

"Cruise missiles are going to affect everyone, not just women."

"Yeah, you're splitting the peace movement!"

"Do you want a lesbian separatist peace movement? Is that what you want?"

"We want everyone to work in the way they find most effective."

"Well, some of us women like working in mixed groups."

"Yes, but some of us don't. We need space to find our own ways of working. They seem to be different. More concerned with personal things—feelings and trust and cooperation, not power-tripping . . ."

". . . and we need space to find our strengths, how to assert ourselves, make speeches and so on—we don't do that in mixed groups."

"Mixed groups are men's groups, only no one calls them that."

"Have one man here and it's just assumed the good ideas are his."

"Us getting strong can only make the peace movement stronger, not split it."

"If your ways are so good, why don't you let us stay and learn from you?"

"Couldn't you be more useful somewhere else?"

"Start another peace camp!"

"I think behind every good woman there should be a good man!"

"Well! My CND group has always supported Greenham. They'd be very upset to hear you'd gone separatist!"

"There's not much women can call their own. It's important for other women to see Greenham as an initiative successfully taken by women. That gives them hope and pride in their own sex, and encourages them to act as well."

"But does it stop Cruise missiles?"

"Look, if you, the men, really support us, why can't you support our decision?"

Voices were rising. It was obvious that we were too large a crowd and feelings too strong to reach an agreement. So all the people actually living at the camp at that time went into a caravan and somehow, with the pressure of all of us waiting outside, reached an agreement. Women only for two weeks, then the decision would be reviewed.

The two weeks passed and the decision was reviewed and confirmed. "It was the best decision we ever made," said Shushu at a much later date. "The men were a problem. They put us in the role of mothers. 'Mummy shows me how to do this,' and always pushing to see how far they could go."

Helen agreed. "The men are so ludicrously protective. When we first talked to Direct Action on the march, they said guard dogs would be set on us! We'd be abused! One chappie wanted us to walk peacefully up to the gate, hand in a posy of flowers and with quiet dignity disappear into the sunset. That's just what we'd have done, disappear, having wasted ten days of our lives. They simply don't think the same way!"

Not everyone was happy though. "I don't think we analyzed the problem properly," said Franny. "Which was those particular men. None of us had the guts to say, 'Shape up or piss off.' When the decision was reviewed, those that disagreed weren't there. It wasn't humane either. People were turning up at night in the dark and in the rain, and having to leave. I felt we were a strong enough group to cope with that and not stick to rigid rules."

"So why did you stay on?" I asked.

"The women felt so strongly about it. Besides, there was the blockade."

THE BLOCKADE

"Isn't this getting a little ridiculous?" the policeman asked. "How many more of you want to get arrested?" Ridiculous to you perhaps, I thought, to me it seems like the most sensible thing I've ever done in my life.

"We don't want to get arrested. That's not why we're here. We're blocking all the entrances to this camp for twenty-four hours to show we intend to close it down, because we object to what's going on in there. If you choose to arrest us, that is your affair."

It was 2:00 pm on a Monday afternoon in March, the first warm day of the year. We stood on a quiet country road, Newbury Church just visible over the horizon, the hedges and trees just touched by a green mist, a lark singing, high and clear, peace. For the third time that afternoon women lay down head to toe to fill a gap in the wire fence enclosing the base. . . .

I'd been nervous about the blockade. We'd talked about it for weeks. It was to follow on from a festival to celebrate the Spring Equinox. While plans for the festival had gone smoothly ahead, because of concern over the threatened eviction we'd done little to prepare for the blockade. So I had arrived at the camp two days previously with a sick feeling in my stomach that we were heading for disaster.

"Don't worry Lynne," Shushu had smiled, patting my shoulder, "We're very organized." And indeed they had been. One group of women had written a small practical briefing, outlining how the blockade would proceed, what to do if arrested, solicitors'[1] phone numbers and so on. A system had been devised whereby every woman involved in the action would register and join a group to do non-violence training. Each gate into the base would have a legal observer who would watch what happened, note the arrests, and relay information to a central point via walkie-talkies hired for the purpose.

All the previous afternoon women had sat huddled in caravans getting to know one another, and deciding how we'd deal with confrontation. Outside the festival had surged around, tap dancers in radiation suits, jugglers, clowns, the Fall-Out Marching Band, all undaunted by the miserable weather. Then I had watched with amazement as two hundred women in the space of an hour managed to work out how to cover seven gates for twenty-four hours, sleep, eat and communicate. It was going to work!

That didn't mean that I wasn't scared as my group walked out to fill the main gate at 6:30 pm: a line of police behind an enormous crowd in front and camera lights glaring in our eyes. We sat down. At six other gates women were doing the same thing, and we waited. The rain poured down steadily but the stream of traffic was absent. The base, it seemed, in consideration of our wishes, had closed itself down. So we settled in, wrapped in rugs and macs, and took turns throughout the night to do four-hour shifts. The cameramen went home. The rain turned to drizzle.

---

[1]English term for lawyers.

Supporters brought hot tea, and entertainers, left over from the festival, went from gate to gate with fiddles and guitars.

Then in the morning, we discovered the base intended to work as usual. The police had created a new gate on a deserted bit of road. Realizing that this made the rest of our blockade meaningless, some from each gate trekked round there.

"This," the police inspector said, "is our gate and if you sit in it you will be arrested." He was very courteous and gave us five minutes to think. The decision was unanimous and the first group of women sat down.

. . . The afternoon wore on. I sat in the dust at the side of the road, sun hot on my face. A line of some thirty women sat opposite me. A line of police faced them. They had changed their tactics and stopped arresting us. They were letting the traffic pile up, then swooping down and pulling us out of the way, letting us back when the traffic had passed. We had changed our tactics too. Five women were too easy to move so as many as possible had formed a strong chain. It was a wearying process. Traffic, mostly gravel trucks, came through every half hour. We were getting good at going limp but it only slowed them down. There'd been some rough treatment: pulled hair, a woman thrown to the ground, but on the whole the police had been friendly, one even sharing his fears about nuclear war with us. Two women were keening, they had done so steadily all afternoon, wailing, "No more war, this isn't a game, think what you're doing."

"We were determined," Sara said later, "that our vision, not theirs, should be in control of that space."

It was growing cold, sun low and red in the sky, the police were pulling barbed wire back across the gap, they were leaving. All the women started shouting and hugging each other. "We've done it! We've done it." Singing and dancing we formed a circle. Then suddenly, spontaneously, silence fell. We stood filling the road. A policeman giggled, but then muffled his radio. They were silent too, for the first time that afternoon with us, not against us.

"Pass a smile around," a woman whispered in my ear grinning. I whispered to my neighbor and watched as the women's faces lit up.

A letter in *Peace News* the following week read:

'The blockade' as a blockade was a failure and. . . . I would say that what I saw symbolically, and actively, manifested was woman's oppression and subjugation . . . they were using their bodies the way they've been used for centuries, lumps of unintelligent flesh booted aside when they got in the way. No attempt was made to seal off the site in a proper pacifist way with glue, padlocks and chains . . .

Angered, I wrote back:

> . . . What mattered was the effect that symbol had on ourselves and the
> people we were confronting. A policeman trying to pull two arms apart in
> a firmly linked human chain has to directly confront his own feelings
> about human contact, handling women not as sexual objects but as
> powerful beings . . . hacking through a chain he can avoid all that. It's just
> the nice easy masculine field of mechanics, no feelings involved. It's that
> objectification, that lack of understanding as to what pain and suffering
> really mean that makes it possible to press a button and annihilate a
> million people, that's what we're trying to challenge. That action meant
> directly confronting these people with our bodies . . . with the compre-
> hension of what violence and power mean in human terms . . . No, we
> didn't "win," but you can't take control till you feel powerful and not one
> of us left that day without feeling stronger and more sure of our power to
> act. Surely not the result of a day of oppression and subjugation.

Two days later I handed in my resignation at the hospital where I was
working. Helen rang me up. "Lynne! You can't give up your job. We
need doctors."

"I consider nuclear weapons a health threat and I'm not confronting
it here in casualty. You're a fine one to talk anyway. Have you been
evicted yet?"

"Not yet, they're applying for a court order. We'll get five days' notice
to prepare our case."

"How's Franny?"

"She's set up a new camp at the construction gate — mixed. Come and
see us."

THE EVICTION

April — the camp looked beautiful. The poplar in the center of the
marquee was sprouting fresh green leaves. Blackthorn blossomed in the
hedges. I stood by the for once unlit fire. "Hello," a voice shouted.
Looking up, Sara's grinning face was just visible through a hole in the
roof. "We're building a tree house for when they evict us. It rests on the
structure so they can't take that down without risking our lives."

"Brilliant!" I said.

Another woman was making a rope ladder, and another binding
rushes together. "For walls," she said. "They come from the Kennett
near Silbury Hill, did you know the land is sculptured in the female
form?"

"No, I didn't. Who are you?"

"Since I've come down here I've called myself Ioma Axe."

"Hello Lynne," said Shushu, "Did you hear about our flying blockades?"

"We've developed a new technique, small blockades as and when it suits us. We did one to greet a visiting American General," Helen added.

"It only ended when an American Serviceman tried to psych us out by revving up his bike and it burst into flames between his legs. He was OK." Shushu went on.

"That's what convinced me I had to stay," Ioma said. "Magic."

"Had you been down before?"

"For the blockade on the 21st and the atmosphere was so good—spider webs woven everywhere and all these different women, Buddhist nuns, women from France, all working together. I just thought 'This is it! This is the place!' " She laughed. "I've had a lot of asthma and before the weekend I'd thought 'I'll probably get pneumonia and die.' Then I found myself saying, 'Go and do it—you're not going to die and if you do—tough!.' "

A small child ran by, a woman spoke to him in German. "That's Beatrice," said Helen. We wandered out on to the grass verge where a star, made from branches and wool woven together, swung in the breeze.

"Do you think the camp has changed?"

"Yes, you've got a lot of women coming now who are much more involved in the women's movement, committed to feminist principles. They're also much clearer on the nuclear issues."

I noticed a small spiral of painted rocks on the grass. "We've started a peace cairn here and at the construction gate." Sara told me. "So that people who can't be here can show they care by leaving a rock, that way they see they're not alone. Rocks and stones are the oldest things. They have a lot of power."

Small signs had appeared around the camp: ASK PEOPLE WHO THEY ARE, DON'T GIVE YOUR NAME TO STRANGERS.

"The council have been here looking around," said Shushu.

Two weeks later a letter arrived from Annie. The council was going to the high court on the 14th of May for an "Order to recover possession of the land at Greenham Common." The case rested on the fact that we had broken minor by-laws. I noticed that one of the by-laws applying to the common stated that no person "should throw or discharge missiles." Some nineteen named defendants and persons unknown were also summoned to say why they shouldn't be evicted.

The court hearing, as we expected, went against us. We spent the night of the 14th blockading the main gate, hourly expecting the bailiffs. The eviction didn't occur that night however, or the next.

The blockade of the main gate continued, women came from all over the country, bringing food, staying a day. We gradually prepared the camp, moving stuff we didn't want to lose and most of our caravans on to a small strip of Ministry of Transport land 100 yards from the main gate. It was wearying, waiting, difficult to keep the fire going or our energy levels high.

On Thursday 27 May, when I had gone home for a few days, a friend phoned. "They've been evicted." I turned on the six o'clock news in time to see Sara being lifted bodily from the cab of a bulldozer.

It took them nine hours to raze the camp to the ground, doing considerable damage to our poplar tree in the process, giving Beatrice mild concussion and arresting five women for causing a breach of the peace in the process. They left the caravans on the Ministry of Transport land alone.

I am sitting in court with twenty to thirty other women filling the benches beside me. Clutching handfuls of flowers, dressed in bright clothing, they are the most cheerful sights there. Three magistrates: two women and one man, straight-faced and neatly pressed, gaze down onto Ioma, Tina, Amanda and Beatrice in the dock, who are surrounded by police. They all look rumpled, having spent the night in the cells, but that didn't stop Sara and Beatrice from bursting into the court singing their lungs out and embracing all the women within reach before being hustled into the dock.

We've listened for two hours to the witnesses for the prosecution, mainly police officers, read from their notebooks as to how the defendants lay or stood in front of a bulldozer, while other women walked round it "tying it up with string." The assistant bailiff has complained of being followed around by "ladies singing," and has told us that "It wasn't for us to decide what was what, ours was to obey orders."

"At what point does anyone take responsibility?" Sara asks from the witness stand. She is speaking in her own defense and has already confused the clerk by stating that she finds the oath acceptable if she may swear to the Goddess, rather than god.

"We are all of us intelligent people. How can we sit around hiding the truth, talking legal jargon? We could all be sitting together using our hearts and minds to deal with the terrible situation we face. Even if you feel that the possibility of a holocaust is remote, why does everyone refuse to discuss it? Today we have heard the bailiff say that he was only doing his job, the reasons for the peace camp being at Greenham Common are not his concern. The police say they are only doing their jobs because they are asked to by the bailiff. The court is here today because the police have brought us here. . . .

"I am charged with disturbing the peace. My whole life is dedicated to peace. I may sing loudly but I do not swear or abuse anyone, I am totally non-violent. I do not eat meat, harm any person or animal on this planet. I try to find harmony with earth, my cycles with the cycles of the moon and planets. I search for peace in a world which prepares for war."

Ioma, Tina and Beatrice follow, reiterating Sara's points. Beside me Jane is weaving a web across the palm of her hand and behind me I can hear humming. The solicitor speaks in Amanda's defense.

"At no point did my client show any violent resistance. I think my client would say that the idea of the Queen's Peace comes from the King's Peace defined during the civil war, not just in the narrow sense as meaning law and order but as a state of affairs where all can live peacefully."

How can one get through to them? They sit on the bench, expressionless, unmoved. The clerk rises. "We ask you to enter a recognizance to keep the Queen's Peace for the next twelve months for the sum of £25. Are you willing to so enter?" He asks each in turn.

"No," says Amanda quietly.

"I follow my own morality as I always have. If these people continue what they are doing I shall continue what I am doing," Sara replies.

"Is that no?" the clerk asks in a tired voice.

"I must follow my own morality."

"I think we must take that as a no. Ioma Axe?"

"I do not accept your wording or your values. I believe I always have kept the peace."

"Will you answer the question, yes or no!"

"No," says Ioma.

"Yes, I will keep the peace as I always have," says Beatrice.

"You may stand down, the clerk says, in a relieved voice, choosing to misunderstand her.

"I'll use my own interpretation of the word peace," says Tina.

"You MUST answer the question," the clerk almost shouts in exasperation. "Yes or no!"

"I'll use my own interpretation." Tina stands her ground.

"Then I must ask the court to decide. "Red-faced, the clerk sits down.

The magistrates confer, the humming grows louder. "That's all we're living for, to try and keep the peace!" Jane cries out to the magistrates. "The rules of this court don't seem adequate to deal with the subject matter in hand," Helen states in a matter of fact tone. "They're living it on a daily basis." Jane continues, "Can you see that? You must stop hiding behind that book and have courage!"

"Seven days," mutters one of the lady magistrates, scarcely looking up.

We're sitting on the steps outside the court, waiting for the van taking them to Holloway to drive by. Jane is still weaving wool, the children are asleep. As to the future? We believe in it. Jane told me this morning that they left the peace cairn alone. Women are planning to come back, and there are peace camps outside military bases all over the country now: Lakenheath, Faslane, Molesworth, Fairford, Caerwent, Burtonwood, Burghfield, Waddington, Upper Heyford. . . . We aren't going away. We'll be there for as long as it takes.

POSTSCRIPT: NO LONGER
LIVING IN FEAR

The landscape has changed. At first there was grass, neat shrubs and verges as in any suburban park, and the women lived in caravans. So they covered the grass with rocks and earth and towed away the caravans. But the women built benders with wood and plastic, weighed down with the rocks. So they tore down the benders and dug up the rocks and widened the road and passed a new law that forbade anyone to build benders. So the women slept out in the open.

And now the bailiffs come to move the women themselves, two or three times a day for the last two years. And still the women stay, not only here but all around the base. Their few possessions are piled in prams and vans, easy to move quickly. Some sleep in the bright red, quick-to-put-up tents, donated by the Quakers, others in Gortex sleeping bags or under quickly strung plastic sheeting. Now they plan to extend the base itself to enclose this small piece of land. Perhaps they have not noticed that the women can simply move across the road.

The most profound effect however is not on the landscape but on the lives of the women themselves. In her five-year association with the camp, Helen, a former midwife and mother of five children, has ended her marriage, come out as a lesbian and consequently had to struggle with her ex-husband for access to her youngest children: "I think he was quite fearful they would learn that there were other ways of living from me. The children themselves went through a phase when they were unhappy about my life. I don't suppose they are delighted with it now but they accept that it's right for me and they know that I care about them. More important the younger ones are not going to grow up regarding lesbians with horror. They don't see as much of me as they would like but I can't do the political work I'm involved with *and* raise my sons. Other women can, I admire them for it."

Not surprisingly her political focus has also changed. "When I first got involved it was very directly because of the missiles. Now I feel that the real problem is getting men to make the fundamental changes that are necessary to allow women to live safely." She points to the rapes of three women at Molesworth allegedly by men involved in the peace-camp as an indication of the urgent need for the Campaign for Nuclear Disarmament to raise the issue of male violence.

Rebecca, who has lived at the camp for the last four years, sees her views "tempered" rather than changed: "My commitment is to feminism—women have a different approach and I've given up trying to convince men that what we say is right. Women need to put energy into the changes they are making for themselves because they're changing faster and with greater understanding. That's where the hope lies. And I've learned to trust revolutionary non-violence. I used to be much more accommodating. Now I don't accept that non-violence can ever be passive. It has to be active and challenging both to oneself and to the thing that you're opposing, because it's an opposing force.

"I'm tireder than I used to be; I've never worked so hard in my life as in the last four years. There's part of me that longs to turn my back on the struggle and just go and do something else. But I certainly don't feel I've sacrificed anything to be at Greenham. I've learned so much about myself and about other women."

Lesley, who left the camp in 1983 still sees it as having changed her life in a way that nothing else has: "The most important thing about the camp for me was the way it energized and strengthened me to work elsewhere. I'm much more confident, I understand issues more clearly and trust my own judgement. Nor am I prepared to be put down or belittled when working in mixed groups. Greenham was a spring board and an eye-opener for me, it made me much more politically aware—not just on the peace issue.

"It brought my husband and son together. They have always had a very conflict-ridden relationship and I'd always mediated. While I was away they had an enormous and cathartic confrontation—yelling at each other on their knees through the cat-flap after my husband threw my son out. Their relationship's grown from there. They now get on incredibly well and love each other very much. It wouldn't have happened if I had been there."

None of the women regretted their involvement and all of them saw the camp as continuing to be effective both in directly confronting Cruise and keeping a constant watch on the base as well as empowering other women. The base has cut back its exercises by 25 per cent this year, Helen pointed out. Recently a *Mail on Sunday* article under headlines of *98 Missiles and 1 Woman* had bemoaned the absence of the thousands of women who "Embraced the Base" in 1982. The article completely failed to understand that the action was organized by a tiny group of women living in appalling conditions.

Rebecca remarked, "It wouldn't be appropriate to call such an action now, not because of a lack of support but because women are far too involved in their own communities in a way they hadn't realized was possible before that action. About once a year I go through a real struggle with myself as to whether I can face another winter at Greenham. Wouldn't it be nice to earn a bit of money and couldn't I be just as politically effective elsewhere. But if I was involved in any kind of political work I'd have to live somewhere and be involved locally and I can go out from here to be involved in other areas such as the Links campaign.[2] This is my home. And I do get something important from living here: a sense of community—from being involved with the struggles we have to engage in everyday; both among ourselves as women struggling for our own freedom and the visible persistence of our struggle against the base, the courts, local prejudice—and from seeing how all these things have changed."

Certainly change has not been confined to the women who have lived at the camp. The deployment of Cruise turned local peace activists overnight from "supporters' of Greenham women—to active resisters. At the beginning Peg who lived with her forester husband in a cottage a few miles from the base "admired but didn't get really involved." After deployment she suddenly realized she was in a position to track them whenever they went out and that's what she has been doing ever since. She acts as a bridge between Cruisewatch—which continues to grow in effectiveness—and the camp: "The convoy passes my door almost every time it goes out and even though I'm busy with the telephone tree and the radio, my husband and I never let it actually pass without taking the banner out. It might seem a small gesture by two pensioners but if you do nothing it is taken as assent." She has watched her family become increasingly involved with the camp. Her daughter sleeps up there. Her grandson speaks up for the women in his local school. "I used to think how lucky people were who could sell up and get away from the base. I don't feel that now, I'm proud to have the women as my friends and that if this evil had to be, it's here, so that at least I can play a positive part. It occupies almost the whole of my life."

Local Mobilization

Newbury Campaign against the Missiles, her local peace group, have not found it so easy. The group can't switch off like other groups. "You can see the bunkers when you go shopping. So how can you forget?"

---

[2]The Links campaign grew out of the connections made between miners' wives and Greenham women, who together with Friends of the Earth and Greenpeace, look jointly at the issues of nuclear power, nuclear weapons and coal communities.

Peg explained. "Half would like to focus on other issues like other groups further away. But Cruise is here and if anything's to be done about it, it's us that has to do it. You're either for it or against it."

The town itself has always in the past preferred to hedge its bets by decrying the women rather than acknowledging the base. Gradually, Rebecca felt, it is dawning on people what the base actually means: "From having drunken servicemen shipped home without standing trial for the damage they've done; from having sirens wail and Cruise thunder by their doors, from having houses flooded as happened last week because of excavations on the base . . ." And, of course, the bombing of Libya frightened people. Rebecca together with five US and British women went into RAF Welford in protest at the use of the cluster bombs kept there. At their trial afterwards, not only did the prosecuter apologize to Rebecca for the police trying to hide the injuries done to her knee, but the magistrate ordered police to return documents stolen from her car and the whole case was written up honestly and at length in the local paper—all unprecedented events in Newbury.

And new women continue to come. There is Donna who drove past the camp while in the Territorial Army in 1983 and thought she'd "really much rather be on the other side of the road." She thought of getting out but didn't like the idea of being courtmartialed. She arrived at the beginning of August this year, saw the convoy and decided to stay. "I thought I should at least put as much energy on this side of the fence as I put on the other."

There is Anna, who came in December having caught "Greenham-itis" from a friend and gave up her job as a shop assistant to come down regularly. "I feel happy and wanted. You can be yourself and don't have to be cheerful. Can you imagine standing beside a till all day? At the moment it feels like I am leading a double life. Old friends know but they don't understand. I'm not interested in drinking and going to clubs anymore. I want something more meaningful in life, and there is that here. When you see total destruction on one side and birds and trees on the other, you realize how precious it is."

The words are familiar, yet the women are just as impossible to stereotype as they have always been. And they come in spite of the fact that police and army violence towards them continues to increase, and in spite of the fact that the camp is a harder place to live. Or perhaps it is because of it. "Obviously," Rebecca pointed out, "when you've been evicted two sometimes three times a day, it's no longer a question of 'I've built my bender and it's safe and cosy for the next few months, so I may as well stay here.' Every woman is confronted daily with whether she wants to move back onto the land. The women who live here now have a stronger commitment to cooperate amongst themselves than before."

"There's this myth that the old guard were acceptable and the new guard aren't," Helen said. "People always want to see the 'Good Old Days' as the best. Yet I don't remember a time when there was ever complete acceptance of women at the camp. The women associated with the camp now are so clear and sure of their personal politics in a way we never were because we just tottered on to the scene and didn't have the confidence. These women came straight out of school with no jobs available and are politicized from day one."

And there's something else. While in five years the idea of women organizing separately at a political level has not yet become acceptable, it has at least become an established fact, and non-violent direct action is seen as a valid tactic in a way that we would have found hard to imagine at that time, as the recent actions against NIREX demonstrate. The arguments for and against bubble away but no longer threaten to split the peace movement. It is Greenham that has helped to create this sort of climate so that the women who come today no longer have to spend their time justifying themselves or fighting for political space. They can get on with what they came to do, confronting the base and the issues it raises.

Five years ago the women who arrived at Greenham stressed their "political" naiveté and their fear for the future. They spoke in apocalyptic terms of the need to inform the public of the threat of nuclear war before it was too late. Now the public are better informed. As Rebecca pointed out, given the damage we've already done to ourselves and our environment, it may still be too late. However the women at the camp today do not seem frightened of the future. On the contrary, they hope that they can change it.

16

The Seneca Stories: Tales from the Women's Peace Encampment*

Grace Paley

My friends and I came to the Seneca Women's Peace Encampment from Vermont. No matter what else we saw in the five days of work/action/arrest/talk, we felt the wide eventful sky above us, a blazing place from which sudden thunderstorms attacked. We had driven south out of the Green Mountains, out of the hills where cows pasture on narrow spiraling terraces down to great flat fields of corn, long barely sloping acres of soybeans. So much horizon!

We came into a careful conservative New York area that had once experienced extraordinary history. In the 1590s, the women of the Iroquois nation had met in Seneca to ask the tribes to cease their warfare. In 1848, the first Women's Rights Convention met in Seneca Falls. During the 1850s Harriet Tubman led slaves north through this country. Her safe house still stands. The towns and countryside of Seneca County seemed to be a geography of American Herstory, where women of color and women of less color once lived powerfully and rebelliously, offering their female leadership in a dream of peace and justice for women—and men, too. In fact, the planned encampment was named just that, the Women's Encampment for a Future of Peace and Justice.

---

*Previously published in *Ms.* magazine (December 1983).

There were many greeters when we passed the Amish farm and made a sharp right into the Encampment. Women poked their heads into the windows of our car to assure us of a welcome, to tell us where to park, where the 'Non-Registration' Booth was, to tell any men in the car that they would be welcome in the large area around the house and garden, but beyond the barn the women wanted privacy and safety. We bumped our car over the terrible corrugations that had once been the earth of a farmer's cornfield. We learned that we were expected to put three hours of work into camp maintenance every day. We contributed $7. We found out quickly that the condition of the soil beyond the parking in the tenting fields was also pretty poor. Corn uses the land up and it was a hope often expressed that this land could be renewed, returned to the fertility of the green farms of the country.

Because of friends from New York and New England who had camped earlier we knew: Seneca was Stories. The story of the flag; the story of the TV camera crew; the story of the woman who climbed the Army depot tower and painted out the words 'Mission First'—leaving the words 'People Always;' the story of the astrologers who advised the protesters on what day and what hour to do civil disobedience; the story of the men who apologized, the women who joined us; the story of the woman who wore a shirt saying 'Nuke the Bitches Till They Glow,' who was moved a tiny bit, so she removed the words 'Till They Glow,' reserving further action for deeper thought; the story of boardwalks and ramps lovingly built to keep us all from twisting our ankles, and all that work—the plumbing and electrical work—done by women, the story of rumor, invention, and absolute factual truth in the lovely combinations that become myth.

Here are some of the stories I lived in or alongside of—and a couple of stories told me so often that I've begun to think I was a part of those stories too:

On Saturday, July 30, about one hundred women left Seneca Falls to walk twelve miles to the Encampment. They carried large cutouts of Susan B. Anthony, Elizabeth Cady Stanton, Harriet Tubman, Sojourner Truth, and other women their walk honored. They intended to show the connections between the everyday killing oppression of women and the battering of our world in man-made war. They walked peacefully through uninhabited miles of field and scrub and small towns lined with American flags. When they came into Waterloo, they saw a huge sign stretched between two houses. It greeted them: NUKE THEM TILL THEY GLOW. THEN SHOOT THEM IN THE DARK.

They turned the corner to cross the Waterloo bridge and were met by several hundred Waterloo citizens, nearly all holding little and large flags, nearly all screaming foul cries and words they hoped would insult the women: "Commies," "Lezzies," "Kill them," "Nuke them." Many carried flagpoles with pointed tips, and their enraged screams and jabbing terrified our women, who, after brief discussion, decided to sit down. (This is often done in confrontations to show that violence is not intended and also to give the sitters a chance to talk quietly about what to do next.) The sheriff, an elected official who had known all about the walk weeks earlier, had no way to control the infuriated crowd that consisted of his neighbors, who were, after all, voters. He offered a detour which made sense to some women. But for the women sitting under the barrage of hatred, it seemed foolish to turn their backs. Besides, they felt somewhat stubborn about upholding their right to walk through an American town without vicious abuse. They thought that right was worth a good deal. Many women tried courageously to look into the eyes of the men and women barring their way . . . to somehow change the confrontation into a meeting. Finally, and ironically, the quiet women were arrested for disorderly conduct while the screamers were allowed to go. One by one, the women were dragged off to become the 54 Jane Does who spent five days in the only jail big enough to hold them all—the Interlaken High School.

Among the women arrested was one prominent Waterloo citizen who was horrified by the behavior of the townspeople. Her daughter was one of the first to come to the Encampment the next day to inform us that many of her neighbors were ashamed, that the hard screaming knot didn't represent them, though it would be seen again and again—at the Seneca Depot truck gate, at the Interlaken High School where thirteen brave vigilers who were keeping a watch at night were surrounded by huge trailer trucks, assuring darkness, invisibility, and terror. Here too, the flags were used to poke and jab at the circle of women.

The green lawn outside the Interlaken High School was a place where lots of play happened, too. In the daylight we pantomimed the August 1 march for our Jane Does watching from distant windows. We played out the fence-climbing arrests, we sang to them and, in fact, sang so well that day by day, the taunters became quieter. If we shouted, they shouted. But when we sang, they listened. I listened myself. We were singing beautifully. And we were saddened for the opposition which tried a couple of songs, worked on "Jingle Bells" but foundered on "America the Beautiful," which we joyfully took up.

A story: one of the vigilers at the Interlaken High School prison was approached by a man who told her he'd been one of the people at the Waterloo bridge. He hadn't screamed, he said, just waved his flag. He asked what the whole thing was about, for godsakes. She explained the reason for the camp, the historical purpose of the walk. "Oh," he said, "I thought you were all sitting down in the road because the VFW wasn't letting any women be part of *their* parade. And I agreed with them. That's why I was mad."

Two days after the August 1 march, I was a greeter at the camp entrance. A big car turned in. Father and son. The father leaned out the window and said, "We came to say we're sorry about everything. That's all." The son spoke through the far window. "We wanted to ask you women how you do it? Those people were really rotten to you. I heard them. They insult you and they call you names and you're so calm. My father and me—we honor you. We don't understand, but we honor you."

Two young women came up out of darkness to join us in our night circle at Interlaken High School. Someone tells me they own or work in a restaurant near the depot. They sit with us as we go around the circle trying to see who will go home and who will sit the night out with a good chance of arrest. The two young women sit with us for about an hour, listening to us listen to one another, then proudly and deliberately walk past their neighbors on the way down to their car. The words, "Traitor, traitor," follow them in a halfhearted way.

A great deal has been written about that hostility at Waterloo as though a country that refuses to pass something as simple as the Equal Rights Amendment would not have pockets of vicious misogyny, as though a nation with tens of thousands of nuclear bombs, Army bases, weapons factories in the midst of unemployment would not be able to raise a furious patriarchal horde.

From that rage of flags that seemed so pervasive in the towns of Seneca County, we must go back to the days before the camp's opening. A Waterloo man came to the already exhausted, worried organizers and maintainers of the camp and said, "Take this flag and place it at the camp entrance, or else we will tell the world, the media, the town, how you refused the American flag." The women met to discuss this—as we were all to meet time and time again in large and small circles. There was so much strong feeling on either side that a committee of fifteen was charged with resolving the problem: five women in strong opposition, five women in determined support, and five easy going intermediate mediators. After seven hours under the only shade tree in that part of the camp, it was suggested that women could make their own flags. And many flags *were* made, not national flags, but painted and embroidered banners with pictures and sayings about our lives—also a couple of handsome handmade American flags—and all these were hung on lines in the front yard of the camp, along the road. However, the flag of the provoker was not accepted. As a result the flag entrepreneurs of Seneca County did an incredible business as anyone driving through the red-white-and-blue towns will tell.

In the Nicastro Restaurant a couple of miles up the road, the Encampment leaflet and vision statement are tacked to the wall right next to two awards to Mr. and Mrs. Nicastro: Parents of the Year. In their guest book we have all written our thanks for the decency of this family to all the women who drank coffee and ate fine celebrating dinners after jail. They allowed their place to be used during the summer for meetings between encampers and the community.

On August 1, about 2500 women marched from the nearby Sampson State Park to the depot. It was a long hot walk, stalled by the sheriff every twenty-five feet or so; he was waiting for state troopers. He feared another confrontation. The angry opposition had already entrenched itself and its flags at the truck gate. But this time a band of very brave Waterloo citizens stood with their children not too far away holding signs that said they'd fight for our rights whether they agreed with us or not.

Once at the gate, women came forward to transform the military steel mesh into an embroidery of banners, dolls, children's photographs, quilts, christening dress, lovers' photos. Then they stepped back, and the women who planned the civil disobedience came forward. Immediately women began to climb over the high fence. I thought it was rather ridiculous, but as I and my Vermont affinity group of six women looked and looked, it became more interesting. It was the riskiness of the fence, I thought—this may be the last fence I'll be able to climb in this life (I'm sixty and I see a fence shortage ahead) so I joined the others and we climbed that fence that looked to us women—young or old—a lot like the school fence that encircled girlhood, the one that the boys climbed adventurously over again and again. We were carted off by young soldiers—many of them black and Hispanic—all of them perplexed, most of them quite kind. There was a physical delight in the climbing act, but I knew and still believe that the serious act was to sit, as many women did, in little circles through the drenching night and blazing day on the hot cement in front of the truck gate with the dwindling but still enraged 'Nuke Them Till They Glow' group screaming "lesbian bitches" from their flag-enfolded cars.

To this gate, the curious citizens of Waterloo or Romulus or Geneva—and folks who'd read of this excitement from forty to fifty miles away—came with their children and their coolers to watch silently, and sometimes speak, asking the hard questions again: "What about the Russians?" or "We have to make a living don't we?"; and sometimes, to say sadly, "Did you really burn a flag and then urinate on it?" No. No. No.

So we *had* troubled them. And we asked: wouldn't it have been wonderful if hundreds, thousands of Germans had sat down before the gates of the Krupp gas oven plants and troubled the contented hearts and minds of the good German people? They might have also asked those first two questions.

On Wednesday, August 3, people gathered at the fairgrounds in Waterloo outside the big corrugated-metal building in which the trial would be conducted. Lot of visible media—meaning TV. Our Jane Does had continued their resistance; they were carried into 'court,' then back out into the yard as the judge tried to conduct one trial after another. They demanded a common trial and dismissal of unjust charges. We, their supporters, were removed from the building. Singing again. Finally the senselessness of individual trials became clear. Three women were allowed to speak for the group. Then the judge dismissed the case and ordered the charges dropped. He, like the sheriff, was an elected official but saw the wind blowing in a different direction. Outside in the terrible heat, I walked among the men and women, the cameras, the stalwart youths standing like statues holding enormous flags on thick flagpoles. And found a group of Waterloo women with cardboard signs. WE SUPPORT YOUR RIGHT TO WALK THROUGH OUR TOWN. THE CONSTITUTION SHELTERS YOU. Our Seneca sisters were hugging them, thanking them for their bravery. "Oh," said one of the women surprised and embarrassed. "We didn't think we'd be so important as all that." "You're the most important of all to us," we answered.

There were so many other events that ought to be written about, and I know will be. But briefly . . . the busloads of women who came all the way from Minnesota . . . the women from Greenham Common in England, and Comiso in Italy, and from the Netherlands and Germany who worked so hard to share their experiences with us . . . the religious women who asked if they could pray in the depot chapel, were given permission, then asked to leave when the pacific nature of the prayers was understood . . . the walk to Harriet Tubman's house . . . civil disobedience actions of Labor Day when women chose to dig a hole under the fence instead of climbing over it.

One of the most important events, and I do think of it as an event in itself, is the local news that the Seneca Encampment became. That news coverage is part of the news I brought home. The combination of stubbornness that is nonviolent action, the peculiar, arduous, delicate process of our constantly public meetings set against the opposition's vituperative rage illuminated the issues. What we talked and acted about was Peace and Justice, and the way we went about it spoke to the word "Future."

One more story: I am waiting to use the phone. There are two phones. I am pretty annoyed with the long gabby calls of the people on line in front of me, until I'm finally close enough to hear a couple. One woman is giving information about her entire affinity group to a contact person . . . someone's dog has to be picked up . . . a mother must be called . . . a job has to be put off. The woman on the other phone is young and in tears. She's saying, "Mom, Ma, please, it's my world they're gonna blow up." Then some silence. Then, "Ma, please, I have to do it. It's not terrible to get arrested. I'm all right. Ma, please, listen, you got married and had us and everything and a house, but they still kept making nuclear bombs." More tears. "Listen, listen, please, Ma."

I wanted to take the phone from her and say, "Ma, don't worry, your kid's okay. She's great. Don't you see she's one of the young women who will save my granddaughter's life?"

17

The Puget Sound Women's Peace Camp: Interviews with Two Activists

Diana E. H. Russell

I met Sandra Jo Palm and Susan James in March 1984, when I spent a one-week vacation at the Puget Sound Women's Peace Camp. I was profoundly impressed by these two women. Their willingness to change their lives radically in order to try to prevent nuclear war inspired and challenged me. Spending a week with women like them also made me realize how attached I'd become to my structured life with its routines and physical comforts.

At forty-eight, Sandra Jo, a Quaker and a feminist, was the oldest member of the Peace Camp. Her interview precedes the interview with Susan James.

SANDRA JO PALM

Because I'd been working for several years in the women's liberation movement and trying to invent new processes, I dropped in to the Puget Sound Women's Peace Camp to participate in a feminist non-violent action. I spent the night there, then went on to another meeting elsewhere. I stopped by the camp again on my way home, and ended up staying for a few days, then for a few more, and it's been eight months now!

Initially I was drawn to the Peace Camp because it felt like a graduate school in women's liberation. We were taking all the things that had been worked out in the early days of the women's movement a step further, so it seemed like a place to grow as a feminist.

You hadn't decided before you came to the Camp to work against nuclear weapons?

Absolutely not. In fact, I didn't focus on that issue for several months. I saw the Camp as a place to do feminist consciousness-raising. This is a great feminist recruiting ground. It also gave me an opportunity to move feminists toward a more radical view of society, and it was wonderful to be around women with similar values.

What do you see now as the relationship between feminism and working against nuclear weapons?

We're facing the likelihood of nuclear war because there's a problem with the whole structure of our society. We won't have war if we restructure it according to feminist principles because we will have other ways of dealing with conflicts. I see the nuclear threat as a symptom of the ills of a society which we have to change in a very radical way. I used to think that we had to change all aspects of society and that it didn't matter which ones we worked on. But I'm working on the nuclear crisis because I've become increasingly convinced that there's about a 50 percent chance of our having a nuclear war.

What convinced you of this?

The first thing was seeing the documentary movie "The Day After Trinity" about Oppenheimer and how he was recruited to make the first atomic bomb and the group of people he gathered around him. Several Nobel Prize winners were involved. They recruited the best brains in the United States, so they had all these brilliant men and some women working on it. What disturbed me most was that only one member of that group of scientists questioned whether they should be making the bomb. That person called a meeting but only very few of the scientists showed up to discuss it. Only thirty-five or so out of the thousands who were involved in making it discussed the ethical consequences of what they were doing. These people appeared to get caught up in the excitement of the project and they continued with it even after Germany surrendered. The realization that nobody said "no" was one thing that influenced my thinking. Somebody has to say no—like to the Cruise missiles being made by Boeing—so *I* did.

But at first it seemed very unlikely to me that we'd get into a nuclear war. I felt that neither the United States nor the Russians wanted one, so it wouldn't happen. I got scared only when I started reading more about this government's plans for a limited nuclear war and their belief that we could survive this, in fact I became absolutely terrified. I read documents that convinced me that our government thought that nuclear war would occur. And the US government had already okayed the dropping of two nuclear bombs. If they'd done this once, perhaps they'd think that it was okay to do it again. After these realizations I knew I had to work on this issue, and as a feminist I knew that there had to be a feminist analysis of why we came to be in this situation and how to tell them that we're not going to cooperate with this.

Why is it important to work with other women on this?

For various reasons women have not had a voice in what is happening to us. We haven't had an influence on policy. We don't have the power and we can't just throw rubber bands at the power; we have to learn the skills that we haven't had the opportunity to develop before. We haven't even had the opportunity to *imagine* ourselves in the roles that are needed. This Peace Camp is trying to develop the skills necessary to bring about change; to work against our internalized sexism, to change our own images of ourselves, and to see that we ourselves can do everything that needs to be done.

Do you think that women can keep nuclear war from happening?

I certainly do. I no longer have the denial mechanism that I used to have, so it's very hard to live with the idea that our lives may end very soon. But I really believe that we have the power to withhold cooperation from the men who are responsible for this situation. There are a lot of women in this world. There are more of us than men. Women can be empowered to stop cooperating with men. Then society will change and we won't have nuclear bombs.

Do you foresee many more women working against nuclear weapons?

Absolutely. And I see women becoming increasingly empowered on this issue. I saw 2000 women come through the Peace Camp in the summer of 1983, and all those women are working in some way right now to stop nuclear weapons. Greenham women have inspired thousands upon thousands upon thousands of women to make a change in their lives and to feel that they can do something about the situation we are in. I'm becoming much more hopeful that an increasing number of women will become aware of the changes that we need to make.

You seem to be able to face the possibility of imminent death and remain hopeful at the same time.

Yes, I feel hopeful because not only women but citizens in general are taking more of an interest in this issue. All the major magazines now have some coverage in every issue on nuclear war. Three years ago there was absolutely nothing on the nuclear threat. There has been a tremendous change in the last few years and the consciousness of our whole country has been raised. Not as much as in Europe, but we're getting there. And women have been increasingly influential in this area of social responsibility, as has the whole religious movement.

What in particular do you see as the role of the women's peace camps in formulating strategy and in enabling women to change this situation?

Right now I think peace camps provide one of the most effective ways of reaching out to radicalize women to a feminist perspective. I think the church is also really effective in reaching women, but the problem with the church is that it doesn't have a feminist analysis. Religious people who work on the nuclear issue don't realize how society as a whole has to change.

How important do you think it is to establish new peace camps?

I think it is very important. If a peace camp were to be established in a major area like the San Francisco bay area, it would be built on the shoulders of other peace camps which have come before. It could become the parent of other peace camps that would spring up all over the United States, or at least in the West.

How have you been affected by being at the women's peace camp here in Puget Sound?

It's changed my life. It's changed all my priorities. I've relegated other things to second or third place. It's changed me in a very personal sense. I've always tithed with the expectation of effecting social change, but now I've become a peacemaker too. I was speaking at a rally in Portland, Oregon and a religious person there said, "Blessed be the peacemakers," and I realized, "Hey, that's just what I am – a peacemaker." That's my full-time role.

Working on peace has reinforced certain things for me. For example, I've had all kinds of reasons for thinking we have to live more simply, and now I've added another reason for doing so. I think that everybody needs to do more political work and that everybody must start giving more. I think we should give at least ten percent of our time and money to make change. One of the ways to do these things is to stop having to spend forty hours a week trying to make it economically possible to maintain an unnecessarily high style of living. It doesn't bring us happiness. It doesn't bring us a longer life. It just means we spend a lot of time working and spending the earth's resources on inconsequentials. Living more simply and not consuming so much has given me a sense of freedom. One of the things I do with this freedom is to work for social change. Being at the Peace Camp has deepened my commitment.

Another way my life has changed is that I no longer do my art work, and sometimes I miss it a great deal. My art was at the gallery level, and it took me a long time to achieve this. Also, I'm now living in a community of women whereas before I lived with a partner and my son in a very nuclear family type of environment. Living in a community means all kinds of changes. I moved away from my family. I don't have a home of my own any more. I don't even have a room of my own. I gave my car away. The normal things of life aren't there for me any more. I don't have a family, a home, or a car.

Do you find that hard?

No, it's very liberating. I feel very free to do anything I want with my life. I feel very light.

Do other women at the camp believe in tithing?

I don't know, but I *do* know that women in the peace camp spend a fair amount of their own money on this work. It's very seldom that they ever ask to be reimbursed for things. There probably isn't a woman at the Peace Camp who doesn't give at least ten percent of her income to this work.

Do you find it difficult to tell other women that you think they ought to be giving ten percent of their time and their money for peace?

No, I say it wherever I speak. I have no trouble with it because I feel so strongly that it's an important message to convey to people.

SUSAN JAMES

Susan James wasn't actually staying at the Peace Camp when I was there, but I met her on several occasions during my week at the camp. This interview was conducted there.

Why do you think nuclear weapons and nuclear energy are feminist issues?

I'm working to end all forms of violence, and I see nuclear weapons as the ultimate expression of violence. As women we fear this and have to face it every day of our lives. I think the connections are there on a lot of different levels. The mentality responsible for military weapons and military forces and the whole military machine is the same as the one that abuses, attacks and batters women. Both involve the same desire to possess and to exert control. I believe this mentality is usually inspired by some sort of machismo, as well as with insecurity and unmet needs, frustrations, and rage that women encounter with men every day. We're fighting the same mentality on the street as when we fight against the war machine.

On a more day-to-day level of economic survival, women are the greatest victims of the misallocation of money for weapons of death instead of for human needs. Two-thirds of single parent families headed by women are below the poverty level. It is women who suffer the most when social services are taken away. And women are the most victimized by a society that devotes most of its resources to war.

We're also suffering on another level, in that we didn't engineer these forces, but we still have to live with that threat over our heads. With a few exceptions like the male-identified Margaret Thatcher and Jeanne Kirkpatrick, we've been disenfranchised from the decision-making process. If you look at the Pentagon and corporate bodies and global leadership, women aren't involved, yet we are very much affected. So, to me it's a feminist issue on those really different but linked levels.

You mentioned unmet needs and anger as being one of the sources of violence that men have. Why would they have more unmet needs than women?

Well, they're their own victims of this world that they've created. If you look at a profile of a rapist or a batterer, you see that they are needy people. This is not to excuse them in any way. But many of them have been abused and they feel a great deal of rage, and they choose women as an acceptable target for their feelings. If you look at the culture on a larger scale, you also see lots of male insecurity. It's not enough that we in the United States have the whole North American continent, we've got to have the world too! The batterer and the male (or male-identified) leader both try to resolve conflicts by means of force. Feminists and women in general live our lives differently, and we recognize where men's violence is coming from.

At the Peace Camp, we try to relate in a different way. We try not to use force to resolve our conflicts. We have conflicts almost every day, but we try to resolve them peacefully. So, at the same time that we're resisting and defying the war machine, we're also building a model of the way the world needs to be. It's on a small scale, but living in this way is necessary if we want to touch all sectors of society. We must be able to demonstrate how to resolve things by means other than by force. Through our use of consensus decision-making, we're saying that the power has been concentrated in too few hands for too long and that this has led us to the brink. Right now, maybe four or five men hold the fate of the earth in their hands because they have the power to push the button. Only one or two people have the power in this country, and that's a pretty big decision for any person to make.

When you started working in this women's peace camp, did you have this analysis, or has it developed since then?

It's developed. I always felt that rape was war against women. In Vietnam, for example, part of winning involved soldiers raping women before they killed them. That was just part of the act of war. In conquering territory the soldiers made sure that they conquered women too. They marked them as theirs before they killed them. I've always had that analysis. But I used to see nuclear weapons as something that men had created; that it was therefore their problem and they needed to clean up their act. I saw that women were being beaten and raped on a daily basis, and I felt that that was where I needed to work. I didn't see why I should, as a woman, put all my energies into trying to stop the nuclear buildup.

But then I started reading more about nuclear weapons and I realized that there were some definite connections that went beyond the notion that here's a bigger toy they've made to hurt us with. I also decided that we have to start getting away from the whole single-issue syndrome; the idea that I can only work on this part, and everyone else is going to have to choose which part they're going to work on; the idea that you have to pick your issue and stick with it, that you're unfaithful if you leave it and go work on something else. That's what we've been doing in the women's movement, instead of seeing that everything is connected. By working on stopping nuclear weapons, I am also helping to prevent violence against women. I started thinking that we need to work on all the different fronts simultaneously, because then we demonstrate how the problems all come from the same source. We're hoping we're showing this at the Peace Camp.

What influenced you to extend your analysis to the nuclear issue?

It was reading about the new first strike philosophy and at the same time starting to hear about the Greenham Common women, and understanding that they're giving up their lives because of actions by my government. I was realizing that people in the United States could bring much more pressure on the US government from within this country, than women in England could exert from theirs—being from a different country and not having so much influence on our government. So I felt *really* responsible to these women because I *am* a citizen of this country and have so much more power than they do, in the same way that people in this country are much more responsible for what is going on in Central America. I was pleased when women started building the same type of camp in Washington as the English women built in England.

When did you join the Puget Sound Women's Peace Camp?

I went to the first meeting in February of 1983. About twenty women met in a living room; it was one of the first organizing meetings for the Peace Camp. I decided that that was where most of my free time would go. After that the meetings multiplied in size, and for the first time for me, I was seeing women I'd never seen at meetings before: older women, many women with children, a few women of color. For me, it was seeing the dreams of the radical feminist movement coming together around this issue. All these women were coming together from all these different places—some from the civil rights movement, some from the peace movement, and some were totally new to any movement. It was really exciting. I wanted to spend all my time doing it. I started driving sixty miles to these meetings two or three times a week. I was also working full-time and eventually I couldn't do both, either physically or in conscience. So I quit my job. I wrote a letter of resignation saying that by international law I was obligated to do everything I could to stop nuclear war, and that I couldn't work there and do justice to working for peace. In the process I radicalized a lot of the people at work. I gave a copy of my letter to everyone saying that I had to quit. After that I worked full-time for the Peace Camp.

What do you mean by saying that international law required you to quit and devote full time to peace?

It was made crystal clear at the Nuremburg Trial that when citizens realize that crimes against humanity are being perpetrated, they are obligated by international law to do everything they can to stop it so that atrocities like the Holocaust will never happen again. The idea is that even though people would have been breaking the laws of Hitler's Germany to save the Jewish and other people who were being killed there, there is a higher law that supercedes the law of the land.

There are many feminists who don't believe in the laws of an international court. But I feel that this approach is a really good educational tool, and that it presents a hope for transforming the legal system in the same way that acts to change the Jim Crow laws were done.

Was that also your line of defense at your trial?

Yes. I think we all touched on it, but some of us were more attached to it than others. Our brief goes into great depth about all the rulings that support this line of argument—how Cruise missiles are the modern equivalent of the ovens of Nazi Germany. When we were arrested I said that there wasn't that much difference between stopping an oven being built for a German concentration camp and stopping Cruise missiles. Because Cruise missiles are built to be used, not to be defensive weapons. They are built to selectively kill off countries in the same way that ovens were used to kill off the Jews.

We also used Robert Sheer's book and the front page of a May 1982, *New York Times* article in which Defense Secretary Caspar Weinberger and Reagan talk about their plans for protracted nuclear war. So we used this kind of contemporary evidence for all the laws that we were breaking.

What led you to extend your politics to issues such as the development of the Cruise missiles?

I started reading, and I really felt like we only had a year left on this planet. When I heard about the Pershing II missiles, I thought, when they get deployed, that is going to be it. If it's only going to take a flock of geese or one computer-error—and there are many such errors each year—and since it only takes six to eight minutes for these missiles to reach Moscow, the Soviet Union has no choice *but* to fire. They simply don't have time to verify. They used to have twenty-five minutes, but now they only have six. So I believe that we only had a year left to stop the deployment of these missiles.

By the time we did the action at Boeing last September I believed that we only had three months left. There were some splits in the camp because there were some women who felt this terrible sense of urgency and who acted on it. Other women felt that we had lived through what is called the Cuban Missile Crisis, and that somehow we would live through this crisis too. So they were thinking in a much more long term way. So there was a sense of despair and deflation when the missiles were actually deployed in December, because we had said we were going to stop the December deployment, but we had not. It felt like the end of the line; there wasn't supposed to be anything after December! But here we are, and it's March, and we're still around.

Do you still have that sense of imminent doom?

Yes. I feel that every day now is a gift. That we live on borrowed time. But I also feel that we are making time because we are unveiling the situations that lead up to crisis. The airliner incident [the shooting down by the Russians of a commercial airplane that had strayed over Soviet territory] really reinforced that the Soviet Union was very paranoid and trigger happy, and that to deploy missiles at the same time that they were that paranoid was like fighting fire with fire.

I am also trying to live life more than I was. Whereas before I was working all the time because I believed we had this time limit, I now think that there may be hope. But I still feel that we're living on borrowed time.

Do you think that, or do you really feel it? Do you actually think, "This day might be the last" or does it vary how you handle it?

Well, I think we all have a lot of defenses. I think I'd find it difficult to live with this knowledge if I thought about it all the time. But I think that deep down I know in my heart, from all that I've read, and from all that I've heard, and from all that I've observed, that it *is* true. But then there is a level on which you have to survive and move on and have hope. So these realizations are always pulling on each other.

When I think about what a maniac Reagan is and how intent he is on having this kind of a Western-type showdown where the US military gets to use their toys, which Reagan can hardly wait to use, then it seems clear that it really is a matter of time. Yet people said the same thing about slavery and the civil rights movement, that racism is with us and that we are never going to see the day when Black people will have a shred of freedom. And people said that women were not going to get the vote. But there are stubborn people who said, "We can pull this off. We have done it before, and we can do it again!" And we've seen some changes. So I also feel we have a history of being able to overcome the improbable.

So what do you think is possible for us to pull off at this time?

Well, walking into Boeing was a kind of affirmation of the fact that there are people here who are thinking about the danger we live under. All it's going to take is for many people to become a part of the movement against it. We don't necessarily have to convince our Congress people to change the rules. Because they're not going to change the laws or disarm when the institutions which support them are making so much money from nuclear weaponry. When corporations are boycotted and workers refuse to be a part of nuclear weapons production, and when they organize and negotiate contracts to this effect, and when people do their tax resistance—when we all just refuse to be a part of the problem, this machine will just wither away and die. I don't feel we can stop it at the top, like pruning leaves off branches. I feel we need to cut it off at the root. We need to move the workers of the world community.

There are many small incidents happening right now where engineers and other workers quit and people do tax resistance, and people put their civil liberties on the line. And I believe there are many such instances happening that we're not even aware of. We find out about a peace camp supporter who left Boeing because she knew about the insane military politics and wouldn't be a part of it. But who hears about the engineers she worked with who are practically dying of ulcers and alcoholism and so forth because their knowledge is eating them away— yet who are unable to leave it? They are dying inside, because they are good people who understood on a human level what they are part of. I think people will begin realizing that they will be healthier and happier when they dissociate themselves from such jobs, or work to change things. And this is happening more than it's ever happened before. We never used to look at corporations or little companies across the world that contributed to the nuclear industries. There was a list of companies that appeared every three or four years, and people who were concerned about nuclear weapons were told to "write your Congress person or write your president." This is what was done to try to influence things.

Now we have less time and more awareness, and we're starting to look around our communities and say, "That company makes the bombs, and that company makes the warheads, and that company makes the missiles, and my next-door neighbor works there and I can talk to him or her." So much has happened in a year or two when you think about it. We need to pat ourselves on the back.

You have explained why you think the nuclear crisis is a feminist issue, and why you consider it so urgent. Why do you prefer to work in an all-women organization?

Why work with women? They're so hard to work with! (Laughs) I wrote an article some time ago about an all-women's trucking cooperative in Arkansas. Part of their reasoning for forming an all-women's collective was that when a woman truck driver rode with a male truck driver and they would stop at truck stops, everyone would assume that she was along for the ride, that she was his recreational toy, just there to see the sights. These women got no affirmation for being women truck drivers. Also, most corporations don't employ women truck drivers. The mixed trucking collective was not educating people about the fact that women could do the job. So the women said, "We are going to be a women's trucking company. When corporate trucking companies employ 51 percent women, men can join us!" When you go to these truck stops and when you are on a road alongside two women in a truck, then people will know that women can be truck drivers. There will be no question in their minds. So that's what they did.

I feel that it's the same situation in the peace movement. When men and women work together in groups, there's still the sense that men do it, and a lot of times they try to do it *all*. So one reason for organizing separately as women is that it makes it real clear to the world that it is women doing this—it's not the women's auxiliary of the group.

I also feel that women understand where the violence is coming from because of our experiences in the world—our experiences of being potential prey. So we understand it better, and we have a better analysis of it as women. We're closer to understanding it because we're closer to its potential to hurt us. Also, as women, we're creating this model for the world to look to. Not that we are necessarily biologically more nurturing and compassionate than men, but we are socialized that way somewhat. So whether it's inherent or learned it is a quality that we have and that is needed in this world. By showing that we are women working together for peace, we're showing the world that compassion in a community can happen.

Do you think it would be a good idea to try to set up women's peace camps in other places?

Yes. Until we have peace camps at each of the companies that are making a business of the arms race, we're not going to strangle this machine. That's what we need to do—cut it off at its root. My dream is that some day peace camps will be as common as McDonalds. We'll be everywhere. And then our work will be done. I think that it is going to take that. We're all going to have to start looking around at our communities to pinpoint the sources of this kind of cancer that's causing our imminent death.

Do you think it's more effective to have a peace camp than demonstrating?

Yes. Because women in a peace camp so obviously have to give up their comforts and their families and their jobs, that it sharpens people's awareness of the urgency of our predicament. It's one thing to picket for an hour, but it's another to live on a concrete pathway or in a field next to a corporate park. It's really amazing to people and it makes them wonder about what's going on inside. They see these women as people like themselves, and they start thinking, "What would compel these nice women to give up so much? Maybe there's something going on here that I should check into." Whereas if you do a picket, it can be effective—it embarrasses the company and you get attention—but people don't really start to think in the same way about what might be going on. With a peace camp they start looking beyond the assumption that the way things are is the way they should be. They start realizing that there may be more to it. One of the ways to provoke such thinking is to give up a lot.

18

Close Encounters with the Criminal Injustice System: The Trial of the Boeing Five*

Susan James

The Puget Sound Women's Peace Camp in Kent, Washington waged a two-year campaign to call attention to the Boeing Aerospace Company's production of Air-launched Cruise Missiles. The camp was organized by several dozen women who felt that the Cruise missile represented a particularly dangerous escalation of the 'arms race.' We also sought to make connections between the US government's military policies and oppression at home and around the world.

Our 24 hour-a-day peace encampment was set up in June of 1983 in an open field across from the Cruise missile factory. More than 2000 women streamed in and out of the camp that summer, pitching a tent, leafletting Boeing workers, and participating in community educational events. In October of that year, the peace camp called for an encirclement of the Boeing complex; more than 1000 women participated.

After several unsuccessful attempts to meet with Boeing officials, in the Fall of 1983 several women from the peace camp planned a secret action to talk directly with Cruise missile workers at the factory.

---

*This is a revised and updated version of an article that appeared in *Peace Camp News* (1984).

What follows is an account of that experience and the trial that followed.

Myself and four other members of the Peace Camp visited the Boeing Cruise missile plant the afternoon of Tuesday, 27 September, 1983 to touch the hearts of the Cruise missile workers, to ask them to think about the implications of their work.

We walked in uninvited, unnoticed, at first. The five of us, Leslie Redtree, Tammy Jo Dunakin, Kris Delaney, Cynthia Nelson and I, had gained easy access to the plant by abandoning our Birkenstock shoes and bright dress for the more subdued look of a typical Boeing employee.

After entering the plant, which was a large, open warehouse with a number of work stations, we fanned out. We walked freely in the plant, talking to dozens of workers for about forty-five minutes. We discovered that Boeing works hard to convince Cruise missile workers of the 'value' of their work. Huge American flags hang from the rafters. On the walls, to boost morale hung signs saying "Welcome to ALCM (Air-Launched Cruise Missile) Country."

ALCM Country, like the world at large, I suppose, is a land filled with people unwillingly involved in a daily struggle between conscience and job security. Time and again, people agreed with me and the other women, were moved by our pleas, by our statements. While challenging the workers on the product of their labors, we offered the workers our love, our respect, our empathy for their dilemma.

We saw dozens and dozens of Cruise missiles in various stages of production. Each could kill two million people. It was almost too much to bear. Toward the end of our 'visit,' when we were corralled by a panicked security guard in an open wire mesh cage, the scene brought us to tears. "What about my son? I don't want my boy to be destroyed by these," Leslie cried.

By walking into Boeing that fine afternoon just to talk, the five of us women broke through the illusion of Boeing Company's authority, of its promise to provide security for these bombs. Boeing's lack of security for 'outside visitors' reveals that we cannot protect or be protected by nuclear weapons, really, in any stage of production or deployment. The fact that Boeing seemingly was not concerned with security says something about our country and our world. Nuclear weapons are protected by us—through our acceptance, our complicity and our inaction.

We all share responsibility for these weapons. Through our visit we felt we were following a higher moral law, established at the Nuremberg Tribunals after World War II, which obliges people to halt potential crimes against humanity. The Cruise missile, a first-strike weapon aimed for use against whole countries represents such a crime. We could not *not* do an action. And by putting our personal liberties on the line, we bore witness to the power people can have when they act out of deep moral conviction.

Following arrest, we were charged with criminal trespassing and criminal impersonation. The latter charge was made because we were wearing crudely crafted Boeing name tags that said 'Cruise Control.' Five months later, the five of us went to trial in Kent, the small, relatively conservative town near the Boeing plant. The trial was widely covered in the Kent and Seattle media.

As the four-day trial of the 'Boeing Five' came to an end, the inevitable, sportsy questions were asked: "Were you acquitted? Did you 'win?'"

The questions were legitimate: trials are a particularly striking example of the larger culture's dualistic fixation on winning or losing. But the outcome of this game can't be neatly tallied. Forget the final score (King County Prosecutor's Office 1, Peace Camp 0). It's meaningless. As the jury's nearly four-hour deliberation session demonstrated, the real gains were made in heightened public understanding of the immediacy of the nuclear threat, and the obligation of all people to try to halt this madness—right away. Faced with this awareness of our precarious situation, the trial caused many to rethink traditional understandings of lawful and unlawful, guilty and not guilty.

At the same time, much was lost in Kent's Aukeen District Court that week. With many of his rulings, the judge, Darrell Phillipson, seemed to ignore prospective witness Sandra Bishop's plea that he operate "not as a court of law, but a court of justice."

We had done some casual research on Judge Phillipson, a youngish man with a good sense of humor. Supposedly, he was fairly liberal and sympathetic on the issue. He indicated early in the trial that he had read a number of articles on the Nuremberg obligation and international law in general. In other words, he knew what the stakes were, and he understood that there was a place for international law in his courtroom. But Phillipson dodged his responsibility as a District Court judge by asserting that District Courts cannot set legal precedents: "This is a court of law, not a court of equity." Not two weeks later, a District Court in another state made national news when its judge ruled that jurors could not be 'struck' on the basis of race. Phillipson must have understood that there were legal bases justifying our action. To recognize them formally, however, would incur the legal and corporate wrath of his peers.

To be fair, Phillipson did *listen* to our reasoning for the international law defense: Cruise missiles are the modern-day equivalent of the ovens of Nazi Germany, first-strike weapons included in the Reagan administration's arsenal for a 'limited' nuclear war. We told the court that *not* taking action would be a crime, since we would be failing to follow a higher moral law established at Nuremberg.

Our second defense, 'necessity,' appeared to be more compelling. We compared walking into Boeing to trespassing into a home ringed with gasoline, which could go up at the drop of a match, to rescue a trapped child. "Cruise missiles are very volatile weapons," I said. "The more we build, the more endangered we are. One spark on the international level and we would all go up in flames. So we saw ourselves as rescuing humanity." We saw our trespass as a necessary act to prevent a greater evil—the construction and use of first-strike nuclear weapons.

Phillipson argued that the connection between talking to Boeing workers and preventing nuclear war was "too tenuous." Implied was that, had we actually *damaged* a Cruise missile, instead of 'merely' talking, we might have had protection under the necessity defense! Equally absurd was the assertion that production of Cruise missiles does not pose an "immediate" harm. A drawn revolver is an immediate threat; a revolver in a holster is not, the judge said.

We were incredulous. Leslie responded, "I have a hard time understanding when the threat is immediate. Once the direction is given (to use nuclear weapons), *then* do we take action? And then we will all die *legally!*"

After Phillipson tossed out two rules of the game, we were left with a defense based on the criminal trespassing statute. The statute includes as elements of crime the concept of "unlawful" action. One cannot be convicted of criminal trespass unless the jury finds that she "knowingly entered or remained unlawfully." Since we believed and understood that there were laws supporting and upholding our action, our beliefs were judged to be relevant to the juror's findings.

As a result, nearly all testimony and witnesses, to be allowed, had to speak to our "state of mind" before and during our visit with the Boeing workers. Documents we had read, life experiences that led us to join the peace movement, and people with whom we had discussed our concerns made up what most media representatives, progressive lawyers, and seasoned activists agreed was a most unusual trial of conscience.

The testimony evolved as an essay in what compelled five women, women who could have been daughters, granddaughters, or sisters of the jurors, to journey to a Cruise missile assembly plant. What brought these women—a writer, a former journalist, a San Juan Islands 'hermit,' a former Cornell University biology student, and a former Navy enlistee—to the Boeing plant and, ultimately, to this 'court of law'?

It's the kind of question bewildered mothers and fathers ask when told their daughters' moral obligations have resulted in civil disobedience. We felt we addressed questions the jurors must have had about the need for such actions with the same gentleness and persuasiveness we would use to 'break the news' to our parents.

On the stand, Leslie Redtree said she grieved for months in her forest home on Lopez Island in Washington State after witnessing the arrival of the first Trident submarine. She recalled attending a meeting on the Federal Emergency Management Agency's proposed plans for Lopez Island in the event of a nuclear attack. Midway into the meeting, she felt her twelve year-old son Bill tug on her sleeve. "Is it coming now, Mom?" he asked. "Is the bomb coming?" Leslie stopped, sobbing. Some of the jurors had tears in their eyes.

Spring brought more horrifying news for Leslie. First-strike Cruise missiles were under construction by Boeing in the Kent valley. Knowing what she did about the nuclear threat, Leslie felt she must leave her home on Lopez and work for a day when she could tell her son with assurance that the bomb was *not* coming.

Tammy Jo Dunakin's path to the peace camp included an encounter with the Navy. "I sort of believed those ads that said, 'It's not just a job, it's an adventure,'" she said. But Tammy knew deep down that the 'adventure' had a sinister side. She grew up watching newsreels of the Vietnam War on television. At first, it was strangers who didn't make it back. Then, a friend of the family who died there gave the statistics new meaning. At the peace camp, Tammy said, she began learning about the horror of nuclear weapons. *Those* statistics took on new meaning when she happened upon a Cruise missile, strapped to a disabled truck on Interstate 5. That innocuous looking cylinder, barely twenty feet long and covered with a tarp, could kill two million people. She recalls wanting to destroy the missile on the spot, but then she remembered that there were plenty more Cruise missiles under construction back at Boeing. Changing attitudes was the key.

Cynthia Nelson, a feminist writer, while studying English at the University of Washington avoided twentieth century literature because it reminded her of another twentieth century creation—the Bomb. As her father, a Seattle police department employee who has been supportive, looked on, Cynthia recounted a military childhood. She knew the family moved around frequently because her father was in the Air Force, but, because he was in the Intelligence Division, "I never understood exactly what he did," she said. Through the peace camp, Cynthia began to understand the secrecy that surrounds much of the military.

Kris Delaney remembered her parents' work to halt the Vietnam War; she saw the same newsreels that Tammy watched. She left her Oklahoma home to attend Cornell University, where she was active in the women's movement and peace work.

I grew up in Iowa, and held a rather naive view of the world until I became active in the women's movement during college. While working as an advocate for battered women and rape victims, I wondered where this lack of respect for the dignity of human life originated. Later, I came to understand that nuclear weapons are the ultimate expression of the violence of American culture.

Through our testimony, we showed people that we, too, had experienced times when the problems of the world seemed too much, when we seemed to powerless to make changes. As women, we hadn't been listened to and valued equally. As children growing up in America, we had been conditioned to think that 'the way things are' was the way it should be, and the people had little power to affect the world in which they lived.

Through the peace camp, and through a study of non-violence, we began to recognize the immense power each of us has, as women, to move the people of the world to an awareness of their own power, to an understanding that their actions really do make a difference. We were allowed to call Jane Meyerding as an expert witness of non-violence philosophy. The courtroom was completely silent as Jane quietly explained the meaning of a life that not only respects the value of life, but forces others to see that they, too, can make changes in their actions to influence the direction we're going; for example, by refusing to be part of weapons production. When workers refuse to lay their hands on death weapons, when people refuse to pay taxes to support the Pentagon, when representatives in Washington refuse to endorse preparations for conventional or nuclear war, the military-industrial complex will be paralyzed.

The vision is not as far-fetched as it may seem, as two other witnesses testified. Fonda Zimmerman, an ex-Boeing employee and long-time Kent resident, told of Boeing employees working on military projects who struggled with the pain and moral dilemma of working on weapons. Those who stayed on suffered ulcers and alcohol problems, Fonda felt, because they knew the implications of their work. Fonda left for lower paying, but far more satisfying, work.

Diana Siemens, at the time a Boeing employee and very active member of the peace camp, talked about the importance of Boeing workers taking action to change things at Boeing. "I don't think the best thing is necessarily for Boeing employees to quit their jobs," she said. "A lot of people don't feel they can do that, but are very concerned about nuclear weapons and Boeing's role in making them. I think a lot can be accomplished within Boeing if the workers get organized." She also talked about how Boeing's work has become more and more 'defense-related' over the ten years she's worked there. "Since the economy is in such sad shape, and commercial airliners aren't selling so well, Boeing has really started to emphasize weapons work, such as MX, B-1 bomber, Cruise missiles, and Stealth," she said. She also noted that other Boeing employees have talked to her about their concerns, because they knew she's involved with the peace camp. They have been supportive of the camp, often asking her how it's going and wishing the peace camp well.

Fonda and Diana showed that we were right to believe that there were Boeing workers who wanted to talk about what it meant to make Cruise missiles.

There were also Boeing workers who clearly did not want to talk to us. On the stand, Mike Yantzer, a Boeing worker called by the prosecutor, testified that he would not have talked to us anywhere. He said he didn't like thinking about nuclear war and he didn't think anything could be done to prevent it.

It's too late. I can't do anything. I really don't contribute to the problem. Some people expressed a similar spirit of resignation when faced with the tasks of suffrage for women and emanicpation for slaves. Support for these movements grew when people were moved to take action from witnessing the actions of others, as with the suffragists' hunger strikes, and with the Underground Railroad, which transported slaves to the relative freedom of the north.

We told the jury during opening statements that we saw our action as continuing a legacy of direct actions taken to correct inexcusable, but sanctioned, injustices.

We know we were heard. A number of people from the media who covered the trial said they admired and understood our work. Although ours was an 'open and shut' trespassing case, the jury deliberated nearly four hours. Clearly, they weren't debating whether we actually trespassed. The questions they sent out midway through the deliberation demonstrated they were considering the moral reasons for our action; they were looking at the law in an entirely new light; one that examined lawful acts based on moral beliefs.

POSTSCRIPT

The jury ultimately found us guilty of criminal trespassing. At the sentencing, we were ordered to perform community service and to pay several hundred dollars in fines and court costs.

We had conflicting ideas on how to respond to this order, and amicably agreed to take different paths. Cynthia Nelson and Kris Delaney decided to perform community service for a Seattle feminist bookstore collective and took up a collection for the court costs, rather than voluntarily subject themselves to a punitive jail system. Leslie Redtree, Tammy Dunakin and I felt we could not in good conscience perform community service for, or pay money into, such an unjust court system. As a result, we spent fourteen days in the King County jail. We fasted for five days of our jail stay to call attention to those who go hungry because of the US's bloated military budget.

Kris Delaney was killed in January of 1985 in an automobile accident caused by a speeding police officer. Leslie, Cynthia, Tammy and I continue Kris' work, each in our own way.

19

Looking Back:
The Women's Peace Camps
in Perspective*

Rachel Lederman

In 1980, women established a permanent peace encampment at Green-ham Common Air Base in England. By 1983, there were at least thirty women's peace camps on three continents at sites of first-strike nuclear technology. The women handed out leaflets and scaled fences; they sat in circles around campfires, in yurts and teepees, and talked about how to stop nuclear war, and how to do it in a women's way.

This grassroots movement was not centrally coordinated. Rather it spread spontaneously, from one community touched by the weapons buildup to another. Individual women who spent time at one women's peace camp would travel to another city or country and talk about it. The actions of women across the land and sea ignited a spark which in each locality grew into a particular flame according to the circumstances, culture and community involved.

*Parts of this chapter grew out of a response that was written by Diana Siemens and myself with collective input from the Puget Sound Women's Peace Camp participants, and was published as "Women's Peace Camps: Feminist Revolutionary Force for Change" in *off our backs* (May 1984). A bit was taken from an article I co-authored with Joan Tierney, "Venceremos! Making Connections Through Coalition Work", *We Are Ordinary Women: A Chronicle of the Puget Sound Women's Peace Camp* (Seal Press, 1985). Also worthy of acknowledgement are Louise Chernin, Nalani Askov, and Cynthia Nelson for many late night conversations. This chapter however expresses only my own peculiar opinions.

Most of the thousands of women who participated in the peace camps never met. They did not communicate consistently through any newsletter. But when a few managed to get together, they shared amazingly similar stories of struggle and hope.

As the women's peace camp movement grew, some women began to raise concerns about it from a feminist perspective. In movement periodicals such as *off our backs* (March 1984) and pamphlets like *Breaching the Peace* (London: Onlywomen Press, Ltd., 1983), they questioned whether this particular resurgence of women's activism in a time of declining radical feminist activity and increasing rightwing backlash, was a return to the doctrine of 'Woman as Mother' cloaked in feminist garments. They asked whether the women's peace movement might in fact be working *against* feminist goals, by subordinating women's specific concerns to the issue of nuclear weapons.

Those feminists saw nuclear war as a diversionary 'red herring'. They worried about whether what they saw as the relative glamor and excitement of the women's peace camps was draining women away from working on specific women's issues. Were women's peace camp organizers encouraging women to play their traditional role, instead of empowering them? Were the camps advancing an anti-feminist, biological determinist rationale of women as natural moms, nurturers and peacemakers? Were the connections being drawn between feminism and non-violence playing into female passivity? The critics perceived the camp women's tactics as flakey and self-trivializing, and questioned whether the actions had any impact on the outside world or were primarily symbolic. Finally, were the camp women working for the liberation of women and other oppressed groups, or were they merely concerned with developing an escapist "women's culture" to which a few privileged women could retreat?

Many of us who had devoted ourselves to the women's peace camps for a year or more were in fact struggling with some of these same questions. At the Puget Sound Women's Peace Camp, after months of rainy 3:00 A.M. security shifts and constant interminable meetings, Boeing was still turning out its two Cruise missiles a day. Cruise were, as far as we knew, being deployed at Greenham and Comiso, while the people of Cuba and Nicaragua were digging trenches to prepare for US air attacks. We were burned out by internal struggles and a protracted encounter with the legal system, and we had ceased to draw in much new energy. And, after striving to approach our work from a specifically feminist perspective, we too had to wonder whether an entirely different message than we had intended was coming across to the public, filtered through the media.

This chapter will attempt to address these questions, by retrospectively evaluating the women's peace camps as a form of feminist action (rather than as a contribution to the peace movement). My analysis focuses on the Puget Sound Women's Peace Camp, which was located in Kent, Washington, near a civilian Cruise missile factory, because this was the camp with which I was most involved (as a founder and long-term core participant). Conversations with women who participated in the Seneca, Wisconsin, Minneapolis, and Greenham Common women's peace camps also added to this chapter, but my knowledge of the European movement is quite limited.

THE WOMEN'S PEACE CAMPS AS FEMINIST ORGANIZING

We can evaluate the women's peace camps as feminist action by looking at how they furthered the feminist goals of organizing and empowering women.

The peace camps organized thousands of women around the nuclear threat, bringing them together to work on this issue in a context that did not compel women to overlook sexism or to deny women's leadership. Most of the women who came to the peace camps were not, by and large, 'stolen' from work on women's issues—many were previously inactive. Some went on from a summer at a peace camp to work for a variety of other causes. They stated that their peace camp experience empowered them to take action, taught them skills, and strengthened their awareness and articulation of how issues fit together and affect them as women. Women who had shied away from political meetings, participated in peace camps by stopping by and washing the dishes or helping to construct a yurt platform. Often, they soon found themselves climbing over military base fences, facilitating meetings, and organizing mass demonstrations.

Women who had only experienced mixed-sex political groups before were initially amazed by our feminist group process. In an early Puget Sound Women's Peace Camp organizing meeting, the original group of six organizers brought a draft for a 'Unity Statement' to sixty newly involved women. We had been pleased with ourselves for finally agreeing on this draft statement despite our quite varied political 'lines'. We hadn't realized that we were actually a relatively homogenous bunch of leftist and feminist organizers compared to the bulk of women who were appearing in exponentially increasing numbers at each successive planning meeting. We met no agreement on *anything* in the statement. At that stage, the political common ground was simply that we all wanted to stop the Cruise missiles, and we all liked the idea of doing it from an all-women encampment. After a long, intense and at times tearful meeting, one by one the new women said that they could not believe that they had been listened to with such attention, and that their thoughts had been given equal importance with those of the more experienced organizers. And, after three weeks of meeting in small groups, the sixty of us were able to reach a consensus on a Unity Statement that did not leave out feminism and the connections that made our Camp unique from other anti-nuclear weapons actions. While this long process slowed down the start of our actual anti-nuclear protest, this consensual process was extremely important to us as feminists. It affirmed each woman's importance to our collective politics, rather than allowing the political statement to be the province of a select group. And through this process, the new women were encouraged and empowered to continue to develop a women-defined analysis and practice, in the context of a women's group and resistance community.

Of course, some of us had previously worked in other parts of the women's movement, so it is true that we were 'stolen away' from those other issues in the sense that we made a choice to spend our time working with the peace camp for a while. While peace camp work had its share of dishwashing and latrine scrubbing to balance out its television interviews and dramatic confrontations, I will admit that there was an excitement involved which drew me away from staffing crisis lines and fighting anti-abortion legislation, at least for that period of time. The excitement, for me, was not the media coverage, nor the adrenalin thrill of direct action. It was the excitement of being able to say, at once, everything I wanted to say: as a woman outraged not only by the specter of nuclear holocaust, but by male supremacy, white supremacy, enforced heterosexism, the rape of the earth for profit, the imperialist government that was preparing to try out its nuclear toys in the Third World and to wage its war with the Soviet Union in the land of my European peace camp comrades. It was the excitement of being able to make these connections in an act of resistance that embodied our visions for the world we wanted to create. It was the excitement of seeing these possibilities capture so many women's hearts at a time when it seemed few women were finding much of inspiration about the women's movement. (And hopefully, the time spent working with the women's peace camps re-energized women who later returned to the 'specifically feminist' work of running the shelters and clinics.)

Finally, it is necessary to respond to the charge of 'stealing women away from the women's movement' by examining anti-militarist and anti-nuclear work *as specifically feminist work.*

MILITARISM AS A FEMINIST ISSUE

Another way we can evaluate the women's peace camps as feminist action is by looking at how they challenged male supremacy by confronting militarism as an aspect of male supremacy.

The women's peace camp movement analyzed war as a way that ruling class men have consolidated global power. An analogy we drew was that rape, battering and reproductive control are enforcers of male privilege at home, while militarism is part of this same approach on a world scale. So, to achieve feminist revolution, women must challenge the nuclear arms buildup, militarism, and imperialism. Conversely, peace can only ultimately be acheived through a feminist revolution that would not just bring 'women's rights', but would redefine power, and reject force as the arbiter of conflicts.

Does applying the word 'feminism' to issues that don't only affect women weaken the word and the movement? Feminist peace activists contended that women cannot achieve liberation *without* expanding our struggle as women beyond the biological issues that *men* have defined as our sphere. We believed that feminism implies a total world view, and that liberation for women, who are members of most other oppressed groups, requires a revolutionary global restructuring of power relations.

Thinking less theoretically, we can approach militarism as a feminist issue because of the direct economic and social impact it has on women locally and globally. At the same time, we recognized women's *power* to undermine the global military machine, which runs on our unpaid and underpaid labor.

We were also criticized on the grounds that this line of reasoning implies a biological determinist doctrine that women are *naturally* superior, peacemakers, and earth saviors. Biological determinism is a mythology created to perpetuate the status quo. But it is not biological determinism to say that there are such things as masculine and feminine values. To contend otherwise would be to discount thousands of years of cultural history. In general, the women's peace camp movement did not say that women's brains are circuited differently from men's. Rather, we put forth the idea that the values traditionally relegated to women need to be reclaimed as central to public society; need to be reclaimed as defined by *women* (as *feminism*); and are presently essential to the survival of our planet.

Certainly, a biological determinist line may have been put out by some women active with the camps, as it has in other sectors of the women's movement. This type of reasoning is a primary way we have all been taught to explain the world, and the women's peace camp movement was composed of many women who thought and said different things: it was not a party with designated spokespeople. But 'Woman as Mom' is not a *necessary* reasoning implied in women's peace camp organizing, nor was it a primary reasoning in actual *collective* statements and actions. For example, the Seneca Women's Encampment Handbook stated:

"We don't think that women have a special role in the peace movement because we are *naturally* more peaceful, more protective, or more vulnerable than men. Nor do we look to women as Earth Mothers who will save the planet from male aggression. Rather, we believe that it is this very division that makes the horrors of war possible." Nevertheless, the question remains as to how we could have been more effective in countering this anti-feminist interpretation of our efforts. Another important question is whether this analysis of militarism as a feminist issue, put forth by an overwhelmingly white movement, implies that women's oppression is primary, thus minimizing the importance of the relationship between militarism, race, and class oppression, and denying the diversity of women's experience.

In the next two sections, I will discuss how the Puget Sound Women's Peace Camp women acted on our politics, and some of the contradictions presented by the peace camp as a form of feminist action in terms of our ability to struggle with these questions, and in terms of our practical effectiveness.

WHAT WE DID

At the Puget Sound Women's Peace Camp we conceived of the peace camp movement as an attempt to organize the withdrawal of women's support from militarism and the reclamation of our power, by forming an international movement while at the same time focusing locally on confronting the first strike technology being developed, produced, and stored in our own backyards. We educated ourselves and the public on the economic power interests behind nuclear weapons and conventional intervention, and the real impact of these phenomena on our communities and on people in other parts of the world. We did not approach nuclear weapons as a single issue, but focused on the connections between nuclear weapons and the violence prevalent in our daily lives, and consequently, on the connections between our oppression as women and that of all non-ruling groups.

The Puget Sound women picked the Boeing plant as our target because Boeing was both our community's number one employer, and a primary nuclear and conventional military contractor. We wanted to call attention to the industrial part of the military-industrial complex, from a pro-worker perspective. We saw an opportunity, by sustaining a long-term presence near the plant, to create a public dialogue that would foster awareness of Boeing's military role and eventually make the workers aware of their ultimate power to stop weapons production. Boeing was manufacturing Cruise missiles and we wanted to take action against the then-impending Euromissile deployment, and to create a "chain of feminist opposition to the Cruise"[1] that was to include a production facility (Boeing), a test site (Cole Bay, Saskatchewan), a transshipment point (Seneca Army Depot, New York), and a deployment site (Greenham Common). The international nature of our action was very important and we tried to maintain communication with our 'sister camps' around the world. We also began to develop connections with women peace activists in Australia and Japan; with Central American women's organizations and with Native American activists.

Feminism profoundly affected every aspect of our work, including our decision-making processes, our development as a community, and our strategies for action. Our internal development and empowerment as women were goals as important as our impact on the outside world. We used principles drawn from non-violence and anarchism, which we found compatible with our goals—not only stopping the Cruise missiles, but ending all forms of violence and abuse. As feminists, our collective agreement about non-violence meant that we strove to act with respect for the spirit within all things, and that we supported the right of all people to self-defense and self-determination, even though we ourselves were not choosing the tactic of armed struggle. In practical terms, we chose non-violence because it seemed the most effective way to confront an opponent armed beyond our wildest possibility, and anarchist methods worked best in organizing women alienated by hierarchical, male-dominated political groups and seeking a unity between politics and spirituality.

Our primary activity was educational work in the local Kent and greater Puget Sound communities. We spoke to everyone from the Lions Club to the Socialist Workers Party, did street theater, and passed out thousands of leaflets. When we spoke to Kent community groups, we spoke about nuclear weapons, Boeing, jobs, and the concept of conversion to civilian production; and about why we were camped outside Boeing as women. When we spoke to other Left groups we emphasized the connections between nuclear and conventional warfare, feminism, racism and capitalism. We held many open educational events at the Camp on a variety of topics. Central America ranked a close second to nuclear weapons-related events. This was because we did not feel that we could work against the future murder of millions in a nuclear war without simultaneously working against the present murder our Government is inflicting on the people of Central America, and without supporting the Central American peoples' struggles for peace and justice.

In the Fall of 1983 the Camp was contacted by activists who were

---

[1]From the Puget Sound Women's Peace Camp Unity Statement.

forming an Emergency Response Network against US intervention. We were contacted both because of individual women's many years of prior work on these issues and because of the Camp's reputation for having expertise in collective, feminist group process and nonviolent direct action. We were asked to take leadership in organizing direct action and to contribute feminist process insights to the newly forming Network. Pickets and demonstrations where the Peace Camp provided all-women peacekeeping and performed street theater evolved into a Network campaign to prevent escalation.

At the same time that Fall, we were organizing a major demonstration and encirclement of Boeing. In September, five women entered the Cruise missile plant and spoke with workers for over an hour before being arrested.

In September we were also forced to move our physical encampment from the city property within sight of Boeing, to a house about a mile down the road. Many women who had lived at the original camp full-time returned to jobs or school. Only a handful continued to maintain the twenty-four hours-a-day 'presence', and the change in location contributed to a change in group focus away from this physical presence. There was an air of discouragement as Euromissile deployment proceeded and the European peace movement was reported by US media to be on the wane. And the more immediate war in Central America was increasingly on our minds, as were local issues such as the murders of over forty women whose bodies were dumped in the Green River which ran behind the Camp.

More and more, our political work took place in Seattle, where the five women who had been arrested in the Cruise missile plant were preparing for their trial and where many of us were involved in coalition work. Besides the Seattle Central America Network, we were part of and played leadership roles in the coalition that organized a Take Back the Night March to Stop the Green River Murders; a coalition against the homeporting of a Navy nuclear carrier in Puget Sound; and a Martin Luther King Day march, to name a few. Many of us saw this coalition work as a way of reaching out beyond our particular, mostly white group, and of acting on the "connections" emphasized in our Unity Statement. Through coalition work, we learned a lot and built respect and trust with a wide range of other groups. However, it was very difficult to try to represent the Peace Camp in a coalition. The Camp had started out as a group open to all women who stayed at or participated in events at a physical place, the encampment. We never agreed to redefine ourselves as a political organization with a specific membership. Coalition work therefore took on the character of personal projects of individual women. Without the physical, energetic and political center the encampment at Boeing had provided, we drifted into doing support work exclusively, rather than continuing to build our own movement, until it no longer made sense for the women who had been the Puget Sound Women's Peace Camp to continue to work together as a group.

CONTRADICTIONS

In May 1984, I wrote in my journal, "I must have spent hundreds of hours in meetings arguing over structure and not planning action. Are the Cruise missiles at Boeing, or here in our hearts? Women attack any woman who takes any initiative. Internalized oppression keeps us on this side of the fence as effectively as Boeing's security force."

I've tried in this chapter to describe the politics of the women's peace camp movement. That this is a contradiction is expressed in the name, Puget Sound Women's Peace Camp. When the Camp was first established, the name referred to a *place*, a physical site across the road from the Boeing plant. Any woman who was *at* the site was a 'Peace Camp participant' with an equal voice in consensus decision-making, meaning that she could individually veto any group decision. Theoretically, our goal was to include every woman in the world as a Peace Camp participant. As time went on, some of us became active in 'representing the Peace Camp' in coalitions, speaking about our work, participating in conferences, and expressing particular politics that went beyond the basic agreements of our Unity Statement. Without any conscious decision on our part, the name Puget Sound Women's Peace Camp began to refer to an *organization*, or at least, other people began to relate to us as such.

Because of our commitment to consensus decision-making, those of us who were struggling to represent this amorphous group and to plan action in the name of the group became concerned with clarifying who was and was not a decision-making participant. At this point, things fell apart. The few women who were still living in the house in Kent still thought that their activities defined the organization because they occupied the physical space, which was no longer even a 'camp.' Others of us thought that an evolution from our focus on Cruise missiles to broader, revolutionary goals was implied by our process and visions. But no consensus existed as to our collective 'next step' past the encampment stage, and we became paralyzed by our confusion about structure and process.

Women had come together because the Cruise missiles, the time line created by impending deployment, and the vision of a women's resistance encampment, together lit a particular spark. Over the Summer of 1983, we were very successful in educating the community about Boeing's role in the arms race, and in educating ourselves to the point where most of us grew to share a multi-issue feminist analysis of the nuclear arms race. But the Camp never moved into a stage of more active confrontation of Boeing's weapons production after the "Boeing five" action, nor into becoming a political group doing self-defined work on other issues in the long term.

Process, group accountability, leadership, and individual autonomy were continual areas of conflict which consumed so much meeting time that they seemed to prevent us from moving ahead with our Boeing campaign or other work.

Initially, this conflict took the form of a split between the women who were most intent on taking immediate direct action against the Cruise missiles, and those who were more oriented toward developing a long-term campaign and a uniquely feminist statement. After the pre-encampment planning stage, some women began to feel frustrated with consensus decision-making in such a large and open group. In contrast to early, more goal-oriented meetings, women with less verbal skills and women with cultural differences in speech patterns began to feel that they did not have equal input in large meetings. Women feared that 'process' in fact meant censorship by those they perceived as the politicos in the group.

This process was important, because these same conflicts came up at most of the women's peace camps as well as in the peace and women's movements in general. Those who participated came out of the meetings with renewed commitment to the group. The catch was that not everyone participated, and a few women never seemed to let go of their anger and mistrust at not having been let in on the action. The group as a whole didn't go on to many more risk-taking actions. Instead of creating momentum, the action drained us.

This may have been because five out of twenty-five core activists became caught up in a ten months foray through the US legal system, while the rest of us went through the changes around our site and coalition work that I have described.

But there was also a deeper problem. We were paralyzed by our feminist group process. The egalitarianism and collectivity that were so empowering at first, became distorted into instruments of internalized oppression as the group lost its external focus on stopping Cruise missile production. 'Consensus' began to mean that no one could take any initiative for fear of being seen as a leader. Thus, the group could go nowhere. We confused our internal power with the 'power over' exercised by patriarchy. Instead of striving for *all* women to become leaders, we fought to keep no one from filling this desperately needed role.

One part of this paralysis was created by our dual nature as a living community and an outwardly-directed political action. These natures were perpetually in conflict. One group of women would plan a meeting agenda aimed at setting political goals and planning action, and another group would arrive with an agenda of working on interpersonal conflicts and exploring group spirituality. Instead of giving time to both, we would then spend our meeting time arguing over the agenda, each side convinced that their focus was more important.

This dual nature was also the source of much of our energy and attracted many women who would not have participated in a conventional demonstration. Many women who participated in peace camps in the US were as committed to creating all-women spaces and 'women's culture' as to political action against nuclear weapons. In fact, in the US the peace camps can be seen as evolving as much out of the women's/ lesbian culture movement as from the inspiration of Greenham Common. They were a step toward bridging the gap between the cultural movement and feminist political organizing. But because our society so rigidly separates the personal from the political, slogans aside, our group was effectively unable to integrate those areas in our minds even though such an integration was so central to the peace camp as a concept.

Unfortunately, we had all brought with us all the baggage of the abusive, women-hating, racist, drug- and alcohol-addicted outside world. Because we were living together, the Peace Camp took on many of the characteristics of a dysfunctional family. These conflicts were especially painful because we also brought with us high expectations that the Camp would be a feminist utopia. Instead, it was simply composed of 'ordinary women.'[2]

Another part of the paralysis had to do with our inability to rationally evaluate the differences between our movement and Greenham Common. Because we were so inspired by Greenham, we wanted to emulate them more than was practically or tactically effective, given our different resources and political situation, and we felt guilty about these differences instead of trying to figure out how to use them most effectively.

The women at Greenham Common have been able to wage a successfully disruptive campaign of constant direct-action against the Air Base. This reflects their larger base of support, more central location, and economic factors that make it easier for British women to actually

---

[2]The PSWPC Unity Statement began, "We are ordinary women . . ."

live at the Camp. The larger base of support is due to the fact that the Greenham women are mostly British women who are protesting US-controlled missiles and bases in their country. Nationalism is on their side. US women are only beginning to realize that it is not our interests that are being protected by the Euromissiles. Furthermore, the Puget Sound Women's Peace Camp was protesting our community's largest employer. Different tactics, and a prioritization of resources were called for.

Our restraint from undertaking civil disobedience actions that first Summer was a good tactical decision. We were never a target of significant community hostility as was the Seneca Women's Encampment, where women immediately began climbing the fence. Thus, we were able to reach more people. Later, more confrontational actions would have been appropriate and effective. But by that time, our group process had thickened into a kind of quicksand we were struggling to be free of and we could no longer make these strategic decisions. For example, a few women, blindly attempting to follow the Greenham model, continued to 'camp' in the Kent house long after the rest of the group's work was taking place elsewhere. This drained the group financially and hampered our process of redefining ourselves. Because we felt guilty about not camping in the mud like our British sisters, we did not decide to get rid of the expensive house for a long time after it had ceased to fulfill any political purpose.

CONCLUSION

By the time we closed the peace camp house in the Fall of 1984 and most of the other women's peace camps in the US had also folded, the United States Government's preparations for a first strike were still on course, albeit with some setbacks. However our impact was undeniable. In Kent, the fact that Boeing was manufacturing nuclear weapons and the impact of weapons production on the local economy were now dinner table conversation. In upstate New York, Seneca Army Depot no longer looked like the friendly base next door. Tall fences, new guard towers, shiny rolls of razor wire, and bothersome low-flying surveillance helicopters proclaimed it to be what it is, the key East Coast transshipment point for nuclear weapons and storage place for the neutron bomb and Pershing IIs. An employment trainer in nearby Ithaca, New York who worked with women in transition between home-making and the paid job market, reported an unprecedented influx of trainees from rural, conservative Seneca County who were spouting feminist ideas. At Greenham Common, US military might had been made a mockery of by the women's determination and creative non-violent tactics. For example, in March 1984, one hundred police officers were used to surround fourteen sleepy women at 1:00 A.M. so that the military could whisk a Cruise missile in and out of the base for a quick 'exercise' before it was blockaded. The women's peace camps played a crucial role in inspiring mass resistance to nuclear weapons deployment all over Europe. And those of us who participated will never be the same.

While our Puget Sound Women's Peace Camp did not prove an optimal format for long-term movement building, it was highly successful in calling attention to local corporate arms contracting, and in getting over 2,000 women involved in feminist action. We have much exploration to do of feminist processes and strategies for social change. The women's peace camps were one attempt by women in several countries to gather before some of the pinnacles of the death and profit-worshipping culture, and to live out a vision for a cooperative, life-affirming future. Within the camps, on three continents, we discovered some of our differences and commonalities, and developed visions to sustain ourselves through the years of hard work ahead.

20

FANG – A Feminist Anti-Nuclear Group*

Diana E. H. Russell

Jonathan Schell leaves an important question unanswered in *The Fate of the Earth* (1982): if we reject our doom, how do we most effectively "rise up to cleanse the earth of nuclear weapons?" The anti-nuclear movement has become a massive international movement now, so this question is easier to answer for non-feminists than it was some years ago. People must try to find a place in this movement that fits their ideology, unleashes their energy, and moves them to make a commitment.

And what should feminists do? The answer is—the same. But suppose there is no such consonant group near where they live? That was the case for me in 1983, so I decided to help *start* the kind of group I wanted. I think there is much to be said for small, feminist anti-nuclear action groups at this time in history. One advantage of a small group is that its members can more easily play a role in decision-making, and actions can be organized more rapidly. I want to offer my experience in FANG, a small all-women's feminist anti-nuclear action group born in October 1983, as an example to other women.

Less than two months old and still without a name, our group felt the need to organize an action in connection with the much publicized TV movie "The Day After." Because most women in our group had jobs they couldn't leave on a Monday, the day after "The Day After," only

---

*This is an edited version of an article that was previously published in *Atlantis: A Women's Studies Journal*, Vol. 12, No. 1 (1986).

five of us participated in the action. Despite our small number, we were observed by many people, and I doubt that they will ever forget us and the message we conveyed. Even such a tiny group can have an impact. And, personally, for me, after twenty years of participating in actions and demonstrations, I had never had so much fun in a political action before. Nor have I ever felt so clearly that I, as one activist, was getting my point across and making a difference. Here's what we did:

Wearing Ronald Reagan masks and raincoats, we "flashed" the phallic missiles that hung between our legs outside the San Francisco television station responsible for making and showing "The Day After." Our demonstration was not intended to convey opposition to the movie, although we were distressed at its failure to provide any information about the peace movement. Our signs read THERE DOESN'T HAVE TO BE A DAY AFTER; PEACE THROUGH NUCLEAR ARMS IS A BIG PHALLACY; STOP MASTURBATING WITH MISSILES; KEEP U.S. PISSILES OUT OF EUROPE; PERSHING II AND CRUISE: SIX MIN- UTES TO A PREMATURE EJACULATION.

With these graphic statements, we hoped to increase public aware- ness of the connection between the threat of nuclear war and men's macho use of violence to resolve conflicts. For example, one rationale for the US decision to build MX missiles was that the Russians' missiles were bigger than ours. Not more powerful — just bigger! We believed that the insanity of the nuclear arms race is, in part, an expression of a phallic competition.[1]

Advance press releases about FANG's action were sent to fifty news- papers, television and radio stations. Not one of them covered the event. Some FANG members had predicted that the male-dominated media would be unwilling to describe or photograph our phallic-weapon im- ages. They were right. Instead of media representatives, three police cars pulled up and five or six policemen told us that it was illegal to wear masks and that we had to remove them. When challenged to provide a citation of the law, the policemen eventually admitted they were mis- taken, and we donned our masks once more. If media censorship had succeeded, this attempted police harassment, at least, had failed.

The Federal Building in San Francisco was our next target. On the way there one of the flashers was hit in the face by a male passerby who presumably felt threatened by our message and appearance. Once inside the Federal Building, guards ordered us to leave on the grounds that we were vulgar and disruptive. Our argument that nuclear weapons and the danger of global nuclear war are the real obscenities appeared to be lost on the guards working there that day.

---

[1]We were delighted when Helen Caldicott articulated a similar view in her book, *Missile Envy*, published the following year (1984).

Most people who saw the Reagan flashers responded dramatically. Some glared. Some laughed. Some cursed. Some blushed. Some made V signs. Some stared blankly. Some applauded. But no one failed to notice us.

Despite the media whiteout, we believe our weapon-flashing communicated the important political message that the nuclear mentality and the masculine mentality are intimately connected. It is because other organizations either fail to see or communicate this connection, or are downright hostile to attempts to convey it, that we started FANG in the first place. Women Against Imperialism, for example, would not permit FANG's Reagan flashers to join their International Women's Week demonstration at the Presidio in San Francisco, maintaining that we were not sufficiently serious.

On 12 December 1983, the day of the deployment of Cruise and Pershing II missiles in Europe, FANG "flashed" again, marching with hundreds of other women in San Francisco. We also demonstrated on 10 March 1984 in commemoration of International Women's Week, and on 15 April, the deadline for Americans to pay our taxes so that the government can pay its military bills.

For the latter action, we made our point by building a seven-foot missile which was worn as a penis by one flasher and supported by others. Another flasher walked in front with a sign that read OUR TAXES WILL PAY FOR THE BIGGEST PHALLACY OF ALL—THE MX. The words on the sides of our large missile were THE MX: GUARANTEED TO DESTROY OUR PLANET. All the flashers had price tags dangling from their own smaller missiles with information on the cost of the Cruise, Pershing II and MX missiles.

On 18 June 1984 we participated in a demonstration in Santa Cruz against the Miss California Pageant with signs such as: WE WANT GIRLS TO BE GIRLS, AND BOYS TO BE BOYS, SO WE CAN CONTINUE TO PLAY WITH OUR TOYS. We stood on the back of a truck and were greeted with wild enthusiasm. The demonstrators appeared to understand immediately the connection we were making between the masculine mentality and the nuclear mentality.

Hopefully, hundreds and perhaps thousands of feminist anti-nuclear groups will begin to emerge all over the country, coming together in coalitions when collective actions are needed. I also hope that the anti-nuclear movement will soon come to recognize at last that an effective anti-nuclear movement must also be anti-sexist and anti-patriarchal. My third wish is that the women's movement itself will become part of a mass coalition of anti-nuclear groups that will organize to eradicate the threat of a nuclear catastrophe. My final wish is that all these changes occur in time to save us and our planet.

21

On the Line*

Hollis Giammatteo

On The Line, a peace walk initiated by women, was an eleven-month journey from the Naval Submarine Base in Bangor, Washington to the Pantex Plant in Amarillo, Texas (the final assembly point for all nuclear warheads in the US) to the Naval Weapons Station in Charleston, South Carolina. We walked along the railroad tracks, following the route of the White Train. This train, once truly and eerily white, travelled the country unseen for twenty years. In 1982, after a tip from a reporter, Jim Douglass, co-founder of the Ground Zero Center for Nonviolent Action, tracked the Train back to its source, the Pantex Plant, and the Tracks Campaign was born. In February 7, 1985, the Department of Energy painted the Train the various colors of the freight lines that haul it through its fourteen host states. The top of it remains white, but it is now known as The Painted Train.

The first day of spring, 21 March 1984, was our departure day and, that morning, launched lovingly by the Ground Zero community from the Submarine Base gates, we headed south toward Portland, a ten-day walk away. Giddy with the challenge of that distance, no one could yet take in the achievement of Texas, 2,700 miles away.

We were eight women, carrying everything in two carts covered brightly with stickers, peace flags and banners, looking not quite of this century, and a little bit like ships. In the carts, the gear and the clothes to last six months; the films and the literature that would constitute

*Previously published under another title in *Atlantis: A Women's Studies Journal*, Vol.12, No. 17 (1986).

our programs, given almost every evening in almost every town along the way.

We had spent from November of 1983 to February of 1984 organizing; the goal, as we saw it, was to broaden the already existing network of communities that vigiled and prayerfully resisted the Train, and to share information with the uninformed, the disinterested, and, to be sure, the opposed. Often this cast us in the role of listeners. We were helped by key groups and individuals in each state, and by March had a pretty firm grasp on our routing, our contacts and our program commitments. There were, of course, some grave gaps in the knowing. Wyoming, for example, presented a 120 mile stretch of desert; Nebraska would prove most frustrating, as town after town and church after church reneged on their sponsorship.

We learned "on the job." Press and media attention forced us quickly to be concise and counter-manipulative. As I got better at shaping our message into the conventional news format, I discovered that effective peace work requires a focus on team work; that press and media and the work are all involved in redefining what is "news." As we walked, I think we honestly witnessed a growing concern in the media not to slough off peace work as not newsworthy. It was becoming OK, publicly, to cover peace, and we insisted on speaking about non-violence and the building of a peace-filled world as well. The Walk was not merely a reaction to an administration pledged to nuclear proliferation in an election year, but was the presence of peace.

I knew from the beginning that ours would be an experiment in community; I just did not know how we would get there, for it is one thing to sit around a table, throwing out words like "trust" and "commitment," and another to be in the experience, caught off guard by a vivid demonstration of someone's very different point of view. Was the Walk about the community, or about specific action? Where did the two meet? If they did not, was it a failure of peace? We had first to recognize that peace is not the absence of conflict. Then we all had to stop judging each other for not being the same. This took a while. We each had, for example, different styles of "confrontation," and it took a while to trust that each would not abuse her right to do her job in her own way, unobstructed and unjudged.

Then there was the magic of the road. We thought often of how the nature of diplomacy would change if everyone made such walking a part of their lives from time to time. For you have no option but to trust your neighbor. We grow by wandering; we open to the amazing generosity of others when we ourselves have little; we step again into the natural world where time and the passing of miles will not be hurried; and seasons and the powerful moods of the sun settle us back to the good humility, and a knowledge strong like a pulse that, if we open to it, we can communicate, fiercely and gently with God.

VANCOUVER, WASHINGTON, 31 MARCH 1984

We are becoming obsessed with the banner. Its message, "White Train Threatens Life on Earth," is grimly offered to the scenery on this small back road, and the wind billows it backward. We were such a tiny group. Several have decided not to walk because of colds, and Maura has gone on to Portland, afraid that her cough is growing into something serious. We five have all we can take of "visibility" tasks, struggling with the banner and push-pulling the carts up the endless hills. Mount St. Helens is pluming in the distance, one flank sooty. Dark, purply clouds gather in an orange sky above her; a funnel takes shape to her right. I pull out my tornado story, and the temperature drops, and we make a turn straight into the rain.

I am suddenly Mother Courage in the modern world, and weary. Unseen on these back roads, I am aware of how useful the press and media are to the work. I get to thinking that maybe the Walk will continue in this kind of void, in the back country, where occasional cars see our gypsy group as crazy women, off to the hills for holiday. A car slows, stops: a woman reads our banner. "White Train *Theaters* Life on Earth," she reads, and nods and puts on a grave face of understanding.

We leave the backcountry and come out to the major highway: hamburgers and 7-11 chains; the malls; six-lane heavy traffic, and exhaustion. It is five o'clock, with six more miles to go. I think I cannot go on, and say as much. Sande, bless her, water streaming down her plastic poncho into her pink tennis shoes, gently explains that her vision is of covering every mile by at least one set of feet. We heal the earth as we go, she says, and even though no one else but we will know it, the chain from Bangor to the East Coast must be laid down link by link, unbroken. She believes in this healing. I look up, through my hats, at the strip—the junk of it, our car culture; the convenience stores and varietal McDonald's; the prefab cubes and emporia of gathering and getting; the utter absence of beauty; the disregard. "I can't heal this," I say.

"Especially this," she says. "It is important."

But they cut down trees for this, and bulldoze hills. I jump the six lanes to go buy beer for later, when, I think, my offended eyes will have earned a long, hot bath and at least two Heinekens.

WASHOUGAL, 6 APRIL

They can be a thrill, these little towns. Our banner and carts create a heartening stir today. Our coordinator came out to walk with us. When this happens, the excitement of those who have prepared for our arrival lifts me out of my private *why*, and I am restored by the symbolic power of the Walk. In our simple, not to be hurried, self-reliant act, we are connecting Bangor, Washington to Amarillo, Texas to Charleston, South Carolina. Are we mad?

Anyway, she is here to meet us, inappropriately shod, of course. People seem to have lost touch with their feet, and relate to the Walk initially as a problem in footwear. This is a small rebellion, our living with one pair of shoes for six months, in an era that has bullied us with choices by making Occasions instead of making Do.

The rain is back. We parade around the business loop at the suggestion of our coordinator, a young woman eager to make of our presence a catalyst for forming a peace group common both to Camas and Washougal. The town reporter is waiting. Two high school girls rush us in a parking lot, and squeeze $10 into my hand. They linger to talk with Terri about organizing students to vigil the Train. We parade; cars honk; V signs are flashed. One salty old man calls out from his car window, "We need more of those White Trains!" We respond with humor, but when it comes to his getting out of the car and yelling at my face, I am not sure what I will do, nor how I feel right now about engaging. I admire anyone who offers a response, though. Even a slur is preferable to indifference: A thought sets into motion other thoughts, banging up against and re-arranging each other.

I am not at home in the media of slogans and contempt. Is the goal to convince or listen? That listening is *not* a passive mode will require some practice, I think. I am not a position, only an act that seeks integrity.

STEVENSON TO WHITE
SALMON, WASHINGTON,
8 APRIL

Last night, a disquieting time. I felt roped in to support M.A. and Ellen at the evening program, while the others went off to rest. M.A. suggested a Beyond War workshop; Ellen, the Train rap. Feeling grimly inadequate and wanting desperately to creep off and write, I offered simply to "be there," a lousy compromise. I am at a loss about what to say in the programs. A precedent has been set; give the history of the Train; recount vigorously and with passion the beginnings of the Tracks

Campaign; show the film, and perhaps, encourage questions. All this is designed to poke and prod and stimulate folks into recognizing the relationship between sexism, racism, classism, and the arms race; or between American Life Style and the Train; *or*, oh, any number of ambitious moral posturings. I feel *I* am posturing. What right do I have to ask people to change their lives?

Every night it seems we re-invent the wheel, though. Should we throw in music; the satirical sketches we have prepared from my musical; meditations and readings? We will never get good at the programs until we get a system going. We ought to have teams that could take walk time off for planning the program. Until we agree on the need for prep time, our presentations will be slip shod and last minute, burdened by exhaustion.

I know that is considered too controlling by some in the group. But what is "too" controlling about it? One's style of presentation is different from another's, and surely we ought to encourage that. Again, it seems easier to react than to initiate, easier to grumble at the precedent than to create a new one.

Besides, I have been hard on myself lately, wanting to be a combination Jesse Jackson—Krishnamurti when I speak. Since this is the first time I have gone on the road as a messenger of peace, the expectation seems a bit steep. At this point, my message of peace could use a little revising. I am, alas, more interested in the casseroles arranged on the table than telling people what to do about the Train. I am more interested in having my feet rubbed than in assuming a responsibility for networking the peace groups from Portland through the Gorge. I am more interested in brushing my hair than in stepping through my haze to answer questions, some of them, disastrous in this mood ("Have you gotten good weather?"), and some of them simply beyond my ken ("What are the comparable nuclear weapons systems in the USSR, and what are you doing about *that?*").

Barbara saves the evening. Our Stevenson connection, she is earnest, present to the intended spirit of the evening, and desires to form a peace group here. Her concerns restore the focus that baby cries, tag and scattered toys threaten to diffuse. We scrape our chairs into a circle, and MA begins with the question, "What is your own experience of war?" Silence. The group bends in collective concentration to the middle. Paula's boys giggle, all but one, who looks 12, going on 48. This is Matthew, a friend of her boys. He is a cartoon-weird type, so very grave he is about the Train, all big-eared and map crazy. When it is his turn to speak, the boys put hands up to bursting cheeks and explode into laughter, running out of the room. Matthew perseveres, a look of pale wonder on his solemn face. His uncle was killed in Vietnam; he will not forget the stories, the return of the body, the funeral. The boys' laughter is sharp in the room. I do not understand, and my eyes meet Matthew's. They have abandoned him, and I want him to know I will hang around.

I am amazed by this group, scattered and baby-talking and seemingly indifferent. Terri is, too. Her story was about losing a great-grandmother to a Nazi concentration camp, tears making her voice quiver. The boys laughed then, too, not at Terri, but out of inattentiveness. She writes me a note in her anger, and we go outside to smoke.

TRI-CITIES AND THE HANFORD RESERVATION (RICHLAND, PASCO, KENNEWISK, WASHINGTON), 17 APRIL

It is humbling to take in gratitude. Last night, a physicist from the Hanford Reservation through Batelle (he has been very brave about taking a moral stance against Batelle's defense contracts, at great personal risk) made On The Line a very special welcome on behalf of the World Citizens for Peace. There are twenty-five or so at the gathering, including young children. I am often touched by their presence because here we all sit, adults, somber or terrified toward eloquence or stiff with rage, sharing our nuclear stories, and the children's innocence is a haunting counterpoint. Their unguarded and joyful expectation that life go on, proceeding from ball to laps to dinner jives well with holocaust, because you cannot see a child's face before the wreck of Hiroshima, and not just go crazy with grief, and want to go say to Casper Weinberger, "We don't want that kind of protection. No enemy is enemy enough to endure that kind of suffering at anyone's hands."

It *is* intense here. The Hanford Reservation, of course, is the economy, has been since World War II and it is a tiny, brave minority that goes against the nuclear tide. And so the intensity in this room is also because our presence gives these brave few strength.

Jim reads his favorite passage from the Gospel According to Luke: the disciples, with much to do are cast out of their safe territory as sheep among wolves. In faith they are asked to make their journeys without money, shoes, material possessions. As he reads the passage, initially lost on me because of the "Go Forth's" and hefty Biblicals, I suddenly realize that he is seeing *us* in this context. First moved, gradually guilty, I think, "I am not doing enough, neither increasing my understanding of nuclear issues, nor going forth without money, food, and especially not without shoes; do not deserve such pulsating respect."

And then something happens. It does not ease my pangs for increased doing, but it lets me accept his intensity, theirs really, for the whole evening is one of gratitude. The Walk moves people regardless of the walkers. The Walk triggers in people their yearning for peace, not as a concept, but as a daily practice. Meeting us releases the power of hope, a deep perhaps untalked about resolve. That is why it is so intense sometimes, and why I have not words to meet it with. Only heart. They are projecting their yearning and believing selves. So, of course, it will not do to answer with a stammering confession of my own inadequacies, or to lessen that charge with a humorous account of my blisters. It will do only to take the power of that gratitude in, let it settle in the heart and travel to the toes and believe that when we, all of us, work, a great force of good is released, like a spirit dispensing hope over our joined and worried souls.

MONTPELIER, IDAHO, 3 JUNE

On the road it is necessary sometimes to *not* be nice. I do not mean that defensively, city street smarts meets the great outdoors. I mean, niceness has nothing to do with describing who we are to those who ask, with bearing witness. Now, niceness has its place, but I need to expand my repertoire, and when I "do" polite, let it issue from respect and not from habit. Mom's Good Girl tapes and Dad's approval are the voices in my head; "be obedient" and "for God's sake, smile" still bicker for attention. In recent confrontations, my insides turn out. First I am angry. Then I try to fix it with that hopeless New Age edict, "Don't be so judgemental." The current confrontation is sparked by the question (asked a dozen times a day), "What about the Russians?" Now, that is a good question, but it is often asked in the spirit of a *coup de grace*. "Ha Ha, what do you know, my stupid girls? Go march there; you'll see what freedom is!" By assuming that we are for the Russians, that that is what it is to be *for* peace, the common concern, however many variables that inform the task of making peace, gets swept away. It is like focusing on the youth and idealism of the student protests in the sixties in order not to take seriously the substantial concerns. It is like confusing justice with what the judge is wearing.

I have got to push through it, though, my knee-jerk rage at being closed out by ignorance like this, and then my silence. A goal—let anger be the fuel, and let my speaking ride it.

Montpelier, "another Mormon town," we are warned, "99%," and this evening we are hosted by the 1% remaining—the civilized, the Presbyterian. They await us, four old women in red pants suits and bright pins, with their kind stew and conditional interest. Also, two old men, who sit behind pillars. The women hover with busy regard. They ask questions and turn away mid-answers in their worry over place settings and where is everyone and will they be in time for dinner?

Helen seems in charge and lines us up by a vat of beef stew and a tray of jello salad. All but two of us are vegetarians, a fine start. We stagger ourselves, politely, among our hosts. I look across at Sande. Her face is very red. She sits beside Carl, who is boasting about the rifle he carries in his truck. She is staring at the wall and has not touched her jello salad.

Ruth and Jerry, meanwhile, represent hope. Sure enough, it is revealed that they have owned, written for and run the town newspaper for some thirty years, and they have just sold it. "We're the town radicals," Ruth keeps saying, and I laugh along with her, missing the derision. I do not know that I am sitting in the middle of a feud.

Helen is telling stories of her girlhood. "When I was a girl," she says, "why, we used to throw the liver and the innards to the darkies. And they were glad for it. *Now* what with the price of meat, who wouldn't be?" There is a stunned silence.

After dinner, Helen wants us to stand up individually and speak. It feels like Ralpha Senderwitz's School of Public Address in Allentown, Pennsylvania. At fifteen I went there, to learn The Drama, and how to speak with poise in public, however inane the subject of my speech. Helen expects little public addresses, well placed between coffee and dessert, and we feel bullied, not to mention underdressed. She asks questions, looks up grandly and announces, "dessert, dessert." She is attempting to treat the evening as a diplomatic exercise, and so charges through it like a hostess to delinquent five year-olds. If she did not remind me of my grandmother, and my own roots where fear, prejudice, and the limitations of experience were, my frustration might be reduced to a clear broth of anger. But this is thick soup, theatre, both which are, of course, the Walk.

Ruth, with her halo of Colette frizz, her direct inquisitive eyes, holds her own at the other end of the table, still muttering, "town radicals"; admonishing, to herself, "they are so conservative, so conservative," off on some private reckoning of the cruelties done them and their paper over the years. Her energy stops there, deadends in slight. Jerry does not say much. He is long and slim, androgynous. He curves in, holding himself off a little to the side. Fifteen years Ruth's elder, this seems part of the town's long sustained reproach. I am out of touch with small town proprieties and grudges.

Michael tiptoes to the table and whispers to his mother, Pat.[1] They

---

[1]Pat, our eastern Idaho coordinator, accompanied us loyally from Pocatello on, running shuttles from her home to us, bringing mail, picnic baskets, and Michael, her nine-year-old son, whenever we were on the road. They walked with us often, her station wagon becoming the Walk sag wag for weary walkers to interchange walking and shuttle

walk away together. Now it is time to be ON, and to try to toughen up the Good Girl recitations toward Train talk and peace, more along the lines of Barbara Deming, less Ding Dong School. Patty starts. I see the fervor in her eyes, and suspect that the ensuing speech might exert an appeal elsewhere. She is passionate, describing the power of witness; the transformation of our values. I am moved. It is a good reminder to me of the long haul commitment to the Walk, and of why I am sitting here in this church basement.

Pat and Michael return. Of all things, she is carrying a mop, and Michael giggles. "Excuse me," she says, "we seem to be experiencing a flood. There is a geyser in the middle of the floor."

The energy geysers, too. Everyone but the walkers is in a flurry of "what?" and "where?" The peace gathering is broken and we few remain inside a comedy of errors, dumbfounded. Helen rushes to the bathroom in an attempt to aid. She flushes the toilet endlessly, and with every flush gallons of raw sewage boil up from the drain in the middle of the room. Michael has a filled bucket, runs for another, and a bucket bridge is started to run the filth up and out of the door. Someone yells, "For god's sake, stop flushing!" and Helen emerges, confused.

There is no peace left in the basement. I head for the stairs, longing for fresh air and distance. Helen grabs me. "Where are you going?" she asks.

I say, "To wait until this is over, and then to be taken wherever I'm staying the night. We're all exhausted."

"You can't go yet," she says. "I've called the town photographer and she's on her way. She's making a very special point to be here. She's already late for a wedding."

"All right," I say, "we'll wait for a little while, but I'd really appreciate getting it organized soon." Again I start for the stairs.

"About tomorrow," she continues, "if some of you could come to Sunday service, we'll let you talk for five minutes before."

Puzzled by Helen's request under these, and any circumstances, I say, "Some of the walkers will be out on the road by four in the morning, and the rest of us will want to be out early to relieve them. So let's leave it at 'we'll see.' "

I corner Ruth, asking if she knows where we are to stay. With her, it seems, those of us not planning to be on the road at four. I ask her can she take us home soon. I am rank, on top of being exhausted, having camped, unwashed for days. My hair, confined under my black Sicilian scarf, is a flattened fright, and my bones ache. Helen overhears,

---

tasks. It was a particularly good arrangement when faced with acts of God, such as hail storms, swarming ground squirrels and plagues of locusts.

tsk-tsking. "You're not dirty, dear, and you don't smell at all." That does it. It seems an ultimate violation of my dwindling stockpile of truths, and I start to crumble.

The photographer arrives. She looks sullen and frankly put out, but that could be because of the mess in the middle of the floor. We file upstairs for pictures, seeking a patch of grass. Our feet are bare and as we walk onto the lawn, we feel simultaneously the dread ooze. We stand in the puddle of sewage. The photographer of course has no idea why we scream, why we arrange ourselves, bristling, in a row by the carts.

"Helen," I smile sweetly, "come here with us. I couldn't possibly have this event recorded without you." She wades through the ooze. I put my arm around her.

There is a time not to be the *good girl*, and so for the rest of the evening I am not, and try to find the boundary between personal integrity and rudeness, crossing over, I'm afraid. Ruth's and Jerry's street is named for them; that fact characteristic of a small town, and their place in it, remarkable to my urban anonymity. Theirs is a large house, split level. We go in and I ask for scotch. Jerry smiles and brings out a bottle.

"Drink as much as you want," he says.

I do.

In the living room, Sande is busy writing; Jerry reads the paper; Ellen and Ruth and I talk. Before this, Ruth and I had talked alone. She was explaining the big house—the space; the towels; the closets full of toys as useful for when the children and the grandchildren came. And then she explained her recent stroke, how it took her a year to learn to read again, and speak; how "ceiling" got all mixed up with "painting," and "shoe" with "plate"; how Jerry had slowly taught her to write and spell, but still there were moments of despair and disorientation.

Now we talk about the town and its politics; about their children, both gone east to practice medicine for the poor, the hungry, the disempowered; and about the Walk. Ruth is stuck on one thing, and that is fear. She cannot imagine walking on the streets at night let alone across the country and I think, because of that, she begins to mother us most oppressively.

I was not sure if it was the stroke that kept her from hearing that we are not afraid, on that level, for our safety, or if it was her own fears, the scars from ostracism. I glimpse in Ruth my own undoing. She has accomplished much: the newspaper; conscientious and successful children; a loving marriage. She surrounds herself with art. Wyeth and Breugel reproductions hang on the walls, and there are shelves of books. Her fear is speaking to my *good girl*, that catch in the throat that happens when I ache to speak out honestly, with conviction, but do not, for fear of ridicule. My parent tapes are in me: "rules and regulations, dear"; the belief that the unconventional is a phase, not the advance toward truth and clarity. Mother's first response to the Walk was, "people will laugh at you." So this is my own peculiar guard that stands before my heart. If I speak out against the "rules and regulations," and with feeling, I will be ridiculed. Now Ruth, here, is fearing for her life; I am fearing for my twisted sense of honor.

Ruth admires us as the ideals she will not practice; the conscience she will not be. I am sad for this. It reminds me that I would greet those who climbed the mountains, or pulled timely, crystalline projects from their dreams as if their lives taunted my limitations. I would get stuck there, in comparison, not in the glad participatory handshake of ingenious humanity. So I feel sorry for her a little and suggest different styles, myriad expressions of peace work, and doing what we can with what we have, and other vague et ceteras designed to reassure Ruth as much as me.

The next morning, she is ablaze with mission. Blankets of laundry appear on the kitchen table, and plates of toast and scrambled eggs. If it were not cold and drizzly, if we were not aware of soon having to relieve the walkers, out in the cold since five, it would all feel like Mom packing us up for summer camp. Ruth administers to needs that she keeps creating in her excitement to be with us. Yes, we eat the toast, the eggs, more toast; we laugh when she returns with Sande from the walkers on the road to whom she has delivered warm cocoa, more toast.

There is tension. Sande knows we should be off; expects each of us to do what we can to facilitate a smooth getaway. But the comforts are seductive; the laundry, slow; the toast, good, and Ruth, a rocket of attention. I sit her down and ask for Helen's, Thelma's and Carl's addresses. Painstakingly she writes them out in a slow tremble. Perhaps I should not have asked. Perhaps writing is too difficult for her hand and memory. I do not want to blunder, and yet feel the pressure from Sande to leave, the impatience of others with this frenzied, stalled morning. She rushes into Jerry in a terrible frustration. He has remained thoughtfully removed, buried in his paper. She cries for help and then returns to her scrawls on the paper. It is taking too much time. The others have cleaned up, gathered our belongings and put them out.

Our ride comes; we are ready. Ruth and Jerry walk us outside. There are tears in her eyes as she says, "When the Train comes, I don't know what I'll do. No one ever turns out. No one cares. I'll be the only one."

I cannot pretend not to understand. I have spent my entire adult life in cities, and am not in touch with the kind of small town conservatism that seems to kill creative and dissenting spirits. I cannot really take in the repercussions of expressing unpopular opinions, of making waves, of insisting on truth from our institutions that are characterized by bland self-interest and hypocrisy. No, I am no saint, just naive, and I say, perhaps blithely, "But Ruth, that's it! Make a sign, a huge sign, 'One Woman For Peace,' and be at the tracks when the Train comes through." I describe my vision—the country holding hands in a 2700-mile human chain, bearing signs, flowers, photographs, candles to the Train when it comes through; not one town dark, allowing the dark passage of the Death Train.

We said that, should she choose to vigil, something would catch fire over time—at the next vigil, three people; and then, a dozen; that consciousness has a way of spreading, the results, perhaps, immeasurable from our own vantage point in time.

We got in the car. Ruth was weeping, and Jerry too. "What is it," she said, "that sign? I'll do it. 'One Woman for Peace.' " And we left her, the image of a tiny, frightened woman, walking out of her house some night to meet the Train with her sign, "One Woman for Peace" held high.

That was more courage, I swear, than mine in the walking, for I was ready to walk, and although I encountered some fears, I did not set out with an agenda of past evils and present insecurities. And there was Ruth, with all her fears exposed, on the verge of being ready. Such love and gratitude I felt that day and wondered, had our *good girl* nauseas intermingled to make a little mutually blessed change?

COKEVILLE TO FOSSIL BUTTE NATIONAL MONUMENT, WYOMING, 5 JUNE

Today I yelled at a drunken man who gave MA and me a lift ten miles up the road toward Fossil. He made me mad, and how much energy can you give to figuring where the alcohol stops and the man begins? Anyhow, he asked a lot of questions, barking them out with that male prerogative, that filling-up-space posture, where they interrupt a lot to make you feel ridiculous, or they change the subject, because they do. It is a posture of "men should speak their minds whatever the occasion; however unsuitable the contents; and in and out of turn." Meanwhile, I take a club to my politeness, calling it the flip side of that prerogative.

So I barked back. I assumed some male prerogative and shouted out my deep convictions, across MA's lap, across his Budweiser and through it, through my *good girl*, those polite concerns over not offending, through my fear of ridicule. I met the barking man on his own terms. I assaulted him with my vision of non-violence. I shouted that, no, I did not need to get my facts and figures straight in order to understand the complexity of the issue; that my life was being messed with, thank you, by a system of violence and oppression, and that no amount of details pro and con, about the Russians and their weapons would take away that knowledge in my heart.

He said if his neighbors were beating on his kids, he would go out and shoot the neighbors. You would not solve that with this non-violence crap, now would you?

I said, "Damn it, yes, you'd better, because if you go shoot your neighbor, then your kids will have learned that shooting *and* solving a problem are the same, and isn't it better to be neighborly and talk so when it comes time to harvest the crop or solve the gopher problem, your neighbor is there ready to help out?"

And wouldn't it be better to talk to the kids, if they're getting beaten, and hear from them how it hurts, and what they want to do?

So it went, this little UN session over laps. It felt good to take my gag off, even though I was swearing, and I thought that might be hypocritical. At least I did not encounter his impossible invective with *good girl* "there there's." We caught up with the group and he got out, too, to get another beer from his cooler in the bed of the pickup.

I am in a gap of should, though; what *should* I be yelling? My reactions to his paranoia; my own loaded facts and figures? By convincing him, I am just convincing me. I am not podium material; I would rather hug than slug, but this kind of politics makes me feel naive and, also, hysterical, like many women who seem to go at issues with their hearts in their voice boxes.

Part 5

WHAT NEXT?

The nuclear industry, powerful, profit-oriented, totally unconcerned about our health, aided and abetted by a government that is its twin, is murdering us and our children every day. And it is up to us, each one of us, to stop it. . . . No time to quibble about survival being a 'white issue.' . . . Massive demonstrations are vital. Massive civil disobedience. . . . Talk with your family; organize your friends. . . . Support those who go to jail. . . . We must save Earth, and relieve those who would destroy it of the power to do so. Alice Walker, *In Search of Our Mother's Gardens* (1983), pp. 344–346.

22

Only Justice Can Stop a Curse*

Alice Walker

To the Man God: O Great One, I have been sorely tried by my enemies and have been blasphemed and lied against. My good thoughts and my honest actions have been turned to bad actions and dishonest ideas. My home has been disrespected, my children have been cursed and ill-treated. My dear ones have been backbitten and their virtue questioned. O Man God, I beg that this that I ask for my enemies shall come to pass:

That the South wind shall scorch their bodies and make them wither and shall not be tempered to them. That the North wind shall freeze their blood and numb their muscles and that it shall not be tempered to them. That the West wind shall blow away their life's breath and will not leave their hair grow, and that their fingernails shall fall off and their bones shall crumble. That the East wind shall make their minds grow dark, their sight shall fail and their seed dry up so that they shall not multiply.

I ask that their fathers and mothers from their furthest generation will not intercede for them before the great throne, and the wombs of their women shall not bear fruit except for strangers, and that they shall become extinct. I pray that the children who may come shall be weak of mind and paralyzed of limb and that they themselves shall curse them in their turn for ever turning the breath of life into their bodies. I pray that disease and death shall be forever with them and that their worldly goods shall not prosper, and that their crops shall not multiply and that their cows, their sheep, and their hogs and all their living beasts shall die of starvation and thirst. I pray that their houses shall be unroofed and that the rain, the thunder and lightning shall find the innermost recesses of their home and

---

*Previously published in Alice Walker, *In Search of Our Mothers' Gardens* (New York: Harcourt Brace Jovanovich, 1983).

that the foundation shall crumble and the floods tear it asunder. I pray that
the sun shall not shed its rays on them in benevolence, but instead it shall
beat down on them and burn them and destroy them. I pray that the moon
shall not give them peace, but instead shall deride them and decry them
and cause their minds to shrivel. I pray that their friends shall betray them
and cause them loss of power, of gold and of silver, and that their enemies
shall smite them until they beg for mercy which shall not be given them.
I pray that their tongues shall forget how to speak in sweet words, and
that it shall be paralyzed and that all about them will be desolation,
pestilence and death. O Man God, I ask you for all these things because
they have dragged me in the dust and destroyed my good name; broken
my heart and caused me to curse the day that I was born. So be it.

This is a curse-prayer that Zora Neale Hurston collected in the 1920s.
And by then it was already old. I have often marveled at it. At the
precision of its anger, the absoluteness of its bitterness. Its utter hatred
of the enemies it condemns. It is a curse-prayer by a person who would
readily, almost happily, commit suicide, if it meant her enemies would
also die. Horribly.

I am sure it was a woman who first prayed this curse. And I see her—
black, yellow, brown or red, *"aboriginal"* as the Ancients are called in
South Africa and Australia and other lands invaded, expropriated, and
occupied by whites. And I think, with astonishment, that the curse-
prayer of this colored woman—starved, enslaved, humiliated, and
carelessly trampled to death—over centuries, is coming to pass. Indeed,
like ancient peoples of color the world over, who have tried to tell the
white man of the destruction that would inevitably follow from the
uranium-mining plunder of their sacred lands, this woman—along with
millions and billions of obliterated sisters, brothers, and children—
seems to have put such enormous energy into her hope for revenge that
her curse seems close to bringing it about. And it is this hope for
revenge, finally, I think, that is at the heart of many People of Color's
resistance to the present anti-nuclear movement.

In any case, this has been my own problem.

When I have considered the enormity of the white man's crimes
against humanity. Against women. Against every living person of color.
Against the poor. Against my mother and my father. Against me . . .
When I consider that at this very moment he wishes to take away what
little freedom I have died to achieve, through denial of my right to vote
. . . Has already taken away education, medicine, housing, and food
. . . That William Shockley is saying at this moment that he will run for
the Senate of my country to push his theory that blacks are genetically
inferior and should be sterilized . . . When I consider that he is, they
are, a real and present threat to my life and the life of my daughter, my
people, I think—in perfect harmony with my sister of long ago: *Let the*

earth marinate in poisons. Let the bombs cover the ground like rain. For nothing short of total destruction will ever teach them anything.

And it would be good, perhaps, to put an end to the species in any case, rather than let white men continue to subjugate it, and continue their lust to dominate, exploit, and despoil not just our planet, but the rest of the universe, which is their clear and oft-stated intention; leaving their arrogance and litter not just on the moon, but on everything else they can reach.

If we have any true love for the stars, planets, the rest of Creation, we must do everything we can to keep white men away from them. They who have appointed themselves our representatives to the rest of the universe. They who have never met any new creature without exploiting, abusing, or destroying it. They who say we poor (white included) and colored and female and elderly blight neighborhoods, while they blight worlds.

What they have done to the Old, they will do to the New.

Under the white man every star would become a South Africa, every planet a Vietnam.

Fatally irradiating ourselves may in fact be the only way to save others from what Earth has already become. And this is a consideration that I believe requires serious thought from every one of us.

However, just as the sun shines on the godly and the ungodly alike, so does nuclear radiation. And with this knowledge it becomes increasingly difficult to embrace the thought of extinction purely for the assumed satisfaction of—from the grave—achieving revenge. Or even of accepting our demise as a planet as a simple and just preventive medicine administered to the universe. Life is better than death, I believe, if only because it is less boring, and because it has fresh peaches in it. In any case, Earth is my home—though for centuries white people have tried to convince me I have no right to exist, except in the dirtiest, darkest corners of the globe.

So let me tell you: I intend to protect my home. Praying—not a curse—only the hope that my courage will not fail my love. But if by some miracle, and all our struggle, the Earth is spared, only justice to every living thing (and everything is alive) will save humankind.

And we are not saved yet.

Only justice can stop a curse.

23

Reclaiming the Discourse: Feminist Perspectives in Peace Research*

Barbara Roberts

Peace research, like most academic enterprises, has tended to focus on the male population and experience of war and "peace," and thus unwittingly to exclude the lived experience of women in daily life, in peace and war, women's practices of peacemaking, and women's insights. Women have become invisible in the discourse, their absence, among the chronicles of "men of goodwill," itself becoming invisible. Despite the best intentions, inattention to over half of humanity has deprived the research of crucial insights and resources. The following survey is meant to identify some of these, and suggest some of their potential.

Women and men have different perspectives on violence, war and peace (Roberts, 1984; Reardon, 1985, 1983; McAllister, 1982; Wiser, 1986; As, 1983). First, the most common form of physical violence in our society is violence against women by men. Second, women suffer more than men from structural inequality and institutionalized violence, within every stratum of society, where force is either historically distant or a last resort; that is, domination and systemic discrimination long enshrined by law or custom (Boulding, 1976, 1977; Boulding et al., 1976;

*This is an excerpt from a longer article, previously published under another title in *Atlantis: A Women's Studies Journal*, Vol. 12, No. 2, (1987).

Roberts, 1983a; Lernoux, 1980; Rogers, 1980; ISIS, 1984). Third, women have little say in the political decisions that lead to war, and virtually none in stopping it once it has started. Women both as civilians and simply as women, are targets for attack, including sexual attack in peace as well as in war. In fact, woman-hating is a fundamental part of military training and militarism (Sampson, 1977; Michalowski, 1982; Eisenhart, 1975; Kamester and Vellacott, 1987; Strange, 1983). Fourth, women are statistically more peaceful than men; despite historical evidence that some women can be as bloody-minded and militaristic as their brothers, there is increasing evidence that, in our time, women as a whole are characteristically more cooperative, nurturing, and constructive than men (Roberts, 1984; Wiser and Roberts, 1985; Gilligan, 1981). This is not to deny that men can (and some do) behave in these ways; indeed, recent research on the Neolithic suggests that these peaceful behaviors and characteristics may have been the norm for both women and men for thousands of years (Eisler, 1987; Gilligan, 1983). Today, however, such men are very much in the minority.

Peace studies, like other disciplines, can benefit from the recognition that women and men have very different life experiences, life chances and life choices. Marxist scholar Phillip Corrigan points out that human capacity is limited or developed by particular social forms in historical circumstances (Corrigan, 1984), and gender has been one of the most significant of these shaping forms. The different life paths of women give us access to different resources from those developed by the male experience; these resources are badly needed today when the existence of all life on earth is gravely threatened.

Violence, whether domestic or national, is based on concepts of sovereignty and hierarchy (Carroll, 1972). It is characteristically (that is, statistically) male to presume that relationships operate by the rules of dominance (*power-over*) rather than mutuality, interdependence (*power-with*), and empowerment (*power-within*). In training himself for vio-lence—whether domestic or national—the attacker must dehumanize both himself and the 'enemy,' so that his normal human awareness of connectedness and kinship between him and his 'target' will not hinder the attack. To dehumanize and objectify, it has been shown, is part of normal masculine training to separate feeling from thinking (Reynaud, 1983; Woodcock, 1984). "Boys don't cry," they are told. Men must act on the basis of 'principles' stripped of the flesh of human relationships, priding themselves on other forms of moral and emotional insulation. This insulation is a common element in boys' contempt for girls and 'sissy' feelings. In at least 10–25% of men, dehumanization develops into violence, in their propensity to dominate, harass, batter and rape women and sexually abuse girls, and in the barrack room (or locker room) training to see the 'enemy' as 'broads,' 'wogs,' 'slopes,' and 'cunts.' Men who won't fight are 'a bunch of women': potential victims for either side (Roberts, 1983, 1984; Eisenhart, 1975).

Getting rid of weapons would not automatically create a peaceful society. The social relations and systems of violence and inequality, and the types of people produced by these systems, would remain. We would still have what Barbara Starrett calls the death pattern or the Vampire (Starrett, 1982). Peace preparations, then, involve more fundamental and revolutionary changes than ending 'war.'

In a brilliant essay called "Peace on earth, goodwill toward women," Alice Wiser warns: "If you are not a feminist then you haven't even begun to think about peace. You've only thought of stopping war or stopping the arms race, of non-war. The distinction between being against something and being for something is enormous." Wiser develops a six-stage model of peacework, each with its own goals, mindset and methods.

1. Anti-war; action from fear and frustration, excitement replacing despair; the problem is political, and 'out there.' This is the stage at which she sees the majority of people in the peace movement today.
2. Beginning awareness of the connection between personal lives and war and peace issues; involvement of social justice and peace activists in personal actions such as tax or military service resistance; simplifying daily life. High burnout and dropout rate, much self doubt.
3. Women emerge as a group, realizing that gender injustice and skewed ways of conceptualizing and acting are pervasive, even in the peace and social justice work we have been doing. Malestream models and methods questioned, search for deep causes of violence, based on lived experience. A new world view, new methods begin development among women. This is the first real peacework. Most men have no idea of this process, and keep doing stage 2 work, saying 'women's issues' are not real peace issues.
4. A new vision of peace begins to be developed. Anti-war work continues, but is seen as a step toward the peaceful world of justice, equality, community. Most men have trouble doing this; women learn fast.
5. Assumption of personal responsibility and often drastic personal change; commitment to risktaking in daily life to root out sources of violence. Learning to live peacefully; remaking institutions and people. Attention to feelings, process, morality and ethics (a la Gilligan, not in some abstract way) is an important part of this work.

6. Collaboratively designing and implementing new systems and structures to make visions reality. Revolution: complete, from the inside out and the bottom up; peaceful, joyous revolution (Wiser, 1986).

Changing the discourse is an important part of anti-war and pro-peace work. Dorothy Smith and others have helped us to see that the discourse in which the intellectual, political, economic, spiritual and even interpersonal business of human society is carried out does not reflect the experiences, perspectives, interests and priorities of women (Smith, 1974, 1975, 1977, 1978, 1979, 1981a, 1981b; Ng, 1982). A major emphasis in past and present feminist thought has been the importance of naming and putting forward all these things and having them seen as legitimate. The discourse of the peace movement reflects masculinist perspectives and methods; elsewhere I have called it the discourse of 'machothink' (Roberts, 1984).

What would it mean to have a feminist discourse in the peace movement, or more accurately in the anti-war movement? For example, it would mean that we personalize the war machine. We locate war preparations as specific acts or decisions taken by individuals whom we name and locate in their work and family contexts. This requires biographical and corporate research of a relatively simple sort. War preparations are immensely profitable for those people who control large corporations involved in weapons and military research, production and sales. They are immensely costly for the rest of us because our taxes pay the millions of dollars of subsidies for war industries. Investment in so-called 'defence' spending creates very few jobs (fewer than almost any other kind of investment), each one of them requiring huge capital costs. Military spending also takes away money needed to provide for essential human needs such as clean water, food, health care, and education (Sivard, 1983; Smith and Smith, 1983; Enloe, 1983). In fact, with the money spent on arms in the world for only a few minutes, all the world's people could be given safe water sources.

Which corporations are profiting directly from militarization? Why are corporations permitted to do this? Who are the men who make the laws that protect the death merchants? Who are the men who choose to make or sell weapons at the cost of hunger, thirst and ill-health for so many other people? (Bokaer, 1984; Sampson, 1977; Easlea, 1983). Do these men have families? Children? These men who are the war planners are preparing the means for not only our deaths but the deaths of their own family members. Changing the discourse means to talk publicly about those facts, and about these men as named individuals making specific decisions, not as abstract parts of the system or unnamed monsters. A feminist discourse on these issues will turn the discussion back to the personal as political, and the political as personal.

A feminist discourse would also mean that we personalize the effects of war preparations on our own lives. Many of the most important parts of our lives are affected by militarization; how we feed, clothe and shelter ourselves, with whom we live under what circumstances, if we have kids and how and by whom they will be cared for; what choice we have about any of the foregoing, and what we can do to complain or change something we don't like (Enloe, 1983). These are all political issues; the limits on our lives are set in large part by the decisions of the men whose own lives and fortunes are tied in with war preparations.

For an easily understood example of how we might talk about war preparations and our own lives, let's assume that all of us reading this are somehow in the same large building and all our kids are together in a big day-care center nearby. Assume that as we go on about our business it becomes clear to us that the men who talk in various rooms nearby are planning to torture and kill our kids. These men use terms like 'destructive capacity,' 'deterrence' and 'theater of operations'—but we now know with certainty that it is our kids in the day-care center they are referring to. And assume that for some reason we can't just go and get them out of the day-care center. First stop and think about this situation. How do we *feel* about this? Do we feel fear, horror, rage, grief, shock, hopelessness and a determination that we will not let this happen? These very intense feelings are as appropriate to our present real-life situation as they are to the hypothetical kids-in-the-day-care center situation described here (Macy, 1983). Returning to our hypothetical day-care center, how do we stop their deaths? Do we continue to carry on obediently with our routine business and allow the planners to prattle on? Do we continue to talk in the language of these men? It seems unlikely. Would we not rather say, "Hey wait a minute, we won't let you do that," or "What do you mean, theater of operation, that's my kid's life, my kid's body you're talking about!" Just as in that hypothetical situation we must insist that the covert plans for our children's deaths be openly acknowledged and our collaboration refused, in our actual situation today we must transform the discourse to insist that the human element be included in any talk about war, talk by anyone at any level for any purpose. The 'human element' includes the effects of their plans on our physical, emotional, spiritual selves; the sights, sounds, sensations and smells their plans imply for us. It includes our feelings about what is being planned for us.

It follows that we must insist that those who calmly discuss war plans without reference to this human context are crazy: mentally ill, insane, out of touch with reality, not to say sociopathic and psychopathic. We must change the ground of the discourse and speak from our whole lives. This is not an abstract academic issue, it is a moral and personal issue. When we allow 'machothink' and 'nukespeak' to define the rules of discourse for us, we are complicitous by our silence. We must name what's going on and who is doing it.

This has painful consequences. First, we'll be attacked, and second, we'll go crazy ourselves because if we think and talk and feel about these horrors we can't stand it. Those of us who have been involved in rape crisis, child sexual abuse or wife battering resistance and support work have already experienced this. Going crazy is appropriate but inconvenient. There are ways to stay sane; despair and empowerment work, support groups, other feminist resources (Oldring, Sydiaha and Blythe, 1987; Macy, 1983; Therapy Now, 1984).

The act of naming is in itself a healing act. Berit As, the Norwegian feminist peaceworker, was invited to the Couchiching conference in 1982. She found it dominated by men preparing for war, who used a number of techniques familar to us to make the peaceworkers feel discredited or crazy; ignoring them, telling them they were wrong or lying, treating them like objects. Berit found herself physically ill and mentally paralyzed after a couple of days, which was awkward because she was supposed to give a talk to the conference. What saved her was to realize that when the machothinkers talked about "theaters of operation" that might be nuked in Europe, they were talking about millions of women, men and children who were Berit's family, friends and neighbors—and she felt a good deal of pain and grief and absolute outrage at what they were planning and how they were describing it. And that is the substance of what she said at her talk. She told us later that this experience had convinced her that we must always speak up and insist that the truth be told about what was going on. It would heal us and help to change the definition of the situation. Moreover, the act of naming is an empowering act. When we name what is going on, we then can more easily have access to our feelings about it. Our feelings are an important source of energy and power (Macy, 1983; Starhawk, 1982; Therapy Now, 1984). As well, naming ends our complicity in the doublespeak which helps to make the potential victims acquiesce in the assault.

We sometimes hesitate to speak up because we do not feel informed about weapons systems, strategies, and military language; we cannot speak easily about the war games played by our 'defenders'. Fortunately we don't all need to become experts on the methods by which the war planners intend to annihilate us, in order to tell them and each other that we will not allow them to do this. This is not to say that facts about the arms race and militarization, about corporate capitalism, the state, government policy, vested interests, etc., are unimportant. They are very important. Most of them are also readily available. What we must do is to insist that these facts are not the only or even the most important information that must be discussed. We must not feel that we have to be able to reel off data about armaments and war in order to discuss peace. We don't need to learn the war planners' pornographic discourse of objectification, dehumanization, hate and death; we need to change it. We are already experts in the most important parts of the discourse we need to use. We live, we love, we learn and work and struggle together, we have hope and joy in each other and in the beauty of the world around us. That is what we say 'yes' to, and what we must speak about. And that, I believe, is where transformation begins.

Women are too often silenced by accusations that we are just being emotional. These accusations can be refuted in several ways. First, our emotions of grief and despair are a sane and appropriate response to the situation; when they are accepted and experienced, they can be positive and useful. Our despair and outrage come from our sense of connectedness to all around us; that same caring and sense of connectedness are a source of great power. Thus, 'being emotional' is not only appropriate, but a pragmatic step toward changing the situation. Second, it is crucial to realize that accusations such as 'being emotional' obscure the power relations inherent in discourse. He who controls the discourse defines the terms in which discussion can be carried out (Smith, 1978, 1977). She who challenges and redefines the discourse is engaged in important and powerful political work. A discourse based in and expressing our lived experience, our connections to others and our 'preservative love' (a commitment to the well-being of creatures at risk, as Ruddick defines it, 1983) for them, is a discourse based on the language of immanence, of power-within, and hence, is full of power (Starhawk, 1982; Roberts, 1984).

How did the discourse of machothink arise? Carolyn Merchant, the historian of science, analyses the intellectual shift in the fifteenth and sixteenth centuries when men removed the life or spirit from the natural world, then began to tinker with the machine they had created, with little care for the damage done to the natural or human environment or the human community (Merchant, 1980; Easlea, 1983). Their tinkering has produced a technology for profit and privilege for a few, rather than for fulfilling basic human needs for all people. Technology is simply a tool; it could as easily serve human need as the greed of its controllers. Our economic, political and social systems exist in their present forms because those who were in charge of their development did not believe that they had to take responsibility for the consequences of their decisions, actions and priorities. This kind of decontextualized thinking is one of the fundamentally necessary conditions for the creation of the planetary survival crises we face today.

We must hook ourselves and the rest of the world, including the natural world, back up together again; reground ourselves in the natural material world and recognize that we are all alive and part of the same web of life: a term which Rachel Carson used more than twenty years ago in *Silent Spring* (1962).

Peace preparations (what I mean by feminist peacework) demand the development of a transformative vision of a peaceful world, and the training of ourselves and others to build and live in it. We must become re-sourceful and reconnected to each other and to our sources of humanity and creation. It is especially important for men to reclaim and redefine male personhood and humanity, because their present forms often make men part of the problem rather than part of the solution. Redefined male personhood would include sharing the world's work, including nurturing, motherwork and housework.

William Blake talked about energy as eternal delight. If, as Einstein says, the power of energy is effectively contained in the material world and this power can be expressed in the formula $E = mc^2$, then our material world and we are a process of eternal delight in which we must reclaim our part. This is doable. The same resources that help us stay sane while we try to stop the insane from killing us, help us to visualize and to rediscover energy and delight. I referred earlier to Corrigan's insights about the development of human capacities in particular social forms and historical circumstances; here I refer to the necessity to explore the 'human capacity' side of the equation, at the same time as we explore and rearrange the 'social forms' side. There are known and effective methods for building peaceful people. We have maps for that exploration. We must not be deterred by the super-rational malestream discourse from exploring moral and spiritual issues or approaches, and we must not attack each other for our differences. Our diversity may help to save us, if we claim it as a resource for the transformation of the discourse, and the transformation of ourselves and our world.

REFERENCES

As, Berit, "A materialistic view of men's and women's attitudes towards war." *Women's Studies International Forum*, Vol. 5, No. 3/4 (1983).

Bokaer, Joan, *Nuclear war: who's in charge?* (Citizens Network, Center for Religion, Ethics, and Social Policy, Cornell University, 1984).

Boulding, Elise, *The underside of history* (Boulder, Colorado: Westview Press, 1976).

_____ *Women in the twentieth century world* (New York: Sage, 1977).

Boulding, Elise et al *Handbook of international data on women* (New York: Sage, 1976).

Carroll, Berenice, "Peace research: the cult of power," *Journal of conflict resolution*, Vol. 5, No. 4 (1972).

Carson, Rachel, *Silent spring* (New York: Fawcett, 1962).

Corrigan, Philip, "Marxism and cultural theory." Paper to the Annual Meeting of the Society for Socialist Studies, Guelph, Ontario, June 1984.

Easlea, Brian, *Fathering the unthinkable: Masculinity, scientists and the nuclear arms race* (London: Pluto, 1983).

Eisenhart, Wayne, "You can't hack it little girl: a discussion of the covert psychological agenda of modern combat training." *Journal of social issues*, Vol. 31, No. 4 (1975).

Eisler, Riane, *The chalice and the blade: Our history, our future* (San Francisco: Harper and Row, 1987).

Enloe, Cynthia, *Does khaki become you? The militarisation of women's lives* (London: Pluto, 1983).

Gilligan, Carol, Interview on the CBC (Canadian Broadcasting Corporation) "Ideas" Program, 19 April, 1983.

_____ *In a different voice* (Cambridge: Harvard University Press, 1981).

_____ "Woman's place in man's life cycle," *Harvard Education Review*, November, 1979.

_____ "In a different voice: women's conceptions of self and morality," *Harvard Education Review*, November, 1977.

ISIS, *Women in development* (Philadelphia: New Society Press, 1984).

Kamester, Margaret and Vellacott, Jo (eds.), *Militarism versus feminism: Writings on women and war* (London: Virago, 1987).

Lernoux, Penny, *Cry of the people* (Garden City: Doubleday, 1980).

Macy, Joanna, *Despair and personal power in the nuclear age* (Philadelphia: New Society Press, 1983).

McAllister, Pam (ed.), *Reweaving the web of life: Feminism and nonviolence* (Philadelphia: New Society Press, 1982).

Merchant, Carolyn, *The death of nature: women, ecology and the scientific revolution* (San Francisco: Harper and Row, 1980).

Michalowski, Helen, "The army will make a man out of you." in *Reweaving the web of life*, edited by Pam McAllister, (Philadelphia: New Society Press, 1982).

Ng, Roxana, "Immigrant housewives in Canada: A methodological note," *Atlantis* (Fall 1982).

Oldring Sydiaha, Joanne and Blythe, Joanne, "The despair and empowerment model: its definition and how it relates to women," *Atlantis* (Spring 1987).

Reardon, Betty, *Sexism and the war system* New York: Institute for World Order, 1985).

_____ "A gender analysis of militarism and sexist repression: a suggested research agenda," *Bulletin of the International Peace Research Association* (Summer 1983).

Reynaud, Emmanuel, *Holy virility: The social construction of masculinity* (London: Pluto, 1983).

Roberts, Barbara, "A peaceful world for women: Peace education taking gender into account," *History and social science teacher*, Special issue on peace education (Spring 1985).

_____ "The death of machothink: feminist research and the transformation of peace studies," *Women's studies international forum* (Fall 1984).

_____ "No safe place: the war against women," *Our generation* (Spring 1983). [Please note: rape proclivity data incorrectly given in this article due to typographical errors; refer to Roberts (1984) for correct data.]

Rogers, Barbara, *The domestication of women: Discrimination in developing societies* (London: Tavistock, 1980).

Ruddick, Sara, "Preservative love and military destruction: Reflections on mothering and peace," in *Mothering: Essays in feminist theory*, edited by Joyce Trebilcot (Totowa, NJ: Littlefield Adams, 1983).

Sampson, Anthony, *The arms bazaar: the companies, the dealers, the bribes, from Vickers to Lockheed* (Toronto: Hodder and Stoughton, 1977).

Sivard, Ruth, *World military expenditures* (Washington DC: World Priorities, 1983).

Smith, Dan and Smith, Ron, *The economies of militarism* (London: Pluto, 1983).

Smith, Dorothy, "The experienced world as problematic: a feminist method," Sorokin Lecture No. 12, University of Saskatchewan, 1981.

_____ "On sociological description: a method from Marx," *Human studies*, Vol. 4 (1981).

_____ "A sociology for women," in *The prism of sex.* edited by J. Sherman and E. Beck (Madison: University of Wisconsin Press, 1979).

_____ "A peculiar eclipsing: women's exclusion from man's culture," *Women's studies international forum*, Vol. 1 (1978).

_____ "Some implications of a sociology for women," in *Women in man-made world*, edited by H. Waehrer and N. Glazer, 2nd Ed. (Chicago: Rand McNally, 1977).

_____ "Ideological structures and how women are excluded," *Canadian review of sociology and anthropology*, Vol. 12, No. 4 (1975), Part 1.

_____ "The social construction of documentary reality," *Sociological inquiry*, Vol. 44, No. 4 (1974).

Spretnak, Charlene, *The politics of women's spirituality* (New York: Anchor, 1982).

Starhawk, *Dreaming the dark: Magic, sex and politics* (Boston: Beacon, 1982).

Starrett, Barbara, "The metaphors of power," in *The politics of women's spirituality*, edited by Charlene Spretnak (New York: Anchor, 1982).

Strange, Penny, *It'll make a man of you: A feminist view of the arms race* (Nottingham England: Peace News/Mushroom Press, 1983).

Therapy Now, Toronto. Special issue on living in the nuclear age (Summer 1984).

Wiser, Alice, "Peace on earth, goodwill toward women," *Atlantis* (Fall 1986).

Wiser, Alice and Roberts, Barbara, Unpublished data on women's experiences in peace-making and conflict resolution.

Woodcock, Bruce, *Male mythologies: John Fowler and masculinity* (Brighton: Harvester, 1984).

24

Women's Peace Caravan

Alice Wiser

Feminist International for Peace and Food (FIPF) was formed in 1983 with women from nearly twenty countries in South America, North America, Africa, the Middle East and Europe. We came together to try to make people aware of the situation of the majority of women from around the globe and to help people see the connection between the way women are treated and the existence of war. These ideas are not new; they were strongly expressed by US women before the American Civil War and by at least 1500 women at the Women's International Congress at The Hague in 1915, as well as being expressed less dramatically, but fairly continually ever since. FIPF wanted to find ways to make this information more widely known.

Our first really big project was the Peace Tent we provided in Nairobi, Kenya for the United Nations End of the Decade of Women Forum in 1985. The Peace Tent was reported globally to have been the heart of the Forum, the place where women from around the world could be heard. The FIPF coordinators of the Peace Tent were Ellen Diederich of West Germany, Barbara Roberts of Canada, Genevieve Vaughan of the USA, and Alice Wiser, a US citizen living in England. Our function was to coordinate the various committees which were formed at an April 1985 meeting of FIPF in Maryland, USA. There were committees responsible for such things as daily programs; logos and artistic work; and archiving. In Nairobi arrangements had to be made for both the living needs of the FIPF women and for renting the tents and necessary equipment. The committees also dealt with finances; acting as a liaison with the government of Kenya and with the UN Forum committee; organizing security during the ten days the Peace Tent was in operation; coordinating arrangements with Women's International League for Peace and Freedom (who cooperated and did a great deal to help the Peace Tent to become a reality); coordinating with other women's organizations; issuing publicity to alert women around the world that the Peace Tent would happen and to invite them to suggest possible programs, as well as participate in programs, and to bring examples of women's work from their countries to display in the Peace Tent. There was also a committee responsible for nurturing and helping the women who would do the actual work in the Peace Tent daily. All of this committee work was done by approximately thirty women.

The Women's Peace Caravan is another of FIPF's projects. There are now three of these caravans on the road in North America and one in Europe. Each caravan consists of a motor home with two women staffing it. The object of the Caravans is to make people aware of the situation of women globally, to make the connection between violence against women and war, and to help people understand what they can do to change this. We speak whenever and wherever we can. We participate in radio and television talk shows, do public speaking, offer workshops, participate in discussions and dialogue with other women and men, and we expose people to women from other cultures so that they can learn from them what life is like where they come from. We stop in shopping centers and at gas stations, and talk to people who come forward to find out about us, we speak on college campuses and in high school classrooms, and we show slides and films. We make ourselves as available as possible in the period of time we are on the road.

The four caravans are organized by different women and work in different ways. In Europe, the Women's Peace Caravan is organized by Ellen Diederich and Fasia Jansen. In 1987 this caravan went to the World Congress of Women in the Soviet Union and toured six socialist countries as well as touring through Western Europe.

In the United States the three caravans are organized by three different women. Theresa Fitzgibbons of New Jersey, who is one of the organizers, takes her caravan primarily to demonstrations and actions to offer support. She frequently participates in the actions and demonstrations herself.

I organize another of the caravans. For the past three years I have had the caravan on the road three to four months each summer and covered approximately thirty states and parts of Canada during each summer. I always invite women from other countries to come on the caravan with me so that at any given time there is always one US citizen, and at least one woman from a foreign country working together. Each summer I work with women from two to six countries for various lengths of time according to our foreign guests' schedules. This caravan also goes to demonstrations and actions but, because of problems for international visitors to the caravan, we choose not to participate in actions that break the law.

Gertrud Kauderer from West Germany, who has worked with me for two summers, helped Ardelle Hough of Wisconsin to organize the third caravan, our newest one that travels in the USA. They organize their caravan approximately the same way I do. They have worked primarily in the northern area from Minneapolis to Maine and in parts of Canada.

In all, we are heard by millions of people every summer. Gertrud and I have particularly prepared ourselves to speak to even the most conservative male audiences and have had some success in being invited back to speak to such groups. We see ourselves as an alternative media, information, and educational service. I am now working with Genevieve Vaughn and Lori Harvey from Texas on a plan to have perhaps ten caravans on the road in the USA during the presidential election year. On these caravans will be women from Europe, Canada, South America, Africa, the Middle East, the Soviet Union, Asia, and the South Pacific, as well as women from the USA. The caravans will travel individually criss-crossing the country with occasional times when all ten caravans meet in one city for a week at a time. This massive organizing job is in progress now.

A state of non-war can be brought about by governments but non-war is not a much healthier state for women than is war. Peace, on the other hand, is an active state that can only begin within the individual and radiate out through personal relationships to the workplace, the places of worship and education, to regional, national, and finally to international relationships. Peace can exist only with a complete reshaping of global society in which we educate ourselves for cooperative work between equals, colleagues.

To have this we must scrap the top-down model of control and power over. The top-down model produces a pyramid shape to society with, at the top, a few, mostly white, Western, heterosexual males maintaining all the power and wealth of the world. Under them come other males, some of color, and perhaps a female or two who fit the male model, who hold the next level of power, control and wealth. That second level is fiercely competitive and adversarial because they all want a place at the top. Those at the top are just as competitive and adversarial because they don't want to lose the places they have struggled so hard to get. Below these levels are ever-increasing numbers of people competing and struggling with each other to climb to the top. At the very bottom are the largest group, the ones with no power and no wealth who make possible the rest of the pyramid, who are the foundation that the people on top need in order to stay on top.

In order to have peace, FIPF envisions a different shape to society, one in which the skills and values that have been assigned to women for the past 5,000 years are the values that shape our society and the ways in which we make our decisions. We do not envision a society without conflict, but rather a society that does not condone or accept violence as a possibility for resolving conflict. Such a society would have a circular shape with all people of all sexes, races, sexual orientations, ages, cultures, weights, heights, and religions participating as equals. We would celebrate our differences, work hard to reshape and restructure our thoughts and languages to be inclusive, struggle to create solutions that are inclusive of the needs and desires of the minority as well as of the majority, implement decisions cooperatively, and listen and take seriously the complaints of those who say they feel left out.

To achieve this circular society of equality, of social justice, of enough for all and not too much for any, we believe we must prepare ourselves to think in new and different ways, to see ourselves and others differently. To these ends we advocate separate women's groups for women to do the work they find necessary to become equals. We advocate that men meet in separate men's groups to do the work they must do to become equals. Additionally men's groups must be formed around those qualities society considers womanly, the qualities of nurturance, caregiving, sharing of feelings and emotions, integration of feeling and intellect, concern for children and others who must be dependent, empathy. We realize it is harder for men because women have a two-hundred year lead on them. But the possibility has been there for them all these two hundred years so they must take responsibility for getting on with it themselves. We must all prepare ourselves to get rid of the polarization the top-down society has produced. Only when we are prepared can we finally come together. The Women's Peace Caravan exists to make these ideas more widely known.

25

Feminist Visions in Action: Interview with Simone Wilkerson

Interviewed by Helene Rosenbluth
Edited by Diana E. H. Russell

. . . I know that there is not going to be nuclear war, because I personally will not allow it to happen. I personally will make sure that my life is used so that this may not happen in my name. Simone Wilkerson, 1985.

Helene Rosenbluth:

I had recently returned from the 1985 International Women's Conference in Nairobi, where I had been quite amazed at the diversity of woman-power and especially by women who applied their creative energies in the anti-nuclear movement. I received a phone call from one of the organizers of Feminists International for Peace and Food. Their idea for setting up a Peace Tent at the Nairobi conference — a neutral space for women from various nations to come and participate in a feminist dialogue — was such a success that they decided to take the show on the road. I couldn't wait to meet these women who were picking up where the "Decade for Women" had left off. I packed up my trusty tape recorder and trucked up the windy road to Topanga, California, to meet the Peace Caravan. It was adorned in peace signs and feminist bumper stickers and was complete with photocopier and computer, and a book with messages from women around the world.

Simone Wilkerson had been travelling throughout the United States for two months with her Canadian/American cohort Alice Wiser. Together they met with women from all walks of life—from Quakers in the Southeast to Republican ranchers in Wyoming—reminding them that all women are peacemakers.

I was particularly impressed with Simone's style. Extremely low-key, she was a housewife from Wales, in her mid-forties, and had left her typically British middle-class life to organize and encourage other women to take responsibility for changing the world. I thought this was a tall order for a rather serious, soft-spoken woman. And yet, after hearing her tale I had no doubt that not only would she succeed, but that she would share this feeling of empowerment with everyone who came in contact with her.

Simone Wilkerson is a constant reminder of the extraordinary power that women possess. According to Simone " . . . it's the power we are taught to denigrate. But we've got to believe in it, because it's the power that will take over the earth and save it."

Simone Wilkerson:

All women are peacemakers, the way they run their families and their homes. You've got to be peacemakers just to keep it together. But what actually happened to me was that I was at home bringing up my two children and living with my husband on the Isle of Wight on the south coast of England when I watched a television program one day called "Protect and Survive." It was about the British government's plan to protect the civilian population in the event of a nuclear war. If a nuclear war occurred I was told to take off four doors from the inside of my house and lean them at a ninety-degree angle against an inside wall because the outside walls might be missing. Then I was supposed to put soft furnishings and cushions and pillows on the outside of this structure. In the 'inner sanctuary,' which I think is a really interesting use of language, I was told to put a two weeks' supply of lighting, heating, cooking utensils, food, and toilet facilities. My husband, my children, my parents, who were living with me, various pets, and myself, were supposed to live there for two weeks until the radiation dropped to a safe level, after which time we could come out and carry on with our lives in true British fashion.

I became more and more horrified and upset and angry as I watched this program, because I realized that what they were saying to me was that in the event of a nuclear war not only must I die, but I must first watch my children die. Because even *I* knew—and I knew very little at that stage—that children die before adults from the effects of radiation. But I couldn't accept this. I didn't bring my children into this world to push them between four doors and watch them die. There is no justification for them to tell me as a mother, "You've got to watch your children die." From that point on I started watching all the TV news programs, listening to everything on the radio, and reading everything in the newspaper about the arms race. I was amazed to learn that I'd been walking through the world with my eyes closed. I sank into a state of despair, and my husband got fed up with me because I was constantly in tears. Every time I looked at my kids I knew that they weren't going to grow up unless we changed the world we live in. So my husband said to me one day, "There's no point in crying like this because it isn't going to do the kids any good, and it doesn't change anything. If you feel strongly about it, you ought to join the local peace group." So I did. And I think he probably often regrets those words, because I'm sure what he meant was for me to go to a meeting once a month.

I live in a very conservative area of Britain and it was very difficult to find a peace group, but I dug one up and started going to meetings. They would have fund-raisers and coffee mornings and write leaflets, and sometimes they'd have speakers to talk about how the weapons worked. And they planned to go on a walk organized by the National Campaign for Nuclear Disarmament where all these people meet in Hyde Park and murder the grass every year. It seemed insane to me. We were faced with imminent annihilation and we were planning to go on a yearly walk again. But when I started to say this to the local peace group, they started telling me that I had to calm down or I'd burn out. At that point I began to question my sanity. My neighbors and the peace movement were denying me my reality, which so often happens to women, and we begin to accept that denial.

Then, in 1981, a friend called me up and told me about a group of women who were living outside the main gates of the American Air Force base at Greenham Common. She said the women needed supplies and that it was only a day trip away from where I was living. "Why don't we go and spend a day there?" she suggested. "We can take food to them and see what it's all about." So that's what we did.

At the same time that I had been becoming desperate, a group of British women who were living in Wales had become fired-up about the British government's decision to take ninety-six American Cruise missiles into our country. This was the final straw for them because, up until that point, it was possible to believe that nuclear weapons were just a deterrent. But Cruise missiles are first-strike weapons. They're designed to start and to win a limited nuclear war. And the American government at that time was openly talking about winning a limited theater war in Europe. As a European this horrified me. In response to the announcement that first-strike weapons would be deployed in Europe, the Russians had said that they would put their system onto something called 'launch on one.' This would enable them to launch a nuclear war in three minutes by computer with no human input. I knew that in one eighteen-month period there had been 140 computer errors in the Pentagon alone and that one of those errors was so serious that three squadrons of planes armed with nuclear weapons had taken off. In the seventh minute the President was supposed to be notified but they couldn't find him. If these planes hadn't been stopped fourteen minutes later, we wouldn't be having this interview. So three minutes to launch nuclear weapons by computer with no human input was totally unacceptable to me and to these women.

Although all this information was in the newspapers, neither the politicians nor the people were discussing it. These women in Wales wanted to focus attention on this dangerous situation so they decided that they would walk 120 miles from Cardiff in Wales to the base at Greenham Common where the first missiles were due to be deployed. So forty British mums and grannies pushed their babies 120 miles in push-chairs. They thought that in doing this they would get so much media coverage that attention would be focused on the Cruise missiles. They planned to have a one-day rally at Greenham and then go home. But after walking for ten days they didn't get into one newspaper or on to one television or radio program. It was as if their march hadn't happened. Although these women hadn't previously been involved in politics or demonstrations, they decided something had to be done. Five of them made the really radical decision to chain themselves to the fence of the air base, and someone called the local police. While they were chained to the fence, the Commander of the base came over and said to them, "What on earth do you think you're doing?" And a white-haired Welsh granny said, "We're chained here as a protest against those American missiles in there." And he looked at her with absolute contempt and he said, "Well that's ridiculous. As far as we're concerned, you can stay there for good." And that's what they did. And they're still there, four years later. It was that spontaneous.

That night about fifteen or twenty women slept out under the stars in their sleeping bags. They decided that they would stay at Greenham Common until something was done about this issue. The only thing that they were asking for was an open, public, televised debate between the leaders of our country, who were making these decisions, and the women of our country, who were going to have to pay the price for these decisions with their lives and with the lives of their children and the people they loved. And they still haven't been granted that request. Our government is so frightened that they won't allow an open televised debate.

These women had been at Greenham for ten days when I arrived. I met all these women who were just like me, and I realized that there was nothing wrong with me. I heard a lot of talk about women's liberation and I went home that night and I didn't let my husband get a word in edgewise. I ended by saying, "I'm going there tomorrow." I didn't ask his permission. I didn't wonder whether he could cope with it. I just knew that I had to go there. It was like instant liberation. What actually happened to me on that day was that a baby feminist was born into this world. And I went to the camp and lived there on and off for the first year.

Nobody was taking any notice of our protests. They weren't taking us seriously. They would come and film the evictions, but they would never allow us to talk about the issues. So one day when they were going to come and film us, a group of us decided that we would take our protest on to the base where it belonged. We planned to walk through the main gate, but when the time came we *ran* through it because we were frightened. The guards didn't know what to do with fourteen women running through like that, so they closed the front gates. We got into the sentry box and started singing songs, and a crowd gathered at the main gates to see what we were doing. The wife of an American serviceman came along that morning and she wanted to go on to the base to do her shopping, but she couldn't get through the crowd that were watching us. So we were arrested and charged with an act likely to cause a breach of the peace because Mrs. Calhoun had been delayed for twenty minutes and was unable to do her shopping. The idea was that if she got angry and hit somebody, that would have been our fault. We were sent to prison for two weeks for that.

However, our action turned out to be a great triumph. We were allowed to bring in expert witnesses to speak on our behalf, and we were allowed to talk ourselves about the fact that our government, along with the American government, was guilty of breaking English law. The 1969 Genocide Act makes genocide or conspiracy to commit genocide a crime under English law. Genocide is defined in that act as causing psychological or physical harm to any large group of people. We claimed that our government was guilty of genocide as defined by that Act because there were so many young people who were severely psychologically disturbed by their fears of a nuclear war. We also claimed that our government, along with the American government, was conspiring to commit genocide by planning to use first-strike weapons.

We went to prison in November 1981, and the following December we called for women to come to the base to embrace the base as a demonstration of protest. It was all done by word of mouth and we didn't think we'd get enough women, so we asked women to bring scarfs so we could link up around the base. When we came out of prison we went down to this demonstration and over 30,000 women were there. We had enough women to surround that base one and three-quarter times. Every women brought with her a symbol of what was precious about her life and every inch of that nine-mile fence was decorated. It was incredibly beautiful. Women hung up their babies' first shoes, or they put up photographs of their children or their grannies, grannies put up photographs of their grandchildren, children wrote poems, and messages were written to the soldiers. And women who hadn't brought anything picked long pieces of grass and wove the word 'peace' on the barbed wire fence. Then we all linked hands. It was such a powerful experience I think many women were transformed by it. We realized that we weren't going to leave matters in the hands of our government any more. I made a vow to myself that day as we linked hands that I personally will make sure that my life is used so that a nuclear war doesn't happen in my name.

We can't blame Thatcher and Reagan for the position we find ourselves in, because it is our fault. Our taxes have paid for these weapons and our silence has condoned them. Women made a vow that day to no longer be silent and to use any creative and imaginative non-violent way to make our voices heard. What was even more moving to me was that the following day, 5,000 women stayed behind to stop that base from functioning. We decided that we would sit down at all nine gates and not let traffic in or out of the base. Five thousand women were willing to go to prison to change the world we lived in. Some of the women who sat down were breastfeeding their babies, some of them were grandmothers, some of them were young teenage women. It was incredible. The police decided they weren't going to arrest us that day so they just dragged us away in the mud. They dragged us by our hair, by one arm, by one leg, by one breast. Some women were severely hurt. I watched my sisters being thrown to one side and then turning around and asking another sister, "Are you okay? Can I help you?" and then silently going back again to sit down at a gate. At the gate where I was, some women went back sixteen times. One very small and frail woman next to me was in her eighties, and I said to her at one point, "Come on, you've got to take a break." And she said, "You young ones can take a break. I'm eighty years old and I haven't got a lot of time left, so I've got to get on with this."

Many of us had not had confidence to stand up against the intellectual arguments about strategies and the reasoning behind the weapons that the men put forth. But I realized that the arguments are silly because nobody can convince me, as a woman, that any other woman is my enemy. I know within my gut that every Russian mother loves her children as passionately as I love my children. Nobody can convince me that another mother is my enemy.

We don't see women in the Third World going on anti-nuclear walks, calling for an end to the arms race. They're too busy trying to feed their children and trying to survive. And yet we spend something like a billion dollars a day on weapons, or some such terrifying amount, while two-thirds of the world's children are starving. And this is done in my name. As a mother I cannot bear to think of another child in another part of the world starving because of my silence, because I condone that happening. I've heard all these arguments about "If you were a woman in Russia, you couldn't speak out like this." Well that just makes me more morally obliged to speak out for the people in this world who *can't* speak out for themselves. Many of us in the West have the privilege of knowing that our children will be fed three times a day, of knowing our children will be clothed and go to school. We have no right to accept that privilege and not use it, because there are people in this world whose children are starving. And it is up to us to speak for those people and to change the world for those people.

But why should we educate ourselves? If we were to face all these facts about how many Cruise missiles there are, about how much money is being spent on nuclear arms, it might be so overwhelming that we couldn't go on. Wouldn't it be less painful to sit back and not get too involved?

The men in the local peace group always used to say to me, "You've got to understand how the weapons work. You've got to read about them. You've got to arm yourself with all these facts." I think that's absolute rubbish. I didn't join the peace movement to find out how the weapons worked. I joined the peace movement to get *rid* of them. I'm not interested in spending my life learning how the Cruise missile works. All I know is that it will kill millions and millions of people in my name, and that's wrong. That's the only truth that I need. We've got to have confidence in the simple truths, then we can undercut all the strategic arguments. I've seen women do that and it's much more powerful than getting into debates about the statistics and the strategy. People can question your statistics and your policies, but they can never, never question your sincerity.

The energy it takes to suppress the knowledge which is seeping into our lives is very draining. It leaves one totally powerless, in total despair. Yes, the pain of global violence is enormous, but once we start *doing* something, once we start connecting, we get in touch with our own power and realize that we actually hold it in our hands we can change the situation. Because the only power that they have is the power that we give them. We elect our governments, we pay their wages, and if we don't acknowledge their power, they are powerless. There have been so many times that we've gone to court and made incredibly powerful statements in an effort to move the magistrates who sit there with bland faces having decided that we're guilty before we've even pleaded our case. Women have decided now that when we are arrested, say for obstructing a road, we are no longer going to acknowledge the jurisdiction of the court. On the day women are supposed to be in court, many are going back instead to repeat their actions. They are denying the courts their authority.

I'm beginning to think that what we've got to do is to practice total noncooperation. This is frightening because it means we are turning our backs on the whole system and saying we do not acknowledge it because it is killing us. But we are turning towards life. Women have got to do this because men are not going to, that's for sure. We've got to be creative and we've got to be really bold. For example, just before the last election I sat talking with a group of about eight women about a party political broadcast we'd just heard. We were struck by the fact that none of the parties were connecting the issues, which is something that men are very good at. This is in this compartment and that's in that compartment and never the two shall meet. We were really angry because nobody was talking about the arms race and connecting it to the fact that we had three million unemployed. So somebody said that we ought to put up our own candidates. And I said, "Yeah, that's a great idea! We ought to run against Margaret Thatcher and present an alternative point of view." So someone said, "Why don't you do it then?" So I said, "Oh, alright." And immediately I'd said it, I thought, "How on earth am I, an ordinary housewife, ever going to take on running against the Prime Minister?" Then someone else said, "And I'll run against Michael Heseltine [the Minister of Defense]."

After we'd made this monumental decision with no money at our disposal, we approached the Green Party in our country and asked them if they would finance the printing of one leaflet. Our leaflet encouraged people to question their thinking, and we delivered it to every house in Margaret Thatcher's constituency. Then we got the four doors that our government has told us to get to protect us from a nuclear war, and we built a shelter in the main shopping street in Thatcher's constituency, and we lived in it for two weeks. We put up a big notice saying that if people voted for the Conservative Party, this would be their new home—the mortgage rates would be very low—and we asked people to come and talk to us. It was an incredible experience because we never went to bed the whole fortnight we were there. We talked with people night and day. We were getting people to question things that they'd just assumed.

There was one man who used to stop every day to talk to me for half an hour on his way to and from work. He would ask about my family and he told me he was married and had two young children. He was a typical British gent working in the city with his bowler hat and pinstriped suit, and he believed in the Conservative Party policies and he believed in defense. He talked about the need for us to protect ourselves from our enemy, the Russians. And I asked him, why, if we needed these weapons to protect ourselves from the Russians, did the British government through the guise of the Central Electricity Generating Board, sell uranium to the Russians? I said it didn't make sense. There were lots of conversations like this until the night before the election. He came up to me on his way home and he said, "Well, Simone, I'd like to say that I'm going to vote for you, but I support Maggie, as you know, so I have to vote for her and you know what that means." I was feeling very tired and very despondent and very emotional, and I looked him straight in the eye and I said, "Yes, I *do* know what that means. It means that you are voting for the death of my children, and what's more it means that you're voting for the death of your own children, and that's a real tragedy." And I said, "I hope you think about that and I hope you can sleep at night and live with yourself." And his eyes filled with tears and he couldn't speak and he walked away in silence. I saw him again after the election, and he said, "You know, I couldn't vote unless I could be sure that what you said was not the case. I couldn't risk it." And he said, "I still believe in the Conservative Party but the next time I go to my local Conservative Party meeting, I have a whole list of questions that I want to ask as a result of our conversations. And I want to thank you for bringing those questions up for me." As far as I'm concerned, the whole campaign was worth that one man beginning to ask questions.

I will tell you another story about five women in the area where I live who went to a meeting where the local government had decided to spend £20,000 (about $36,000) to update and renew the local bunker for the protection of local government officials. At the same meeting it was decided that the same local council was going to stop the building of a hospital because they'd run out of resources. We were so mad, we decided we had to do something. We tried to get a meeting with the local council but they ignored our letters to them. The bunker has a one-story house over it to disguise the entrance. The local peace group planned to have a vigil at the fence of this bunker, but before it had started, I and four other women climbed over the fence and went up onto the roof and chained ourselves to the roof. We hung up a big banner telling the population that the local council planned to spend money on the bunker and stop building the hospital. The police came and were really angry, and the local council came out and they were really angry, and the local peace movement was also really angry, and they were all trying to persuade us to come down from the roof. But we refused. They asked us what we wanted in order to get us down from the roof, and we said we wanted to speak to a local council official. They had to go to find one, and when he arrived we told him that we wanted a definite date for a meeting before we would come down from the roof. So he went off and made some phone calls and he came back and he said, "Okay, you've got a meeting on Friday morning at 10 A.M."—which was three days later. So we got down off the roof but we left our banner up. We got a few other women to come along with us to the meeting that Friday morning. The local council's plans were published all over the papers because we had made them public. Because of this, and because we put our case so strongly at the meeting, two weeks later we heard that they'd totally revoked their decision. They decided not to spend any money on the local bunker. And that's the power that women have. We were five women who decided to say no and mean it. And I know hundreds of stories like that.

The success story of Greenham Common is that in 1981 when the women first went there, very few people in Britain knew what a Cruise missile was or understood why it was different from previous weapons. Very few people knew what was going on at Greenham Common. I would say that ninety percent of the population in Britain now know what a Cruise missile is, they know why it's different, and they know what's going on at Greenham Common. Unlike the people in Germany, they cannot say, "But we didn't know what was happening." They have been faced with a truth and they are now faced with a choice. We have made the invisible visible. When I first went to Greenham Common, it was a fence around a green field. Now there are ten or eleven layers of razor barbed wire, they've got huge watch towers there, they've got searchlights which stay on all night, and they've got armed guards with police dogs. When they stepped up the armed guards and patrolled the fence with weapons because the American forces came to visit them, a member of the Labour Party asked the Minister of Defense in the House of Commons if he would give an assurance for the safety of the women at Greenham, who were using their democratic right to demonstrate. And our Minister of Defense said, "I categorically refuse to give any such assurance. Indeed, these women will be shot if they continue crossing that barrier into the base."

We've defeated ground-launch missiles. We didn't stop them coming to our country, which I thought maybe we would do at one time. But we've defeated them because the idea of Cruise missiles is that they are put on transporters and carried in convoy from Greenham along our British country roads to be deployed in some secret place where they can't be verified. But every time they have had this convoy go out on exercises, the women have tracked every inch of the movement that that convoy has made. They've followed it and found out where it's hidden and painted slogans on all the convoy vehicles. There's an organization called Cruise Watch which comes out all over the country in the middle of the night to do this and then publishes its findings. So ground-launch Cruise missiles have been totally defeated. That is the power that women have.

I think that we as women have got to get back in touch with our powers as individuals, because we could be the most powerful people on earth if we choose to be. It's not a power over someone else that we want to get in touch with, it's not the power of patriarchy, it's the power from within ourselves. Men are absolutely terrified of this power. We also need to see the links between nuclear weapons and domestic violence against women and torture and rape and incest and pornography and the psychological violence which denies us our reality on a personal level and on the political level. Because nuclear weapons are just a manifestation of a wrong way of thinking, a way of thinking that we have to change.

I have to say that I'm being moved more and more to political separatism, because until men get their act together, I don't want to put my precious woman's energy into any man. Everywhere I go I keep meeting these women who say, "My husband would never rape, my husband would never treat women in that way, my husband treats me equally. He does the washing up, he does the cooking. He is totally sympathetic to the feminist movement and to feminism." And I hear men saying that too. My answer is, "Well, what is he doing publicly to point the finger at his brothers who commit these acts of violence?" Just before I left my country this time there was a court case that was in all the national newspapers. An old man had viciously raped an eight year-old girl. All the evidence was there, it was a sewn up case, but the judge, who was a man, said of the defendant who had committed this crime in his summing up that he was a lonely and frightened old man, and he gave him a twelve-months' suspended sentence. I want to know where all those wonderful sympathetic, feminist men were then. I want to know why they weren't out on the street outraged at that decision and why they haven't removed that judge from his position because he's not fit to be in it. When I see men taking on that kind of responsibility, then I will begin to deal with them again. Because they have to pick up the responsibility for what their sex have done to our sex for centuries.

In order to be a peacemaker, what kind of visions of peace do you have?

I would like to tell you a couple of short stories that reveal how I began to see my vision. A few years ago the Greenham Common women called for a demonstration of ten million women over a ten-day period. If they couldn't get to Greenham they should withdraw their labor wherever they were for ten days and vigil or demonstrate or whatever in their own areas to show their support. Many of us went to Greenham for two of those days. The police were ready for us because they no doubt remembered when we had over 30,000 women there and we shook down miles and miles of the fence. They'd shipped in the riot vans and they had extra riot police on duty and there were soldiers there with their guns and there were police dogs, and policemen on horses, and all these policemen in their riot gear. When the women arrived they totally ignored the base and the police. They visited each others' tents, they met old friends, they met new friends, they spent time together, they talked about their visions, and they envisioned, and for me that was so powerful because it was denying the police their power. Had we gone into confrontation with them, that would have acknowledged their power. So for ten days they were there with nothing to do. They must have felt really silly, and they were unnerved at being totally ignored.

There was another vision I had about the weapons. A whole group of us were talking just after the deployment of Cruise missiles about whether it would ever be possible to send the weapons back. And I thought about that and I imagined those men remaining there like silly little boys guarding their rusting weapons while the world had moved on.

I think it's important that our life becomes our vision. The year after the first walk to Greenham over a hundred women walked 120 miles from Cardiff in Wales to an American submarine tracking facility called Broady. One day I went ahead of the walk with another woman to leaflet the villages to let them know why we were doing this. It was in a tiny village in the Welsh mountains and we were on the main street when we suddenly heard this singing coming from behind the mountain. The villagers became aware of this singing which was growing louder, and then this column of color appeared like a Nomadic tribe of women coming down the mountain with all these bright ribbons, and they were singing their joy. It was such a powerful image. And that's the unique way that women work. I've seen walks where the men chant their slogans and you see the people in the towns close up and tense. But because it was this wonderful band of color, and this wonderful singing and this celebration of life, before people even knew what it was about they were already open; they were smiling and saying, "Oh, look at this, isn't it lovely? What's it about?" "It's the peace movement." "Oh, really!" And immediately their barriers were down. It was really beautiful.

Before the next walk I will describe to you occurred, I had lost a baby which was a very difficult thing for me to cope with. Also, two days before this walk was due to take place, one of my lifelong friends was murdered. She was in bed with her four year-old daughter when a young man walked into her bedroom and shot her. Her six year-old son woke up in the room next door and went screaming for help. When people arrived at her home the young man had shot himself. Nobody knows why he did this. There was no emotional involvement between them, he'd obviously just gone bananas. The four year-old child had to be taken to the hospital because she had shrapnel wounds down one side. I had known this woman all my life. We were very, very close. I'd been going through a period of dealing with violence in my own early life and having to sort out what it meant, and it seemed to me that Sherry's death was just a manifestation of all that violence. I was shattered. So I wasn't going to go on the walk.

A friend rang me up the day after Sherry's murder and I told her I couldn't face the walk. She said, "You *have* to go." She was so adamant about it and she got another friend to come and take me there. It was a walk that had been planned by a few women for our own spiritual purposes, but over a hundred women came. The walk required us to cross Salisbury Plain where there are military firing ranges. The military practice up there every day, fifty-two weeks of the year. There were over a hundred women on the walk and we soon realized that the police were going to try to stop us. But we made up our minds that we were going to do this, and we did it. The police would line up in front of us and they'd say, "You can't go this way, you've got to go that way." And they'd try and direct us down the hill. And somebody would say, very quietly, without any confrontation, "We're going to go that way." Then the police would link arms and say, "You can't go through here." And some woman would say, "Okay women, let's sit down for a nappie [diaper] change," because there were lots of babies with us. We'd sit down and change the babies' nappies and sing a few songs and drink tea, smoke cigarettes, exchange stories, and rest. The police would relax and then gradually the women would get up, then hold hands and snake our way through the police lines and carry on walking exactly where we wanted to. This happened time and time again, and it was totally without confrontation.

On the last day of the walk, nobody was ready to leave. Somebody started a circle and every woman went over quite spontaneously to join it. The police were waiting for us to start walking because they knew we were going to go over the firing ranges again. Somebody started up a chant and we kept going around in this circle and chanting and then somebody broke the circle and we spiraled in and out, holding each others' hands all the time. It was like a moving wheel of women. And the military was so freaked out about this that they flew helicopters really low to try and disperse us, but not one woman looked up. Even though the helicopters were so low that they were blowing on us, nobody broke the spell, nobody broke the chant, we just went on doing it for over an hour. We were building up energy, and once it was built up we started walking and we knew we were going to go where we wanted to go. That's the magical way that women work. We have to get in touch with this power that we've been denied, this power that we are taught to denigrate and not believe in. We've got to believe in it because it's the power that will take over the earth and save it.

I don't live at the Greenham Common camp any longer. I work by going around and talking to women. I don't talk about the arms race any longer. I talk about global violence. There are women in this country who are victims of rape, victims of incest, victims of male violence, both physical and psychological. We're bombarded with violence from day one and the damage it does us is untold. Woman are the walking wounded. I think we need to gather together in women's spaces to help heal ourselves and to help heal the earth and to find the strength to nurture each other through that process. I've paid a real price for the things that I've done. The first thing that happened when I became visible was that a lot of our friends stopped asking my husband and me out socially either because they were totally opposed to what I was doing or because I was a social embarrassment to them. So my husband paid a price too. Then when I went to prison, he was the one who had to face people on the streets and deal with it. Even though the choice I've made to leave my family has been hard on my husband and on my children, I have to show my children that not only is there an alternative that we create with our words and our vision, but that we have to live our vision. And if I don't set that example to them, who will? If I stay in my marriage I am saying to my daughter, "If you happen to get married, then you have no choice." I'm not willing to say that to her. What I had to do was to take total control of my own life in order to get in touch with my own power and be effective, both on a personal level and on a political level.

What is the connection between women working for peace and peace walks? Is there something particularly feminine about walking?

When you walk, you're changing the people with whom you come into contact and you're also changing yourself. You become very strong as a group. You learn a lot about working and getting on with people, about peacemaking with each other, about overcoming differences. At the same time, you're a public witness and you're able to go through areas and talk about the issues you want to talk about.

I've been asked to organize the British part of a peace walk through Central America. It's going to be a mixed walk with men participants as well as women. We're proposing that the men who are coming on the walk should walk in the middle, protected by women, and that when we come to any confrontations or conflicts, only the women should deal with it. So if the men of other countries we're walking through come with guns to attack the men on our walk, they will first have to kill the women. That for me is the ultimate image of the women's peace movement — women surrounding and protecting the men for their own good. We've got to contain them. We've got to show them the alternatives.

Some of us came up with another visionary idea at a conference in Halifax. We found out that the smallest nation being represented within the United Nations is Belize. They have a population of roughly 160,000. So we thought that if we could get 160,000 women's signatures, we would go to the United Nations and declare ourselves a global nation of women in exile behind all borders. We'd point out the fact that we are not represented by any government or economic structure in any nation at the moment, that we are excluded from any meaningful participation in the policy-making and decision-making process. Therefore we would demand full member status in the UN and representation on all UN bodies as a global nation in exile.

When I got back to Britain, I was talking to women about this idea, and one of the women said, "The UN is celebrating forty years of failure because its peacekeeping force, which is just another army with weapons, has failed to bring about global peace." So we decided that we would have a petition to ask the UN to fund a United Nations Women's Peacekeeping Team to go into areas of conflict without weapons and without uniforms to help bring about global peace. Those are the kinds of visionary ideas that women come up with.

I know that you are travelling in a peace caravan at this time. What do you hope to gain by travelling throughout the United States?

We've got to become story-tellers, we've got to communicate in those ways again. Eventually I would like to see the peace caravan going right across the globe. If this one is a success, Feminist International for Peace and Food, who have funded this peace caravan, hope to have a fleet of ten on the road in this country. It's an extension of the nomadic tribe of women wandering the earth again. We've tried on this trip to go to small towns where peace groups don't normally hit town. For example, we went out to the first MX missile site with Lindy Kirk-Bride, the wife of a rancher in Wyoming. It's deserty land there, and we got stones and made a magic circle with the women's peace symbol inside it on the side of the road so everybody driving past would see it. Then Lindy's little daughter, who was about six, spontaneously went and sat inside the circle and I tied suffragette ribbons on the fence. At the end of this ceremony, tears were pouring down Lindy's face when she said, "I cannot tell you how important your visit has been. I've been trying to decide whether or not to give up my work for peace and I'm not going to give up now."

We went to another place in Salt Lake City where we'd spoken at a Quaker meeting in the morning. And this Quaker woman said to me, "I went home after the meeting this afternoon and I told my husband that I'd quit my job. I told him that I don't know what I'm going to do yet, but I'm going to put my life into changing the world in the way that you do." That's an incredible point for a woman to come to after an afternoon meeting. She's going to go through a lot of pain with that decision, because people do. But she's going to find incredible hidden strength. The peace caravan has that kind of value because we can touch people who are feeling very isolated and down.

One of the problems with the peace movement is that it often finds itself talking to itself. I think it's also important to talk to the 'unconverted.' I spoke for two hours on a very right-wing phone-in radio show in Texas. The first caller was extremely abusive and accused me of being a communist and ranted and raved and I couldn't do anything but listen because I was too frightened to open my mouth. In the end he just wound down. I suddenly realized that he was really frightened and genuinely concerned. So I said to him, "I appreciate your fear. I know that your concern is genuine. But I'd like to ask you a question. If you were frightened of an intruder coming into your family home, would you wire your windows and your doors with explosives so that when the intruder came through the windows or the door, he would be blown up, along with your home and all the people that you love?" And he said, "No of course I wouldn't. That doesn't make sense." I said, "But can't you see that is what your President has done? He has wired your home with explosives." I think it was because I was able to listen to him and to have respect for his genuine concern instead of just being angry at his point of view, that he was able to listen to me. It really taught me a lot about the need to be able to listen to where those people are coming from.

How do you measure the success of a peace caravan?

If only one woman changes her life because of a meeting, I consider that success. When you know that you have in some way empowered women, made them feel that they are important, that they do have the power to bring about change, that's what I consider success.

26

Beyond Nuclear Phallacies

Diana E. H. Russell

Many feminists involved in anti-nuclear work believe it is important to recognize the connections between the nuclear crisis and many other issues, such as racism, imperialism, classism, poverty, militarism, and sexism. Many feminists also feel that this understanding of the connections should be demonstrated in actions. During the week I spent at the Puget Sound Women's Peace Camp, for example, the members of the peace camp participated in a "Take Back the Night" march in Seattle to protest a series of murders of local women by the so-called Green River murderer. Indeed, the group had helped to organize the event. Some members also participated in a teach-in on the immorality of US intervention in Central America. The only action specific to anti-nuclear work that I recall during that week was the participation of a few peace campers in the farewell send-off ritual for an all-women's peace walk across the United States (see chapter 21).

The Peace Camp women gave a party for me during my stay there, and because of my work on violence against women, they invited women from rape crisis centers, battered women's shelters, and child sexual abuse agencies. As we went around the circle introducing ourselves, a couple of the women said they felt bad that they had been so inactive on the nuclear issue. A member of the Peace Camp responded reassuringly: "But the work you are doing *is* anti-nuclear work. It's all connected."

But is all work to end violence against women anti-nuclear work? While my chapter on sexism, violence, and the nuclear mentality also stresses the connections between violence against women and the nuclear crisis (see chapter 7), I don't believe that work on any form of violence against women constitutes anti-nuclear work, or that opposition to Reagan's policies in Central America will help to stop a nuclear war. If we could afford to take a very long-term perspective, if we had more time, then I would agree that action on a multiplicity of issues contributes to a nuclear-free world. But unless we diminish or eradicate the nuclear threat, we may not be around to work on other issues. I understand the fears many feminists feel about single issue campaigns, particularly in light of the failure of the suffrage movement to transform itself into a more radical, multi-issue movement after the vote for women was won. But the totally unprecedented character of the nuclear predicament, which holds the world hostage to the whims of a few leaders, means that we must respond to this crisis in unprecedented ways.

Some people have no choice but to spend all their energies on the most immediate survival issues, making it impossible to attend to the problem of global survival. But this is not the case for the majority of women in this country. While we must recognize the connections between different forms of oppression, our survival requires that more of us focus our actions on preventing a nuclear calamity. This does not mean that we should define our anti-nuclear work in a narrow way. Working for a nuclear-free world includes confronting the problem of dichotomized sex roles and male dominated institutions, for example. But to be most effective more of us need to confront sexism in the context of anti-nuclear war.

FOUR IMPORTANT STEPS

In an article on pornography and the women's liberation movement, I have argued that there are four distinct and crucial steps in dealing with a social problem (1980). First, we need to *recognize* it. Many problems are never recognized as such. For example, the murder of women—femicide—is still hidden by the word homicide. In fact, there is very little murder of women by women. When women are murdered, the perpetrators are almost always men. We have to recognize femicide before we can consider its causes and decide what we can do about it.

The second step involves acknowledging our *feelings* about the problem we have recognized. Simply to recognize rape, woman-battering, and the misogyny in pornography, and not to *feel* outrage, involves an unhealthy kind of short-circuiting.

Next, we need to try to understand the *causes* of the problem. If, for example, we conclude that rape happens rarely and that a few crazy men are responsible, the implications for action will be different from actions based on the belief that rape is an extreme acting-out of the socially-sanctioned male role.

Finally, there is the question of action—what to *do* about the problem and how to inspire and empower people to end whatever social problem we are addressing.

APPLYING THESE STEPS
TO THE NUCLEAR ISSUE

I believe that most feminists recognize nuclear weapons as a problem, but that few are willing to face the extent to which our lives are jeopardized by it. My hunch is that most women who believe that the danger of nuclear obliteration is less of a threat to women's lives than rape, battering and incest, simply aren't educated on this issue. Certainly, that was true in my case.

A poll of more than 1,200 people in the Northern Californian communities of Palo Alto and Stockton was conducted a week before the showing of ABC's television movie "The Day After," and again three days after it. This poll concluded that the movie changed very few people's views *(San Francisco Chronicle,* 14 December 1983, p. 48). Two of the other findings are far more remarkable. First, 75 percent of those polled "believed, both before and after seeing the show, that their chances of dying from a nuclear blast or fallout fell within the categories of 'somewhat likely,' 'likely' or 'very likely.' " Second, 90 percent of viewers before and after the broadcast were optimistic that nuclear war can be prevented. That fully three-quarters of the population polled believed that there is some likelihood that they will die in a nuclear disaster shows that many of these people *are* willing to face the predicament in which we live. They are not deniers—at least not intellectually. This finding might lead one to think that Palo Alto and Stockton are hot beds of dedicated anti-nuclear activity. On the contrary, the nuclear disarmament movement is not particularly strong in these locations. How can so many people remain passive in response to these two beliefs? The answer may be that in the case of the nuclear crisis, *feeling* about it may be an even more serious obstacle than *recognizing* it.

Another explanation for this passivity may be a sense of powerlessness. In Patricia Gwartney-Gibbs' 1984 random sample survey of 468 University of Oregon students, for example, she found that only 2 percent strongly agreed that "a nuclear war will never happen. No one is that crazy" (17 percent checked "somewhat agree" and 81 percent disagreed with the statement "somewhat" or "strongly" [1985, p. 9]). Only 8 percent disagreed with the statement that "the possibility of a nuclear war is a critical (if not the most critical) issue of our times," and a majority of the students strongly agreed with it (58 percent). As reported in chapter 1, in a similar survey conducted at the same university in 1987, Lach and Gwartney-Gibbs also found that the women students surveyed were significantly more pessimistic about the probability of a nuclear war and the likelihood that the US would survive such a war than were men students. But the overall recognition of the danger of nuclear war by these students, particularly the women students, didn't translate into action because of their sense of powerlessness (Lach, personal communication, June 23, 1988).

Before people will be moved to action, they have to get in touch with appropriate feelings about the issue, but they also have to feel that what they do can make a difference. In recognition of this, some women have developed techniques for helping people do "despairwork" followed by "empowerment work" (for example, see Joanna Macy, 1983 and Chellis Glendinning, 1987).

Helen Caldicott describes how, after quitting her job as a pediatrician because it seemed futile in the face of the nuclear threat, she was "very depressed and lost for several weeks" (1984, p. 19). She compares the stages people experience when confronting the truth about the nuclear threat with those faced by people who are seriously ill or dying.

[M]any people when faced with the imminent prospects of nuclear war will enter this grief process. It is extremely painful psychologically and most people avoid these feelings if they possibly can, but only if people will let themselves experience the true gravity of the nuclear peril will they even be motivated to alleviate the situation (1984, p. 303).

Caldicott further suggests that:

The angry phase is the most constructive period because anger is a very powerful emotion and can be channeled into constructive areas. . . . The last stage, acceptance, is also a useful phase, for when people have stopped battling with reality, they have more energy to devote to constructive solutions to their dilemma (1984, p. 303).

Intuitively it makes sense that many people are motivated into action following their emotional acceptance of the true danger of a nuclear catastrophe—assuming that they aren't too overwhelmed by feelings of powerlessness.

The third step in dealing with a social problem involves understanding its causes. Because of the widespread failure to recognize the role of sexism in the nuclear crisis, the goals of anti-nuclear organizations have often been too limited, and most feminists have not contributed their energies to the struggle, *as feminists.* Some of the feminists who are active in the peace movement feel they must put aside their feminism in order to work for a nuclear-free world; I suggest that instead they recognize the valuable contribution that their feminist perspective can make toward solving this problem.

Many people agree that the best way out of nuclear despondency is to become engaged in anti-nuclear actions. Consciousness alone will not save us. Committed, persistent, determined, courageous actions are our only hope. Part 4 of this book provided several accounts of what some feminists in this country and England have done to try to prevent a nuclear disaster. Hopefully they will inspire more feminist actions.

The women's liberation movement has changed the consciousness of vast numbers of people in this country—and the world—with regard to rape, woman-battering, incest and extrafamilial child sexual abuse, and pornography—to name a few of our achievements. Although these problems are far from being solved, we can take pride in having created a massive shift in awareness, generated with minimal funding and in the face of considerable resistance. I believe that we can be equally effective in pointing out the connections between the masculine mentality and the nuclear mentality, and the connections between nuclear threats and other types of male violence. But first we must deal with our own resistance to working on the nuclear issue.

OVERCOMING OUR RESISTANCE

(1) Because the nuclear crisis affects everyone—not just women—many feminists do not consider it a women's issue.

Charlotte Bunch is one prominent feminist who argues that we need to work *as feminists* on all kinds of issues, not just those traditionally considered "women's issues" like reproductive rights, child care, rape and woman-battering (Bunch, 1987). There are feminist perspectives on militarism, on poverty, on racism, on intervention in Central America, on discrimination against the elderly, on nationalism, on pedagogy, etc. Yes, the nuclear crisis is everybody's issue—not just women's. But it is surely a women's issue too! And, as already emphasized, a proper understanding of it requires a feminist analysis.

(2) Because many people and groups—disrespectful of the seriousness and urgency of women's oppression—have discounted our struggle and tried to co-opt us to work on other issues, we have become suspicious of all attempts to get us to work on problems that are not primarily women's problems.

This is a reaction that I understand, from the inside, since I have frequently felt suspicious on exactly these grounds. I do think that we need to be very careful about what exceptions we make. But I also think the nuclear threat must be seen as an exception: (a) because our not doing so will increase our chances of dying in a nuclear war; (b) because a feminist analysis of the nuclear threat will only be made by feminists and will be most effectively communicated by us; and (c) because we can be active on this issue without abandoning our feminism. Just as working against pornography from a feminist perspective is another way of working against rape and raising awareness about misogyny, so working against the nuclear threat is an opportunity to point out the lethal nature of patriarchal politics and the necessity for eliminating sexism along with nuclear weapons.

(3) Many feminists prefer to work with other women in groups or organizations that follow feminist process as well as feminist principles. Because there are very few all-women's feminist anti-nuclear organizations, many feminists haven't become actively involved in the nuclear disarmament movement.

Why have so few feminists been willing to initiate the kinds of groups and organizations they prefer? I believe it is because we are apt to consider women-only groups as acceptable only for work on rape, woman-battering, reproductive rights, and pornography, for example, but not for "larger" issues involving men as well as women. Here "separatism" is seen as divisive and anti-male. Few men are interested in working on women's issues, as narrowly defined. But many men become upset and threatened if women prefer to work on other issues in all-women's groups. And many women will plead their cause whenever men are threatened, particularly when the men are allies in a shared struggle.

An experience I had at a Livermore Action Group (LAG) meeting in August 1983 offers some insight into why many feminists may be uncomfortable working in all women's anti-nuclear organizations. LAG regards itself as feminist, and many feminist affinity groups have been active in it. LAG prides itself on applying principles of feminist process, such as sitting in circles and being sensitive to what is happening on a feeling level during meetings. About 150 people were present at this particular LAG meeting. A decision was made to break up into small groups to discuss certain agenda items. A woman asked if it were possible to have one of the small groups be an all-women's group. After a surprised silence in the room, the facilitator gave his permission for this to occur.

While I was disturbed by the surprised response to this request, I was more distressed when only six women chose to participate in the women's group, despite the fact that the women's movement has shown how empowering working in all-women's groups and actions can be. This suggested a strong norm in LAG against exclusively women's groups, despite this organization's efforts to be sensitive to issues of sexism. I am in no way opposed to feminists working with men in anti-nuclear organizations. I *do* object to any antagonism to, and non-validation of, all-women's groups including anti-nuclear ones.

(4) Because so many of the women who have been involved in the peace movement have not been feminists, many feminists have come to associate women peace activists with non-feminist politics.

Women peace activists' traditional emphasis on their roles as mothers and grandmothers as being the key motivators for their participation in the peace movement has alienated many feminists, who are both weary and wary of women's discounting of their own importance compared to that of their children or grandchildren. Furthermore, those of us who are not mothers, whether childfree by choice or not, have felt invalidated by this rationale.

Similarly, many women activists in the anti-pornography movement participate because they consider pornography to be sinful and immodest. Most feminists who oppose pornography do so, of course, for different reasons. Often anti-pornography activism is so deeply associated with conservative, prudish, or right-wing sentiments that the anti-woman and sexist nature of pornography is minimized or obscured. As I wrote in 1978, "We have been so put off by the politics of these people, that our kneejerk response is that we must be *for* whatever they are against" (1980, p. 301).

While anti-nuclear women have not alienated feminists to the degree that many of the conservative women working against pornography did (and do), feminists' association of peace activists with traditional sex roles and traditional lifestyles has created an obstacle to our involvement in the nuclear disarmament movement. It is also true that at least some of the non-feminist women who have been active in the peace movement have been blatantly anti-feminist.

(5) Because most anti-nuclear organizations are male-dominated, many feminists have not been willing to work in them. Creating a nuclear-free world is such a gigantic and ambitious undertaking that many feminists who have chosen to participate in such groups have tried to tolerate the sexism that occurs there rather than disrupt proceedings with their objections.

There have been many accounts of sexism in the peace movement. Many of the contributors to Pam McAllister's anthology, *Reweaving the*

Web, express hurt and anger as a result of such experiences (1982). The feeling that women must swallow our objections to sexism is not, of course, confined to the anti-nuclear struggle. I remember experiencing this self-censorship many times in working with various anti-South African apartheid groups in this country. Not wanting to undermine the work of the group by pointing out sexist attitudes and practices, I chose to drop out instead.

(6) Many women, including feminists, have silenced themselves because they believe that it is necessary to know a great deal about technology, the politics of the arms race, and international diplomacy, for their anti-nuclear efforts to be valuable.

As Simone Wilkerson points out in chapter 25, we have often been manipulated into thinking that opposing nuclear weapons requires considerable technological expertise. Some women have even come to believe that we should not allow our attitudes and actions regarding nuclear weapons to be influenced by our emotions. Helen Caldicott has said that she is often accused by men of being too emotional about nuclear war. I love her response to this criticism. "It is absolutely inappropriate," she writes, "to be unemotional as one contemplates the fiery end of the earth" (1984, p. 301).

(7) In a few cases women are so bitter and angry about sexism and the oppression to which men have subjected us that they don't want to lift a finger if their actions might help save men.

This attitude is similar to the one expressed by an Afro-American woman in Alice Walker's "Only Justice Can Stop a Curse" (see chapter 22). Although this attitude may be understandable when one hears the experiences of the women who feel this way, to increase the risks to our own lives, as well as to the survival of the entire planet, out of anger toward men, or white people, or the ruling class, is self-defeating.

Jonathan Schell eloquently articulates the choice before all of us, women and men, Blacks and whites, poor and rich, feminists and non-feminists:

> Two paths lie before us. One leads to death, the other to life. If we choose the first path—if we numbly refuse to acknowledge the nearness of extinction, all the while increasing our preparations to bring it about—then we in effect become the allies of death, and in everything we do our attachment to life will weaken: our vision, blinded to the abyss that has opened at our feet, will dim and grow confused; our will, discouraged by the thought of trying to build on such a precarious foundation anything that is meant to last, will slacken; and we will sink into stupefaction, as

though we were gradually weaning ourselves from life in preparation for the end. On the other hand, if we reject our doom, and bend our efforts toward survival—if we arouse ourselves to the peril and act to forestall it, making ourselves the allies of life—then the anesthetic fog will lift: our vision, no longer straining not to see the obvious, will sharpen; our will, finding secure ground to build on, will be restored; and we will take full and clear possession of life again. One day—and it is hard to believe that it will not be soon—we will make our choice. Either we will sink into the final coma and end it all or, as I trust and believe, we will awaken to the truth of our peril, a truth as great as life itself, and, like a person who has swallowed a lethal poison but shakes off his stupor at the last moment and vomits the poison up, we will break through the layers of our denials, put aside our fainthearted excuses, and rise up to cleanse the earth of nuclear weapons (1982, p. 231).

Unfortunately, as already mentioned, Schell doesn't suggest how we might best go about cleansing the earth of nuclear weapons. I would like to explain why I believe civil disobedience is a particularly effective strategy for women to use, whatever issue we are organizing around.

THE EFFICACY OF CIVIL DISOBEDIENCE

Many women anti-nuclear activists have already engaged in civil disobedience. A few feminists have also been arrested for acts of civil disobedience in protest against pornography and violence against women (for example, Nikki Craft, Ann Simonton, Melissa Farley, and their wonderfully creative and daring companions-in-action in different regions of this country). Nevertheless, only a small minority of feminists have engaged in civil disobedience as feminists, or feel open to engaging in it.

I believe civil disobedience lost some of its appeal as an effective strategy because the victories of the Civil Rights movement in this country seemed so short-lived and insufficient. But white women are obviously in a very different situation from Black people, and I believe some of these differences make civil disobedience potentially much more effective for women of all ethnic groups to use in all-women or primarily women's actions. For example, when minority group men and women engage in civil disobedience, the often nonexistent goodwill of the white majority determines whether or not demands are met. In contrast, women from all classes and ethnic groups not only constitute a majority of the population, but they are integrated into the male world, particularly in the family, so that they cannot be isolated and ghettoized in the same way that members of minority groups have been. When women are arrested for their protest actions, their husbands and men friends have to deal with the consequences. They have to take care of children and/or the household—itself a consciousness-raiser. Those who are not already concerned about nuclear war are *made* to care about the issue, at least in this indirect way, because they are negatively affected in ways they can recognize. Often when activists are at risk because of their political actions, the political commitment of those who love them increases. Thus, our integration with the male population, a factor that is often a strategic weakness for us in undertaking militant feminist actions (because the males in our lives frequently discourage or stop us), becomes a strength.

This is not to say that those women who are less integrated into the male world—particularly lesbians—don't have an important place in this struggle. Such women have the advantage of not having to deal with sexism and male resistance at home, which is why they have played and continue to play such a key role in the women's liberation movement in general. This may also be why so many lesbians have been among the first to take the risks involved in civil disobedience.

Civil disobedience is a particularly suitable strategy for women because most of us feel more comfortable engaging in non-violent actions. This strategy is therefore much easier for us to practice than for many men. Thus a factor that is often considered a tactical weakness for us—a common unwillingness to meet violence with violence—also becomes a strength. If we are badly treated by the police in this situation, we may gain all the more support for our cause.

Despite Sonia Johnson's conclusions that "what we resist persists" (1987, p. 27), and that those who participate in civil disobedience along with other resistance strategies like demonstrations, pickets, and petitions, become unwitting accomplices in what we are opposing (1987, p. 26), she provides an additional reason why civil disobedience is a particularly potent method of action for women. Johnson observes that each woman who had participated in such actions was "euphoric" and "high with admiration for herself" (1987, p. 21). "They all felt bigger and nobler, capable of so much more than they had thought. Each had caught a glimpse of her true stature and was ready to grow into it as fast as possible" (1987, p. 21).

Because women have been socialized to obey the law and to obey men generally, practicing civil disobedience can be exceedingly liberating. Civil disobedience "can teach us," Johnson writes, "that the inadequacies we fear are mostly imaginary" (1987, p. 22). Having so often been socialized to see ourselves as inadequate, women need experiences that teach us this lesson.

The depth of our concern about an issue can sometimes be measured by our willingness to pay a price of some kind; for example, the inconvenience and indignity of arrest. The suffragettes' fight is a case in point. But if the tactics used scare and threaten the public, as did many of the actions of the Weathermen or the Symbionese Liberation Army, for example, then they are likely to backfire. Civil disobedience shows commitment and concern in a very dramatic yet relatively non-threatening way. For all these reasons, and more, I strongly disagree with Johnson's view that civil disobedience and other resistance strategies make us accomplices in what we are fighting against.

Women have been taking life-and-death risks for centuries. Simply by being women, we risk being raped. Many of us are harassed at work or beaten at home because we are women. Some of these risks we cannot avoid. Some risks perhaps we can. Continuing to live with a violent husband or lover, for example, is very, very risky. Indeed, marrying someone we barely know, or even someone we know very well, can be very risky in a society that often does not recognize rape within marriage, and in which the interests of males are legally and culturally entrenched.

Hopefully, the time has come when women will stop taking as many personal risks—where these are avoidable (like staying with a dangerous partner)—and will take more *political* risks. By taking more political risks now, like those that civil disobedience entails, women may need to take fewer personal risks later on. And let us remember Margaret Mead's wise words: "Never doubt that a small group of thoughtful, committed citizens can change the world. Indeed, it's the only thing that ever has" (Paulson, 1986, p. 114).

REFERENCES

Bunch, Charlotte, *Passionate Politics* (New York: St. Martin's Press, 1987).

Caldicott, Helen, *Missile Envy* (New York: William Morrow, 1984).

Glendinning, Chellis, *Waking Up in the Nuclear Age* (New York: William Morrow, 1987).

Gwartney-Gibbs, Patricia, "Student Attitudes Studied," *Lane County Nuclear News Bureau*, Vol. 3, No. 5 (1985).

Johnson, Sonia, *Going Out of Our Minds: The Metaphysics of Liberation* (Freedom, CA: Crossing Press, 1987).

Lach, Denise and Gwartney-Gibbs, Patricia, "Attitudes Toward Surviving Nuclear War," Unpublished paper presented at the National Women's Studies Association Meetings, Minneapolis, Minnesota (June 23, 1988).

Macy, Joanna, *Despair and Personal Power in the Nuclear Age* (Philadelphia: New Society Press, 1983).

McAllister, Pam (ed.), *Reweaving the Web of Life: Feminism and Nonviolence* (Philadelphia: New Society Publishers, 1982).

Paulson, Dennis, *Voices of Survival in the Nuclear Age* (Santa Barbara: Capra Press, 1986).

Russell, Diana, "Pornography and the Women's Liberation Movement," in *Take Back the Night*, edited by Laura Lederer (New York: William Morrow, 1980).

Walker, Alice, *In Search of Our Mother's Gardens* (New York: Harcourt Brace Jovanovich, 1983).

ABOUT THE EDITOR

Diana E. II. Russell obtained her BA from the University of Cape Town, South Africa in 1958; a Postgraduate Diploma from the London School of Economics and Political Science (with Distinction) in 1961; an MA from Harvard University in 1967; and a PhD from Harvard University in 1970.

Diana is a Professor of Sociology at Mills College, where she has taught since 1969. She is author of *Rebellion, Revolution and Armed Force: A Comparative Study of Fifteen Countries with Special Emphasis on Cuba and South Africa* (Academic Press, 1974), *The Politics of Rape* (Stein and Day, 1975), author and coeditor of *Crimes Against Women: The Proceedings of the International Tribunal* (first published by Les Femmes in 1976 and republished by Frog in the Well in 1984), author of *Rape in Marriage* (Macmillan, 1982), *Sexual Exploitation: Rape, Child Sexual Abuse and Workplace Harassment* (Sage Publications, 1984), and *The Secret Trauma: Incest in the Lives of Girls and Women* (Basic Books, 1986). *The Secret Trauma* won the 1986 C. Wright Mills Award which is given annually by the Society for the Study of Social Problems for outstanding research in the social sciences.

Diana was one of the main organizers of the International Tribunal on Crimes Against Women in 1976. She was also one of the founders of Women Against Violence and Pornography and Media in 1977, FANG in 1983, and the Mills College Faculty and Staff Divestment Committee in 1985. She has been arrested twice for her participation in political demonstrations, once in South Africa in 1963, and again in England in 1974.

Diana is currently at work on a book, *Lives of Courage: Women for a New South Africa,* based on her interviews with women in the South African liberation movement. It will be published by Basic Books in 1989. She is also co-editing a book with Dorchen Leidholdt, *No Safe Place for Women:*

319

Feminists on Pornography, to be published by Pergamon Press, Inc., in 1989. And she is co-editing another anthology with British feminist criminologist Jill Radford titled *Femicide: The Politics of Woman-Killing* to be published in 1989 by Twayne Publishers in the US and by Open University Press in England.

CONTRIBUTORS

Rosalie Bertell received her PhD in mathematics from the Catholic University of America, Washington in 1966. She is the author of *No Immediate Danger: Prognosis for a Radioactive Earth* and has also published over eighty academic papers, addresses and articles in environmental, peace and health journals and books. She has been called as an expert witness before the United States Congress and has testified in licensing hearings for nuclear power plants before the United States Nuclear Regulatory Commission. A member of the Order of Grey Nuns, she now researches low-level radiation as Director of Research of the International Institute of Concern for Public Health in Toronto, Canada, and campaigns internationally against the dangers of nuclear technology.

Carol Cohn has a PhD in Social and Political Thought from The Union Graduate School. She is a Research Associate at the Department of Psychiatry of the Harvard Medical School and a Senior Research Scholar at the Center for Psychological Studies in the Nuclear Age, in Cambridge, Massachusetts, where she is currently working on a book about the language and thinking of defense intellectuals under a grant from the John D. and Catherine T. MacArthur Foundation.

Gary Delgado has a PhD in Sociology from the University of California at Berkeley. He is the author of *Organizing the Movement* published by Temple University Press in 1986. He is currently working as the general organizer of the Center for Third World Organizing in Oakland, California.

Patricia Ellsberg has been active in the peace movement for twenty years, in partnership with her husband Daniel Ellsberg. Currently she is a board member of the World Policy Institute and the Elmwood Institute and is engaged in formulating positive alternatives to our present foreign policy.

Barbara Gerber received her EdD in counseling psychology from Syracuse University. She has been a professor of Counseling and Psychological Services at SUNY at Oswego since 1965. She has also served as Dean of Professional Studies and is currently Chair of the Teacher Education Task Force. She was a founding member of the National Women's Studies Association and served as a member of the Coordinating Council from 1981 to 1987, as Treasurer from 1982 to 1985, and as publisher of NWSA Perspectives from 1985 to 1987.

Hollis Giammatteo is a writer whose fiction, nonfiction and poetry have appeared in publications such as *The North American Review, Vogue, Feminist Studies, Prairie Schooner, Nimrod, Calyx* and many others. Hollis is the recipient of the 1988 PEN/Jerard Fund, "given for a distinguished nonfiction work-in-progress by an emerging woman writer" for *On the Line,* an early excerpt of which appears in this anthology. She lives in Seattle, where she teaches writing with the Gold Mountain Institute, an association of writers who teach, founded by Natalie Goldberg.

Susan Griffin is the author of *Women and Nature: The Roaring Inside Her* and *Pornography and Silence.* She is a Schumacher fellow. Her play *Voices* was awarded an Emmy. She holds an MA in English literature and an honorary PhD in Human Letters from Starr King School for Divinity. She is currently at work on a book called *The First and the Last: A Woman Thinks About War.*

Susan James is a feminist internationalist who traded in a career in journalism for a life of solidarity work. She currently works as a counselor with children who have witnessed or experienced domestic violence. Susan also works as an activist with the Seattle chapter of the Committee in Solidarity with the People of El Salvador (CISPES), a national organization working to stop US intervention in El Salvador.

Lynne Jones qualified as a doctor but resigned from her medical post in 1982 to work full-time for peace. She has travelled throughout Europe, getting to know women working for peace in several countries in East and West Europe. Lynne has also lived off and on in the United States, where she took part in the Women's Pentagon Action. She has worked with women's peace groups in Britain, particularly the camp at Greenham Common. In 1984 Lynne returned to medicine, and is currently training as a psychiatrist in Oxford. She writes regularly on peace and human rights issues, and remains fully involved with the peace movement.

Rachel Lederman was an organizer of both the Puget Sound Women's Peace Camp and the Seneca Women's Encampment for Peace and

Justice. She now lives in the San Francisco bay area, where she continues to work in the feminist and anti-imperialist movements. She is an attorney, an artist and an anarchist.

Rhoda Linton has a PhD from Cornell University in Research and Program Evaluation Studies. She is currently a core faculty member at the Union Graduate School of the Union of Experimenting Colleges and Universities. She has written an article entitled "Seneca Women's Peace Camp: Shape of Things to Come" for a forthcoming book, *Rocking the Ship of State: Toward a Women's Peace Politics*, edited by Adrienne Harris and Ynestra King.

Elissa Melamed was born in New York City and received her bachelor's and master's degrees from Radcliffe and Harvard, and her doctorate in psychology from Columbia Pacific University. Her book, *Mirror, Mirror: The Terror of Not Being Young*, was published in 1983 by Simon & Schuster. In 1985 Elissa was tragically killed in a fluke accident when she was hit by a motorcyclist. Her major interest before her death was in the empowerment of women for peace, a subject about which she wrote and spoke extensively.

Sandra Jo Palm is a porcelain ceramicist and a feminist non-violent activist. She has been active in the following movements: civil rights, anti-apartheid in South Africa, disarmament, women's, lesbian, and non-US intervention in Central America. She is currently a member of the movement for a New Society, Women's Skills and Resource Exchange, and AHIMSA.

Grace Paley is a member of the Literature and Language Faculty at Sarah Lawrence College and author of *Enormous Changes at the Last Minute* as well as three other books. She won the title of First New York State Author and has received a Guggenheim Fellowship as well as many other honors and awards. She was one of the organizers of the Women's Pentagon Action and has worked with the War Resisters League.

Fran Peavey, author of *Heart Politics,* is a consultant on personal, community, and international social change. She also performs comedy about global issues as the Atomic Comic. Fran did her doctoral work in innovation theory and technological forecasting at the School of Instructional Technology, University of Southern California. She taught at San Francisco State University in the Department of Educational Technology for two years.

Annie Popkin, teacher, photographer and community activist, received her PhD from Brandeis University for her thesis, "Bread and Roses: An Early Moment in the Development of Socialist Feminism," part of which appeared in D. Cluster's *They Should Have Served that Cup* *of Coffee: Seven Radicals Remember the 60s.* She has taught Sociology, Women's Studies and Ethnic Studies at the college level in Boston and the San Francisco bay area. She also leads "Unlearning Racism" workshops in schools, workplaces, and community organizations.

Barbara Roberts received her PhD in history from Université d'Ottawa in 1980 and now teaches women's studies at Institut Simone de Beauvoir, Université Concordia, Montréal. A member of the Feminist International for Peace and Food, she was a coordinator of that group's Peace Tent at the Nairobi NGO Forum and has been active in Forward Looking Strategies implementation activities. She has published extensively in the areas of ethnic/immigration studies and peace studies, and is currently working on a book on women's peace activism in twentieth-century Canada. She is also co-authoring a book on the Peace Tent.

Helene Rosenbluth is a radio producer for Pacifica Radio in Los Angeles and is the creator of the award-winning documentary "The Family of Women: Stories from a World Gathering." This five-part radio program is based on interviews conducted at the International Women's Conference in Nairobi. The series and the interview with Simone Wilkerson are available on tape from the Pacifica Tape Archives, 5316 Venice Blvd., Los Angeles, CA 90019.

Barbara Smith is a Black feminist writer and activist. She co-edited *Conditions: Five, The Black Women's Issue* and *All the Women Are White, All the Blacks Are Men, But Some of Us Are Brave: Black Women's Studies.* She is the editor of *Home Girls: A Black Feminist Anthology* and the co-author of *Yours in Struggle: Three Feminist Perspectives on Anti-Semitism and Racism.* She is a founder of Kitchen Table: Women of Color Press.

Charlene Spretnak has an MA degree in English and American Literature from the University of California at Berkeley. She is author of *The Spiritual Dimension of Green Politics; Green Politics: The Global Promise* (with Fritjof Capra); *Lost Goddesses of Early Greece;* and is editor of an anthology, *The Politics of Women's Spirituality.*

Penny Strange has done a variety of badly-paid work for good causes since graduating from Oxford University, including the Save the Children Fund, *Peace News,* and the women's movement. She now lives in rural Wales with her two sons and earns her living by exercising her passion for gardening.

Third World First is a development group which has grown out of the efforts of students in higher education in England to understand international poverty and to combat it through campaigning against it.

Alice Walker has been active in the struggle to prevent nuclear war for many years. Her most recent books are a children's book, *To Hell With Dying,* and a collection of essays, *Living by the Word.* She recently completed a new novel, *The Temple of My Familiar,* to be published in 1989.

Alice Wiser is finishing her PhD at the University of London in Social Psychology. Her dissertation topic is "Women as Peacemakers: A Social-Psychological Approach." She has interviewed women in nearly forty countries, lectured and run workshops in ten countries, and helped to organize several international women's conferences. She is currently writing a book with Barbara Roberts and Mary Anne Beall about the Peace Tent at the End of the Decade Conference in Nairobi, Kenya in 1985.

Michele Whitham is a Senior Lecturer in the Field & International Study Program at Cornell University, where she has been honored with the New York State Chancellor's Award for Excellence in Teaching, the New York State College of Human Ecology Distinguished Teaching Award and the Presidential Scholars Award for her teaching of organizational and community development to students involved in fieldwork. Michele has published work on experiential education, empowerment and women's development, and is currently finishing a law degree at the Cornell Law School.

SELECTED BIBLIOGRAPHY
ON FEMINISM
AND THE NUCLEAR CRISIS

Aronoff, Phyllis, "Reflections on Militarism, Feminism and Peace Work," *A Women's Studies Journal*, Vol. 12, No. 2 (1987), pp. 4–9.

Becker, Norma and Paley, Grace, "Feminist Organizing in the Peace Movement," *War Resisters League News* (May-June 1984).

Bertell, Rosalie, *No Immediate Danger: Prognosis for a Radioactive Earth* (London: The Women's Press, 1985).

Blackwood, Caroline, *On the Perimeter* (New York: Penguin Books, 1985).

Boulding, Elise, "Perspectives of Women Researchers on Disarmament, National Security and World Order," *Women's Studies International Quarterly*, Vol. 4, No. 2 (1981), pp. 27–41.

Breaching the Peace: A Collection of Radical Feminist Papers (London: Onlywomen Press, 1983).

Brown, Wilmette, *Black Women and the Peace Movement* (Bristol, England: Falling Wall Press, 1984).

Brock-Utne, Birgit, *Educating for Peace: A Feminist Perspective* (New York: Pergamon Press, 1985).

Buehler, Jan, "The Puget Sound Women's Peace Camp: Education as an Alternative Strategy," *Frontiers: A Journal of Women Studies*, Vol. 8, No. 2 (1985), pp. 40–44.

Cabasso, Jackie, and Moon, Susan, *Risking Peace: Why We Sat in the Road* (Berkeley, Cal.: Open Books, 1985).

Cagan, Leslie, "Feminism and Militarism," in *Beyond Survival*, edited by Michael Albert and David Dellinger (Boston, Mass.: South End Press, 1983).

Caldecott, Leonie, and Leland, Stephanie (Eds.), *Reclaim the Earth: Women Speak Out for Life on Earth* (London: The Women's Press, 1983).

Caldicott, Helen, *Missile Envy: The Arms Race and Nuclear War* (New York: William Morrow, 1984).

Cambridge Women's Peace Collective, *My Country Is the Whole World: An Anthology of Women's Work on Peace and War* (London: Pandora Press, 1984).

Cataldo, Mima, Putter, Ruth, and Fireside, Byrna, *The Women's Encampment for a Future of Peace and Justice* (Philadelphia: Temple University Press, 1987).

Chapkis, Wendy, *Loaded Questions: Women in the Military* (Amsterdam, Washington DC: Transnational Institute, 1981).

Cook, Alice, and Kirk, Gwyn, *Greenham Women Everywhere* (London: Pluto Press, 1983).

Costello, Cynthia and Stanley, Amy Dru, "Report from Seneca," *Frontiers: A Journal of Women Studies*, Vol. 8, No. 2 (1985), pp. 32–39.

Deming, Barbara, *We Cannot Live Without Our Lives* (New York: Grossman Publishers, 1974).

Easlea, Brian, *Fathering the Unthinkable: Masculinity, Scientists and the Nuclear Arms Race* (London: Pluto Press, 1983).

Eisler, Riane, "Violence and Male Dominance: The Ticking Time Bomb," *Humanities in Society*, Vol. 7, No. 1/2 (1984), pp. 3–18.

Elshtain, Jean, *Women and War* (New York: Basic Books, 1987).

Enloe, Cynthia, *Does Khaki Become You? The Militarization of Women's Lives* (Boston: South End Press, 1983).

Enloe, Cynthia, "Feminists Thinking About War, Militarism, and Peace," in *Analyzing Gender: A Handbook of Social Science Research*, edited by Beth Hess and Myra Marx Ferree, Newbury Park, Cal.: Sage Publications, 1987).

Fieseler, Beate, and Ladwig, Ulrike, "Women and the Peace Movement in the Federal Republic of Germany," *Frontiers: A Journal of Women Studies*, Vol. 8, No. 2 (1985), pp. 59–64.

Feminism and Nonviolence Study Group, *Piecing It Together: Feminism and Nonviolence* Devon, England: Self-published (2 College Close, Buckleigh, Westward Ho, Devon), 1983.

Froese, Patricia, and Nielsen, Sharon, "Gender and Attitudes Toward the Peace Movement and Nuclear Disarmament," *Atlantis: A Women's Studies Journal*, Vol. 12, No. 1 (1986), pp. 129–135.

Glendinning, Chellis, *Waking Up in the Nuclear Age* (New York: William Morrow, 1987).

Harford, Barbara, and Hopkins, Sarah (Eds.), *Greenham Common: Women at the Wire* (London: The Women's Press, 1985).

ISIS Collective, "Women for Peace," *Women's International Bulletin*, Vol. 26.

Jones, Lynne (Ed.), *Keeping the Peace: Women's Peace Handbook* (London: The Women's Press, 1983).

Kelly, Petra, *Fighting for Hope* (Boston, Mass.: South End Press, 1984).

King, Ynestra, "All Is Connectedness: Scenes from the Women's Pentagon Action USA", in *Keeping the Peace*, edited by Lynne Jones (London: The Women's Press, 1983).

Koen, Susan, Swaim, Nina, and Friends, *Ain't No Where We Can Run: Handbook for Women on the Nuclear Mentality* (Norwich, Vermont: WAND, 1980).

Lundberg, Norma, "Making Sense of War: Demythologizing the Male Warrior" *Atlantis: A Women's Studies Journal*, Vol. 12, No. 1 (1986), pp. 97–102.

Macy, Joanna, *Despair and Personal Power in the Nuclear Age* (Philadelphia: New Society Press, 1983).

Mansueto, Connie, "Take the Toys Away from the Boys: Competition and the Nuclear Arms Race," in *Over Our Dead Bodies: Women Against the Bomb*, edited by Dorothy Thompson (London: Virago Press, 1983).

McAllister, Pam (Ed.), *Reweaving the Web of Life: Feminism and Nonviolence* (Philadelphia: New Society Publishers, 1982).

McDonagh, Celia, "The Women's Peace Movement in Britain," *Frontiers: A Journal of Women Studies*, Vol. 8, No. 2 (1985), pp. 53–58.

Michalowski, Helen, "The Army Will Make a Man Out of You," in *Reweaving the Web of Life*, edited by Pam McAllister (Philadelphia: New Society Publishers, 1982).

Michel, Andrée (Issue Ed.), "La Militarisation et les Violences a l'Egard des Femmes," *Nouvelle Questions Feministes*, Vol. 11/12 (1985).

Nelson, Lin, "Promise Her Everything: The Nuclear Power Industry's Agenda for Women," *Feminist Studies*, Vol. 10, No. 2 (1984), pp. 291–314.

Nzomo, Maria, "Women, Third World and International Peace," *Atlantis: A Women's Studies Journal*, Vol. 12, No. 2 (1987), pp. 40–46.

O'Dell, Jack, "Racism: Fuel for the War Machine," in *Beyond Survival*, edited by Albert, Michael and David Dellinger (Boston, Mass.: South End Press, 1983).

Puget Sound Women's Peace Camp Participants, *We Are Ordinary Women: A Chronicle of the Puget Sound Women's Peace Camp* (Seattle, Wash.: The Seal Press, 1985).

Quistorp, Eva, "Starting a Movement: Frauen fur Frieden" (Women for Peace, West Germany) in *Keeping the Peace*, edited by Lynne Jones (London: The Women's Press, 1983).

Reardon, Betty, *Sexism and the War System* (New York: Teachers College Press, 1985).

Roberts, Barbara, "The Death of Machothink: Feminist Research and the Transformation of Peace Studies," *Women's Studies International Forum*, Vol. 7, No. 4 (1984), pp. 195–200.

Roberts, Barbara (Issues Ed.), *Atlantis: A Women's Studies Journal*, Vol. 12, Nos. 1, 2 (1986, 1987).

Seller, Anne, "Greenham: A Concrete Reality," *Frontiers: A Journal of Women Studies*, Vol. 8, No. 2 (1985), pp. 26–31.

Sherwin Susan, "Feminism and Theoretical Perspectives on Peace," *Atlantis: A Women's Studies Journal*, Vol. 12, No. 1 (1986), pp. 136–141.

Special Issue: Women and Peace, *Frontiers: A Journal of Women Studies*, Vol. 8, No. 2 (1985).

Stiehm, Judith, *Women and Men's Wars* (New York: Pergamon Press, 1983).

Stoltenberg, John, "Disarmament and Masculinity" (pamphlet) (Palo Alto, Cal.: Frog in the Well, 1978).

Thompson, Dorothy (Ed.), *Over Our Dead Bodies: Women against the Bomb* (London: Virago Press, 1983).

Tobias, Sheila, "Toward a Feminist Analysis of Defense Spending," *Frontiers: A Journal of Women Studies*, Vol. 8, No. 2 (1985), pp. 65–68.

Warnock, Donna, "Feminism and Militarism: Can the Peace Movement Reach Out?" WIN, (15 April 1982), pp. 7–11.

Wiser, Alice, "Peace on Earth, Good Will Toward Women," *Atlantis: A Women's Studies Journal*, Vol. 12, No. 1 (1986), pp. 123–128.

"Women and Militarism," *Connexions: An International Women's Quarterly*, Vol. 11 (1984).

Woolf, Virginia, *Three Guineas* (New York: Harcourt Brace Jovanovich, 1938, 1966).

INDEX

329

MEN'S STUDIES MODIFIED The Impact of Feminism on the Academic Disciplines
Dale Spender, editor
WOMAN'S NATURE Rationalizations of Inequality
Marian Lowe and *Ruth Hubbard*
MACHINA EX DEA Feminist Perspectives on Technology
Joan Rothschild, editor
SCIENCE AND GENDER A Critique of Biology and Its Theories on Women
Ruth Bleier
WOMAN IN THE MUSLIM UNCONSCIOUS
Fatna A. Sabbah
MEN'S IDEAS/WOMEN'S REALITIES
Louise Michele Newman, editor
BLACK FEMINIST CRITICISM Perspectives on Black Women Writers
Barbara Christian
THE SISTER BOND A Feminist View of a Timeless Connection
Toni A.H. McNaron, editor
EDUCATING FOR PEACE A Feminist Perspective
Birgit Brock-Utne
STOPPING RAPE Successful Survival Strategies
Pauline B. Bart and *Patricia H. O'Brien*
TEACHING SCIENCE AND HEALTH FROM A FEMINIST PERSPECTIVE
A Practical Guide
Sue V. Rosser
FEMINIST APPROACHES TO SCIENCE
Ruth Bleier, editor
INSPIRING WOMEN Reimagining the Muse
Mary K. DeShazer
MADE TO ORDER The Myth of Reproductive and Genetic Progress
Patricia Spallone and *Deborah L. Steinberg*, editors
TEACHING TECHNOLOGY FROM A FEMINIST PERSPECTIVE
A Practical Guide
Joan Rothschild
FEMINISM WITHIN THE SCIENCE AND HEALTH CARE PROFESSIONS: Overcoming
Resistance
Sue V. Rosser
RUSSIAN WOMEN'S STUDIES: Essays on Sexism in Soviet Culture
Tatyana Mamonova
TAKING OUR TIME: Feminist Perspectives on Temporality
Frieda Johles Forman, editor, with *Caoran Sowton*
RADICAL VOICES: A Decade of Feminist Resistance from *Women's Studies
International Forum*
Renate Klein and *Deborah L. Steinberg*, editors
EXPOSING NUCLEAR PHALLACIES
Diana E.H. Russell, editor